Public Relations

Dedication

To Aylin. Thanks for helping me through … the Summer of 2002.
(Paul)

To Anita and Denis Murray for their help and support over many years.
(John)

Public Relations

Contemporary issues and techniques

Paul Baines
John Egan
Frank Jefkins

Routledge
Taylor & Francis Group

LONDON AND NEW YORK

First published by Butterworth-Heinemann

This edition published 2011 by Routledge
2 Park Square, Milton Park, Abingdon, Oxon OX14 4RN
711 Third Avenue, New York, NY 10017, USA

Routledge is an imprint of the Taylor & Francis Group, an informa business

First published 2004

British Library Cataloguing in Publication Data
Baines, Paul
  Public relations: Contemporary issues and techniques
  1. Public relations – Management
  I. Title   II. Egan, John   III. Jefkins, Frank
  659.2

Library of Congress Cataloguing in Publication Data
A catalogue record for this book is available from the Library of Congress

ISBN 0 7506 5724 3

Transferred to Digital Printing in 2012

Contents

Foreword

This is a timely book because the PR industry is in something of a crisis. It formally recognized this in March 2002, when *PR Week*'s PR and Media conference concluded that 'the PR industry must seek to win back its credibility by divorcing itself from spin doctoring'.

The crisis has been some time in the making. It can reasonably be said to have begun with the social changes in the late 1960s, which not only usefully brought the demise of deference – i.e. unearned respect – but encouraged a new irreverence. This rapidly turned nasty and brought an increasing cynicism to bear on our institutions and their leaders and their works. The death of deference also spawned single-issue pressure groups, notably on environmental issues, who embarked on perpetual campaigns through an often complicit media.

Not surprisingly, the media were themselves affected by the changes in values and became more demanding, intrusive and arrogant. Technology reinforced the pressure on institutions, notably by screening events as they happened into our sitting rooms and increasing the pace at which the nation's affairs were conducted. It produced a proliferation of media outlets and increasing competition, which have in turn ushered in what is called 'dumbing down' – the trivialization, cheapening and coarsening of news treatment. And 'dumbing down' generated the cult of the so-called celebrity, which is a very loose definition of anyone who has, however fleetingly, appeared on the TV screen.

Media proliferation, competition, 'dumbing down', the cult of the celebrity and the increasing nastiness of the media also brought a proliferation of PROs as institutions and individuals sought to protect themselves from rampant journalism, exploit the opportunities offered by the changes or, more constructively, to manage relations with them. As with all rapid growth, we acquired PROs the industry could do without.

Over the past 25 years, PR in Britain has certainly become more central to institutions' and government's thinking and operations, though there is still a long way to go in the average organization. Many, perhaps a majority, are light years away from the Institute of Public Relations' (IPR) definition of PR: 'the planned and sustained effort to establish and maintain good will between an organization and its publics'. Many PROs would privately testify to this because of their organization's negative attitude to communication in or outside a crisis.

We should not assume that because PR, as a multifaceted means of establishing and sustaining a reputation, has made great strides under the pressure of society's rapid evolution from its deferential state that it is generally, let alone enthusiastically or intelligently, employed. Indeed, for all its advances, it has suffered a setback because of the way PR and presentation have been practised by the Blair government over its first six years. That setback was highlighted by *PR Week*'s conference in 2002.

There is, of course, a great deal of confusion over what constitutes 'spin' and consequently the work of the 'spin doctor', a term coined by a *New York Times* journalist in 1984. It is to be distinguished from PR, as defined by the IPR, by its lack of ethics, restraint or judgement, its obsessive preoccupation with finessing situations, clever dickery and immediate palliative effects rather than with longer term reputation. That is exactly what we have seen from the British government since 1997.

It has led to a serious loss of trust in the government – a feeling that it is 'all spin and no substance', as Labour MPs have acknowledged, and a high casualty rate among 'spinners'. Their ultimate cynicism was revealed by Jo Moore, who advised the Ministry of Transport immediately after the terrorist atrocities in New York and Washington that 11 September 2001 was 'a good day to bury bad news'. Now, even the government's leading spinners who remain concede that they went over the top.

The crisis that they have created in the PR industry was not ended but merely interrupted by the Iraq war. We shall see the battle for PR integrity joined in the years ahead.

The value of this pretty comprehensive tome, apart from its timing, is that, while covering the waterfront of PR practice, it reveals the struggle already taking place by interviewing active participants. It is designed to make the student think as well as teach him or her the philosophy, detail and mechanics of PR. If, unsurprisingly, I don't agree with everything it has to say, I would advise students to read Richard Quest, of CNN, on PR as it is offered to a journalist. He more often than not hits the nail on the head.

In short, this book is about a growth industry which is operationally patchy and less than firmly rooted in the ethics implied in the IPR's definition of the craft. I hope its authors Paul Baines and John Egan will eventually be credited with improving matters, allowing Middlesex University Business School to bask in their glory.

Sir Bernard Ingham

Preface

This text has emerged as a result of work undertaken by both authors principally in the area of political marketing and relationship marketing research over the course of the last six years. In addition to this research element of our work at Middlesex University Business School, the authors have also been involved as practitioners in marketing Middlesex University Business School, particularly for corporate and academic programmes, domestically and overseas, and developing the university's reputation. This textbook had a strong foundation to build on, and was originally commissioned as an updated version of the Second Edition of Frank Jefkins' *Public Relations Techniques* (Butterworth-Heinemann, 1994), particularly in its structure and focus, although much has changed in the interim. The unique feature of the original book was its balance between theoretical and practical aspects of the public relations discipline and its contemporary focus. We have made special attempts to maintain this whilst including actual material from current projects that we have been involved with, in addition to case studies to highlight the nature of PR in practice. To further strengthen the book's appeal to practitioners, we have included five interviews with a number of eminent PR practitioners and academics.

We feel that the public relations discipline has changed considerably over the course of the last 20 years, and particularly since the beginning of the 1990s. As the number of potential sources of media has fragmented and multiplied, so has the importance of the cult of the personality and the PR stunt. The celebrity is of increasing importance in communicating a brand's values in an integrated communication campaign. Crisis management is taken more seriously as a result of the terrorist threat that has emerged since 11 September 2001, and sponsorship and sports marketing are now huge areas in their own right. Public relations as a discipline has moved centre stage in many boardrooms as the importance of this function has been recognized, and as its link with corporate performance and reputation has become increasingly clear. This text aims to outline some of these changes and provide the reader with an insight into the world of contemporary PR practice.

We are fortunate to have had input from numerous eminent contributors, particularly our interviewees. We hope that their contributions give the text more of a flavour of the PR industry and practices therein. The text attempts to cover, in brief, the major theory and techniques necessary for someone relatively new to public relations or someone who has been working in public relations but wants to know more about why they are doing what they are doing! As such, this text is a useful guide for practising public relations officers either as those who commission work from public relations agencies or as those who run their own PR departments.

The text considers distinct public relations topics, chapter by chapter, in five parts. Part 1 contains an introduction to the public relations industry and attempts to provide the reader with an insight into the psychology of communication within the PR field, as well as a flavour for what public relations actually is. This section is concluded with an interview with Kevin Moloney from Bournemouth Media School, focusing particularly on the definition of PR and how it is changing. Part 2 illustrates the public relations planning process and the way in which public relations activities are organized using real-life examples and cases. This section is concluded with an interview with Marie Owens, Director of Communication at Middlesex University, looking particularly at the PR planning process. Part 3 deals with the process of managing media relations, writing press releases and other ways of generating publicity. The section concludes with an interview with former Chief Press Secretary to Margaret Thatcher and veteran journalist, Sir Bernard Ingham, who concentrates on media management, as the discipline has come to be known. Part 4 considers particular techniques in public relations campaigns. This section concludes with an interview with Richard Quest of CNN, focusing particularly on broadcast media. Part 5 covers specialist areas of PR such as sponsorship, lobbying and financial PR. This is an important section of the text, since many of the changes in the PR industry are driven by work conducted in some of these specialist areas. This section concludes with an interview with Dianne Thompson from Camelot Group, who examines critically the public affairs process. The book also includes the codes of conduct of both the Institute of Public Relations and the International Public Relations Association.

We suggest that the book will be particularly useful for PROs who are new to their positions and who want a practical understanding of what the job entails. However, the text contains sufficient theoretical material to provide experienced managers with new insights into their industry and the way in which it is changing. The text is also useful for undergraduate and postgraduate students studying public relations on degree programmes and professional programmes such as the CAM Certificate and the IPR Diploma.

We welcome any constructive comments on how you feel our text can be improved. If you would like to contact us, please e-mail us at p.baines@mdx.ac.uk or at j.egan@mdx.ac.uk. We hope you enjoy the text!

Paul Baines
John Egan
Middlesex University Business School, London, UK

About the authors

Dr Paul Baines

Paul is Principal Lecturer in Marketing and Director of Business Development at Middlesex University Business School in London. He holds bachelors, masters and doctoral degrees from Manchester School of Management at UMIST. He is a Chartered Marketer and a full member of the Market Research Society. At Middlesex University, he has been a past undergraduate curriculum leader with responsibility for developing and monitoring undergraduate marketing programmes. He has taught on a variety of courses, at both undergraduate and post-graduate levels, including strategic marketing, consumer goods marketing, business-to-business marketing, marketing research, political marketing and introduction to marketing courses. Currently, he teaches a postgraduate course in strategic marketing.

He is the author and co-author of numerous journal articles and book chapters, and frequent contributor to international conferences, on the use of marketing techniques in non-conventional services environments, particularly for political parties and candidates. He is co-editor, with Bal Chansarkar, of *Introduction to Marketing Research* (MU Press), co-author of *Contemporary Strategic Marketing* with Ross Brennan and Paul Garneau (Palgrave Press), and co-author, with Bal

Chansarkar, of *Introducing Marketing Research* (John Wiley). Paul's recent marketing research consultancy projects include projects for a number of organizations, including a high-profile football club, a large aerospace maintenance company, a national charity and an advertising agency.

John Egan

John Egan is Principal Lecturer in Marketing and Head of Marketing Services at Middlesex University Business School. John is a Chartered Marketer and full member of the Chartered Institute of Marketing. He is a Fellow of the Royal Society of Arts & Commerce and a member of the Institute of Direct Marketing and the Academy of Marketing. He has taught on a variety of courses, at both undergraduate and postgraduate levels, including marketing communications, direct marketing, retail marketing and service marketing management. He currently shares his lecturing duties with heading the team responsible for marketing the Business School.

John has considerable industry experience, having spent over 20 years with retailers such as Bloomingdales (New York), Hudson Bay Company (Canada), Chinacraft, Garrard, and Mappin & Webb before joining the Business School in 1997. He is the author of *Relationship Marketing: Exploring Relational Strategies in Marketing* published in 2001, and numerous journal articles and conference papers on subjects including relationship marketing, political marketing, retailing and marketing communications. He is also a member of the editorial board of the *European Journal of Marketing*.

Frank Jefkins

The late Frank Jefkins was the author of the highly successful text, *Public Relations Techniques*, on which this book is based. He was highly regarded in the field of public relations, illustrated by his receipt of the Sir Stephen Tallents Medal from the Institute of Public Relations for 'exceptional achievement in, and contribution to, public relations practice'.

Acknowledgements

We would like to express our gratitude to all those who have generously supplied us with information, examples and illustrations for this book. A number of quotations have been taken from the press and other publications, and these have been acknowledged in the references at the end of the book.

Our thanks are due to: Kevin Moloney at Bournemouth University Media School, Sir Bernard Ingham, Richard Quest of CNN, Marie Owens of Middlesex University and Dianne Thompson of Camelot Group plc. All were happy to discuss their areas of practice and contribute their ideas to an important component of the book. In addition, we would like to thank Carole Baines for her work on transcribing the interviews and in formatting and sub-editing the manuscript prior to publishing, and Joyce Clancey for her continuous help and support. Paul Baines would also like to thank Martine and Brad Spence, who kindly loaned him their house in Canada, and generous support, during the Summer of 2002, to work on the manuscript whilst teaching a course at the University of Ottawa. John Egan would like to thank his family for putting up with him as he hid himself away on this project. In particular, Anita and Denis Murray, whose help and support throughout the year have been invaluable.

We would also like to thank the many anonymous reviewers for their helpful comments, many of which were incorporated into the final manuscript. Thanks particularly to those reviewers who made specific recommendations on material to be included to improve the text. We would like to thank the team at Butterworth-Heinemann, particularly Nicki Kear and Holly Bennett, and various others in the marketing and production departments at BH.

Our thanks are also due to the Institute of Public Relations for permission to reprint the Code of Professional Conduct in its latest version and the Global Alliance for Public Relations and Communication Management for permission to reproduce its global protocol on ethics.

Part 1

Defining Public Relations

Chapter 1

Introduction

LEARNING OBJECTIVES

At the end of this chapter you will be able to:

■ define public relations;
■ explain how public relations techniques reduce hostility, prejudice, apathy and ignorance;
■ contrast PR with public affairs, advertising and marketing;
■ recognize the main factors involved in a PR campaign.

The professionalization of the PR industry

Public relations is often referred to as a new, young profession or business, but this is not really so. PR techniques have been used in different forms for centuries. Edward Bernays, considered to be the father of modern public relations and a nephew of psychoanalyst Sigmund Freud, argues that the rulers of ancient Egypt, Sumeria, Babylonia, Assyria and Persia all used personal and political publicity (1952, p. 13). Bird and animal symbols on the sails of Phoenician and Viking ships could be regarded as early examples of corporate identity schemes. Over the centuries, the funnels of steamships, stagecoaches, trains, taxis and buses have been painted in identifying colours. Emblems on shields and the uniforms of armed and other uniformed services were similar forms of corporate identity. This kind of identification and distinction has grown up into systems of logotypes, typography, uniforms, dress and badges, colours and the liveries of transportation, of which the modern airline is a prime example. For instance, British Airways courted controversy during the Thatcher administration when it incorporated ethnic designs in place of its British Ribbons on its planes' tailfins to denote its 'glocal' approach (i.e. both global and local).

Government and public services have been among the leading users of public relations techniques in the last century. Lloyd George, as Chancellor of the Exchequer, used public relations to explain the new old age pension scheme in 1912, and the first president of the IPR, Sir Stephen Tallents, used public relations to promote the Empire Marketing Board between 1926 and 1933. At the end of the century, the British Labour Party, under the direction of Peter Mandelson and Alastair Campbell, reorganized the campaigning department to align it with the concerns of voters, and to improve its press relations. Mandelson had argued during his tenure as director of campaigns in the 1980s that 'press and broad-casting contacts must be dramatically extended beyond the parliament-ary press lobby' (Mandelson, 1988). Voter concerns were identified partly through the endeavours of Philip Gould, who conducted focus groups to assess the mood of voter groups in swing voting regions of the country (Gould, 1998). The results were fed into policy development and news management programmes. In the USA, political PR was already well established. To some extent, the British Labour Party's campaign app-roach was based on that of Clinton's US Democratic Party, where several Labour officials (including Gould and the party's general secretary, Margaret McDonough) had temporarily worked.

Globalization, the fall of communism as a competing ideology and business context, the increased competition that has accompanied deregulation in major markets, a greater understanding of the importance of consumers, particularly by consumer themselves, and the dual fragmentation/globalization of mass media have all affected public relations activity. The result is that it has become increasingly systematized and research-led over the last century, as has its business counterparts marketing, advertising and human resource management.

Public relations has developed very rapidly in recent years, partly because management of various commercial and non-commercial organizations have discovered a need for public relations activities. There has also been a considerable increase in the means by which public relations messages can be conveyed – for example, through satel-lite, cable and Internet media – as the mass media generally has paradoxically fragmented and globalized simultaneously. It may also be true that the terms 'public relations' and 'public affairs' themselves imply something unduly special, but organizations of all kinds have been communicating for centuries. Modern public relations has, how-ever, refined the techniques, integrated the action and given it a name, so that it is now a distinct discipline. Public relations has been organized professionally by the Institute of Public Relations (IPR) in Britain and the Public Relations Society of America (PRSA) in the USA. By 2002, the IPR had around 7000 members and the PRSA had around 20 000 members.

The British public relations industry has seen an increase in demand for consultancy services over the last 20 years, although there has been a downturn in business at the turn of the new millennium. Total billings declined in 2001, with some estimates indicating a drop in industry income of around 15 per cent (Anon., 2002a), probably as a result of the downturn in the telecommunication, media and technology sectors generally. PR has been used to promote new industries (e.g. the computer industry, medical imaging equipment), new services (e.g. Internet banking), new technologies (e.g. Sony's PlayStation), and new kinds of media (e.g. Internet and cable television). This upsurge in demand over this period created a need for more able and versatile staff. But professional training for PR professionals is still relatively underdeveloped. Realization that on-the-job training is insufficient for the healthy growth of the profession, and its ability to provide efficient, cost-effective services, has ensured the urgent attention of the professional bodies. Degree courses in PR continue to run at Bournemouth University Media School, Leeds Metropolitan University, Manchester Metropolitan University and Stirling University, for instance, among many others. The London Chamber of Commerce and Industry (LCCI) continues to develop interest in its public relations courses.

PR personnel have also raised their importance within their organizations as PR roles, and particularly that of the press officer, have gained increasing acceptance. Management is now much more likely to recognize the need to be involved in communications and PR directors are now much more likely to have a seat on the board. Modern public relations calls for people with a holistic view of business, who can act as advisers to management on a great variety of issues. Recruits to the industry are frequently second- or third-time career people, although there is now an increasing number of younger entrants, with university, CAM, LCCI or IPR qualifications or their counterparts in other countries.

Broadly, the public relations practitioner needs to possess the following personality traits and attributes:

- Ability to communicate.
- Ability to organize.
- Ability to get on with people.
- Personal integrity.
- Imagination.
- Willingness to learn.

Integrity is particularly important, since PROs are 'rated ... below politicians and journalists in terms of public trust' (Haywood, 2002), mainly due to the bad name given to the function by 'spin doctors'. The latter are government and political communication specialists seasoned in defining media-friendly perspectives on events or programmes, which tie in with their own organizational objectives.

Public relations practitioners need to have some knowledge of many ancillary subjects. For example, these can include:

- Media, both existing mass and created private.
- Printing.
- Photography, video, CD-ROM, DVD and other audio-visual, and visual, aids.
- Exhibitions.
- Marketing research.
- Sponsorships.

In addition, the ability to plan, budget and direct programmes is also fundamental (see Chapters 5–11). So, public relations practitioners need more than the ability to prepare press releases and entertain journalists, especially when many journalists and editors argue that very few practitioners are capable of writing a publishable news release! An adversarial situation between the media and public relations practitioners has developed as a result. PROs don't always help this situation by sending unsolicited press releases by fax and e-mail of little possible editorial value in the hopes of gaining column inches or news air time. Editors usually welcome the faxing of urgent material that they have invited, but the general distribution of releases by e-mail and fax has become an abuse of the privilege. The solution is to carefully cultivate a network of journalists and editors, to develop strong mutually trustworthy relationships with them, and to discuss possible press releases with one or two trusted sources before general release. If an event or communication is regarded by them to be a story, it can then be sent out to everyone else in the network, the next day. This kind of strategy, however, can sometimes alienate those journalists who are provided with the information later. After all, journalists are interested in getting a story first because it establishes their reputations and sells papers or stimulates advertising. Writing press and feature articles is covered in further detail in Chapters 14 and 15.

Public relations defined

The purpose of professional public relations is to create *understanding*. It is unlike advertising, whose main aim is to generate awareness and sales, or propaganda, whose aim is to suggest (in the true meaning of the word) what individuals should believe. Some commentators confuse public relations with these two very different forms of communication.

In many parts of the developing world, public relations techniques have been adopted because of the urgent need to educate people about new public services, and in order to introduce new lifestyles. It is important at this stage to establish a clear understanding of what public relations is all about. The IPR define public relations as: '*the planned and sustained effort to establish and maintain goodwill and mutual understanding between an organization and its publics*' (cited in Jefkins, 1994).

PR's importance lies in emphasizing the need for *planning, sustained effort* and *mutual understanding*. A lot of public relations is ineffective, and not cost-effective, precisely because it is haphazard and unplanned. Thus, management skills become fundamental. Sometimes, PR is criticized as being intangible and a waste of money. Of course, it can be if it is not planned and conducted properly, with clear objectives and assessable outcomes. Unlike advertising, which may have short-term campaigns, public relations activity should be sustained to be effective. Finally, there should be *mutual* understanding.

Most PR commentators would agree that public relations should aim to achieve consensus between an organization and its publics, but Holtzhausen (2000) argues that a PRO should strive to identify the tensions between the organization and internal and external publics. Through the identification of tensions, practitioners will promote and create situations in which new meaning is produced through difference and opposition. One could argue that Benetton used just such an approach in its advertising campaigns during the 1990s.

In public relations, organizations receive as well as transmit information. They must listen as well as speak.

In this regard, one definition of public relations emphasizes the role of research in the design of PR programmes. This is known as the Mexican Statement because it resulted from an international conference of public relations organizations held in Mexico City in 1978. It is a more comprehensive definition than those discussed previously:

> Public relations practice is the art and social science of analysing trends, predicting their consequences, counselling organization leaders, and implementing planned programmes of action that will serve both the organization's and the public interest.
>
> (cited in Jefkins, 1994)

The statement spells out the full role, nature and responsibilities of the public relations function. The statement outlines five important considerations in the PR process. These include:

- *Analysis of trends.* Before we can begin the planning emphasized in the IPR definition, it is necessary to investigate the current situation that the company finds itself in and its relations with its publics.

Questions that need to be considered include: what opinions or attitudes exist? What is the extent and accuracy of awareness? Is there understanding or misunderstanding? Does a good, bad or false image exist? Those publics concerned may consist of the community, employees, suppliers, distributors, consumers, financial institutions, politicians, civil servants, academics and a whole host of influential opinion leaders. A PR campaign needs to be planned with a full understanding of the trends that will influence the organization's future. Once communication problems and needs have been ascertained, the PRO can plan appropriate communication solutions. Much public relations work is about effecting change (see Chapter 25, on internal PR). PR department managers or consultants cannot recommend a programme and expect money to be funded for its execution unless a clear need for it, based on the organization's situation, has been conveyed. Sometimes, PR practitioners (in-house and within consultancies) present management with a distorted concept of the situation, which might be no more than an optimistic belief of the organization. This kind of wishful thinking is commonly known as '*the mirror image*'. It can lead to an ineffective PR campaign.

- *Predicting the consequences*. Once the situation has been studied, the consequences can be predicted. Generally referred to as the process of 'issues management', the PRO's task in this regard is to identify how publics will react to particular events. For example, in the European airline industry, the trend has been towards decreasing ticket prices for short-haul travel and increasing competition as airline alliances develop. The 11 September 2001 attacks exacerbated this overcapacity, as demand plummeted in the months after the attacks. The role of the PRO in this context is to explain why redundancies are fundamental and necessary, both to the survival of the company and the survival of existing employees.

- *Counselling leaders*. The advisory role of public relations is important. There are two aspects of public relations management. One is management of the in-house department or the consultancy, and client services, and the other is working with top management of the organization. Giving advice to leaders can range from personal advice on a day-to-day basis to attending committees consisting of managers or board directors. In many of our most successful companies there is a one-to-one relationship between the chief executive officer and the public relations director, the most prominent example of which has been the relationship between British Prime Minister, Tony Blair, and his press secretary, Alastair Campbell. Equally, US President Bill Clinton's relationship with his press secretary, Mike McCurry, was fundamental to his continuing popularity during his second term. Having conducted the research and assessed the findings, the PR practitioner's task is to advise management on what needs to be done. The campaign plan requires diligent attention to the planning of the workload in terms of hours and use of materials, resources and expenses.

- *Implementing planned programmes of action.* Implementation of the planned programme, including opportunities to report progress, and to be flexible if circumstances change, are fundamental to the effective PR plan. The programme should have strategic, measurable, actionable, realistic and timely objectives (see Chapter 7). The extent to which these objectives are eventually achieved should be either obvious or measurable.
- *Serving the public interest.* The programme should also serve the public interest. In other words, it should be socially responsible and ethical. It should not exploit or corrupt the integrity of the media. If the practitioner is a member of his or her professional body (e.g. the IPR or PRSA), he or she will be expected to uphold a code of professional conduct. As a manager this relates not only to external relations but also to a refusal to accept instructions to behave unethically. Some employers and clients take it for granted that the public relations practitioner can be used to manipulate the media. Armed with the code of conduct, the professional PR practitioner should refuse to accept such abuses.

Whilst the ineffective PR practitioner is responsible for the conflict involved in the adversarial relationship with journalists, it is also true that journalists can often create false ideas of, and expectations, for PR initiatives. Press dislike for public relations is exemplified, for instance, when a politician visits a disaster area, where even a sincere action might be mocked and subsequently is unfavourably reported. A visit by the British Prime Minister, Tony Blair, and the hapless transport secretary, Stephen Byers, to the site of the Potters Bar train crash in 2002 was absolutely fundamental. The media had been increasingly reporting stories of mismanagement in the rail industry and government failings on safety issues. Conversely, the New York Mayor, Rudolph Guiliani, galvanized the press during his visit to Ground Zero, the site of the World Trade Center, after the terrorist attacks of 11 September 2001. These initial and subsequent visits to the site ensured continued support for the victims in the immediate aftermath of the attack from around the world. Of course, the PR function does not only deal with crisis management problems. As it seeks to generate understanding amongst the media, it uses photo-opportunities and soundbites for other purposes also. These are often mocked by the press, particularly in the political PR context. Interestingly, the media find themselves increasingly using this material as political parties become more experienced at news management.

The comparison of public relations with advertising and propaganda is often confused. Public relations works best when it is perceived to be unbiased. It should deal in facts, not fancies. To succeed, both advertising and propaganda attempt to create positive associations amongst their audiences with their messages. While advertising puffs up 'truth' through self-enhancement and exaggerated claims, propaganda vehemently denies the credence of other perspectives despite the dubiousness of its own claims. In contrast, public relations techniques are often used to reduce negative associations as well as to create positive ones. This is done by attempting to create understanding. This does not deny the role of persuasion, or rhetoric, in modern public relations, it simply outlines that PR has to be believed to be effective, mainly because its messages are often then conveyed as fact by third-parties.

The primary objective of public relations

The object of public relations is frequently thought to be the achievement of a favourable image, a favourable climate of opinion, or a favourable mention by the media. That is a misunderstanding. Organizations are never able to please all of the people all of the time. But they can achieve *understanding*, amongst their major publics, which is very different from approval. Good examples of organizations that seek to generate such understanding include those in the nuclear (e.g. British Nuclear Fuels Ltd.) and oil and gas industries (e.g. Shell, Esso/Exxon). Some organizations have very good relations with the press. Virgin, Richard Branson's group of companies, generally enjoys very favourable relations with the British press, projected, as his company often is, as the champion of consumer values. The model outlined in Figure 1.1 illustrates the stages of public mood that a public relations programme may deal with. The task is to move public opinion from downright hostility through prejudice, apathy and ignorance towards interest, acceptance, sympathy and ultimately empathy. In order to move up through these stages, the PRO must help publics become more knowledgeable about the company and its perspective. This helps to generate understanding amongst publics and drives the transfer process. The process is circular, as successive publics influence each other. PROs frequently enter the public mood at the stage of hostility, although they could enter at subsequent stages, mainly because publics are usually suspicious of an organization's motives, until they are clarified, and because of an innate fear of change. Each of these stages of public mood is considered further in isolation.

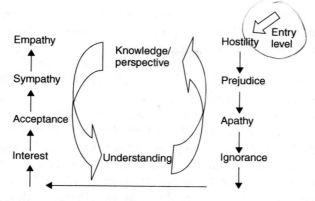

Figure 1.1 The public relations transfer process.
Source: adapted from Jefkins (1994)

Hostility

What is the extent of the nature of hostility towards the organization, its people, activities, products or services? In the case of the Union Carbide/Bhopal crisis in 1984 – detailed in Chapter 26 – hostility amongst the Indian media was substantial. The hostility may be irrational, based on fear, misunderstanding or false information. In this case, although there were numerous reasons for the release of noxious substances in the air, Union Carbide were seen to be partly to blame for not implementing adequate safety procedures, as was the Indian government for allowing the development of slums around the factory.

The public may feel threatened by an organization or by what it does, yet no genuine threat may exist. It may be that dislike remains but it is possible to achieve an attitude of tolerance. In recent times, many ideas which were once hated have now won sympathy if not support. In developing countries, new lifestyles have been adopted which were once resisted, while in the industrialized world new technologies have won, or are winning, approval.

Prejudice

This word literally means to prejudge, to form an opinion or attitude without considering available information. Can we convert prejudice into acceptance? BT is a good example of this. It has been blamed for the late development of broadband services in the UK. Yet whilst the government demanded that it open up its network for broadband use, it was prohibited by government from offering entertainment products on its telecommunication networks until 2002. Many potential users regard BT as overpriced, yet they have no understanding of its need to adhere to government pricing regulations.

The task of converting prejudice is not a simple one. Such attitudes can endure for a long time. For instance, success and affluence seldom change working class people's attitudes, as we usually see in election voting patterns. Prejudices can survive lifetimes, as we can see in disputes all over the world. The IRA believed until well into the 1990s that the British government wanted to maintain rule over Northern Ireland. It was not until secret meetings took place between John Major's security service representatives and IRA operatives that this misunderstanding was cleared up; namely, that the British interest was self-determination for the province.

From a business perspective, such prejudice is frequently illustrated in the travel business. Travellers are now taking holidays in countries towards which they were once deeply prejudiced (e.g. Russia, China and Japan). The French authorities maintained a ban on British beef, after it was linked to several deaths, even though the EU had removed its own ban. The continuing French ban was subsequently declared illegal by the European Union. However, a more cynical observer might well say that the French continued the ban not because they were prejudiced against the safety of British beef products, but because the French wanted to ensure that they supplied the domestic market for beef, a £250 million market for British beef at 1996 volumes (Baines and Harris, 2000).

Apathy

Hallahan (2000) argues that inactive publics (for the PR definition of publics, see Chapter 8) are usually ignored and forgotten by PROs. He argues that PR strategies should aim to enhance motivation and ability to process information. To do this, it might well have to create opportunities to communicate. With non-publics, PROs either should ignore them, or create a reason why they should involve themselves and communicate this. Once they become aroused, he argues that PROs supply information that addresses concerns and clarifies misunderstandings.

People are, however, naturally conservative. They have a self-protective resistance to change. If public relations activity is to achieve understanding, it has to break down this unwillingness to want to know. Apathy may deter a person from considering taking a holiday, for example, to India. Whilst advertising might generate the initial awareness of the opportunity to holiday in India, the public may feel that India's relations with Pakistan, and possible nuclear confrontation over Kashmir, make it too dangerous a place for holiday-making. The role of public relations would be to convince potential holiday-makers that it was not too dangerous and that, indeed, the risk was minimal.

Ignorance

Inevitably, sometimes people are ignorant about a subject. For instance, in high-technology markets, this is frequently the norm, where consumers and other publics have limited understanding of what the organization is trying to do. An example might include outlining the benefits of a new on-line trading system for small businesses. Such situations require the use of public relations to educate the market, before the advertising and direct mail campaigns can begin.

At the beginning of a new product or service launch, most people are ignorant of what any organization offers, so it's important to prepare the market to ensure it is more likely to respond to subsequent advertising. Such a process may occupy 18 months to two years work, depending on the complexity of the product or service, before advertising starts. Many products and services have failed because market education activities were not undertaken.

Interest

PROs are often particularly good at generating media interest in causes and new product/service launches. Such interest may be sparked by writing newsworthy press releases in such a way as to present the new idea as novel or unusual, or in a novel or unusual way. Alternatively, interest may be generated directly with particular publics through exhibitions, house journals, sales or distributor bulletins, through broadcast news reports or through industry seminars. A co-ordinated marketing communications campaign incorporating PR and supportive advertising may be key to stimulating initial interest.

Acceptance

Although publics generally might not agree, or might be unsure, of a company's actions, this type of campaign is designed to bring about a public's acceptance of a particular problem, often as a precursor to their agreement. Employee relations disputes might well bring about this type of campaign after a recent recession or crisis has occurred.

The PRO's role might be to explain that the company had few other choices but to lay off staff and that, in doing so, this ensured a large number of other employees' jobs. The union might not agree with the actions undertaken, but hopefully they will accept that action was necessary.

Sympathy

This stage requires the PRO to move public opinion into a broadly supportive mood. Whilst sympathy is generally a supportive attribute, it also constitutes a level of emotional detachment. A PR programme might need to effect attitude changes or at least a greater understanding of the salience of issues in public opinion. Charitable organizations frequently attempt to move public opinion in this direction for their particular causes (e.g. the NSPCC's Full Stop child abuse prevention campaign or the National Heart Foundation's Save a Life campaign).

Empathy

This stage is rarely totally achieved. It denotes when public opinion is almost or perfectly congruent with that of the management of the organization. Attitudes and opinions of the public are in line with those of the management of the firm. Recently, in the market research industry, there has been focus on customer empathy, a practice of determining not only whether or not customers are satisfied, but how they feel at the same time. In times of crisis, empathizing with public opinion is imperative if the company wishes to emerge from the crisis in a positive light. Empathy is a stage beyond sympathy, connoting total involvement with what an organization is trying to do. The Harley Davidson organization would probably argue that it has managed to develop customer empathy through its super customer engagement programme. Whenever Harley Davidson organizes an event, people come flocking to them from all over the world. Sometimes, political organizations, religious orders, sports clubs and pop bands achieve this kind of support, often through skilful event management designed to reinforce customer identification with the cause, product or service. Clearly, in such cases, one could argue that a cult has developed.

From these comments on the four negative states of hostility, prejudice, apathy and ignorance, and the four positive states of interest, acceptance, sympathy and empathy, it should be clear that before planning, budgeting and recommending a public relations programme, it is essential to research public opinion. Some or all of these states may exist. Equally, there may be acclaim rather than hostility, tolerance rather than prejudice, enthusiasm instead of apathy and wisdom instead of ignorance. Such an ideal situation is unlikely. Public relations is concerned with the development of *understanding* by the provision of information and perspective.

Is understanding really the primary purpose of public relations?

There are those who insist that public relations is, and should be, a form of advertising; that it is a cheap substitute for advertising (earned or free media, as it is sometimes called in the US). The media often tend to regard public relations stories as advertisements. Unfortunately, too many of them actually are!

It is true that most public relations people work in-house, and not in consultancies (the opposite of advertising practice), and it is also true that the greater part of public relations activity is conducted outside the commercial world. Public relations has an enlarged role to play in not-for-profit organizations, principally because of the increased accountability placed on managers in such organizations by their publics. Example organizations include central and local government, NGOs (non-governmental organizations), political parties, trade unions, professional institutes, voluntary bodies and trade associations, the police, the armed forces, the fire and ambulance brigades, the health and social services, charities, special interest societies, and clubs, sports clubs and societies.

A PRO might be trying to create understanding of a hospital's work in heart transplant surgery, or the achievements of police working in multiracial regions, or the tenets of Islam (rather than the militant version propagated by fundamentalists). Equally, they may be involved in generating publicity for a new car product launch. Either way, they are concerned with disseminating information and perspective to their publics, in order to create understanding of what their organization is trying to achieve. This is the primary objective of public relations. Understanding is best achieved when:

1. Top management understands PR practice and knows exactly what it needs to communicate. The chief executive is literally the organization's chief PRO.
2. PROs are answerable to their chief executives, and may be board directors or consultants who serve an appreciative top management.
3. Good media relationships are developed based on mutual frankness and respect. Practitioners understand how, when and why editors

need material, and editors know who they can rely on to supply what they want, when, and how they want it.

Comparing and contrasting PR with its sister functions

Understanding how public relations contributes to the work of an organization is frequently best understood by considering what it does not do, or how it differs from other functions. These include public affairs, marketing and advertising. Many organizational charts do not show the PRO in an independent role. Sometimes, the PRO comes under the marketing services manager or may be a part of the job specification of particular directors, managers and executives. Figure 1.2 outlines the organization chart for Bass, the brewer (Wilson, 2001). The full-time PRO occupies a senior role in the corporate affairs department, and has line management authority over both the media relations and public affairs functions. The PRO services all functions of the organization but reports directly to the chief executive.

Public relations and public affairs

Some unnecessary confusion has been created by the use of these two expressions. Public affairs is sometimes used to mean simply public relations. An American euphemism, it has been imported into Britain. Whilst public relations is generally regarded as the umbrella term for organizational communication activities, the more commercial and

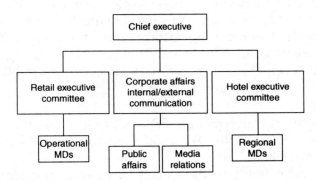

Figure 1.2   Public relations at Bass.
Source: Wilson (2001)

perhaps marketing-orientated communications now tend to be defined as public relations. Nowadays, regulatory affairs, parliamentary liaison and lobbying tend to be subsumed under public affairs. Public affairs activities are generally those that involve dialogue with government for purposes of public policy-making, legislation and regulation. This topic is considered in further detail in Chapter 29.

Public relations and marketing

This is a more controversial topic. Kotler and Mindak (1978) outline five different models of how PR and marketing relate to one another: marketing and PR are distinct but separate; separate but overlapping functions; marketing is the dominant function and PR a subset; PR is the dominant function and marketing a subset; and marketing and PR are converging functions.

Some view marketing as distinct and separate departments within the organization. It could be argued that PR sometimes concerns organizations that might not be engaged in traditional marketing activity, e.g. political parties. However, even such organizations have now developed marketing departments that include advertising (often aligned with membership development or income generation departments). Charities generally have their own marketing departments as well. Whilst there are similarities between the two, the difference between the two is highlighted well in the following quote:

> Marketing deals with markets and public relations with publics. Organizations can create a market by identifying a segment of the population for which a product is or could be in demand. Publics create themselves however, whenever organizations make decisions that affect a group of people adversely.
>
> (J. E. Grunig, cited in Briggs and Tucson, 1993)

Often, within universities, there is both a corporate communications department and a marketing services department. Nevertheless, although these departments might well have different remits, they frequently report to the same boss: often the pro-vice chancellor for corporate affairs in the UK context. There are those who see public relations as a subset of marketing. PR, it is argued, is a component of the communication mix along with sales promotion, personal selling, advertising and direct marketing. An American academic, Martha Lauzen, assistant professor at San Diego State University, argues that marketing is attempting to subsume all PR's roles and functions. She defines this as marketing imperialism:

> Marketing imperialism is the intrusion of marketing into the activities traditionally within the domain of public relations.
> (Lauzen, cited in Briggs and Tucson, 1993)

Examples might include corporate identity schemes, cause-related marketing and corporate social responsibility initiatives, and sponsorship. But public relations activity principally aimed at an organization's customers is differentiated in this text by its denotation as marketing public relations. This topic is considered further in Chapter 28. Some might argue that PR should be the dominant function in relation to marketing because it considers all stakeholders, whereas marketing is mainly focused on the customer. Finally, marketing and PR could be seen as converging functions, particularly in markets where public opinion (that driven by the mass media) has considerable impact upon corporate image (e.g. the pharmaceutical market and anti-retroviral drugs in South Africa) and this is likely to impact upon profitability in the long term.

Really, it depends on what role marketing plays within a particular organization, and the power structures that develop within, and between, the two departments *vis-à-vis* the chief executive. If marketing has a strategic role, the PR function is more likely to come within its remit. Nevertheless, even in that scenario, public relations still has a role to play in every stage of a co-ordinated marketing communications campaign.

Public relations and advertising

Several comparisons have been made between public relations and advertising. To emphasize and distinguish the differences between the two, let us consider four distinct areas in which these differences occur. They are:

1. The people addressed (i.e. the target audiences or publics).
2. The media through which these people are addressed.
3. The costs and methods of payment.
4. The purpose of the communication.

I The people addressed

Advertising campaigns are usually concentrated on the largest number of potential buyers. Public relations programmes are dispersed among different groups of people. Advertising addresses the target audience, whereas public relations might address many publics. While advertising is aimed mostly at distributors, users and consumers in order to sell, and to suppliers in order to recruit and buy from them, publics can include stakeholders other than suppliers, customers or buyers. Not all organizations are involved in industry, trade or commerce. We have already mentioned that most public relations exists outside the business world, and to substantiate this claim here, in greater detail, ignore some of the non-business organizations in which the public relations function is particularly important:

- The police, armed forces, prison service, fire brigade, ambulance services.
- Hospitals and other health services.
- Universities, schools and other educational establishments.
- Societies, institutes and associations representing special interests, including professional and trade bodies.
- Churches and various religious organizations, such as missionary and denominational educational societies.
- Cultural organizations, e.g. libraries, museums, art galleries, symphony orchestras, and choirs and choral societies.
- Sports clubs representing every kind of amateur and professional sport.
- Political parties, political societies, trade unions.
- Central government, ministries and departments.
- Local government authorities.
- Charities and voluntary bodies ranging from Marie Curie Cancer Care to the Royal National Lifeboat Institute.

Many of these organizations also use advertising techniques to raise funds, recruit employees, and inform customers and consumers, but they are usually non-profit-making and so advertising has traditionally played a secondary role, perhaps because there is seldom the available budget for this activity or because it is regarded as less necessary. Notable exceptions to this include the NSPCC Full Stop Campaign. It is interesting to note that, despite its success, it was criticized in certain quarters as wasteful expenditure.

2 The media

Table 1.1 illustrates the different media used by the advertising and public relations functions for comparison purposes. If the lists are compared side by side, it is clear that there are differences in the use of some similar or identical media, while there are many media used only by advertising, and yet more which are specially created for public relations purposes. The latter may be called private or sponsored media and they are seldom mass media, whereas advertising generally exploits mass media.

Table 1.1 An advertising and PR media comparison

Advertising media	Public relations media
i. Display and classified ads in consumer magazines, trade, technical and professional journals	i. News stories, feature articles, newspapers, pictures for the press. Internal and external journals
ii. Commercials (film or videotape) and advertising films for transmission on television and cinema screens. Sponsored TV/radio programmes	ii. Videotapes, slides, cassettes, corporate video by satellite, video news releases, CD-ROM, DVD. Sponsored TV/radio programmes
iii. Radio commercials	iii. Taped radio interviews, studio interviews, phone-ins, news
iv. Posters, signs, buses and other ambient advertising media	iv. Educational posters, in-house posters
v. Public, trade, permanent or mobile exhibitions	v. Public relations aspects of all exhibitions and private exhibitions
vi. Sales promotion schemes	vi. Educational literature and other printed information
vii. Point-of-sale displays	vii. Sponsored publications
viii. Sales literature, leaflets, brochures, catalogues	viii. Seminars and conferences, spoken word sometimes combined with video shows, slide presentations and exhibits
ix. Direct mail	ix. Press facility visits, works visits, open days
x. Door-to-door mail drops of sales literature, samples, cash vouchers	x. Annual reports and accounts, company histories
xi. Sponsorship for purposes of advertising or direct marketing	xi. Event management, e.g. floats at carnivals, awards of prizes, sponsorship of events and causes
xii. Special forms of advertising, aerial, shopping bags, other novelties	xii. Corporate identity livery, symbols (logos), colours, typography, uniforms, dress, badges

The lists in Table 1.1 are by no means complete, but they help to show that advertising and public relations can communicate differently by means of different communication media. There has, however, been a continuing trend to integrate marketing communications activity such that advertising and public relations programmes contribute to each other's objectives.

3 Costs and payment

In marketing it is usual to refer to above-the-line and below-the-line. Advertising is regarded as above-the-line, whilst PR, sales promotion and direct marketing are below-the-line. The historical reasons for this are explained in Box 1.1. To explain the advertising agency commission

Box 1.1

The terms 'above' and 'below' the line developed because of the nature of the commission systems, and methods of billing, used by agencies for much of the twentieth century.

Companies would earn their money advertising work not from the advertiser but as a commission from the media owner. The media owner would invoice the agency less the commission, whereas the agency would charge at full cost. Thus, the agency's fees were 'above' the line – included in the total and not as an extra.

If the agency offered a company other services (e.g. sales promotion, PR), these would be extra costs and designated below the line.

system more thoroughly, agencies may be recognized (or accredited as it is called in some countries) by bodies representing publishing houses and broadcasting stations or contractors. It is more convenient for the media to deal with a small number of space and air time buyers (e.g. advertising agents) than with large numbers of advertisers. Commission is seldom adequate and agents commonly charge their clients a supplementary percentage. Agents also earn commission on work which they subcontract in order to produce advertisements, e.g. typesetting and photography, but in some cases, e.g. printing, the supplier does not deduct a commission but adds a percentage which represents the agent's handling cost. Thus, whereas it could be cheaper for the client to buy print direct, it would not be cheaper for him or her to buy space or air time direct. The advertising agent's sources of income are various and complicated. There are some agents who reject the commission system and work more professionally for fees representing hours and expertise. There are also media independents which only plan and buy media and agencies that only do creative work.

Public relations consultancies, by contrast, do not generally accept commissions. They are mainly selling time (e.g. man-hours and expertise) and materials and expenses. The hourly or daily rate for public relations services covers salaries, overheads and profits, and is often paid as a retainer. Costs associated with advertising agency and public relations agency services are outlined in Table 1.2.

4 The purpose
Generally, advertising and public relations functions have tended to work to different objectives. More recently, with the introduction of integrated marketing communications programmes, their purposes have become increasingly intertwined. Generally, public relations aims to

Table 1.2 Comparison of advertising and PR costs

Advertising costs	Agency payment
Advertising space in the press	Commission on space, air time, screen bookings, poster site rentings
Airtime on television and radio	Charges for artwork and costs of production
Rental of poster sites	On-costs of work farmed out to suppliers (e.g. printers)
Screen time at cinemas	Discounts from suppliers (e.g. photographers, film, videotape, DVD, CD-ROM makers)
Stand space at exhibitions	Fees for work which bears no commission
Production costs of: (a) Press advertisements (b) Television commercials (c) Radio commercials (d) Cinema screen commercials (e) Exhibition stands (f) Print, display material	

Although commissions were the traditional method of agency payment, the number of clients using this method has declined significantly in favour of a combination of methods including (Smith, 2002):

- Commission rebating – where the client received a rebate on the inclusive commission price
- Fees larger companies in particular are moving to retainers or project fees
- Pay by results – some agencies (usually the young and aspiring ones) are prepared to gamble on the success of their work

Public relations costs	Consultancy payment
Time – salaries	Fee based on hourly/daily rate
Materials – stationery, postage, photography	Recovery of cost of materials, usually at cost, but sometimes with handling charge
Expenses – travelling, hotels, hospitality	Recovery of expenses at cost

educate and inform in order to create understanding, whereas advertising seeks to inform or remind in order to persuade and sell. The two may be related in the sense that it is difficult or excessively costly to persuade and sell if prospective buyers lack knowledge and understanding of what is being advertised. Public relations can often be a precursor activity to advertising. The success of the advertising may also depend on the corporate image and the reputation of the advertiser, which also requires publics to have knowledge, understanding and, perhaps, previous experience.

The Tate Modern launch case study: an IPR excellence award winner, 2001

The Tate Modern communications team was a winner of an IPR excellence award in 2001. Their winning submission to this award is reproduced here, in abridged form, to provide readers with an indication of what the organization of a PR campaign involves. It provides details of the campaign's background and objectives, strategy and plan, target audience, campaign execution and implementation and, finally, the results and evaluation of the campaign, and why it was so successful. It clearly outlines those aspects of a campaign that a PRO would need to consider when writing a PR campaign plan.

Background and campaign planning

Tate Modern opened to the public on 12 May 2000. It was the first new national museum to open in London in a century. It became the first national museum for modern art in London and was supported by a Millennium Commission project funded by the National Lottery. Housed in the former Bankside Power Station, Tate Modern displays the Tate collection of international modern art from 1900 to the present day. There is a full range of special exhibitions and a broad public programme of events throughout the year. The ex-power station has been transformed into a modern museum by Swiss architects Herzog and de Meuron. The former Turbine Hall now marks a breathtaking entrance to the gallery. At night, a light-weight luminous roof is a unique addition to the London skyline. The objective of the Tate communications team was to ensure that the launch of the new Tate was covered sufficiently by both the national and international media. It also wished to broaden appeal, double attendance, be seen to be worth the entrance fee, differentiate the new Tate from the original by calling one Tate Modern and the other Tate Britain, achieve international acknowledgement and involve the local community. Each of these objectives is considered further in Table 1.3.

In conjunction with PR consultants, Bolton and Quinn, the Tate communications team secured the support of high-profile endorsers and key members of the media. An editorial column in the *Financial Times* ran from 1997, as the Tate Modern was still fund-raising. The campaign achieved a build-up of interest through strategically generated editorial coverage at all major stages of the project.

Table 1.3 Objectives of the Tate Modern campaign

Objective	*Further Details*
Broaden appeal	Make modern art more accessible and less elitist by attracting people who intend to come to galleries but who rarely do
Double attendance	In figures, the Tate communications team set sights on doubling the attendance to Tate
Be seen to be worth the money	Needed to ensure it was seen to be a project worth the money compared with other millennium projects
Clarify Tate Britain	Position Tate at Millbank as Tate Britain before launching Tate Modern. Tate Britain was dispatched two months ahead of Tate Modern
Achieve international acknowledgement	Ensure the attention of the international media, particularly those in New York and Paris, which already have well-established modern art museums
Involve the local community	Involve local residents and community groups so that they could benefit from the new gallery

Campaign execution and implementation

The communications team wished to attract a wide audience to Tate Modern, so it was necessary to secure the support of television, the mid-market papers and crucially the tabloids. Favourable coverage in the tabloids was arranged through events such as the black-cab drivers preview. In a special preview session, 20 000 black-cab drivers in London were invited to a preview especially for them. The idea was that this would enable the 'cabbies' to explain and talk about the gallery to their passengers. An ingenious idea, since it is likely that they would frequently be asked for directions and to be driven to its location. The Tate communications team distributed press releases and photographs. In March 2000, *The Observer* did a special supplement to launch Tate Britain, and *Vogue* magazine printed its own feature in May. The Tate Modern team also managed to secure a four-part documentary on Channel 4 on the architecture and building project, in addition to four art documentaries on BBC2, whilst the actual opening by the Queen was covered live on BBC1. GMTV hosted their breakfast show from the Tate Modern. Working with PR agencies in France and New York, the Tate communications team was able to secure extensive international coverage and specialist art world press throughout the world. In its corporate identity programme, The Tate logo, designed by Wolff Olins, was applied to all items of print, the website, merchandise, signage and

Table 1.4 An outline of the key audiences and the advocacy mechanisms adopted

Target Audiences	*Key advocacy mechanisms*
Media: press, broadcast (television and radio), national and international	Enlisting the support of high-profile endorsers and key members of the media
Government	Lobbying government to ensure Tate Modern entry was free
Artists	Involvement of British artists (important in international context)
Art critics (national and international)	A range of private views and tours for all sectors throughout the project were arranged.
Art enthusiasts	Communication liaison and involvement
Art 'beginners' (e.g. cab drivers) – see below	through the set-up of visitor centres. The *raison d'être* for the Tate Modern was explained
Local Southwark community	Prior to the main press days, a private view of the museum for local residents and press was arranged

uniform at both the Tate Modern and Tate Britain. The PR programme was supported by other marketing and advertising activity. Table 1.4 outlines some of the key ways in which the Tate team communicated with their audiences.

The creative content of the campaign was enhanced by collaborations with British artists, one of the campaign's stated objectives. A fanfare by Sir Harrison Birtwistle was commissioned for the Queen's formal opening of the museum and Tracy Emin produced a front cover for *The Observer*'s British Art supplement. Celebrities were invited to the opening party (e.g. Madonna, Mick Jagger, Kylie Minogue and Claudia Schiffer).

Results and evaluation

The campaign's initial objectives were achieved. The media campaign was successful in ensuring favourable tabloid coverage. Between 12 and 17 May 2000, the Tate Modern had 317 column inches of space in national print media, making it the fifth biggest story that particular week. International media coverage was also extensive. The approximate total audience reached through national television alone during April, May and June 2000 was estimated at 126.7 million. Thirteen articles in the tabloids represent a potential reader audience figure of approximately 32.5 million. In addition, 5.25 million people visited Tate Modern in its first year (more than double the team's expectations). Over 1 million of these came in the first six weeks. The website was initially registering an average of 24 million hits per month. By May 2000, the website was receiving around 10 million hits per day.

Chapter 2

The psychology of public relations communication

LEARNING OBJECTIVES

At the end of this chapter you will be able to:

- describe the basic elements involved in the mass communication process;
- outline the main means of communication in PR;
- explain the meaning of source credibility and attractiveness;
- explain psychological reactance theory and its relevance to PR.

The psychology of the mass communication process

The purpose of public relations is to create understanding by imparting knowledge and information. This process requires the PRO to select the most appropriate media and techniques for the particular task at hand. For instance, if a workforce is becoming increasingly unhappy with its remuneration package, then it is better to communicate with them through internal meetings, newsletters and the intranet than it is through editorial coverage in local newspapers, for instance. Equally, if the Prince of Wales wants the British public to accept that Camilla Parker-Bowles may well become his wife, then it is important for his press secretary to convey the couple in a positive light. This would be best achieved through favourable editorial coverage, which would be facilitated through the organization of appropriate events (e.g. charity work, royal occasions and photo-opportunities). So the selection of the media channel by which we need to communicate with a particular public is imperative. Why is this so?

Often, people do not understand us and what we do either because they have not received, or comprehended, information that we have disseminated. Messages can be conveyed through the press, radio, television, video, exhibitions, the Internet and the spoken word, but it all depends on how effectively the message is transmitted and received. We should consider that, in any one day, we receive thousands of messages. Consider, for instance, a typical working woman in London might well be woken by her clock radio, blurting out adverts for the local DIY store and furniture retailer, for instance. Whilst she eats breakfast, she may encounter advertisements on either Channel 4 or 5 or ITV, and she might well listen to the morning news programmes. Picking up the morning post, she opens direct mail from, say, charities and financial service organizations. On her way to the rail station, she might encounter many billboards advertising, among other things, L'Oreal. On the tube, reading the free paper to avoid eye contact with the other passengers, she will likely encounter many press adverts and editorial coverage concerning commercial products. After arriving at work, she will probably have been subjected to hundreds of messages begging for her attention. By the time she goes to bed, this could literally be thousands. So the PR message may often be lost in all the other messages that we receive. When we consider that we are recipients not only of commercial messages, but also social and interpersonal messages, we start to realize just how sophisticated the communication, memory and perception processes of the human brain must be.

If we paid attention to all these messages, wouldn't we go mad? We think you probably would. But our brain ensures that we only take account of those messages that we find meaningful in some way. This process of screening out interesting information from the clutter is known as *selective attention*. We are interested only in certain types of products, so men would not generally be interested in adverts about lipstick, for instance, although marketers for cosmetic firms are trying hard to get them to wear moisturizer. Consider this phenomenon in your own life. If you are looking to book a holiday, look how interested you become in messages about flights or package tours. The same goes for the couple who have just bought a house. Adverts for washing machines have never been, or are likely to be again, so enticing! The messages that we ignore, often referred to as clutter, are effectively communication 'noise', since they can distort the way in which we receive other more meaningful messages.

If we not only avoid exposure to certain messages, but actively seek others (e.g. requesting a catalogue), this is known as *selective exposure*. We

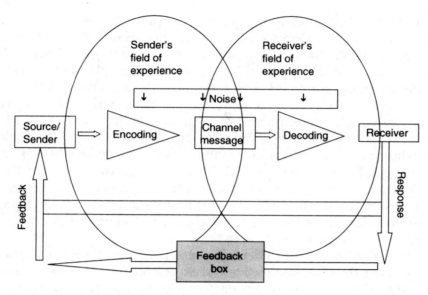

Figure 2.1 The classical model of the communication process.
Source: Smith (2002); based on Schramm (1955)

may also be seen to selectively expose ourselves to certain kinds of messages through the media we choose to read or watch. For instance, some people do not read newspapers (and so will not see press advertisements). Some people do not listen to the radio very often or read different types of magazines. Figure 2.1 illustrates the basic communication process.

From the diagram, and using a public relations communication example, we can see that a message (e.g. a new vaccine has been developed to cure the AIDS virus) emanates from a source (e.g. a pharmaceutical manufacturing company), is encoded (into a brief for a PR agency which is subsequently formatted perhaps as a video news release), passes through a message channel (e.g. CNN; say, Richard Quest's business news programme – see interview with Richard Quest from CNN on pp. 290–7), is then decoded (into an editorial feature) and is received by the television-watching public. So there are numerous opportunities for the message to be received differently from that intended. Note that further communication is based on the response of the recipient and feedback and that the communication does not occur in isolation, but in a system where others are also communicating, and creating distracting 'noise'.

Why is communication sometimes so difficult? Part of the reason is because people generally do not like to read things they can only just barely understand, and the same goes for listening to audio messages and watching audio-visual images. People prefer reading matter that requires no effort in reading and to listen and watch straightforward news bulletins. As such, it is important to keep messages simple. This may be the reason for the growing 'soundbite' and photo-opportunity culture in Britain, where PR companies provide journalists with ready-made commentaries for their editorial and news bulletins, and with photos, video releases or photo-opportunities. In Britain, the difference in style of writing between popular tabloid newspapers and the quality broadsheet newspapers is stark. Compare, for instance, the difference in literary style between the *Sun* and the *Daily Telegraph*. Of course, these newspapers have very different readerships in terms of size, demography and socio-economic status. So, it is important when writing a press release to tailor that release to the audience of the newspaper you are sending it to (see Chapters 14 and 15).

Communication is also difficult because the recipient of the message does not have the same knowledge and experience (not necessarily less or more, just different) as the communicator. This may partially explain why people 'turn off' when listening or viewing messages. Communicators talk about needing *'overlapping fields of communication'* in which both the sender and the receiver are talking the same cultural language. Knowledge and experience develops with familiarity and repetition. People have different personalities, which in turn affects the formation of their attitudes, opinions and values. This is what makes communication so difficult. Two people may perceive the exact same message differently. This is because they hold different opinions, attitudes and values. Let's outline what opinions, attitudes and values actually are.

Opinions are best described as those quick reactions we tend to make to opinion poll questions about current issues. They are usually held with limited conviction, often because we have not yet formed or fully developed an attitude. This is not to say that pollsters always question people about opinions; if we hold a strong view, our perspective on an issue is probably linked to a formed attitude. Worcester and Mortimore (1999), Chairman and Managing Director respectively of market research firm MORI, explain that opinions are the 'ripples on the surface of the public's consciousness, easily blown about in the winds of political comment and attention by the media... They are unlikely to have been the topic of discussion or debate between them and their relations, friends and work-mates'. Attitudes, however, are held with conviction, over a longer duration and are much more likely to influence behaviour. Conversely, values are even more strongly held. They tend to be linked to our conscience, imbued through the familial socialization process, culture and religion, and are frequently formed as infants.

The opinion poll, a measurement tool designed to systematically and objectively measure public opinion, was developed by George Gallup and first employed in the 1936 US Presidential election (Anon., 1991). It is an important device, particularly in public relations, because it allows us to determine how messages are being received by our intended publics. It is important in planning PR campaigns, particularly in situation analysis (see Chapter 6) and implementation and control (see Chapter 11). Whilst quantitative research, traditionally carried out by telephone or street interview, is generally used to measure opinions and attitudes, values require the use of qualitative research, such as focus groups or depth interviews.

Communication is part of the learning process, and public relations is about informing, educating and creating understanding. In order for the public to understand what we are trying to convey, messages often need to be repeated, since people usually forget them over time, particularly the specific arguments or message presented. The general substance or conclusion of the message is marginally more likely to be remembered (Bettinghaus and Cody, 1994, p. 67). Thus, political parties have coined the term to be 'on message'. This outlines the need to continually repeat messages, slogans and mantras (assuming that they are resonating with the public, of course!) through various communication media simultaneously. Senior executives of the central committees of political parties have occasionally insisted that MPs check with their party's media centre first before they conduct a television interview or issue a press release. This has not always been heeded, principally because MPs have tended to believe that they are perfectly able to construct their own interview. However, messages tend to have more resonance with the public if strong, believable arguments are presented and repeated. In advertising, if weak arguments are presented, the measured attitude towards the advert declines towards unfavourability. Where the message is novel, favourability increases until recipients receive messages for the third time, when favourability begins to decline (Bettinghaus and Cody, 1994, p. 86).

Message receipt is also affected by peer group pressure, intended or otherwise. The publishing of opinion polls during elections has long been banned in various countries (e.g. France), precisely because they are believed to impact upon the final vote. Thus, members of groups tend to conform to a group norm, enhancing the self-image of the recipient and increasing the feeling of group identity and belongingness. It is important for the PRO to understand that their intended publics may have their own cultures and subcultures, which impact upon how the message is received. Some messages are deliberately aimed, not at the ultimate recipient, but at 'opinion leaders' such as religious, cultural or social leaders who have influence over the target group. A number of public relations campaigns have leveraged the persuasive power of reference group membership through word-of-mouth campaigns. The producers of the film, *The Blair Witch Project*, initially marketed the film at minimal cost through their website and using viral marketing techniques (i.e. e-mail requesting users to send on information to other interested parties). Only later did they employ advertising. Word-of-mouth communication is so power-ful precisely because we usually trust our friends' and colleagues' opinions. According to Duncan (2002, p. 558), if you receive a recom-mendation about a film from a friend you are 1000 times more likely to go and see the film than if you had seen an advertisement. But what does this have to do with PR?

The answer is that group influence impacts upon public relations and vice versa in a number of ways. Generally, journalists are organ-ized as a group for press conferences and if it goes well, journalists are more likely to report a favourable article or broadcast, especially if their colleagues intend to do so. For this reason we often refer to the media as 'opinion formers'. Secondly, in marketing public relations (see Chapter 3), consumer audiences can be excited through word-of-mouth communication when organizing or sponsoring exciting cul-tural (e.g. music, art or sports) events. A good example of an event promoted through word of mouth is the annual Virgin music festival aimed principally at teenagers and people in their early twenties. Designed to raise the profile of the Virgin group, the festival also pro-vides a venue to sell some of the Virgin stable of products (e.g. cola, vodka and energy drinks) and has benefited from the mass popularity of the Glastonbury festival. Any large-scale organized event provides the attendee with a feeling of being part of the event, of belonging to it. Rallies for political parties and party conferences are designed to provide members with a feeling of belonging to the party; to ensure that they work harder to win the election campaign in their con-stituencies. House journals (see Chapter 23), meanwhile, are intended to institute feelings of group membership. They are particularly effect-ive when they include details of well-known staff. Examples might include marriages, births, deaths and retirements, but might equally include opinions about topics of interest, e.g. the organization's mis-sion or its human resource policy. Internal PR is covered in more detail in Chapter 25.

Means of communication

We can also influence memorization (also called 'front-of-mind' aware-ness in that you are attempting to get your message to the forefront of the target's mind) and the persuasiveness of our messages by changing the way we communicate. Generally, there are five different means by which we communicate. These are:

1. *Through words, whether printed or spoken.* According to Erickson et al. (1978), powerful speech, defined as incorporating conviction, is more persuasive than powerless speech, defined as incorporating hesitancy, submissiveness, uncertainty and the use of the questioning tone. This has important ramifications for how interviewees react to interviewer's questions on news bulletins and programmes, for instance. Of course, it is not just how something is said that impacts upon persuasiveness; it is also what is said by whom. We have mentioned 'opinion formers' and 'opinion leaders' and will be returning to the important topic of source credibility later in this chapter.

2. *By sound, such as music or sound effects.* Jingles are often used in advertising but they have also been used in PR. A good example of its effective use was during the Labour campaign for the 1997 British General Election when Tony Blair played *Things Can Only Get Better* at virtually every rally. Of course, radio appearances and news releases read out on radio will often appeal to radio listeners, but the PR practitioner should bear in mind that listeners are often doing other things whilst listening to the radio – for instance, driving or working. Radio news outlets should be chosen carefully to ensure that they appeal to an appropriate audience. For example, Bath University might well target Bath Radio with news of its new course developments or conferences being held, but it would be futile to try to obtain national news coverage of these items unless they were of wider public appeal.

3. *Through movement, such as action in films, video or TV, or by gestures and body movement.* Video news releases (see Chapter 21) have often been used particularly effectively. Greenpeace used this method whilst their protesters occupied Shell UK's Brent Spar oil platform in order to ensure that it was not taken into the North Atlantic for dumping. Churchill's backward two-fingered V for victory gesticulation was perhaps one of the best examples of body movement intended to convey his uncompromising approach to defeating Hitler in the Second World War.

4. *By the use of symbols such as corporate identity logos, badges and signs.* Certain shapes, creatures and people carry significant meanings, as can be seen in badges, trade marks and logos. Animals are particularly popular, the lion most of all. There are many products called Lion, and of course Singapore has been branded the 'Lion City' to increase its appeal to tourists. Uncle Sam is a national symbol of America. Other countries adopt animals and birds, especially the airlines – for example, the kite of Malaysian Airline System. The McDonald's 'Golden Arches' symbol is recognized worldwide, as is Microsoft's windows

emblem. The creation of an appropriate symbol helps publics and consumers to remember the company and what it stands for. The topic of corporate identity is covered in further detail in Chapter 28.

5. *Through the use of colours, which evoke different effects and meanings.* The language of colour varies round the world and is important in communications. The Chinese have a language of colour, with red representing prosperity and happiness, yellow meaning joy and wealth, but blue meaning sadness. When the Japanese tried to sell pale blue sewing machines to the Singapore Chinese they failed miserably. In the West, black is the colour of mourning, but in some countries it is white. Imperial Tobacco is rebranding its 'light', 'mild' and 'ultra' brands according to the colour of their packaging after the EU's European Court of Justice decided to ban the use of these descriptions in relation to cigarettes as part of its forthcoming Tobacco Products Directive, due to become law in 2003. Davidoff Lights will become Davidoff Whites, whilst Lambert and Butler Lights will be renamed Lambert and Butler Gold, and Lambert and Butler Ultra Lights will become Lambert and Butler Blue (Kleinman, 2002a).

In educated societies we may use all of the above forms of communication. However, in some societies these forms of communication may not exist, or they may have special significance. For instance, the sheer size of populations and land areas can affect communication. In the Namibian Presidential election campaign in December 1999, the main parties competing for the presidency had to communicate with voters in 13 different regions of the country, many of whom speak different languages. Although the official language in Namibia is English, only 7 per cent of the population can speak it. Afrikaans is the common language of most of the population and about 60 per cent of the white population, whilst German is spoken by 32 per cent of the population, and the indigenous populations speak Oshivambo, Herero and Nama (CIA, 2003). Communication in the election campaign was principally achieved through radio broadcasts in various regions of the country in various languages. Clearly, when conducting public relations campaigns in overseas countries, it is important to bear in mind the nature of the host country's languages and forms of communication.

Problems with understanding language

In some countries English may be a major second language, as it is in Hong Kong and Malaysia, or the predominant language, as it is in Singapore. English is a second language in Indonesia, where there are many English-speaking people from Australia, Britain, Canada and the

USA. English predominates in Nigeria, but there are also newspapers in Hausa and Yoruba. There are famous English language newspapers in India, e.g. *The Times of India*, but also others in Indian languages. In overseas countries, the communication difficulty is magnified because of language and socio-cultural differences. Even countries as culturally close as the USA and UK may have difficulties with understanding and have been described as 'two countries separated by one language'.

Multi-language countries present many communication problems. Even when English is spoken, the speaker's vocabulary may be limited. This can result in people misunderstanding words that they do not know and gaining the wrong meanings from what they are reading. Some words have very different meanings in other countries. It is very difficult to promote the Irish Mist brand of whiskey in Germany, where *mist* means dung!

In developing countries, whilst it might be possible to obtain editorial coverage in a newspaper, it may be less likely that the general population will read the article. The degree of literacy will differ from country to country. An interesting example of public communications takes place in Accra, Ghana, where postmen or messengers carry oral messages between village and town people, arranging marriages, land deals and all kinds of business matters entirely by means of memorized messages. It is a remarkable example of effective communications based not only on information dissemination, but also on understanding and trust. Although we might generally be able to understand the communicator (the source), we might not trust or believe them. We turn to this topic in the next section.

Source credibility and attractiveness

Credibility is the extent to which the recipient perceives the source, the originator of the message, to possess relevant knowledge or experience and trusts the source to provide unbiased, objective information (Belch and Belch, 2001, p. 173). The credibility that we as receivers bestow upon a source has an impact upon how we integrate, and internalize, the message into our memory system. If message recipients have a highly negative view of a particular company, product or event, it is fundamental that someone who is respected is used as the source of any messages. This has important ramifications for PR specialists, particularly during times of crisis management, for instance (see Chapter 26). If a particular agency has a good reputation for handling crisis situations and they are hired by a company during a crisis, the media are much more likely to believe the side of the story that they convey. Max Clifford has been particularly successful at obtaining column inches in the major tabloids for his clients (including Antonia Da Sancha) precisely because journalists trusted him to provide interesting and newsworthy stories.

Conversely, Jo Moore, a Labour spin doctor, was forced to formally apologize to Britain's victims of the 11 September 2001 bombings in America when she suggested that, because of the disaster, the following week would be a good time to release any bad government news. Shortly afterwards, she was forced to resign. She had simply lost her credibility with journalists.

From a public relations perspective, the fact that newspapers and broadcasters convey a company's perspectives on its products or services or statements ensures that the general public is more likely to believe the message conveyed, since it is apparently filtered through the 'lens' of the media. The major broadcasters (e.g. BBC and ITV) are required under regulations and their constitutions to be unbiased. Thus, broadcast news is more likely to be trusted than its press counterpart. Press journalists and editors are under no such compunction to remain impartial and frequently pursue a particular editorial line. This occurs especially in relation to political parties and issues (e.g. the *Daily Telegraph*'s unashamed pro-Conservative and the *Daily Mirror*'s equally unashamed pro-Labour stance). So when Richard Quest from CNN discusses a major positive change in British Airways' airline security, this is more credible than if British Airways themselves state this in advertising copy.

Source attractiveness also impacts upon the persuasiveness of the message. Audiences tend to view sources as more attractive if they are similar to themselves, if they like the source, and the more familiar the source actually is to the audience. At BT's broadband summit, effectively a product launch for their broadband Internet service held at their headquarters in central London in summer 2002, Nick Ross was used as compere. Nick Ross is known to most people as the TV presenter on the BBC's *Crimewatch* series, and was an effective choice not only because he is a skilled presenter, but because he is used to dealing with difficult questions. He was asked difficult questions from many members of the audience, who were upset at what they regarded as BT's intransigence in developing the broadband network. However, by ensuring each received an appropriate and measured reply from the relevant BT personnel, he helped to persuade the audience to some degree of BT's perspective.

The perceived authority of the source is also important since it can induce deference in the audience. Thus, PROs should ensure that they ask the right people to speak at press conferences or in live broadcast media interviews, particularly where the person is an authority within the organization. Thus, PROs may ask experts to take part in product launch events, for instance. Remember the point made earlier in the chapter about the nature of how one speaks and whether or not people are persuaded by it? These two concepts are essentially interlinked: perceived authority is at least partly a function of how one speaks and composes oneself, as well as how well-known one is in a particular field of endeavour. If, however, we feel that we are being forced to believe something regardless of whether or not it is a credible message, we might instantly reject it. This phenomenon is known as 'psychological reactance'.

Psychological reactance theory

This theory suggests that people may feel resentment and anger when an organization or person acts to restrict their behaviour. But what has this got to do with public relations? Well, there are frequent occasions when PROs tell journalists not to ask specific questions about embarrassing subjects. This often leads the journalists to make their own enquiries into the company or to write negative editorial simply because they are being kept in the dark. CNN's Richard Quest illustrates this factor in the interview outlined at the end of Part 1, when he states that when he was asked by a PR agency not to ask a particular CEO a question, he asked it anyway, and told the PRO in no uncertain terms that he would ask whatever questions he liked. In the same interview, Richard Quest also outlines how the British Royal Family has become more amenable to journalists, whereas in the past they have tended to make no comment. This has ensured that they get better coverage because journalists have something more positive to write about.

When journalists feel that they have been deceived, however, all trust is lost and they are very unlikely to write up a company's perspective in a good light. Lying to journalists, of course, is not as infrequent as one might imagine. The former Secretary of State for Northern Ireland, Peter Mandelson, resigned after he allegedly lied about a loan from fellow government colleague, Geoffrey Robinson, the former Paymaster General. Particular problems have arisen in the US as companies have released false financial statements, e.g. Enron and Worldcom. Such practices are looked upon dimly and the US government has now enacted a Social Responsibility Act ensuring that perpetrators are severely punished for making erroneous financial statements. Companies that do make false statements tend to do so when they are in trouble, e.g. financial problems or in a situation where they have been negligent. However, a golden rule of crisis management is that one must not make false statements (see Chapter 26). Lying will destroy the trust and any goodwill that you might have had with the journalists concerned.

Chapter 3

Marketing public relations

LEARNING OBJECTIVES

By the end of this chapter you will be able to:

- explain the PR–marketing relationship;
- understand how public relations techniques can support the marketing function;
- outline how PR techniques might be used during the six stages of the product/service life cycle.
- explain how PR techniques can be used to support specific marketing activities (e.g. branding, vertical communications activity, and customer retention and loyalty programmes).

The PR–marketing relationship

Both the in-house public relations manager and the public relations consultant may encounter and have to resolve problems concerning the relationship between public relations and marketing. In America, the term 'marketing public relations' has been coined to illustrate that there are other forms of public relations. Public relations is concerned with numerous activities, with industry, the charitable and public sectors and commerce; much does not have a direct link with marketing (e.g. crisis management, regulatory affairs). Nevertheless, many public relations consultancies today are becoming increasingly marketing orientated, particularly in the area of corporate image and branding, as they see greater profits in these activities. Marketing divisions of companies are making increasing use of these consultancy services. This chapter outlines how public relations can support the marketing function.

From the in-house point of view, much depends on the role of the public relations manager. Does he or she report to the CEO or service the marketing department (or other departments)? Which is the ideal and most appropriate role? There is no harm in public relations coming under the authority of the marketing director, if the public relations manager enjoys independence as a specialist. Such a situation is common in the banking industry. Managers frequently place public relations conceptually in the promotion box of the marketing mix's four Ps (i.e. product, price, place and promotion). Such categorization can hide the wider role of PR as a form of communication designed to aid in generating understanding amongst publics rather than just achieving awareness and publicity. When working in the marketing field, the public relations manager can, therefore, suffer from misunderstandings about his or her true role as a particular kind of communicator.

Public relations' role in the marketing mix reconsidered

Marketing and public relations have much in common. Both involve human relations and require strong communication and interpersonal skills. The public relations manager can make practical contributions to marketing strategy when it is understood on both sides that public relations techniques can be useful in all aspects of the marketing mix. Yet, the marketing mix concept has become increasingly discredited in service markets, which usually now make up at least 60 per cent of most Western countries' gross domestic product. It offers a 'checklist' or 'toolbox' approach (Grönroos, 1994) and is usually unable to account for the nuances associated with service markets, where interaction, trust and credibility are key parameters in retaining and acquiring new customers. The new marketing approach or, some argue, old approach relabelled, is more focused on relationship marketing (RM) or customer relationship management (CRM). PR techniques can be used to engender trust and credibility. Thus, in a competitive marketplace, marketing PR is becoming increasingly important. Research has indicated that the traditional marketing mix approach can prove very restrictive (e.g. Gummesson, 1987) in strategy development, particularly as it appears unsuited to the modern dynamic environment (O'Malley and Patterson, 1998). Telecommunications, banking and air transport are all increasingly turbulent service environments. In the late 1990s and early 2000s, public relations has had an increasingly important role to play in all three industries in the UK. Whilst telecommunications companies, particularly the mobile operators, have been dealing with 'churn' (i.e. customer registration, then deregistration) and increased competition resulting from deregulation, banks have been tackling increasing levels of competition from, among many others, supermarkets (e.g. Sainsbury's, Tesco) and insurance companies (e.g. Prudential's Egg). The major national carriers in the European air transport industry have been particularly troubled, as low-cost carriers such as Ryanair and EasyJet eat into their passenger volumes. Marketing public relations has played an important role in all three cases. For instance, telecommunications companies have moved into new media markets offering broadband connectivity (e.g. BT's division, BTOpenworld) and have used public relations specialists to launch new products (e.g. BT's Broadband Summit). Meanwhile, in a stroke of genius, easyJet managed to become the subject of a new, consumer reality TV series, *Airline*, showing the difficulties airline personnel faced when dealing with customers demanding unreasonably high levels of service for the economy price they had paid for their ticket.

These three industries, however, have all been hit by other problems, dealt with by other types of public relations activity. The major European telecommunications firms (e.g. Deutsche Telecom, the Dutch operator KPN, and BT) have all been struggling over the last couple of years under heavy debt loads, arising as a result of diversification into new markets, and the purchase of 3G licences. This eventually ensured that they were downgraded by credit rating agencies such as Moody's. For the likes of BT, this took a heavy toll, since it meant that its interest payments increased and future equity offers became less attractive. In this environment, financial public relations activity became paramount. Banks also required the services of public relations specialists, particularly in the corporate image field as the sector has consolidated (e.g. HSBC and its takeover of Midland Bank, Lloyds Bank and TSB, Halifax and the Bank of Scotland). Meanwhile, in the airline industry, national carriers (e.g. BA) have required considerable crisis management help as a result of the 11 September terrorist attacks and the subsequent downturn in their passenger volumes, particularly to the Far East and the USA, which has precipitated considerable downsizing and route rationalization.

Marketing public relations is therefore an important component of public relations, but should not be seen solely as an *optional* element of the communication mix. It could enter into product development, reflecting the feedback received from the media and various publics about products and services, ranging from complaints to suggestions and demands. For instance, the content of a package holiday could be changed because of unfortunate experiences in the past that required assistance in dealing with enquiries from the media. Motoring correspondents may have criticized certain design defects of a motor car. Such feedback can assist product development, for public relations acts as the ears, with its own market intelligence networks, as well as the voice of an organization. Public relations techniques can often be appropriately adopted in any of the following situations:

- Product/service design and conception – dealer relations programmes conducted by the PR department might provide useful ideas, e.g. a car dealership might provide the manufacturer with a new idea for a financing package.
- Product/service life cycle management – dependent on the place of the product/service in its life cycle, PR can be used to generate awareness initially or reposition the brand, for example.
- Market or marketing research – public relations research, particularly media monitoring of competitor activity, can be invaluable information in the development of the organization's marketing and strategic plans.
- Naming/branding and positioning/repositioning – because of its strong relationship with the mass media (i.e. principally press, radio and television), the PR department often knows how new branding and positioning strategies are being played out in the mass media, an important opinion leader in determining, ultimately, public opinion on such topics.
- Corporate/brand/product image programmes – public relations agencies are increasingly being used to design branding strategies ahead of their advertising counterparts. They have an important role to play for the same reason as above.
- Pricing decisions – the public relations function is of particular value to organizations where pricing is regulated (e.g. telecommunications, electricity and water industries), since the regulatory or public affairs component usually deals with this relationship.
- Packaging decisions – again, the public relations function is of particular value to organizations where packaging or labelling is regulated (e.g. toys, food and tobacco industries), since the regulatory or public affairs component usually deals with this relationship.
- Distribution programmes – PR personnel will frequently develop vertical communication programmes to enhance trade relations incorporating brochures, contests and events.
- Financial public relations – particularly during mergers and acquisitions, or periods of recession or other times of stock market interest.
- Industrial relations – PR has a major role to play here in ensuring that management's perspective is heard and to monitor how the firm is perceived in the press during strikes and other periods of industrial unrest.
- Test marketing – in some industries (e.g. pharmaceuticals), it is fundamental to generate product/service awareness through market

education campaigns often supported by the PR function, at the test marketing stage.

- Advertising – PR is generally used to support advertising; for example, BT's broadband launch summits (see page 36), which complemented its subsequent advertising campaign.
- Sales promotion – PR personnel may well be useful in helping to devise customer retention, maintenance and loyalty schemes which can often link into sales promotion initiatives.

Thus, there are opportunities for public relations to support marketing programmes throughout the preparation and conduct of a marketing programme. Indeed, if PR, advertising, sales promotion, personal selling and sponsorship (and other communication activities) are integrated (i.e. they work to the same objectives), they are more likely to work for the benefit of the company. In this chapter, a few of these elements are selected for discussion, to elaborate on how marketing public relations is conducted.

The product/service life cycle

Marketing strategy takes note of the position of a product or service in its life cycle. The traditional six-stage product life cycle (PLC) shows a product passing through stages of development, introduction, growth, maturity, saturation and eventual decline. Whilst fashion goods are designed to last a few months, a motor car with minor modifications should last for years. This does not refer to the life expectancy of individual products, but to the selling life of the total production. In the case of a motor car, a new model will be designed to replace the old model when sales fall below a given acceptable level. Products like Coca-Cola, Robinson's squash and Wrigley's chewing gum may have an indefinite life cycle. The same could be said for life insurance and fixed line telephony services. Different kinds of public relations activity will be required at each of the six different stages of the life cycle. For example:

1. *Development*. In this stage, PR personnel work closely with R & D to ensure compliance with government regulations, to raise awareness amongst the media of the project's existence, and to develop internal and external networks to support a potentially successful project. The focus at this stage should be on stakeholder compliance. In other words, what do the various parties (e.g. regulators, shareholders and employees) think about the new project? Internal PR is important during this stage.

2. *Introduction*. At this stage, PR may or may not be part of an integrated marketing communications programme, but will usually involve product launches, press releases and conferences, and events for supply chain intermediaries to raise awareness of a new product or service's existence. Where the product or service is novel or complex, a marketing education programme may be undertaken, with product demonstrations and personal selling at conferences or seminars of customers and supply chain intermediaries.

3. *Growth*. During this period of increasing competition and rapid growth, PR will partly need to focus on internal public relations and relations with supply chain intermediaries, as the business expands. Firms may require additional financing at this stage and PR personnel may have a role to play here in ensuring that the business prospects are reported positively in the financial press.

4. *Maturity*. PR functions here to maintain sales but also to identify future opportunities for new product or service development. This might well come from monitoring competitor activity in the mass media or from events organized through the PR department. PR personnel will usually have to explain the financial implications and the nature of the company's long-term business prospects to stakeholders at this stage. Jim Beam Brands employed PR agency, BursonMarsteller, to attract younger drinkers in the stagnating bourbon whisky market, particularly in the Czech Republic, Germany and Austria. In a PRCA (Public Relations Consultant Association) award-winning campaign, it developed the Real Long Weekend campaign, allowing drinkers the opportunity to win chauffeur-driven tours of clubs and sporting events in the Jim Beam airstream vehicle specially fitted with the latest electronic gadgetry and, more importantly, a bar (Anon., 2001a).

5. *Saturation*. When the rate of profit increase becomes negative as demand drops, industries often begin to consolidate as they vie for the remaining business. PR has an important role to play during mergers and acquisitions, particularly in managing sensitive compliance issues with regulatory and competition authorities, but also in explaining the rationale to shareholders and to suppliers and customers alike. PR also might serve to describe additional uses for a product to maintain revenues or to feed back information on new product/service ideas obtained through trade relations programmes. PR may well have to start dealing with the press because of industrial relations problems. This largely depends on whether or not the firm has new products or services to replace lost revenue in the pipeline.

6. *Eventual decline*. The objective of the PR function at this stage is to end the product or service's life gracefully and describe new opportunities

that the company is involved with, assuming it is. If it is not, PR personnel may be dealing with industrial relations problems or shareholder and/or city financial concerns.

There are variations on the traditional life cycle, which have an impact in terms of what public relations techniques need to be adopted. For instance, there is the recycled PLC, which applies to projects pulled out of decline as a result of improvements, or other changes such as repackaging or price-cutting. There is the leapfrog effect when one model is replaced immediately by another higher performance product or service, and the staircase effect when new product uses or new services are introduced. The classic example of the staircase effect PLC is nylon, but it can also be applied to shipping, insurance and banking, which have diversified their services over the years. Changes in behaviour of the life cycle provide special opportunities for public relations activity. Thus, here is a good example of how the public relations practitioner can work closely with marketing, for the public relations strategy will depend on the sort of PLC experienced by the product or service. The four types of PLC are shown in Figures 3.1–3.4.

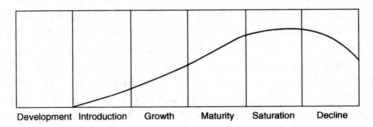

Development   Introduction   Growth   Maturity   Saturation   Decline

Figure 3.1 Traditional product life cycle.
Source: Jefkins (1994)

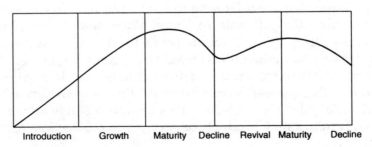

Introduction   Growth   Maturity   Decline   Revival   Maturity   Decline

Figure 3.2 Recycled product life cycle.
Source: Jefkins (1994)

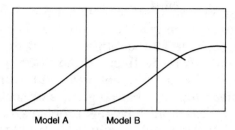

Model A   Model B

Figure 3.3 Leapfrog effect product life cycle.
Source: Jefkins (1994)

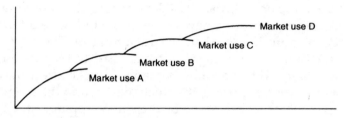

Market use D

Market use C

Market use B

Market use A

Figure 3.4 Staircase effect product life cycle.
Source: Jefkins (1994)

Product/service/brand naming

One of the most elementary, yet most important, aspects of marketing communication is the generation of the name of the company and its products or services. Years ago, it was natural to use the founder's name as the name of the company (e.g. Ford, Cadbury, Guinness). In creating a company name today, it is necessary to consider what the name communicates to its publics, particularly if these publics may include overseas markets. Choosing the right company name is an exercise in public relations. Some of the best company names are simple initials (e.g. IBM, BBC, BP). People may not always know what the letters stand for (e.g. IBM – International Business Machines), but they do have a clear image of what they mean in terms of products or services. Names given to late 1990s Internet banking services also have been rather curious – for example, Prudential's Egg and Abbey National's Cahoot!

A simple device, which helps names to be pronounced and remembered easily, is the use of vowels (a, e, i, o, u), and the use of syllables to frame these, to produce rhythm. These could be short words (e.g. Oxo), but three-syllable names with good use of vowels (e.g. Rentokil, Texaco Minolta) are good examples. In spite of their strangeness in Europe or America, Japanese names have this quality, e.g. Fuji, Honda, Sony and Kawasaki.

In the globalization era, there has also been a move away from explicitly naming the company after its country of origin. For example, British Petroleum, British Home Stores and British Airways have become BP, BHS and BA respectively. In addition, names need to be acceptable worldwide, so should not have unfortunate, different or maybe offensive meanings in other languages or societies. Names like Coca-Cola and Elf, for example, have few problems, but the company at first called Malaysian Air Lines encountered problems because MAL suggested sickness to French-speaking people.

In deciding on a name for the corporation or its range of products and brands, the public relations manager can offer valuable advice, for he or she should be sufficiently broad-based regarding the company's affairs to see all the implications of a new name. If the public relations department had been more involved in the renaming of The Post Office to Consignia, the organization might not have had to renounce the name (back to Royal Mail). When a name is changed, it can affect the attitudes of recruits, employees, the trade, the stock market and the media. People may be suspicious of a new name or they may applaud it. Credibility, reputation and confidence are all at stake if an inappropriate name is selected. Table 3.1 indicates some of the qualities a good name should possess, providing examples.

It is important to consider whether or not the name lends itself to advertising, whether in the form of a logotype or trade mark, or typographically in advertisements, on labels and packs and in sales literature? FCUK – French Connection UK's brand – with its vulgar connotations, links well with the nihilistic, anarchistic lifestyles of many young people today. It is worth remembering that a short name can be displayed more boldly than a long one. This could be important on, say, a label on a small or narrow bottle. HP suits its slim brown sauce bottle very well.

When Gerald Ratner, head of the Ratner's jewellery chain, announced that his company's products were 'crap', in the early 1990s, his business sank and he was replaced as chairman. The impact upon the business was so severe that it subsequently changed its name to Signet to avoid association with his remarks. Names like Viagra and Post-it! display distinctiveness and may ensure that a press release announcing a product launch is more likely to be read and reported on by press correspondents. The 'green issue' now also plays a big public relations role in packaging, since there are EU directives to consider (e.g. recycling and the fast food industry).

So, naming and branding exercises require public relations input because communication, corporate identity, corporate image, trade and customer relations, and many other aspects of public relations are all involved. This is when the knowledge, experience and advice of the PR

Table 3.1 Important considerations when product/brand/company naming

Consideration	Reason	Example
Memorability	Customers more likely to use service if it is. More likely to become part of their 'evoked set' of related products/services/companies. It is more likely to spark the interest of innovators and early adopting customers if it is memorable.	Asda (supermarket) Egg (Internet banking) Freeserve (ISP) FCUK (retailing)
Image	The name might convey what the organization is about. If it does, it is important to determine amongst multiple publics exactly what that impression is.	Rentokil Consignia (retailing) Iceland.co.uk (retailing)
Distinctiveness	The name may differentiate the company, brand or product from its competitors or it may convey a special property.	Post-it! (office supplies) Viagra (pharmaceuticals) Kodak (electronics)
Packaging	The labelling may be of particular importance to the public relations team because of the necessity to comply with particular regulations or because it can offer a competitive advantage if certain labelling is adopted (see examples).	The Body Shop (not tested on animals claim) Iceland (GM-free food – without genetically modified material)

practitioner can be valuable to top management or marketing management or both, especially at meetings where early discussions are being held on future developments. The opposite sometimes occurs though, with disastrous results; the public relations people are only called in to write a press release on the name change when everything else was decided months before.

PR can have a substantial impact on new product/brand launches. When youth and consumer PR agency S. Punk and its sister events company, Cunning Stunts, worked with BMW to launch its revamped Mini, they targeted bars and clubs around the UK with romantic handwritten messages inserted into matchbooks, urging people to ring the Mini hotline. This tied in well with the advertising campaign illustrating couples enjoying their love affair with their new Mini (Cowlett, 2002).

Metcalfe and Rose (2001) state that PR can particularly benefit a new pharmaceutical product launch if media tool-kits are distributed to appropriate correspondents incorporating a news release, fact sheets, product photos and a product insert.

Pierach (2002) argues that PR as a function, however, does not yet deserve a place at the branding table because it isn't sufficiently involved in brand planning. He argues that PR firms need to become more comfortable with discussing metrics beyond media impressions and advertising recall. They need to input their expertise in establishing relevance and third-party credibility. Cowlett (2001a, b), on the contrary, believes that PR agencies are doing just this, by poaching planning professionals from the advertising industry. She outlines how Interflora, the flowers franchise, has begun using PR planning to reposition flowers among 20- to 25-year-old females as a fashion accessory.

Vertical communications

Public relations can offer significant inputs to trade or dealer relations programmes dealing with supply chain intermediaries supporting, among other functions, the sales force, advertising and sales promotion aspects of the marketing mix and the marketing operation more generally when it is in action. Fraza (2001) reports a survey where distributors agree that sharing customer/sales information can lead to better production cycles, leaner inventories and increased sales. However, they only work with suppliers that they trust. Public relations has a significant role to play in building this trust. Public relations contributions, in vertical communication programmes, may include the following projects.

Organizing exhibitions

It may be either a trade or a public show, but an exhibition is an opportunity to show distributors a company's latest products and to meet them face to face. It could be advertised by inserting a ticket in a trade magazine (or in the external house journal mentioned on page 49), by sending a ticket direct, or by having tickets given out by travelling sales representatives. An exhibition or seminar may well be proposed by the PR manager specifically for supply chain intermediaries. These could well be initiated by the marketing department, but the PR manager's experience in organizing events, knowing of suitable venues, and arranging visual aids will be valuable to the marketing manager.

Training events for supply chain members

The PR manager's skills can be helpful at training events, as with the production of tapes, slides and videos. These may be used on training courses, or for portable counter display units carried by sales representatives. Training can also be incorporated in the external house magazine. Proficiency certificates can also be awarded for display at the distributors' premises after attendance on appropriate training courses (e.g. Microsoft Certified Software Engineer courses).

Organizing works visits

These events might also be organized by the PR manager and can also be a form of training, since distributors are able to learn at first hand how products are manufactured, and how quality control procedures are applied so they are knowledgeable when talking to customers. Sometimes, factory visits are required by the buyer before they purchase (e.g. Tesco buyers usually demand this when purchasing food products). Vineyards frequently arrange events for wine-sellers and tour operators arrange visits to particular resorts for travel agent representatives. A company's staff are better able to recommend the product if its employees have seen or experienced the product or service for themselves.

Producing external house journals

Published solely for the trade, these can be circulated to wholesalers, retailers, franchisers, agents and brokers according to the kind of business and the kind of distributor used. The content should be of value to these special readers, and not merely publicity for the company. It is also important to keep distributors aware of company news that will encourage understanding of the supplier. Features can be published which will help the distributor to sell the company's products or services, and this can range from educating distributors so that they are knowledgeable when dealing with customers or clients, to advising them on shop display or general business management advice, e.g. warning of impending legislation.

Managing press relations

In industrialized countries, where there is a substantial range of trade publications, PR practitioners are usually fully exploited in developing press releases and organizing press conferences. This usually includes: writing news stories about the company, its products/brands and their packaging and advertising campaigns; feature articles; personality stories about new appointments; interviews; works visits for journalists; press receptions; and invitations to exhibition stands, as well as releases and pictures for exhibition press rooms. All this needs to be done in close co-operation with the marketing department. Public relations input to the organization of exhibitions is discussed further in Chapter 22.

Contests supporting promotions

These have proved popular in a number of trades. A typical example is a contest based on the best window dressing or in-store display contest in which the retailer submits a photograph of his or her display (e.g. mobile phone retailers). Other contests may be based on sales figures, run on a regular or seasonal basis according to the nature of the trade. Contests can also be incorporated into trade magazines. They have the public relations effect of encouraging supply chain participation, and they have the marketing effect of advertising. The organization of contests, choice of prizes and award ceremonies, with media coverage in the trade and local press, all require the skills of the PR practitioner.

Sales force relations

Field sales representatives often feel neglected and remote from their company's central headquarters either because they are, or because they travel frequently around the country or internationally. Ultimately, this distant proximity can be harmful to the maintenance of good sales force relations, as salespeople start to acquaint more with their customers than their own organization. Often, the salesperson is the first, and major, contact that a company might have with its supplier. The company will be judged on this person. Part of sales training should be the public relations role of presenting a uniform image of the company without destroying the individualism of the sales representative. Some of the ways in which the PR practitioner can service the sales function are as follows:

● Through the corporate identity scheme – this includes developing uniform business cards, vehicle liveries, letterheadings, price lists and other sales literature, to present the company physically. This is discussed more fully in Chapter 28.

- By producing a special house journal, newsletter or bulletin – when produced solely for the sales force, such a journal can concentrate on topics of specific interest, e.g. salesperson of the year, product/brand of the year, or new suppliers. Field sales representatives are seldom interested in the domestic affairs of factory or office staff, which usually appear in staff newspapers, and may pay little attention to these publications.

- By producing audiocassette bulletins, or CD-ROM, or DVD presentations – such material is even more convenient than printed bulletins, having the advantage that the sales representative can play them on the road, train or in the airplane cabin. They have more curiosity value than a piece of print that can be glanced at quickly. The Internet is fast becoming the medium of choice for these bulletins.

- By organizing regional and national sales conferences – these can be useful get-togethers, and with his or her organizing ability, knowledge of venues, and access to videos and other visual aids, the public relations manager can again help the sales manager. It can also be useful for the public relations manager to meet and talk with sales representatives. There may be opportunities to glean public relations stories, especially in servicing companies where news of new contracts can be valuable. Moreover, these meetings give the practitioner the opportunity to develop internal lines of communication, and to explain to sales representatives what kind of material he or she is looking for.

- By sending the sales force press clippings – usually of notable company events or information. The PR practitioner may also send *reprints* of published feature articles. They are useful since they can be shown to customers. It is important for salespeople to know what is going on within their company, otherwise ignorance can present a poor image to potential buyers.

- By writing and presenting the corporate plan – it is important that sales representatives are familiar with the current business position and the intended direction of their business, because customers may have read about these in newspapers or the trade press and want to discuss them. The report and accounts can be explained in the house journal, or on an audio, video, CD-ROM or DVD presentation. At Cisco, corporate presentations appear on the desktop of personnel at certain pre-specified times, perhaps with a speech by the chairperson.

- By informing sales representatives of communication plans – this information will help salespersons to persuade their customers to buy ahead of the demand. The supply of media schedules and (pulls) of press advertisements can be devised, even storyboards of forthcoming TV commercials. Ideally, sales representatives should see TV commercials before their customers do. Previews can be arranged at regional sales conferences, for instance.

Customer retention and loyalty

Usually, sales promotion activities are used to develop and maintain customer loyalty. Examples include collecting Air Miles by using the Shell credit card. Of course, sales promotion is not a subset of PR, it is a discipline in its own right, although sales promotion agencies are increasingly moving into domains traditionally handled by PR agencies, such as sponsorship. However, there can be a PR role to play, if a sales promotion scheme fails to please and provokes disappointment or complaints. Inexperienced or overzealous brand or product managers could organize schemes that fail to ensure an adequate supply of prizes, or those that it supplies might not be delivered sufficiently quickly to meet the huge demand for the offer. This happened in the 1990s in the UK, when Hoover announced that buyers of Hoover products would be eligible for a free flight to the USA. It certainly did not anticipate the demand it caused. Hoover thought it had included enough provisos in the rules to prevent too many take-ups of the offer. Of course, it had not. The 'offer' was arranged through a small travel agent, which quickly went bankrupt, leaving Hoover to pick up the pieces. Sales promotions schemes provide the PR practitioner with opportunities for press stories, ranging from trade press releases about the scheme to announcements of prizewinners of competitions, particularly in the prizewinners' local press. The price war between the *Daily Mirror* and *Sun* newspapers in early 2003 was claimed to have been won by the *Sun* in press releases carried by many marketing trade papers. The target public here was potential advertisers.

But companies also need to service the customer after they have purchased a particular product or service. This is frequently where many a marketing strategy has come unstuck. In the car market, manufacturers guard the company's reputation and corporate image carefully. Sometimes, they might send out customer-focused magazines to the new car buyer. This kind of interaction is important because the new buyer has invested a significant amount of money in the product and will be wondering whether or not the purchase was worthwhile. This state of mind is known as cognitive dissonance. Such a magazine helps to reinforce that the customer has made the correct decision. It breeds satisfaction, admiration, recommendation and above all repeat purchase. It creates trust, confidence and reputation, which are major objectives of public relations. The PR department has a significant role to play when a company needs to organize the recall of a defective product (e.g. Ford and Firestone tyres on the Explorer – see Chapter 26). Sometimes the frankness and helpfulness with which a recall is handled can turn an apparently bad situation into one of respect and appreciation from customers whose interests or safety have been preserved.

Chapter 4

The public relations industry

LEARNING OBJECTIVES

At the end of this chapter you will be able to:

- explain the advantages and disadvantages of using in-house personnel;
- explain the advantages and disadvantages of using consultancy personnel;
- outline why organizations might need to appoint a PR consultancy;
- describe the process of appointing a PR consultancy;
- detail how good client–consultancy relationships are developed and maintained.

Introduction

Although the consultancy seems to be the most glamorous side of public relations, a minority of public relations personnel actually work in consultancy practices. The in-house PRO, public relations manager or director is the predominant practitioner, especially if he or she services the communication needs of the total organization. There are advantages and disadvantages in the internal and external roles, but the reason for the dominance of in-house personnel lies in the nature of the work. To do a proper public relations job it is necessary to have an intimate knowledge of the organization, and of the industry or business it is in. It is also necessary to have well-established lines of communication within the organization. This can sometimes be distinct from advertising, which may only concern itself with the marketing department, but needs expert outside services such as media buying and creative. Nevertheless, with the more recent movement to using integrated marketing communication strategies, even this distinction is lessening. The in-house public relations manager has to be a jack of all trades, employing different skills, e.g. writing press releases, event management, media relations.

This chapter will be devoted to a comparison between the strengths and weaknesses of an in-house public relations department and a consultancy. For the sake of comparison, the ideal situation will be assumed of an independent public relations department and an independent PR consultancy. We shall begin by briefly comparing and contrasting the advantages and disadvantages of adopting an in-house approach against employing a PR consultancy.

Consultancy versus in-house PR operations

Table 4.1 provides an indication of the advantages and disadvantages associated with setting up your own in-house PR operation compared with employing a consultancy. In practice, most organizations do both. The in-house team may be of varying size and, thus, smaller departments may supplement their team with a retained consultancy to perform certain functions. The consultancy may be used to provide an outside opinion, to augment an unusually busy in-house department, to undertake work for which it is specially qualified, or for occasional ad hoc assignments. This chapter is a discussion of the extent to which PR operations should use in-house resources compared to consultancy resources rather than asking the question of whether an organization should adopt one approach over the other. Note that sometimes one of

Table 4.1 Illustration of the advantages and disadvantages of developing an in-house PR operation versus employing a PR consultancy

In-house		Consultancy	
Advantages	*Disadvantages*	*Advantages*	*Disadvantages*
Offers a full-time service	Lack of impartiality	Independent, unbiased	Provision of a partial service
Good lines of communication	Narrower range of experience/lack of training	Varied experience	Lack of relationship intimacy
Continuity of personnel	Poor person specification/job description	Proximity to media sources/publics	Divided loyalties
Better value for money			Lack of specialized knowledge/ inexperienced staff
Proximity/access			

the categories has both advantages and disadvantages for a similar item, appearing contradictory, e.g. whilst consultancies are described as having varied experience, they are also described as having a lack of specialized staff. In fact, what this really shows is that it often depends on the PR consultancy. They are varied in their offerings. Some are full-service consultancies, others are very specialized, e.g. Lanson Communications (see Chapter 24, on financial PR).

Each of these advantages and disadvantages are considered in the following sections. First, the advantages of an in-house department are outlined, followed by the advantages of employing a consultancy. This allows for an easier comparison between the two approaches.

Advantages of an in-house public relations department

In this section, discussing the advantages of an in-house operation, it is assumed that the PRO is an independent departmental manager with direct access to the chief executive. However, advantages depend very much on the status of the PRO within the organization. Status is seldom given but has to be earned. So, experience, training, qualifications, success, personality and grade or salary bracket will all contribute to the PRO's status and acceptability. The person who complains about their lack of status is either in the wrong job or has yet to establish him or herself fully in it.

A full-time service
The in-house PRO, and his or her staff, can provide a full-time service. This may not be limited to office hours, nor will he or she be subject to the limitations of a consultancy fee, which is based on hours worked, and therefore acts as a deterrent for undertaking more speculative PR work. Time still has to be planned, of course, but does not have to be shared between different clients according to the size of fee in each case. The extent to which the PRO is actually capable of fulfilling the demands of the organization's internal clients depends on the capabilities and size of the PRO's team and the importance of the conflicting demands placed on the PRO by those internal clients. He or she may not actually be able to cope with the workload and so may employ a consultancy for some of the work that needs to be undertaken.

Good lines of communication
Public relations work calls for an intimate internal operation. The PRO needs to develop and maintain good lines of communication throughout the organization, whether this is on a regional, national or international

basis. This is so that information can be obtained quickly, or the PRO can be informed when something occurs of public relations significance. He or she is an integral part of the organization who needs to know, and be known by, everybody. It will be very helpful if he or she is the internal house journal editor, or the editor is in the department, because this will provide continual access to people throughout every division, department and location. To maintain these intimate contacts, the in-house PRO should pay visits to the organization's locations, attend conferences and meetings, visit exhibitions and generally become immersed in company affairs. Some of this may occupy leisure hours. The consultant is unlikely to get so closely involved, if only because the fee will not permit such expenditure of time.

Continuity of personnel

Company personnel tend to stay in their jobs longer than consultancy staff, perhaps growing up with the company. The PRO may have transferred from another sector of the company and is likely to have been trained in the industry. This continuity gives them greater knowledge of the subject and greater familiarity with the company. It helps to give others (e.g. journalists) confidence in him or her, especially when information is needed. This will also give the PRO more authority when dealing with the media, because he or she will be recognized as being more of an expert in the subject than the consultant might be. This can be a serious problem when a consultant takes on a new account, even if the principles are the same, particularly when the consultant is junior within their organization.

Better value for money

Being housed within the organization's headquarters, knowing people and able to move about easily and confidently within the organization, the PRO can often work very economically. Jobs can be dovetailed, such as researching material for feature articles while working on the house journal, or finding material for the house journal, video and photographic library whilst also engaged in other activities also requiring these elements (e.g. media relations). It will cost a lot to staff, equip and finance a PR department initially when compared with the typical monthly consultancy fee, but there is likely to be greater value for money in the longer term in developing an in-house operation, providing appropriate staff are used to staff the operation.

Proximity/access

Working closely with management, the in-house PRO is in a strong position to demonstrate the value of public relations. Management is more likely to understand and appreciate public relations than when dealing with a remote outsider. The PRO has immediate access to those with the information or who make the decisions. This can be important in crises or controversial situations. Moreover, the PRO is also in a position to put the media in touch with his or her seniors.

Advantages of employing a public relations consultancy

This section considers what the competent consultancy has to offer. It is assumed that they are independent, versatile and experienced. Nevertheless, some consultancies are more independent than others. The same goes for their degree of versatility and experience.

Independent, unbiased advice

Advice can cover scores of communication topics concerning the entire range of a client's activities, internally and externally. This can vary from a possible change of company name, how to deal with a proposed relocation, how to conduct public relations overseas, the effects of new legislation EU directives, or a Competition Commission report, how to make representations to a Parliamentary (or Senate) Select Committee, what sort of video system to set up, how to distribute video news releases, to how to deal with a takeover bid. The company benefits by receiving more critical advice from an organization that has a less insular perspective. It might, for instance, see the benefits of a takeover bid and advise accordingly.

Varied experience

To a large extent this depends on how long the consultancy has been established, but since it services a number of accounts its experience will be spread over their different and special needs. Collectively, this experience is likely to be greater than that of any individual client. The spread of media will be greater, the problems dealt with will be more diverse, and the activities engaged in will be more varied. One client may require television coverage, another may be engaged in exhibitions, and yet another may make great use of video or the Internet. Experience gained from serving one client might be useful in serving another client. Over the years, the consultancy will have gained a rich store of experience, just as any professional service does. In fact, a consultancy is likely to be appointed according to its record of past work, possibly in the same or related field. In buying consultancy services, the client should ensure that they examine qualifications, experience and record of past work. These should be among the selling points that the consultancy will present to potential clients.

Having worked for a number of clients over a period of years, the consultant is more likely to be experienced in the use of a variety of macro- (i.e. the commercial mass media) and micro-media (i.e. videos, house journals and private exhibitions). See Part 4 of this text. The consultant will be aware of the opportunities offered by new media and technology. Knowing people in the media means knowing *who* they are, *what* they want and *when* they want it.

Proximity to media sources/publics

Location may be an important asset to the consultancy. Many clients are outside the central business district and some may be located in remote parts of the country. Conversely, consultancies are usually located close to the media. Thus, in the UK, a large proportion of PR agencies is in London. In the US, New York City has a high proportion of PR agencies located there. Having a central location will become less and less important in time, as Internet PR becomes more commonplace.

Consultancies are often located near to printers, photographers, video-makers, exhibition designers, web designers, research units and other suppliers required from time to time. Usually, these suppliers will be independent of the PR consultancy, but if there are any financial associations, these must be disclosed. Similarly, if suppliers give discounts or commission to consultants, this information should be made available to consultancy clients. Because of the variety of its experience, the consultancy is likely to know the supply market very well. This makes its work more efficient and competitive.

Disadvantages of an in-house public relations department

This section deals with the disadvantages of developing and maintaining your own in-house department.

Lack of impartiality

A serious disadvantage can be the tendency for the PRO to be uncritical and biased, partly out of loyalty or zeal and partly because of pressure from management (especially if the PRO is located in the marketing department, where there is bound to be a promotional attitude to public relations). It may be that he or she honestly feels enthusiasm about the organization and what it makes or does. To achieve credibility and acceptance by the media, this tendency not to be impartial has to be curbed. It depends on the professional status that the PRO has achieved. The PRO who is merely a puppet of management will be less respected. Much depends on how much management needs and respects the PRO's expertise.

Narrower range of experience/lack of training

One inherent weakness may be the narrowness of the industry or business the PRO is in. Thus, they might not have experienced a broad span of public relations activity and experience. The PRO may be in, say, food or textiles or engineering, which require contact with a limited section of the media, or confine him or her to only certain kinds of public relations activity (e.g. press relations only). The in-house practitioner may never edit a house journal, make a video, deal with broadcast journalists, organize seminars or write feature articles, and could be out of his or her depth if the company diversified or acquired other interests. A lack of experience may arise when the in-house person has been transferred to public relations from another job within the company. They may have received no formal training in public relations. An example could include journalists, who might well be good at writing press releases but relatively poor in the project management skills required for planning and implementing PR campaigns. The profession is not helped when inappropriate appointments are made. They encourage the cynicism of the media.

Poor person specification/job description

Similarly, public relations duties may be assigned to an existing executive such as a marketing, product, personnel or commercial manager who might know relatively little about good public relations, particularly crisis management, financial PR and corporate identity schemes. They may well treat it simply as marketing PR (see Chapter 3). Even if such a person is aided by a consultant, because of the steep learning curve, he or she could be a liability in the early stages of their new job. For example, they may damage press relations by flooding editors with news releases that are more like advertisements than news stories.

In some large organizations (e.g. multinationals), an executive who is being groomed for top management may be put in charge of public relations for a fixed term. While it shows recognition of the need for top management to understand public relations and to be good communicators, it is unwise to place an unskilled and unqualified person in *control* of the public relations function. Such an executive should be trained first, perhaps by attending a university postgraduate PR course. Equally, management may misunderstand public relations to the extent that it employs a PRO for crisis management reasons only, either to shield top management from the media, or to act as an apologist for management inadequacies. It can also happen in developing countries where management is inexperienced and frightened of criticism.

Ensuring the person specification and job description, or in some cases simply a job specification, is right for the particular function required is fundamental. However, they may not exist. Very often the PRO, once in the job, has to prepare and present his or her own job specifications. Figure 4.1 provides a detailed job specification for a PR manager for the BBC.

This detailed job specification not only outlines the tasks required of the job, it also quantifies aspects of them. In addition, it outlines the experience and skills necessary to be successful in the position. It details the importance of the environment, and the diplomatic skills necessary when working with talented people. It also indicates the importance of the flat management structure (matrix), implying that team working will be particularly important in achieving the department's aims. The job specification would be made available to any prospective applicant who requested it and would also be made available on the website.

It is important to outline the main aspects of the job in any recruitment advertising to ensure that only suitable applicants apply for the job. This ensures that the organization's and potential applicants' time is not wasted. Figure 4.2 provides an outline of an example job advert. In the example shown, the advert outlines the importance of the parliamentary liaison programme. Thus, those PR professionals without experience in this area should either take a crash course in lobbying or public affairs, or not bother applying.

Disadvantages of the public relations consultancy

This section considers the disadvantages of contracting a PR consultancy from the client's perspective.

Provision of only a partial service

The consultancy has only its time to sell at so much an hour or per day, and so it has to be rationed among personnel in proportion to the varying fees paid by different clients. If there is no extra payment, extra work for one client can only be done by taking time away from another client. Consequently, a consultancy may provide only a partial service. The strict economics of consultancy finances need to be understood by clients before they engage consultancies. If £10 000 represents 100 hours at £100 per hour, the client should expect no more, and neither should the consultant give more. Clients are sometimes apt to think that because they have appointed a consultant they have hired that consultant's services full time. They have not. They have merely bought a share of the consultant's time along with a number of other clients. The only full-time service might occur if the consultancy seconded a member of its staff to a client to work in-house on a full-time basis.

Manager, Press and Public Relations
BBC Marketing and Communications
Location \ Birmingham
Salary \ c£40,000

PURPOSE OF JOB

To lead team of BBC publicists and assistants in the creative, dynamic and proactive promotion of the BBC in the Midlands & East in line with agreed priorities for BBC Marketing & Communications and BBC English Regions. To act as Press & PR consultant to Controller, English Regions and his HQ team. To work with the BBC Birmingham Management team to raise the profile of the BBC in and around the city, and the profile of BBC Birmingham to the wider BBC.

ORGANIZATION

Reports to Head M&C, English Regions/Head of Press & PR, Nations & Regions/Head of Publicity with strong editorial dotted lines to the other two. A further dotted line to the BBC's Head of Press on sensitive and/or contentious issues. Directly manages a small team of publicity professionals on grades 3 – 7.

KEY RESPONSIBILITIES

Working to editorial and marketing priorities as follows:

1. A mix of local/regional programme and project promotion in conjunction with the BBC Regional publicists (35% of workload)
2. Network programme promotion with the BBC Network publicists, as dictated by the M & C colour-coded priority system within the framework of 12 Monthly and 40 Weekly priorities (25%)
3. Working with English Regions marketing staff to maximize marketing opportunities with the general public (10%) in Birmingham and the West Midlands
4. Providing back up to the Head of Community Affairs on Birmingham and West Midlands outreach activities (20%)
5. Providing a pro- and reactive service to Controller English Regions/Head of Centre BBC Birmingham, including liaison with Ariel (10%)

Specifically:

1. To lead and coach creativity in all activity
2. To ensure fully integrated campaign working and planning, working collaboratively with colleagues in other M & C disciplines and Worldwide
3. To manage a discretionary budget
4. To organize and oversee a regular and agreed programme of BBC PR events in the Midlands & East
5. To advise and support the Band 7 publicists on the proactive placing of publicity material in newspapers, magazines and the wider media
6. To ensure that BBC key messages continue to reach an ever-widening and diverse audience
7. To be responsible for fast and efficient damage limitation on behalf of BBC Birmingham, programmes made at the centre and in the wider Midlands & East regions
8. To act as spokesperson for Controller, English Regions and provide him and his HQ team with a corporate Press service, including fast and efficient damage limitation in conjunction with the BBC's Head of Press, as required and some internal communications work
9. In conjunction with London-based Publicity Managers, assess and oversee the workload of the BBC Network Publicists
10. In conjunction with the London-based Publicity Managers, ensure that the BBC Regional Publicists have adequate time to work on Top 12/Top 40 network priorities
11. To contribute to the development of shared Nations and Regions communications strategies and contribute wholeheartedly as a member of Head of Press & PR, Nations & Regions' editorial group
12. Also to contribute wholeheartedly as a member of the BBC Publicity leadership group

Figure 4.1 Example of a job specification: British Broadcasting Corporation.

Source: BBC (2002)

Example Organization

The Example Organization is responsible for this, that and the other <details of the organization's remit here>.

As temporary Head of the Communications Branch, you will be responsible for managing the corporate communications of the Example Organization. Key areas of responsibility include developing and implementing communication programmes for our key publics, co-ordinating relations between the Example Organization and its key partner organizations, contributing to the development and implementation of the parliamentary relations programme, and acting as the company's central spokesperson.

Outstanding oral and written communication skills, as well as excellent interpersonal and influencing skills are essential. A professional qualification in public relations or related discipline, experience of working in or with public sector organizations and an understanding of current policy issues in the Example Organization's Industry.

Post will commence in Day X, Month Y, Year Z. Salary will be in the Range £25,750–£32,500 per annum

Application packs are available from Human Resources, Example Organization, Example House, 101 Example Terrace, Example Town. Telephone: <telephone contact> or Email <contact@address.com>.

Committed To Equal Opportunity

Figure 4.2 Example PR employment advert.

Lack of relationship intimacy

Since public relations concerns the communications of the total organization, and lines of communication need to be developed and maintained with directors, managers, executives and others in responsible positions, there can sometimes be a lack of intimacy in the client–consultancy relationship. The consultancy, while on the one hand enjoying a city location, may also suffer from being remote from the client. Public relations managers, like a country's intelligence service, require numerous scattered informants to be effective. Such relationships take time to develop.

Divided loyalties

Whilst the consultancy usually only offers a partial service, it is thus able to offer only a share of its time and expertise, according to the fee, to its client. Conversely, the in-house PRO provides a full-time service and is loyal to only one employer. The divided loyalties of the consultancy, swapping its staff between projects depending on requirements, may lead to misunderstandings, particularly when a client demands service and consultancy staff are busy servicing other clients.

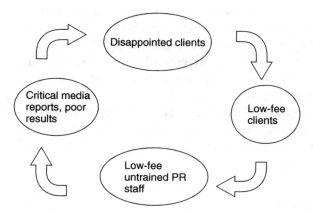

Figure 4.3 PR vicious circle.

Lack of specialized knowledge/inexperienced staff

Although the principles of public relations are generally applicable to any client, consultancies service clients in numerous trades and industries, and cannot be expected to have expert knowledge in them all. It takes time to acquire an understanding of a client's business and clients are apt to get impatient and critical. If the consultancy staff is new or young, the situation may be worsened. The quality of the consultancy service may suffer when low-grade junior staff with little or no training are used. This may rise when consultancies charge low fees to cover inadequate programmes either because clients do not have the confidence to buy objectively planned schemes, or because consultancies do not have the confidence to recommend them.

If the consultancy attracts only small budget accounts, it has to then rely on cheap labour. This can create a vicious circle in which low-salary staff service low-fee accounts, perhaps producing highly critical media, poor results and disappointed clients (see Figure 4.3). However, it is encouraging that many consultants now sponsor employees to take the appropriate PR qualifications or postgraduate training.

Client attitudes to consultancies are sometimes poor. This may be due to the consultancy's failure to cost a programme properly, or because it has attempted to get the account at any price, perhaps with the hopes of increasing charges at a later date. Perhaps the greatest weakness with some consultancies is that they aim to please the client instead of being candid about its shortcomings.

Types of consultancy

Figure 4.4 provides details of the top ten global PR firms by revenue in 2001. These organizations are either independent or owned by large diversified marketing services companies. Most of them are based in the US, in New York. The top ten consultancies provide a wide range of PR services but consultancies can also be specialist.

Before we discuss hiring a consultancy, it is useful to outline the different types of PR consultancy that exist. The different types of PR consultancy include the PR department of an advertising agency, the PR subsidiary of an advertising agency or marketing services organization, the specialist or independent PR consultancy, and the freelance PR consultant. Each of these categories is considered in this section.

PR department of an advertising agency

A number of advertising agencies, especially in the provinces, now offer public relations services. Indeed, many former advertising agencies are chipping the word advertising from their names as they seek to create full-service communications agencies (e.g. Saatchi & Saatchi). In some countries, where demand may be less than it is in Britain or the USA, it is not uncommon for advertising agencies to offer public relations services. A thoroughly good service may be provided, but it all depends on whether the agency is merely trying to augment advertising campaigns with some press relations, or whether the public relations department is headed by an able professional practitioner who can also undertake other aspects of PR beyond marketing PR.

PR subsidiary of an advertising agency or marketing services organization

In this type, a separate sister organization operates in its own right, has its own clients, which may or may not be agency clients, and is responsible for its own profitability. Examples include WPP's Ogilvy PR or Omnicom's Fleishman-Hillard. There will be linking directorships, chairmanships or partnerships with the advertising agency. It may operate under a name distinctly different from that of the advertising agency or marketing services company. For instance, Omnicom's PR and marketing service holdings (excluding advertising) operate under the name Diversified Agency Services (DAS). An advantage of this type of consultancy is that it can draw on the back-up services of the holding company's studios, print production, photographic libraries and other facilities.

An occasional problem, however, with less experienced clients is that they do not always appreciate why they have to deal with different executives from what, to them, is the same firm. They may also become

CONSULTANCY
HEADQUARTERS, LOCATION

1. FLEISHMAN-HILLARD INC.
ST. LOUIS, MO, USA

2. WEBER SHANDWICK WORLDWIDE
LOS ANGELES, CA, USA

3. HILL & KNOWLTON, INC.
NEW YORK, NY , USA

4. BURSON-MARSTELLER
NEW YORK, NY, USA

5. INCEPTA (CITIGATE)
LONDON, UK

6. EDELMAN PUBLIC RELATIONS WORLDWIDE
NEW YORK, NY, USA

7. PORTER NOVELLI INTERNATIONAL
NEW YORK, NY, USA

8. BSMG WORLDWIDE
NEW YORK, NY, USA

9. OGILVY PUBLIC RELATIONS WORLDWIDE
NEW YORK, NY, USA

10. KETCHUM, INC.
NEW YORK, NY, USA

Figure 4.4 Top ten PR agencies worldwide (by revenue, 2001).

Source: http://www.workinpr.com/industry/agency/pr_find.asp

confused if one part of the company operates the commission system and the other charges fees. There can also be problems with consultancy–client relations, where different people servicing the same account provide a different level of service.

Specialist and independent PR consultancy

Some consultancies (e.g. Lanson Communications) specialize in particular classes of PR work (e.g. financial PR or crisis management). These agencies are generally, but not always, independent. They are essentially free of parental advertising agency, or marketing service holding company, ties. Nevertheless, the consultancy may have a working arrangement with an advertising agency. The large PR firm, Burson-Marsteller, actually operates its own advertising service. Many of its clients may not require advertising at all, while some of their public relations programmes may require some advertising capability (e.g. corporate advertising).

Freelance consultants

In recent years, the freelance consultant, handling ad hoc assignments, has become more prevalent. Anyone can call him or herself a freelance consultant, so a firm considering hiring one should ensure that they possess the right experience, training and qualifications. Their service could be ideal when short-term service is required. They could augment the in-house department from time to time. Their fees are usually modest because they have low overheads. Probably the best way to judge the proficiency of a freelance consultant is to check whether they are members of the IPR or PRSA, or their particular country's professional PR association. Since membership of these bodies usually require years of experience and particular qualifications, it helps to ascertain their professionalism.

Reasons for appointing a PR consultancy

A company is likely to employ a public relations consultancy when the volume of work does not justify having a full-time public relations department. When the client can justify a full-time department it will usually cease to use the consultancy. It may, however, also use a consultancy either to augment its busy department, or to handle specialized or ad hoc public relations work. There are thousands of PR consultancies in the UK. Many are small, but the larger ones have their own trade association, the Public Relations Consultants Association (PRCA). The members of the PRCA are company or corporate members. The Institute of Public Relations (IPR) has individual elected members, some of whom may work as freelance consultants. The names and addresses of PR consultants can be found in the Hollis Press and Public Relations Annual.

An organization might appoint a PR consultancy for a number of reasons. These include the following:

● Because the organization has not reached a level of expenditure on public relations that justifies the cost of developing and maintaining its own public relations department.

- Because management needs counselling on short-term communication problems, requiring a report and recommendations.
- To provide a media relations service.
- To provide a central information service.
- To plan and execute a complete public relations programme.
- To organize press conferences, receptions and facility visits.
- To handle ad hoc assignments.
- To provide specialist PR services, e.g. crisis management, corporate identity schemes.

Where the organization commissioning the PR consultancy requires specialist PR services, perhaps on an ad hoc basis, these could include:

1. House journal editing, design and production.
2. Website development.
3. Financial public relations during takeover bids or flotations.
4. Print design, e.g. educational literature, annual reports.
5. Public affairs, e.g. advising clients on legislative procedures and lobbying ministers, MPs, MSPs, MLAs and civil servants, at Westminster and in Brussels, Luxembourg and Strasbourg or in Washington, DC.
6. Fund-raising and/or sponsorship.
7. Crisis management, and many others!

How to appoint a consultancy

When choosing a consultancy, the client should look beyond the principal or managing director, and check the credentials of the person that will actually handle the account. Is the account executive well trained, experienced and competent, possibly holding professional qualifications? It is important to check the credentials of a consultant because the profession is not subject to registration. Anyone can call him or herself a public relations consultant. A great problem when appointing a public relations consultancy is that negotiations are usually conducted between the top people on either side, but once the contract has been signed the day-to-day liaison is usually passed down the line to executives who are unknown to each other. These executives should be present during the negotiations and presentations, otherwise they may fail to work together properly. Client–consultancy relations can be delicate, relying on the compatibility of personalities, and must be excellent if an account is to be serviced successfully.

The buying of consultancy services calls for an understanding of what is required and what can be supplied. Lack of this understanding may result in a client not appreciating the range of services available, nor their value and necessity. Too often, clients think only in terms of purchasing media relations aimed at winning favourable coverage. Consequently, they sometimes provide consultancies with inadequate briefs. The consultancy will need to ensure it presents a variety of services in the form of a planned and fully costed proposal.

To obtain a practical proposal from a consultant, it is best for the client to draw up a short list of around three to five likely consultants. Consultancies promote their services through competitive advertising in the press and by direct mail. Advertisements are placed in trade journals, business newspapers and directories, stands are taken at appropriate exhibitions, and audio-visual devices are used for presentations. Some consultancies issue newsletters and other publications for circulation to clients and prospects. In Britain, *PR Week* has greatly helped in making public relations services capable of being widely publicized. Some consultants may be known to the organization. Addresses (and client lists) can be obtained from the PRCA *Public Relations Yearbook* and the *Hollis Press and Public Relations Annual*. In the US, a list of agencies can be found on the www.workinpr.com website or the website of the Public Relations Society of America (www.prsa.org). There *may* be good reasons for appointing a consultancy that also services rival companies, provided this is agreed between the rivals, simply because the consultancy has experience in the same industry. Confidentiality, of course, must be maintained. Public relations consultancies sometimes develop a reputation for dealing with accounts from particular industries (e.g. the banking or high-tech industries).

The selected firms should then be visited for initial discussions, assuming that they are interested in bidding for the account. To determine whether they are interested or not, a letter should be sent to the chief executive, managing director or business development director. By having the consultancies write a proposal for the account, the client can assess the quality, experience and compatibility of the consultancy staff. This professional approach to the engagement of a professional service is fairer to both sides. Unfortunately, the consultancy will usually receive no recompense if it does not win the contract, so staff time is usually carefully organized into bidding for new business and working on existing accounts. A large proportion of consultancy working hours are spent on administering the business, including looking for new business, recruiting and training staff, and dealing with suppliers.

When appointing a consultancy, it is essential to understand how the work will be costed and charged out, what the hourly or daily rate is, and whether fees will be charged monthly or quarterly in advance. It is a serious consideration when appointing a consultancy. Figure 4.5 provides further important criteria for evaluating which PR consultancy

EVALUATION CRITERIA	EXCELLENT 3 POINTS	GOOD 2 POINTS	FAIR 1 POINT	WEAK 0 POINTS	TOTAL
SERVICE LEVELS AND PERFORMANCE					
Responsiveness					
Enthusiasm					
Budgeting					
Industry experience					
Approach to measurement of outputs					
Client references and case studies					
Subtotal					
COMPETENCE OF ACCOUNT STAFF					
Qualifications and training					
Management skills					
Compatibility					
Subtotal					
CONSULTANCY CHARACTER AND ETHICS					
Mission, vision and values of consultancy					
Established and proven					
Strategic thinking					
Creativity and innovation					
Industry recognition/awards					
Subtotal					
FINAL TOTAL					

Figure 4.5   PR consultancy evaluation form.

Source: adapted from Workinpr.com (2002)

to take on under three headings: service levels and performance; competence of account staff; and consultancy character and ethics.

The above table should be used to determine which consultancy has the closest fit with the organization and appears most capable of fulfilling the brief. The evaluation criteria range from the degree of responsiveness that the consultancy shows to the potential client during the bid process, to the qualifications and training of the staff that will be handling the account, to the reputation of the consultancy for handling accounts in a creative and innovative way.

The client–consultancy relationship

How does the client work efficiently with the consultancy? How can an effective partnership be developed with an outside service, probably located some distance from the client's head office? Sometimes, the client does not know what they want or what can be done for them. This is compounded when there are misunderstandings and arguments over disputed bills. The best way to avoid such conflicts is for the contract to be based on a fully budgeted, detailed proposal set out in full at the start of the partnership, documenting jobs, workloads, hours, fees and costs. If the consultancy believes it may need to alter the work in any way, this should be negotiated with the organization before the week proceeds. Regular monthly contact meetings (with contact reports distributed afterwards to all concerned whether in attendance or not) should be held where expenditure can be reviewed and agreed as necessary. If extra work is required, supplementary budgets can then be approved.

In the event of a dispute over payment, an excellent way of resolving it is to show the client a copy of the timesheet. Clients do not always appreciate how much time has to be spent on different jobs. They are apt to judge the cost of media relations, for example, by the physical evidence of press cuttings. However, press cuttings are best evaluated by their quality and effect rather than their volume.

Good client–consultancy relations can be maintained by ensuring that account handlers are compatible with the organization's PR, by both organizations learning how the other works, when the PR consultancy augments the client's organization, when consultants operate efficiently, and when a good flow of information is maintained between the two parties. Each of these areas is considered next.

Compatibility

In any relationship with an outside consultant, providing any sort of professional service, it is often true that the supplier of a service is only as good as the client permits him to be. When relations deteriorate to the extent that the contract is not renewed, it is often because the representatives of the client and the consultancy are incompatible. The client representation can seldom be changed, and so it is vital that from the time of initial negotiations and presentation of proposals that the right account executive is assigned to the account. It is surprising how often incompatibility can lead to friction between a PR consultant and its client. The account executive should not appear to be superior in any way to the client but, at the same time, the client should respect the account executive's time! The successful management of a consultancy may therefore depend on how carefully personnel are deployed to satisfy the quite irrational demands of clients. An account executive disliked by one client may be received warmly by another. This is a perennial problem. Of course, the head of the consultancy somehow has to get on with every client!

Learning how each other works

The client should get to know the rest of the staff within the consultancy, especially if some perform special tasks, such as lobbying or financial PR. The account executive should visit offices, plants and other client locations to learn more about the client's business. Each should try to learn as much as they can about the other's business. If the client representation is not an in-house PRO but, say, the marketing services manager or a product manager, it will help the relationship if the client takes the trouble to learn more about how a PR consultancy operates. Conversely, the account executive should study the client's industry or business. This may require considerable reading because the client could come from any trade, industry or profession.

Augmenting the client's organization

The consultancy should not be seen as an isolated outsider, but as an extra arm, an extension of the existing organization. This encourages mutual confidentiality. When the client trusts the consultancy and shares secrets with it, the relationship becomes stronger. Good relations can be developed if the client takes the consultancy account executive into their confidence, keeping him or her regularly updated on new product development and company policy. The account executive might be introduced to top management and invited to attend meetings so that he or she is accepted as a confidant. Managements sometimes worry that because account executives tend to be less permanent than their own company staff, and because consultancy staff is external to the organization, they should not divulge company information. Consultancies should maintain client confidentiality at all times.

Efficiency

A frequent cause of criticism by clients is that account executives are late for appointments, and out-of-town clients often make early-morning demands. Out-of-town people take punctuality for granted because they live close to their jobs, whereas city-based consultants are usually commuters who suffer from the vagaries of public transport. These contrary experiences have to be harmonized so that conflict does not occur. Perhaps the client could come to town occasionally, or the account executive should stay overnight in order to make that 8.30 a.m. appointment.

Another bone of contention is over the prompt approval of material submitted by the consultant, whether it is a news release, a speech, plans for a press reception, copy for a house journal, or proofs of printed material. Unless it is explained to them, and impressed upon them, that there are deadlines or that delay will incur extra costs (such as overtime at the printers), clients are apt to be casual. The success of much public relations work depends on timing, and can be destroyed by a lack of urgency. Managing a client can often call for great tact and patience, coupled with persistence. A consultant should never be afraid to fire a bad client and vice versa.

Sometimes, the consultant has to contend with a client who insists on a number of people vetting, approving and maybe even rewriting a press release. Whilst it is essential that facts be checked for accuracy, an approved version may actually end up unpublishable following this process. The ideal situation occurs when the client is willing to admit that the consultancy knows best, which is why it has been hired. Good client relations depend on trust and frankness, not bullying and subservience.

Good flow of information

A very important element in good relations is that both sides should keep the other well informed. The consultant can keep his or her eyes open for things that may be valuable to the client, such as White Papers, survey reports, articles in the press or programmes on radio or TV. The client should also feed relevant information to the consultancy. This could include the following elements:

- News about research and development work, information about prototypes of new products, and reports on tests (such as by independent laboratories).
- Details of supply or production problems, including trade and industrial disputes, import, political or legal difficulties.
- Relocation or new location plans, and any redundancy or recruitment problems.
- Company publications such as house journals, videos, annual reports and accounts, catalogues, price lists and sales literature.
- Advertising media schedules and pulls of advertisements.
- Samples of new products and their packaging.
- Details of changes in products, prices and packaging.
- Lists of stockists or agents.
- Information about changes in distribution methods.
- Information about new appointments and changes in key personnel.

Defining public relations, with Kevin Moloney, Principal Lecturer in PR, Bournemouth Media School

Kevin Moloney worked in public relations for some 17 years and has spent the same time teaching and researching it at Bournemouth University. He worked in the manufacturing industry in Lancashire, at a university in the Midlands and did consultancy in London. He has published *Lobbyists for Hire* (Dartmouth Publishing Company, 1996) and *Rethinking PR: the Spin and the Substance* (Routledge, 2000). His over-riding impression of the industry since 1970 is growth, influence and opportunity.

Interviewer: What I would like to talk about is what PR is, defining PR, especially related to advertising, lobbying, marketing, and so on.

Kevin: We will start with the highest level of generality, let's call it persuasive communication. For me PR is always persuasive, certainly by intent if not by outcome. We could say that PR is non-paid-for persuasive communication and then we could go up another notch of differentiation and talk about non-paid-for persuasive communication through many and varied channels. I think that would include everything from event management to press releases and to lobbying. PR has an amorphous quality, an amoeba-like quality, a shapeless quality which may annoy purists; it may annoy the IPR, and it may annoy the academics, but to those who do it, it is one of its strengths.

Interviewer: Tell me more about its amorphous nature, explain what you mean.

Kevin: OK, looked at as a technique, it is the event-managed, it is the press release, it is the one-page, well-written brief put in front of a minister or senior civil servant. The form of the persuasive communication is so very varied, so shape-changing and, of course, to get modern, PR now has another repertoire of change – the Web.

Interviewer: How would you say PR has evolved over the last 20 years?

Kevin: I came into PR in 1970 and have about halved my time in doing it and in teaching, and researching it. The things that occurred to me are as follows. First of all, the oldies in the 1970s would not believe how pervasive public relations has become. Everybody has got one, from the crook, the celebrity to the Prime Minister. In the 1970s it was a corporate activity, which meant big business, and government activity. Secondly, how many more PR channels there are now; how PR thinking is done inside a promotional culture with so many more outlets. It is done by the press release; done by lobbying and also done by the great protest, the great demonstration outside Parliament, or on marches through London. A third change is who outside big business and government is now doing it? Trade unions, pressure groups, resource-poor groups, individuals with a grievance, celebrities. Today, there is more of it; it is more visible, and it is a near universal activity.

Interviewer: So you think the cult of the celebrity has been increasing?

Kevin: That is one of the drivers for more PR. Another is what I would call accelerated pluralism. In the sweep of our history in the UK since the 1960s, the variety, the number, and the intensity of values and of interest groups expressing them has increased greatly. It has been an accelerated growth and today you have groups for so many causes (for example, environmental, animal welfare groups, health groups) that did not exist in the 1950s. Our culture then was monochrome as regards value and interest groups: now it's Joseph's technicolour dreamcoat. That is the foundational platform, that great company of voices, the foundational platform from which, on which, public relations grows.

Interviewer: You talked about PR being a mechanism for persuasion; can you compare it to advertising for me and discuss some of the different ways in which it is persuasively different and its form is different?

Kevin: First of all, as regards status, in the 1970s, I think a bright young thing would have gone into advertising for a career and staked money on advertising as being the best form of persuasive communication. I think that is challengeable now. I think the bright young thing might well go into public relations. In fact, if you look at the educational world, there are some 15–20 institutions that do PR courses for two or three thousand students, and how many advertising degrees are there in this country? There are about two or three.

I think PR status has gone up and what strikes me again and again is how plastic, how variable in its format a press release, a managed event is, versus the advertising format. How flexible PR is. It has escaped the boundaries of the tabloid and the broadsheet press, into which most advertising is forced. It has escaped the 60- and 30-second slot on television. It has escaped the A5 size and A3 size fliers. Our greatest strength looked at from a PR doer's point of view is that flexibility.

Interviewer: What about persuasion? Looking at the psychological process, how does it differ from advertising?

Kevin: First of all, I think PR persuasion is more culturally adaptable. You can behave, act, in a PR way. You can use the culture, the language of the street, in PR messages. You are more constrained in advertising. You can put into a play, you can put into a radio series, a PR message. You listen to what the current themes are in our political and popular cultures. You listen to what language is today and you can shape those themes and that language into a script and that is PR. It is much more flexible than advertising, but also there is an unattractive side to this. That is, its plasticity; its pervasiveness makes public relations invisible and many people have noticed that, in some ways, that is the greatest persuasive element for public relations. It is done to me and you, but you are not sure, you don't know when and by whom. You may have objections of conscience and you can have serious objections about this invisibility in a democracy. But at the moment we are talking practice and that invisibility is a great asset working for effective PR.

Interviewer: You have talked about some of the great changes that have taken place over the last 30 years; what particular campaigns do you feel have been particularly effective?

Kevin: I look at everything with a certain awe, not positive much of the time, done by Max Clifford. He is iconic. The amount of space he gets for himself, for his clients, is formidable and I think he shows how pervasive, how visible, public relations is today. Name one famous advertising man/woman today, and you are hard pressed. Max Clifford comes to the dramatic fore very quickly as Mr PR.

Another campaign I remember is the whole New Labour campaign, and hence the emergence of Blair and Campbell [Prime Minister and Press Secretary]. A third campaign which sticks in the mind is Brent Spar [when Shell UK intended to dump its oil drilling platform into the sea] and the ability of a relatively poorly resourced pressure group to outwit a global multinational. The David and Goliath aspect of this contest is another element that allows for creativity. One does not easily forget those shots of small boats buzzing around the oil buoy and being water-shelled by big tugs on guard; nor the twisting and diving in front of the tugs and then the protestors clambering up as mountaineers on the outside of the Spar. It's made for television. It's made for the mass media. How can advertising act so pervasively, so creatively and flexibly? Today is the age of PR.

Interviewer: Tell me how the Internet is changing the face of PR.

Kevin: All of us who observe PR keep hold of a little caution because there is an enthusiasm and a sort of selling operation behind the Internet. But I note, for example, that Urban 75, which is one of the best designed and most used anti-capitalist protest websites in the UK, is well written and flexible, with regular updates. It is the work of one man basically; it is extremely well designed; it's close to popular culture and it's sharp, often in a very crude way, about political and social developments. Look, if I was a resource-poor, under-financed protest group, the Web represents a big billboard for me and the skills needed to do it are that blend of editorial design and writing skills, with the skills of persuasion, that the PR communicator has.

Interviewer: OK, but what about the fact that the PR–Internet relationship is quite complex. For instance, you will pick up a piece of paper that has a message and you will see that message but on the Internet, the recipient of the message has to find that out for him or herself.

Kevin: Yes, and I think that is a problem that is common across all groups using the Internet. It is endemic in the Internet system I would guess and this is where creativity or common sense comes in. When you come to think of it, good website publicity and audience building depends on good traditional publicity in print and in the media. In the first instance, you have to get the PR message onto paper, onto the television screen, or passing through word of mouth before you can get people to go electronic with you. There is a self-generating element after that and that has to do with the technology of linkages. The starting point in many cases is pre-electronic technology.

Interviewer: What would you consider to be a good example of a recent Internet PR campaign?

Kevin: There is one at the moment that is talked about quite a lot – it is Stop Esso. It is well designed, it is frequently updated, it earns itself a lot of press publicity, but how effective it is, God knows. That is a research project. I certainly would not believe anything that is put out by either side until the data analysis was done.

Interviewer: What is the future of PR, how will it change in the next, say, 10 or 15 years?

Kevin: My guess is there will be more of it. What's the phrase about 'the debate in the marketplace intensifies through competition between interests'? There is probably going to be more pluralism of values and groups, and there will be more use of the Web one would guess. I think we can watch out for bursts of creativity in the PR message and in its delivery form.

Interviewer: Let's enlarge on that.

Kevin: I was just thinking of stunts or, more politely, managed events. By the way, as far as I can make out, no one has done any research about the PR stunt. I'm thinking of one at the 2001 General Election in the UK. Do you remember the Labour Party had a bulldog dressed up with a Union Jack [the British flag] and they were making a point about the pound and the Euro?

Interviewer: I think they were also trying to take away the image of the bulldog from the Conservatives as well.

Kevin: Indeed, they were incorporating patriotism into their PR. That lives in the memory as it gained acres of print coverage and it had a carnivalesque quality – excessive, creative, individualistic and those qualities may be in more of our PR over the next decade or so.

Interviewer: Give me some idea of the creative side of things in terms of possible changes in the way the PR message is constructed.

Kevin: I am probably stumped there. Let's construct this answer together.

Interviewer: It's difficult I think, because it depends on which aspect of PR you are considering. Can we talk about the stunt a little more? It seems to me that, as you have mentioned, that has increased considerably. I suspect that the tobacco manufacturers will have to make much more use of PR than they have done in the past because of the removal of sponsorship.

Kevin: Indeed, and that has just reminded me of another reason for growth of PR. PR takes us, in a sense, underground. If you are forced well below the visible advertising line, as smoking is going to be, you resort to PR techniques.

Interviewer: That would almost make it regarded as less effective, wouldn't it?

Kevin: If you turn it into a cult, no. To go underground, to connect with themes and moods of popular culture, to get taken up by youth figures, change agents inside popular culture – all that can lead to great stickiness, great memorability of an idea and spread its distribution. To go underground, to associate with popular culture today is a lightning way to large audiences. One of the most interesting books I have read recently is where the author took the characteristics of epidemics and tried to translate them into measuring rods, into rules of thumb for the spread of ideas in popular culture, in fashion, in the spread or tracking down of drugs, or in being law abiding. I think that sort of combination of popular culture and creativity is going to be a growth area for public relations.

Interviewer: Who is your PR hero?

Kevin: What a question. Do you have to like your hero?

Interviewer: No. I don't think so.

Kevin: I thank you for that. I think Max Clifford [freelance celebrity PR consultant] and Alastair Campbell [Press Secretary to the Prime Minister] because they are effective. I do not like much of what they do, but the amount of publicity, the amount of messaging, the attention they attract is remarkable.

Interviewer: Why do you think Campbell is as successful as he is?

Kevin: Because he is an excellent public relations guerrilla fighter. He knows what it is to be on the other side to politicians and what the intense trench warfare between journalists and the public relations is like. And long may it live. That trench war is an indication of the health of democracy. Because he has been on the other side to PR, because he's an ideologue of Labour, because he had that personal break of luck because he knows so many people, and he happened to catch Blair's eye, he's turned into the formidable guerrilla PR fighter that he is and it is not to be completely dismissed when it is said that he is better known than half the Cabinet and twice as powerful.

Interviewer: Let's go back to where we started about the nature of PR. We discussed how it differs from advertising. Is PR a subset of marketing or does it exist in its own right?

Kevin: It is a subset of marketing; it is also a subset of politics and it is a subset of popular culture.

Interviewer: I think I would like to explore popular culture a little more. What are the major aspects of popular culture at the moment and how should a good PR person take advantage of it?

Kevin: We can easily connect with marketing. After that we connect with politics. With marketing, if you were marketing high technology, with the technology of the moment, you would be daft not to go to the clubs, not to walk along Oxford Street, not to go to the bars and listen to the 16- to 25-year-olds, because what they are actually doing with the technology, the language they use to do that, is the raw material out of which good marketing, and the PR aspects of good marketing, comes. The story is probably apochcryphal but it captures an essence: the Nokia people went to the [presumably noisy] clubs and listened to the teenagers, where they discovered text messaging.

Interviewer: I was under the impression that it was originally invented by a couple of engineers to send each other messages.

Kevin: Well, there we have two urban myths.

Interviewer: Can I ask you to sum up contemporary PR in one sentence?

Kevin: Contemporary PR is the most pervasive and creative, classic form of persuasive communication in our sort of society today.

Interviewer: Thank you, Kevin.

Chapter links

Part 2

Public Relations Planning and Management

Chapter 5

Managing planned public relations programmes

LEARNING OBJECTIVES

After reading this chapter you will:

- recognize the importance of planning and control in the PR process;
- acknowledge the benefits of critical path and D-day planning to the effectiveness and efficiency of a PR operation;
- recognize the potential effects of the PR plan on the resources of the company;
- be able to discuss the important elements of the PR plan.

Objective planning

In Chapter 1, two definitions of public relations (the IPR and the Mexican Statement) were introduced. Both lay emphasis on planning public relations programmes, and the latter adds to this the responsibility of 'analysing trends' and 'predicting their consequences'. The key in these definitions is the fact that PR does not just happen but rather is a process that is planned and controlled (Ace, 2001). To these definitions we can now add another (Jefkins, 1994), highlighting the importance of 'objectives':

> Public relations consists of all forms of communication outwards and inwards, between an organization and its publics for the purpose of achieving specific objectives concerning mutual understanding.

The stress here is on 'specific objectives'. If there are specific, measurable objectives it then becomes possible to evaluate results. This makes public relations accountable, cost-effective and tangible. These are important management responsibilities, whether the programme is operationalized by an in-house public relations manager or by an outside consultancy.

Public relations management is not concerned with haphazard 'off-the-cuff' efforts, 'playing it by ear', or short-term troubleshooting or 'fire-fighting' exercises, or with vague, intangible public relations to achieve favourable this or that. To be successful, and justify the effort and cost, a public relations programme has to be organized like a marketing strategy, an advertising campaign or a production schedule. The programme should be planned to cover a reasonable length of time, such as a financial year. Some large organizations prepare three-year (or longer) programmes. Like other programmes, it needs to be planned well in advance and in line with corporate and divisional plans. Thus, if the financial year begins on 1 January the time to plan the programme for the forthcoming year may be in August or September of the previous year. The PR plan is more than an executive level tool. As with all marketing communication tools it must be planned and integrated into the corporate communications plan (Ace, 2001).

It may be argued that public relations departments have to deal with the unpredictable (see Chapter 26 on crisis management). It is undoubtedly true that a few things may be unpredictable, such as a crisis situation, but no business can operate on a day-to-day basis. For example, the British government sets out its plans in the Queen's Speech and the Budget Speech, but in the course of the year all manner of unexpected issues will occur that will require attention and adjustments. There are a number of ways of dealing with the unexpected. From experience, and even anticipation, it can be estimated that a certain amount of time will have to be allocated for such eventualities. A typical example is a press office facility designed to deal with enquiries whose nature cannot be known in advance. Secondly, there can be a contingency fund to allow for expenditures that cannot be forecast. Thirdly, the programme can be reviewed and amended on a rolling basis at monthly contact meetings.

Certain required actions will be known because they will be based on the declared objectives of the company. If, for internal marketing purposes, a house journal is to be published, it has to be written, edited, designed, printed and distributed regularly. The launching of new products or services will be expected, and the public relations programme may include activities that will precede or run in parallel with these launches. The programme may have to be dovetailed with many already planned events, such as participation in an exhibition, the announcement of company results, sponsorship of events, a relocation programme, an opening ceremony or the celebration of an anniversary.

If the year's work is not planned and costed, the likelihood is that a muddle of unconnected things will be attempted, so that in the end nothing is done properly and it is impossible to assess any results. This can only breed scepticism about the value of public relations. It can lead to budgets being cut, staff being reduced and consultancies losing contracts. If there is a definite, objective programme, however, it is possible to tailor the supply of manpower and resources, and to operate within constraints. Unless there are major costs, such as producing videos, touring a mobile exhibition, publishing a large-circulation frequently-published house journal or large sponsorship expenses, material costs will be comparatively small. Similarly, hospitality and expenses should be a modest proportion of the budget. The primary cost will be time as expressed by either in-house salaries or consultancy fees.

Submission of a public relations programme

In an efficiently run organization, the staff PRO will be expected to present a recommended programme and budget for the forthcoming financial year. When making a presentation to a client, a consultancy should present a detailed programme of proposals supported by a fully costed budget, so that the client knows what can be expected for the money and the consultancy knows what it may expect to be paid. The agreed proposals should form the basis of the contract of service.

Even when top management does not expect a programme and budget, it will enhance the professional standing of the in-house PRO if a businesslike approach is initiated by volunteering this information. This will enable the allocation and the control of expenditure of time and money, and establish quite clearly the scope and limitations of resources. It will clarify priorities and establish what can or cannot be done, helping to deter higher management from imposing extra work on the PRO unless other work is cancelled, extra staff or funds are provided, or the department is augmented by the outside services of a consultancy.

Taking any typical day in the life of a busy PRO shows that he or she deals with outgoing work in preparing for a press reception, receives unpredictable and time-consuming phone calls, and relies very much on an efficient personal assistant. Work may not be confined to office hours. Many of these actions are slotted into an overall plan of operation, particularly if they are time-specific. Unless the flow of contributory actions is sustained, deadlines will not be met.

Critical path analysis

The overall plan (or important subsections of it) may be represented by a critical path analysis chart. This may look similar to Figure 5.1 or may be created through a planning software program (e.g. Microsoft Project). The items set out in this example are fictional as they relate to a case study, but they typify a 'real-life' situation. The chart demonstrates how each job has to start and finish on certain dates along the line (that may be vertical or horizontal) in order to arrive at the completion of the task or year's work. The line represents the start and finish of the work, and resembles that for the construction of a building as used on building sites. An active critical path analysis chart would have dates for each job, running from, say, 1 January to 31 December. As noted, in addition to using critical path analysis for annual plans, it can also be applied to single assignments such as the organizing of a press reception.

D-Day planning chart

For a separate job or event, such as a press reception, where the preparation may be spread over three months or more, a D-Day planning timetable can be plotted, working back from the event to the first action. This may be done manually or with the use of relevant planning software. This diary of actions or responsibilities will help the organizer to plan the sequence of tasks leading up to the event and that cannot occur unless this sequence has been followed. Once written down, the D-Day plan provides a checklist of things to do, and it can be associated with a budget of all the items that have to be ordered or bought. We shall return to this in Chapter 10, on budgeting.

Before approving a programme, management may ask a number of questions and it would be advantageous to try and forecast what these may be. These might include:

- What objectives are most crucial to achieve?
- What are the benefits to be achieved?
- What will it cost?
- Who needs to be involved?

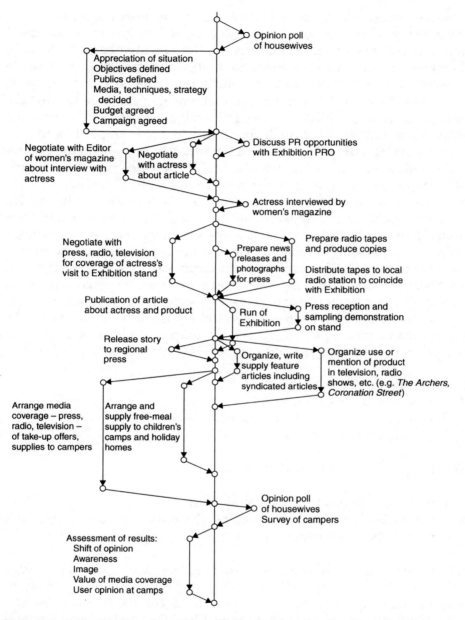

Figure 5.1 Critical path analysis. The placement of product in some media may be restricted by regulation.

- Will it cause disruption or require resources from other departments?
- Do any people/groups oppose the plan?
- What will happen if it is not carried out?
- What are the alternatives?

These questions could be asked of either the in-house PRO or the consultancy. However good your plan is, it has got to be accepted and you will need to take into account the potential barriers. It pays, therefore, to anticipate resistance and doubts, and to do more than that – understand the implications of the likely questions. If the above questions are re-examined, it will be seen that management is concerned not only about what the PRO plans to do *himself* or *herself*, but also how the scheme affects *other* people in the organization. For example, it is all very well proposing publication of a house journal, but people in the organization will have to spend time writing for it. If a video is proposed, various people will have to give up their time for the shooting, and if a technical seminar or even a press reception is planned it will involve company speakers and spokespeople. A public relations programme is unlikely to be conducted without involving other company personnel, unlike an advertising campaign, which is frequently created and placed by outside people. This means 'opportunity costs'. Although the staff may be made available to the PRO at no actual cost, they may have to be pulled off other assignments and resources spent to cover their absence.

Analysis, planning, action and control are the basic building blocks for any management planning process. Cutlip et al. (1994) enlarge upon this when they suggest that PR planners involve themselves with:

1. Defining the problem.
2. Planning and programming.
3. Taking action and communications.
4. Evaluating the programme.

Two things are therefore necessary:

- a practical plan has to be drawn up; and
- it has to be capable of overcoming the objections of those whose approval and authorization are required.

It is no good saying 'Why don't we do this?' Top management will want to know why the proposals are being made, what they are likely to achieve, how this supports the higher level company objectives and what they will cost. It is a selling proposition. This is clearly understood by a consultancy that is seeking business, but it may not always be seen like this by the full-time staff PRO. Because he or she is already appointed, employed, salaried and pensionable, it may not be recognized that this status and security relies on selling management a sound investment! The PRO is never irreplaceable or even, sometimes, appreciated. There is therefore a difference between a PRO who is not responsible for initiating and recommending what the in-house department will do, and the PRO who is responsible for managing by objectives and is in control because proposals have been approved.

Controls – essential paperwork

The best way to control time for an agency or internal work load analysis is to use a simple daily or weekly *timesheet* on which the take-up of time is recorded. This may be recorded manually or electronically using proprietary or bespoke software programs. This discipline will provide a regular check on the amount of time spent on particular jobs, and it can be an early warning system if more time is being consumed on a job than was estimated in the agreed programme. In the case of first-time jobs, it will be a guide to future planning.

Timesheets are essential in a PR consultancy, so that time may be rationed according to the different fees paid by different clients. This works both ways, helping to ensure that a client gets the time to which they are entitled, and warning the consultancy of excessive usage of time. As previously noted, it is easy to allow a given amount of time to, say, the organizing of a press reception, but in practice it will be scattered in small portions over a period of perhaps three months, as shown by the D-Day timetable and thrown up in the daily timesheets. If too much time is spent on one job it means that less time can be given to another. The solution may not lie in working late, or taking work home, because some jobs can only be done when other people are available during their working hours. The effect of keeping timesheets can encourage an understanding of how much time ought to be spent on any given job, thus imposing a kind of productivity control.

The public relations manager's or account executive's administrative staff may collect the timesheets at the end of the week, keep running totals of time expended, and compare them with target totals for the job. Alternatively, the data may be input directly into the computing software system operating at that company. Efficient computer-based *management information systems* have the additional advantage of producing pre-defined management reports. Without such control, a consultancy could go out of business. It is even possible for such a control system to reveal that a client is an uneconomic liability and that the account should be relinquished. There are clients whose fee represents only a day or two's work a week, but whose demands are for a full-time service that is far beyond the scope of the fee.

A second form of control is the use of *job numbers*. Different organizations have different systems but tend to follow a number of general guidelines. Each individual job, such as a piece of print, a photographic session or the production of a video, is given a job number, perhaps prefixed with an identifying letter. Thus, if a consultancy has 12 clients, the job numbers might be coded A to L to identify each client. The in-house PRO can use one letter for the organization, or separate letters for different divisions, departments or subsidiaries. This job number is raised as soon as the job starts and goods or services are being ordered. Suppliers (e.g. photographers, printers) must be aware that they must not accept orders (verbally, on the telephone, in writing, by fax and so on) unless they are identified by a job number.

With such controls in place, suppliers can then put job numbers on their invoices, thus identifying work that has to be charged out to clients. The significance of this is apparent when a photographer invoices a client for a number of assignments, each of which may be on behalf of a different client. Without the job numbers it can be very difficult for consultancy staff to identify items and make sure that they are recovered. The job number system is a form of control that helps supplier, consultancy and client, and ensures a smooth flow of payments.

Contact reports

Good management requires that *contact reports* should be written and distributed after any meeting, whether it is purely internal or a meeting between a consultancy and its client. The PRO or the account executive should write the report and submit it as soon as possible after the meeting so that misunderstandings are avoided.

A contact report is a special form of *minutes*, being a brief account of decisions taken with individual responsibilities clearly stated. Verbatim reports are unnecessary, laborious and tedious.

At the top of the report there should be a description of the meeting followed by the distribution list, which may include people not present at the meeting. The items in the report should be brief statements of topics discussed and decisions taken. On the right-hand side of the sheet there may be a vertical line, and to the right of this may be entered the initials of the people who have to take some kind of action. If the agenda of the meeting quotes job numbers, these can be repeated on the left-hand side of the contact report.

If this report is submitted quickly, any disagreements can be settled and the report can be revised. The reports can be filed, providing a valuable record should any queries or problems arise later on. The collection of contact reports makes an excellent source of information when writing a report of the year's work, whether by the PRO or the consultancy account executive. Again, it is good management practice to produce an annual report, if only in one's own interest. If the public relations programme has followed an objective plan, the annual report can conclude with an assessment of the results of the year's work.

Six-Point Public Relations Planning Model

So far, we have discussed the wisdom of planning a public relations programme, and some of the ways of managing and controlling this programme. In this and the next six chapters, we will discuss and analyse the actual planning process. The Six-Point Public Relations Planning Model devised by Jefkins (1994) has been updated in this edition. It follows the basic planning outline (analysis, planning, action and control) and, it may be interesting to note, the categories closely resemble those noted in the Mexican Statement. The six elements are:

1. Situation analysis.
2. Defining objectives.
3. Defining publics.
4. Media selection.
5. The budget.
6. Implementation and control.

Listed numerically in this way, the model gives the impression that there is a linear progression. In reality, some aspects may take place simultaneously and look more like that described in Figure 5.2. In

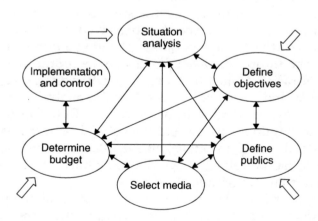

Process can begin at these points ⇨

Figure 5.2 The interrelated PR planning process.
Source: Jefkins (1994)

addition, certain parts may appear 'out of turn' in some situations. There is, for example, often a given budget rather than a developed budget, as suggested by this model. This should not divert the planner from following a logical sequence in the initial planning stage, as this may highlight potential constraints. The number of possible objectives, for example, may exceed the ability to meet them, often because of the limitations of the budget. There may also be more publics than media to reach them. The practical and the possible replace the desirable and the idealistic. A problem in public relations is the temptation to attempt more than is feasible. In the end, it comes down to what can be done with the available time, money and resources.

Public relations can be extremely efficient in terms of *return on investment* and it is remarkable sometimes how much can be achieved with a modest outlay. This does not imply that public relations is a cheap alternative to, for example, advertising or sales promotion. There are, however, times when public relations is more effective and more economical simply because other tools are the wrong medium for a particular type of communication. Indeed, all PR programmes should be part of an *integrated marketing communications* (*IMC*) plan, where the right mix of tools is chosen for maximum effect.

As an introduction to the subsequent chapters, let us look briefly at the six elements of the Six-Point Public Relations Planning Model.

Situation analysis

Sometimes called the *communications audit*, we are concerned here with determining the current image, i.e. the sum total of how the organization and its products or services are perceived externally. Unless we know where we are now, it is pointless planning a public relations programme for the future. For example, it may be found that the organization has attracted unjustified negative criticism, perhaps *hostility, prejudice, apathy* and *ignorance*. The result of this analysis may be that the *current image* may be found to be at variance with the *mirror image* (see Chapter 6 for definitions of 'current image' and 'mirror image') fondly but unrealistically held by management. Management's assumptions about the external perceived image seldom wholly match what people actually think about an organization.

The nature of public relations is seen to be about solving *problems* and changing *attitudes*, which is rather more complex than the bland one so often advanced of seeking favourable images, favourable coverage and favourable climates of opinion. In this respect, we might take issue with those who abuse public relations by seeking these simplistic aims. Real life just isn't like that. Much of public relations has to deal with creating *understanding* of difficult, unpleasant and unpopular situations and issues. This is very true of organizations that serve or supply a large market, ranging from public authorities to private utilities (such as British Telecommunications and British Gas) to the manufacturers of fast-moving consumer goods (FMCGs).

Defining objectives

PR objectives should support the organization's marketing objectives, which in turn should support the overall company and/or corporate objectives of the organization. Objectives should be SMART (Strategic, Measurable, Actionable, Realistic and Timely). In practical terms, PR departments arrive at potential objectives through discussion with the directors or managers in charge of the departments, divisions or subsidiary companies. This would also be a practical approach for a public relations consultancy if it were called upon to serve the total organization, and were permitted to conduct such internal research.

The list of possible objectives is likely to be too long to be undertaken in its entirety, and priorities will have to be decided upon. This should be on the basis of their support of company objectives and (where pre-set) to fit the budget. It is better to apply this restraint at the planning stage, otherwise the public relations effort will be spread too thinly over too many tasks and that can only invite failure to achieve worthwhile results. The simple logic here is that if the public relations programme has clearly defined and measurable objectives, it is then possible to assess the results.

Defining publics

A long list of publics can be assembled. It will be different from the groups targeted for other purposes – for example, for advertising. These targets are fewer and relate to such groups as are defined by social typologies, age or income bands, or other segments of the market. The public relations publics may range from school children to politicians, and not be limited to trade, consumer or user groups. PR publics are not wholly to do with sales or profitability *per se*, but may reflect other considerations of the organization, such as political support, market status, shareholder considerations, etc.

Not only will a budgetary constraint apply, but also the ability to reach every public. Some may be reached *en masse*, as when a television audience is comprised of many publics. Other publics may have to be reached by individually created targeted media, but will the budget necessarily permit this in every case?

Media selection

This leads directly on from the definition of publics and begs the question whether the media available will reach our various publics? In an industrialized country with a wealth of newspapers, magazines, radio and TV stations, the media may be ready-made. In developing countries, however, such media may not only be meagre, but capable of reaching only the urban, educated, literate, monied and elitist minority of the population. In either kind of society, it may be necessary to create special media to reach certain publics.

Much of the PRO's or consultant's skill will be in using or devising the right media, and this requires an extensive knowledge and understanding of the most effective media in terms of influence, circulation, readership and audience figures plus comparative costs. It is pointless to refer vaguely to 'the press', 'the nationals', 'the local press', 'the trade press', 'TV', 'radio' or 'the Internet'. These are meaningless generalities.

The budget

A budget may be set, or one may be developed to cover a proposed programme (often called an objective-led budget). Either way, it will require a careful estimate of the workload (time), materials and expenses. This is where the experience of the public relations practitioner will be important. From experience, it will be known how much time it will take to carry out various tasks, and the PRO should be precise in seeking estimates and capable of judging the merits of competitive quotations. The PRO has to be a skilled buyer of many services, such as design, printing, photography, artwork, exhibition stands or materials, videos, etc.

Implementation and control

Management of the implementation of a campaign is of crucial importance. Slippage of time in one area may cause problems in another. It will also be necessary to decide how the results can or will be assessed. Evaluation is a vital element of public relations planning and this is increasingly recognized by PR practitioners. The industry is making attempts to standardize evaluation systems, and *PR Week* has included a new category (the Proof Award) for this purpose (Harrison, 2000). There may be a continuous assessment, as with the evaluation of media coverage, or it may be some kind of test at given intervals or at the end of the campaign. Some results can be recorded, observed or experienced, and are apparent. Others, like change of opinion, awareness or attitude, may require an independent marketing research survey. These may be 'one-off' (perhaps prior to and after a campaign) or rolling programmes. Research may reuse the criteria used in the first place to establish the current image or the extent and nature of hostility, prejudice, apathy and ignorance. Continuous research conducted or subscribed to already for marketing purposes, such as omnibus surveys, consumer panels or dealer audits, may provide evidence of the effect of public relations results.

Assessments will also be related to the measurable objectives, and when these are realistic and practical the vagueness of intangible public relations will be absent.

Strategic dilemma of consultancies

A subject that has aroused some discussion in the past is the fact that 'clients want outside PR consultants more for their arms and legs than their heads'. Leader comment in *PR Week* (8 October 1992) was provoked by research conducted by Countrywide Communications, who studied the public relations activity in 43 of the top 150 companies and 83 similar companies. Only 29 per cent regarded strategic counselling as an important consultancy service. Similar findings resulted from a survey in 1990 by Smythe Dorward Lambert, while a *PR Week* survey in July 1992 had 'highlighted the rise of the senior in-house communicator with access to the highest levels of management'.

These reports are of some significance in managing public relations programmes. Who is most or least capable of strategic management, the in-house PRO or the outside consultant? The bulk of public relations work is conducted by in-house units. The consultancy either provides a media relations service for small clients or specialist services for big ones, but with the exception of some of the larger and superior-staffed consultancies, they are rarely permitted to conduct complete campaigns. This is inevitable because public relations needs to be an integrated function within an organization, servicing every department, and working at boardroom level.

Chapter 6

Situation analysis

LEARNING OBJECTIVES

After reading this chapter you will be able to:

■ recognize the different 'images' that may exist inside and outside the company;
■ understand the reasons for undertaking a communications audit and situational analysis.

Appreciation of the situation

An objective public relations programme cannot be planned seriously without detailed knowledge of the current situation. This is because public relations is not only a problem-solving business, but also needs to be the eyes and ears as well as the voice of an organization. It needs to have its own intelligence service, and it thrives on feedback. Recalling the IPR definition, public relations is concerned with *mutual understanding*, and that requires an inflow as well as an outflow of information.

There is a definite need to be very cautious of internal management's convictions about external knowledge or opinions. Management may be entertaining illusions. A public relations campaign should not be based on hunches. A public relations practitioner needs, at times, to be a pessimist but not a cynic, at other times an optimist but at all times a realist.

Communications audit

An organization should, as part of its *integrated communications strategy* (and as a prelude to an *environmental analysis*), conduct a regular *communications audit*. The scope (and therefore the cost) of such an audit may vary over time depending on the specific requirements. During a period of change, the audit may be very extensive compared to that required for an annual situation analysis. The communications audit may be performed internally or by outside consultants who can offer professional and independent advice. According to Ace (2001): 'In addition to communications needs, patterns, flow, channels and technologies, a communications audit examines content, clarity and effectiveness, information needs of individuals, work groups, departments and divisions; non-verbal communications and corporate culture issues and communication impacts on motivation and performance.'

A communications audit unfolds in several stages (Ace, 2001):

- *Planning and design*. Involves sampling all marketing communications from every part of the organization.
- *Research and measurement*. Starts with informal exploratory research and moves to more formal information gathering. This stage involves gauging the effectiveness of your communications and feedback systems.
- *Analysis and reporting*. After examining the information gathered in the previous stage, an analysis is conducted to determine how well the communications satisfy the needs of the organization.

The *communications audit* will feed directly into the *environmental analysis* discussed later in this chapter. Before proceeding with this analysis, we should clarify the differing meanings associated with the word *image*, as this may be useful in clarifying our thoughts as to what information is being sought.

Image

The word *image* is one of the curses of public relations, and is liable to mean different things to different people. Image in the broadest sense is the impression people have as a result of their knowledge and experience. Ideally, in public relations we would like everyone to have a uniformly correct impression. This is never the case, as every individual will have their own unique perceptions of the organization. The image can be only what it is, warts and all. There may be, however, occasions when a poor or false image exists simply because people are either uninformed or misinformed.

There are different kinds of image to consider:

Mirror image

Mirror image is how internal management think outsiders see the organization. From the confines of the chief executive's office or the boardroom, it is assumed that outsiders have a particular view of the organization. This may be based on top management's pride or self-confidence, or on a situation that once existed. In public relations, however, nothing can be taken for granted or can be expected to last forever. The alert practitioner has to be sceptical about any information supplied by an inside source.

Current image

An aim of the situation analysis is to establish the *current image*. This is the one actually held by outsiders, and this may well conflict with the illusionary internal *mirror image*. The current image is a consensus of people's perceptions based on what they may or may not know, or on their good or bad experiences. It is quite possible for different images to exist among different publics. The community, staff, distributors, consumers, stockbrokers, academics and politicians may each hold quite separate images of the organization. A public relations campaign should be planned after analysing trends and (to quote from the Mexican Statement) predicting their consequences, in relation to all the different current images of the various publics. For example, the image of a motor car manufacturer may be very different depending on whether you are a sales agent, an owner, a motoring correspondent, a motor insurance assessor, a service mechanic or an investment analyst. The relevance of the current image, and its disparity with the mirror image, will have great bearing on how a public relations programme should be planned.

Wish image

If the PR programme is designed for a new and unknown organization or an organization that is going through a process of repositioning itself in the marketplace, the aim may be to create a *wish image* in the minds of our publics. There are numerous examples of organizations who, sometimes quite dramatically, reposition themselves. Recent examples include 'New Labour' as a centre-left party and BP as an environmentally friendly company. The danger here is the temptation to project a biased or overenthusiastic image.

Multiple image

We may also have to consider the *multiple image* and its implications. The multiple image can be a great handicap. It occurs when representatives of the organization each create a personal image of the organization so that there are as many images as there are people. In situations where there is personal contact between the customer and the salesman, the customer's image may depend on whether that representative is smart or untidy, punctual or late, obliging or unhelpful, and so on. This is a particular problem in service industries, where the delivery of the service involves a high degree of interface with staff with a range of experience, capability and backgrounds. The answer to that dilemma is sales training to develop uniformly good behaviour. It is also one reason why chain stores, banks, supermarkets and building societies are given identical-looking premises, and a corporate image identity scheme is introduced so that, through the use of a logo, house colour, vehicle livery, uniforms or dress and other standard physical appearances, a common image is created. This is done particularly well by airlines that establish an identical image wherever and however they operate on the ground or in the air. The physical *corporate identity* scheme contributes to the mental *corporate image* and reduces the threat of a confusing multiple image.

Optimum image

It may be necessary to accept that, because of the complexity of the subject, the most that can be achieved is the *optimum image*. With this kind of image the aim is to try to establish a reasonably accurate impression of the organization, product or service, a layman's view perhaps of something very technical or complicated.

Corporate image

Finally, there is the *corporate image* which, as mentioned above, is the way the organization itself is perceived by outsiders. This should not be confused with *corporate identity*, although the terms are sometimes used interchangeably. According to Harrison (2000), corporate image can be represented as a jigsaw comprising of *corporate identity, personality, reputation* and *values*. An organization's *corporate identity* lies in its physical manifestation (e.g. its logo, company colours, house styles, etc.). *Personality* is the sum of its characteristics as perceived by the outside world and is often described in terms of human characteristics (fun, dynamic, dull, benevolent, etc.). *Reputation* is what people believe based on their own or other's experience and generally relates to the way an organization conducts its business (e.g. value for money, quality, etc.). *Values* describe the organization's standards and ethics, and will frequently be included in the organization's *mission statement*.

Situation analysis methods

1 Marketing research

When it is necessary to understand the state of awareness, opinion or attitude amongst one or more 'publics', marketing research should be carried out. There are many ways that marketing research can be approached and a vast array of different techniques – see Webb (2000) for a comprehensive range of marketing research techniques. Most straightforward is the *opinion poll*, where a sample representing the public or publics concerned are asked questions calling for Yes, No, Don't know or other simple answers. The results can be represented graphically, and often subsequent polls (known as *tracking polls*) are conducted to measure improvement or shift. The trends can also be presented in tabular form to record the results of the public relations programme (see Table 6.1).

Alternatively, you can ask the respondent their reaction to statements using a Likert scale (see Figure 6.1). The Likert scale was devised by Rensis Likert in 1932 and is sometimes referred to as a summated scale, as scores for individual items are added together to get an overall score.

Table 6.1 Change in party support during the campaign

		Con (%)	Lab (%)	Lib Dem (%)	Other (%)	Con lead (%)
20–22 April 2001	ICM/*Guardian*	33	47	14	6	−14
30 April–1 May 2001	MORI/*Sun*	32	50	13	5	−18
1–6 May 2001	NOP/*Daily Express*	31	51	13	5	−20
2–8 May 2001	Gallup/*Daily Telegraph*	32	49	13	6	−17
Average pre-campaign		32	49	13	6	−17
Result		**33**	**42**	**19**	**6**	**− 9**
Campaign change		**+1**	**−7**	**+6**	**0**	

Source: Worcester and Mortimore (2001)

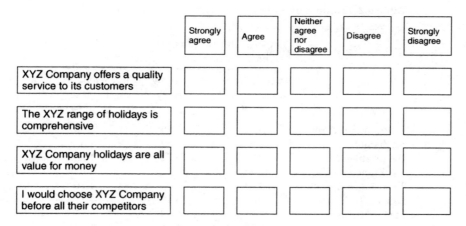

Figure 6.1 Example of a Likert or summated scale.

The sample may be a *quota sample*, where specific numbers of people of chosen sex, age and social grade groups are found by interviewers, or a *random sample*, where names and addresses are taken from a list at regular intervals, and these identified respondents interviewed. Random methods of sampling require that the probability of each unit of the sample (usually a person, household or street) be preselected in advance. The random sample, providing a cross-section of the chosen universe or population, is the more accurate method. It is, however, usually larger than the quota sample, and a number of additional attempts (varying depending on the methodology used) are usually made to contact each named respondent before a replacement is used. Consequently, the random sample is more costly than a quota sample. The interviewer is responsible for finding the right people to fit the quota sample, whereas with the random sample the actual respondents are preselected.

Another form of research is the *image study*, which seeks to make comparisons between the sponsor and rival organizations. This can be conducted by prearranged telephone interviews with an appropriate sample, say, of buyers, decision makers or specifiers of an industrial product. They will be asked their opinions of the different organizations over a range of issues. The results of the study can be presented in tabular form, such as in Table 6.2.

An inexpensive form of research is as part of an *omnibus* survey that a research firm mails to a preselected panel of respondents. This form of research enables the costs to be shared with the other companies participating in the omnibus survey. With omnibus surveys, individual companies usually pay for one or more questions on a general survey

Table 6.2 Example of an image study

Company	Respondents' overall impression of airline maintenance services		
	Number of respondents	Average score	Standard deviation
Lufthansa Technic	42	7.95	0.88
SR Technic	28	7.89	1.07
BA Engineering	34	6.72	1.70
Air France Industries	29	6.59	1.32
TEAM Aer Lingus	43	6.48	1.10
Sabena Technics	27	6.40	1.21
FLS Aerospace	49	6.38	1.15
Sogerma	25	6.26	1.54
ARL	6	5.50	1.66

Fifty-five respondents (maintenance service decision makers) from the European airline industry were asked to rate various aspects of aerospace maintenance services in January 1998 on a score from 1 to 10, where 1 was very poor and 10 was excellent. This table represents their views.

Source: Baines (1998)

(e.g. MORI Omnibus Survey). Knowing the market, a research firm could bring together compatible co-sponsors.

As noted previously, there is a wide range of techniques available to the researcher from simple surveys to depth interviews, from panel or syndicated research to focus groups. The introduction of the Internet and other e-technology has added another dimension to this confusing array. Understanding marketing research, the different methods available, their strengths and weaknesses, and the kinds of service offered by different research firms, is the responsibility of either the PRO or the PR consultant. Advice may have to be given to employers or clients on the use of independent research, why it should be conducted, what it is likely to produce, what it costs and why it is a good investment before planning a public relations programme.

When it has been decided to carry out a study, the PRO or the consultant must be capable of working closely with a research unit. The choice of the type of research, the medium (face to face, Internet, etc.), the sampling frame (who will be interviewed and perhaps where) and the structure of the questionnaire (the information required and the questions to be asked) must be discussed.

It is a PR management responsibility to write the research brief and co-ordinate the research up to and including the final report. This is because the researchers may interpret the results differently from the practitioner.

2 Desk research

Existing information should not be overlooked, whether internal or external. Internal departments hold valuable information in the form of sales figures and salespeople's reports, while other studies may have been carried out by the marketing department (e.g. the *communications audit*) or the research and development department. Published and subscription reports (e.g. *Mintel, Dun & Bradstreet* and *Ovum* – Ovum report on telecommunications and new media), or those of the Central Statistical Office and trade associations, may provide indicators of the situation under review. The company's own annual report and accounts will also include information on policy, prospects and the company's performance.

3 Complaints

A valuable source of information in any organization comes from feedback on the extent or nature of complaints, both from the trade and consumers. It will pay to discuss this subject with those within the organization who receive complaints, such as the customer services department or the sales office. In the case of a manufacturing company, a survey of distributors may be useful, and a sample of retailers might be sent a postal questionnaire or asked to take part in a telephone survey. The format of the questions should be worded carefully so as to elicit praise as well as complaints.

4 Financial situation

It may not be sufficient to read the financial pages, financial journals and the daily share prices to appreciate the financial situation, and better to meet institutional share buyers (e.g. managers of pension funds and unit trusts), stockbrokers and particularly investment analysts who produce reports on companies as investment prospects (see Chapter 24, on financial PR). With the diverse range of publics of concern to the PRO, the financial health of the company becomes of considerable importance. Financial weakness can affect not just investment but employment, trading opportunities and other areas of the business.

5 Media attitudes

Feedback in the form of press cuttings received regularly from clipping agencies, or scripts received from firms who monitor broadcasts, can be very revealing. Known as *media monitoring*, it seeks to answer questions such as:

- What are the media saying (or even are you being ignored)?
- What is the quality of coverage?
- Do they get it right?
- Are they critical or sympathetic?
- What sort of press are rivals receiving?

Media attitudes may also concern direct press relations. Are editors unhappy about the quality of press material they have received from the company? Do they feel sidelined and unable to interview top people? Unintentionally (or because of the poor practice), the company or a former consultancy may have prejudiced editors and broadcasters against the organization. One such investigation by a PR consultancy showed that editors had been writing to the client's advertising manager for information and, since he had filed their letters in the waste bin, these editors had received no information and so had omitted the company's products from important features and supplements.

The situation regarding media relations may be critical to the success of a future press relations campaign within the proposed PR programme. Unfavourable situations may have to be resolved very quickly. Editors and journalists tend to change jobs fairly frequently, and old contacts may have been lost. New staff may be unfamiliar with your organization, products or services. Keeping up-to-date lists of contacts, therefore, becomes of critical importance.

6 Employee–management relations

The attitudes and perceptions of staff are of considerable importance, as they are likely to influence the perceptions of many other publics (customers, suppliers, etc.). An impartial, confidential and independent survey can be useful here, and this is usually included in communications audits, often revealing that management is unaware of employee attitudes. Bad industrial relations leading to strikes have resulted from 'grapevine' information and unfortunate misunderstandings rather than from genuine grievances. While it is perhaps not the place of the PRO to get involved in trade union negotiations, it is nevertheless true that public relations can provide a safety valve if there is a good flow of information throughout the organization. A study may reveal the need for better internal communications, whether in the form of more open management or improved communication techniques, such as a more independent and participatory house journal.

In those organizations where staff are in direct contact with customers, these individuals perform a particularly important public relations role and therefore need to be kept well informed. It is people at the staff–customer interface that are the company's best image-makers! An example of this in action is at Harley-Davidson Europe. This company believes that the best way to develop its corporate image and justify its premium pricing policy is a strategy of 'super-customer engagement'. This empowers employees at all levels of the company to consider the customer's needs as paramount.

7 Community relations

How is the organization regarded by the people who live and work in the locality or the community at large? Again, this is something that is often taken for granted or, worse still, ignored. People play various roles in the community. The local shopkeeper may be a husband, parent, ratepayer or an influential member of a local club or society. Most people play many roles and according to these roles they could have a variety of attitudes for all kinds of reasons. For example, a company that ran an express bus service for its employees had very bad relations with pedestrians, parents, schoolteachers, the clergy and the police following a series of accidents in which children were injured.

Community relations can therefore be very delicate and controversial, and a wide-ranging survey could produce some unexpected revelations. A company may be able to operate far more efficiently if it takes the trouble to find out how it can be a good neighbour. Football clubs, for example, have to understand the concerns of their local communities. They will frequently provide programmes for local schools and engage local residents in planning issues. Good neighbourliness can also help with staff recruitment.

If you fail to find out what the community thinks, bad relations could be perpetuated out of ignorance and indifference. The next time the company seeks planning permission from the council it might be surprised by incomprehensible objections, simply because it had developed over time wide-ranging hostility from a broad spectrum of different publics. A current example is the hostility that is sometimes aroused when a supermarket chain seeks local planning permission to build a huge new store. The application usually includes offers of improved amenities that councils are loath to dismiss. These benefits may be countered by local residents and tradesmen who mount a bitter protest against the development. An example of this is the concerted opposition to a fifth terminal at Heathrow Airport.

As we have noted previously, the Mexican Statement goes beyond 'analysing trends' to 'predicting their consequences, counselling organization leaders and implementing planned programmes of action'. This implies that the results of appreciating the situation must be interpreted. What will happen if wrong things are not put right or if corrective action is not taken? This is where the PRO or the consultant adopts an advisory role, and offers a plan in the form of recommendations to solve the communication problems uncovered by the research.

Chapter 7

Defining objectives

LEARNING OBJECTIVES

After reading this chapter you will be able to:

- understand the importance of objective setting;
- recognize the different ways objectives may be developed;
- understand the importance, and process behind, making objectives measurable.

Importance of defining objectives

The situation analysis, the directives of management (through corporate, business and marketing objective setting) and the needs of various departments within the organization combine to provide the basis for the PR department's objectives. The importance of setting these departmental objectives cannot be overstated. The public relations manager or consultant cannot plan without objectives and without objectives results cannot be assessed. It is at this stage that the process of deciding priorities and applying constraints begins. It immediately raises a number of questions:

- What do we want to achieve?
- Have we the means of coping with all these objectives?
- Over what time frame are we working?

The plan may be for six months or one, two or three years. Some objectives will be short term, others will require continuous, or longer-term endeavour. In all cases, however, objectives should (Cutlip et al., 1994):

- give focus and direction to those people in the organization charged with developing programme strategies and tactics;
- provide guidance and motivation to those who implement the programme;
- spell out the outcome criteria to be used for monitoring and evaluating the programme.

SMART objectives

An important feature of all objectives is that they should be SMART. That is they should be:

- *Specific*. Objectives should relate to specific outcomes not to vague and woolly statements of intent.
- *Measurable*. If you do not quantify your objectives you cannot know whether you have been successful. Measurable objectives are at the heart of the control process. (Setting measures is not always easy, particularly if it involves soft, intangible or subjective factors – for example, satisfaction. Towards the end of this chapter is a section devoted to turning general/broad objectives into measurable ones.)
- *Actionable*. Objectives must be actionable and, ultimately, achievable. For a company to set itself the objective of becoming market leader may either be wholly unachievable or require such resources as might bankrupt the organization.
- *Relevant*. The objectives should be relevant to the thrust of the business as a whole. For example, taking again the objective of market leadership, this would be irrelevant to an organization whose mission is to service a limited number of customers with high quality products.
- *Timely*. Objectives should be set to agreed time-scales.

The development process

If lines of communication have been established within the organization, the PRO will have little difficulty in arriving at a list of potential objectives. The consultant will be able to do likewise if he or she is able to talk to departmental heads, but may have to rely on information from the client when doing this. Table 7.1 outlines some of the priority areas and the appropriate heads of department/managers a PRO might need to understand and communicate with.

Table 7.1 Departmental communication priority areas

Priorities

Personnel Manager

- Need to develop the recruitment profile of the organization at events (e.g. universities, colleges, schools via careers advisers).
- Redundancy problem. Need to explain company policy, internally and externally.
- Relocation plans. Need to explain advantages to existing staff of moving with the company.
- Share issue. Need to advise employees about investing in the company. When there is a new share issue employees may be offered shares at a special price.
- Induction of new recruits. Need to produce support material such as booklets, slides, CD-ROMs or videos and update the recruitment pages of the company website.
- New appointments. Will there be new senior appointments that need to be publicized?

Production Manager

- Works safety. Need to explain safety-at-work procedures.
- New production equipment, techniques. Need to notify trade market of advantages/improvements.
- New quality control methods, in answer to complaint. Possibility of news material.
- New factory, and need to arrange official opening.

Company Secretary

- New share issue, rights or debenture issue. Need to keep the money market aware of the company's corporate and financial affairs, and ensure proper awareness prior to issue of prospectus, bearing in mind Stock Exchange rules on publicity.
- Acquisitions and mergers. Need to announce these if and when they occur.
- Takeover risks. If the company is endangered by possible predators, need to strengthen shareholder/investor relations. Has the share price fallen, or is it too low? Can it be raised or stabilized if the money market is better informed about the merits of the company?
- Change of name or new brands. Is the company about to adopt a new name that will require publicizing?
- Legislation. If the company is likely to be affected by new legislation, does this need public relations action/lobbying (see Chapter 29)?

Export Manager

- New overseas sales territories. Is public relations required, either through home agencies such as the Department of Trade and Industry, or through overseas or international media?
- New overseas subsidiaries, licensing arrangements, agents. Need for overseas public relations. Advise new overseas employees on company history, policies, etc.
- Overseas orders, contracts. What is anticipated, and how can public relations be used to make them known?

Table 7.1 (*Continued*)

	Priorities
	● Role of external magazine, documentary video and company website. Are there production or distribution implications for the public relations department? ● Overseas exhibitions. Need for public relations to support participation, both through government agencies and in the countries where exhibitions are being held. ● Overseas visits. Do company personnel travelling abroad on trade missions or personal visits require public relations support?
Sales Manager	● New sales organization, appointments. Need for trade press releases. ● Sales conference(s). Need to contribute presentation on public relations. ● Incentive schemes. Need for public relations support, e.g. in-house journal. ● Trade deals. Need to make known to trade press. ● Dealer relations. Efforts needed to educate trade about products, e.g. works visits, company websites, etc.
Advertising Manager	● Advertising schedule. Need to know where and when advertising will be placed, and possibilities for supply of supporting editorial stories (part of *integrated marketing communications* strategy). ● Sales promotion material. Need to issue pictures and stories to press. Possibility of special public relations for special promotions such as prize contests (part of *integrated marketing communications* strategy). ● Advertising/marketing and trade press. Need for feature articles about new campaigns. ● Other functional agencies (advertising, sales promotion, direct marketing, etc.). Need to co-operate with them. Do advertisements satisfy corporate identity requirements? Do advertisements enhance goodwill?
Research and Development Manager	● What new products/prototypes are under test? Do test reports need to be published or announced? ● Research techniques. Need to make known company's research resources? Feature articles to be written? ● Independent testing. Is a product under test in an independent laboratory, and should the results be made known? ● New materials, components, ingredients, recipes? Need to make known such new uses or additives. Will publication of research results add to the reputation of the company?
Marketing Director	● Marketing plans for existing or new products. Need to provide supporting public relations, possibly including market education.

Table 7.1 (*Continued*)

Priorities

	● New packaging? Need to make known in trade press. Feature articles in marketing press. ● New prices? Need to announce (and justify) them to trade and consumer media. ● Customer service. Need to make known newly introduced after-sales services. ● Sponsorships. Need to organize public relations activities and support of various kinds.
Chief Executive Officer	● Company plans and policy (and the need for all objectives to support company objectives). Need to know forward planning, especially in order to be well-armed with knowledge and information if media make enquiries. ● How does CEO view the importance of objectives gleaned from discussions with departmental heads? ● CEO's personal plans and activities. Need to organize public relations where appropriate. For instance, CEO may have other activities that can reflect well on the company, e.g. participation in a conference, trade association or voluntary body.

At this stage no 'measurements' are included as, for the moment, we are looking at general requirements. When the list of objectives is finalized, however, a means of measurement must be incorporated unless their completion is obvious. It is also important to be clear what are objectives as opposed to strategies and tactics. At this review stage they are mixed together. One way of distinguishing them is to describe them as:

● Objectives – where we want to go.
● Strategies – how we are going to get there.
● Tactics – the operational aspects of the strategy.

If we use the Personnel Manager's first broad requirement as an example, the distinction between objectives, strategies and tactics become clearer. The original discussion suggested that there was:

Need to develop the recruitment profile of the organization at events (e.g. universities, colleges, schools via careers advisers).

In effect, this can be broken down as follows:

● Objective – development of the organization's recruitment profile.
● Strategy – recruitment events (more/different/larger, etc.).
● Tactics – type, place, presentation, etc.

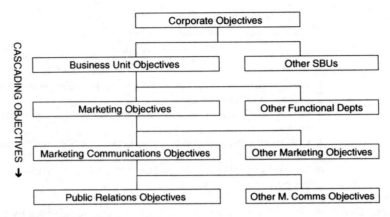

Figure 7.1 Cascading objectives.

With the exception of the Chief Executive Officer, who may be visited last in order to consolidate ideas, incorporate the wider business objectives, select priorities and share confidences, the first eight individuals in the example are not in any order of merit and each may be visited as and when convenient appointments can be made. Another method is to assemble everyone at a discussion meeting when objectives can be tabled and priorities can be agreed. In an organization where objectives are 'cascaded' down through the company (see Figure 7.1), a system of reporting may replace (but may not be as effective as) personal contact.

From the items set out from each departmental head, it will be obvious that not every issue requires regular and continuous public relations, but may be fitted into the overall programme. Some may be combined under single headings such as 'trade press' or 'financial public relations', and time and resources can be allocated to them according to their importance.

The lists are not exhaustive, and are set out merely as a thought-provoking exercise. Here we have concentrated on a large manufacturer, but quite different considerations may apply in other organizations – for example, service industries. There are some aspects such as staff training, a new corporate identity, crises management and parliamentary liaison that have not been mentioned, but could involve very important public relations objectives for certain organizations. There could also be matters of a corporate nature such as social responsibility that may be included.

Turning broad objectives into measured objectives

We consider again the example used previously of the 'Need to develop the recruitment profile of the organization at events (e.g. universities, technical colleges via careers advisers)'.

Improving the 'profile' of an organization may appear difficult to measure at first sight. If research data already exists (perhaps through a rolling research programme that seeks to establish the company's profile on, for example, an annual basis) on the number of people who are aware of the organization and their opinion of it, both of these measures could be used to make the objective measurable. For example:

To increase awareness of the organization by 50 per cent and increase satisfaction levels by 30 per cent in a 12-month period.

If this type of 'rolling research' is not available then, as a last resort, other proxy measures may have to be used. For example:

To attend 50 per cent more recruitment events in the next 12 months.

Although not a direct measure of an improving profile, an assumption has been made that greater visibility will improve the profile of the organization. This is called a *proxy measure*. But it is also a *'process objective'* as opposed to an *'outcome objective'*. Some PR practitioners always set *'process objectives'* (e.g. the distribution of X number of press releases) for their programme. These are, however, rarely strategic and either describe the tactics, or means, rather than the consequences or ends (Cutlip et al., 1994). Alternatively, *'outcome objectives'* (awareness, satisfaction levels, etc.) specify the results that the PRO hopes to achieve. By themselves, process objectives have little value *unless* previous evaluation has shown that these communication processes contribute to desired communication outcomes (Hunt and Grunig, 1994).

Cutlip et al. (1994) use examples to illustrate the elements and form of useful programme objectives:

1. Begin with 'to' followed by a verb describing the direction of the intended outcome (i.e. to increase, to decrease or to maintain).
2. Specify the outcome to be achieved. There are three possible categories of maintanance or change: what people are aware of, know or understand (knowledge outcomes); how people feel (predisposition outcomes); and what people do (behavioural outcomes).
3. State the magnitude of the change or level to be maintained in measurable terms.
4. Set the target date for when the outcome is to be achieved.

Chapter 8

Defining publics

LEARNING OBJECTIVES

After reading this chapter you will be able to:

- recognize the importance of defining an organization's 'publics';
- explain who these publics may be;
- understand the theory and practice behind reaching an organization's publics.

Publics

Public relations departments are rarely concerned with the 'general public' *per se*, but with a range of communities made up of individuals or groups with some particular interest or some other connection. The mosaic of many different ethnic, racial, religious, geographic, political, occupational, social and special interest groupings that would be included make the concept of 'general public' of little value in PR (Cutlip et al., 1994).

The term *publics* is a very meaningful expression and one peculiar to public relations. 'Publics' is part of the jargon of PR, an invented word not often found in an orthodox dictionary (it can, however, be found on the Marketing Dictionary website – www.themarketingdictionary.com). Publics are groups that are deliberately targeted and are those 'people, internally and externally, with whom an organization communicates' (Jefkins and Yadin, 1998). In simple terms, the mission of the public relations function is to build working relationships with all of an organization's publics (Center and Jackson, 2003).

The identification of the 'publics' of public relations is fundamental to the planning of a PR programme, for unless the publics are defined it is impossible to select the media that will best convey our messages to them. It may be necessary to list all possible publics in order to decide priorities if and when constraints of budget, manpower and other resources may have to be applied. The problems and, therefore, the potential publics will vary from one organization to another, and indeed it may change within an individual organization over time. To establish priorities and the media with which to communicate with them, we must first distinguish *all* the publics we would like to communicate with in an ideal world free of constraints. Some organizations will have such a diversity of minority group publics that it would be costly to try to reach them all. Others will have majority group publics who can be reached simultaneously through the mass media, especially if there is considerable *role playing* by overlapping groups.

Role playing

Individuals can play many roles. A man or woman may be a city office worker, a partner, a parent, a motorist, a golfer, a gardener and an amateur photographer who enjoys motoring holidays abroad. Such a person may read a certain newspaper, listen to his car radio and watch television, and is easily reached by the mass market media. Now, supposing an organization such as a bank, building society, travel agent, rose grower, camera dealer or car ferry operator wanted to reach some of the publics represented by this person's different roles. It could do so very easily because such players of several roles enjoy the same popular media. This would not necessarily be the case if people with more specialized interests had to be reached. For example, those who drove performance cars, played in golf championships, grew orchids or enjoyed making home movies.

The example of a bank and its publics may help explain the role playing of its potential customers and the means of reaching them through the existing mass media. The bank's commercial objective may be to lend money to people who require finance for the purchase of houses, home improvements and extensions, motor cars, photographic equipment or holidays at home or abroad. The public relations' objective may be to educate relevant publics (in some measurable way) about the bank's services. The role-playing aspect is important because it will show that many of the bank's prospects or publics are in fact the same people playing out different roles at different times. They can be reached simultaneously through the same media with the same public relations' effort.

Understanding the nature of publics helps the public relations manager or consultant to determine the feasibility of reaching them economically within a tight budget. Mass media may be the answer in certain cases but, in order to reach a specialized minority, it may be necessary to create the media to reach certain audiences. This media may include slides, audio- or videotapes, CD-ROMs, house journals, educational literature, private exhibitions, seminars or internal (intranet) websites.

Basic publics

No list of publics is likely to suit every organization. Indeed, part of the organizational analysis (see Chapter 6) is defining the company's unique profile. The basic publics that apply to most commercial organizations may be generalized as follows:

1. The community.
2. Potential employees.
3. Employees.
4. Suppliers of goods and services.
5. Financial markets.
6. Distributors.
7. Customers.
8. Opinion leaders or formers.
9. Other publics.

Public relations' publics can be seen as spreading through the entire organization, taking in aspects of the operation – for example, production and finance – not normally associated with the marketing function. According to the nature of the business, the nine basic publics can be subdivided or extended. Each of these groupings is considered below.

The community

In broad terms, the community consists of the organization's neighbours within which the organization operates. They may live or work close to the company's factory, office, store, distribution warehouse, research laboratory or wherever the organization is in contact and/or influences and/or is influenced by those around it. Some complex organizations will have many premises of different kinds, and have relations with, and various different effects on, a number of disparate communities. An example of this is an airport, where some members of the community will suffer from aircraft noise, others from road congestion. On the positive side, some will benefit from improved transportation links, while still others will take advantage of the increased job opportunities. Sensible companies are careful to develop and sustain a 'good neighbour' policy. After all, the community may contain actual or potential customers, employees and their families.

The activities of any company have the potential to affect the community in some way. Noise, dirt, fumes, smells and even the very presence of the organization may provoke antagonism. People object to all sorts of premises. They could be potentially dangerous chemical works, waste disposal plants or superstores, however attractively designed and landscaped. Most people recognize that these types of facilities are required within the society but 'not in my back yard'. Deliberate efforts may be made to overcome these problems and to make the organization acceptable. Tall chimneys, garden frontages, tastefully obscured buildings, waste disposal or conversion plants and noise abatement all contribute to better (if not strictly good) relations. More overt public relations activities such as open days, participation in local events and the regular supply of company news to the local press may be evident. Many factories, particularly those with a craftwork element, will encourage visits. Opposition may come from a lack of trust in, or knowledge about, the company. Nuclear power plants, such as the BNFL's Sellafield plant, try to develop better relations by inviting visitors to tour their facilities.

Community relations can be matters of delicacy and diplomacy but, as with so many public relations activities, they also represent corporate thoughtfulness. Public relations is about human understanding. The department store will try not to offend the job applicants it does not employ as they could be customers. Form-filling formalities may keep the accounts department happy but may make the return or exchange of goods difficult from the customer's perspective.

Some organizations take great pride in their community relations, supporting local theatres, musical festivals, flower shows, sports events and being seen to be a responsible member and patron of the local society (see Chapter 27, on sponsorship). In fact, some are great benefactors and throughout history have paid for churches, schools, hospitals, libraries, art galleries, parks and other important parts of the infrastructure. A visit to the websites of larger corporations (e.g. McDonald's, British Airways, Sainsbury and BT) will frequently show that organization's level of community support.

Potential employees

Many future employees may live in the vicinity of the workplace. They may be relatives or friends of present staff, local students, or employees in other local firms. Recruitment may be from local schools, colleges and universities, and it may be important that information about career opportunities is supplied to careers masters, advisers and appointments officers, as well as internally on the company website. Most universities, equally concerned for the employability of their graduates, organize career events to which local and national organizations are invited. These events may be augmented by video or CD-ROM displays, visits to plants and student weekends at training centres, such as those organized by some banks. In this respect, public relations techniques may be seen as being allied to the efforts of the personnel and training departments.

Other employers and industries may be sources of recruitment. Redundant workers may be attracted and trained in new jobs. Where skilled staff are scarce there will be competition for recruits. Vacancy advertisements alone will not always succeed: applicants of the right type will emerge more readily if potential employees are aware of the merits of the employer seeking recruits. Public relations is about reputation and the potential applicant will want to know, perhaps above almost anything else, if the company is a reputable employer. Young people may be deterred by prejudices towards certain industries, as we have seen with engineering and chemicals. In this case, public relations is about correcting false ideas.

Employees

Compared with other north European countries, Britain has tended towards lack of worker participation in management. Old-fashioned craft unions tended to maintain a 'them and us' culture that hardly encouraged ideal industrial relations, and companies seemed content to live with it. Although the methods employed to resolve industrial problems are still open to debate, the outcomes appear to be more constructive and involve less combative employer–employee relationships. In addition, more open management, training in new technologies, the encouragement of communications from the bottom up, the use of worker participation schemes, explanations of annual reports, accounts by means of house journals and videotapes, and so on are improving internal communications and relations.

Another factor that has led British (and indeed worldwide) management to a consensus on the value of good employee relationships has been the growth of service-based industries. Whereas in the 1960s and 1970s manufacturing companies represented the majority of UK jobs, by the turn of the century 70 per cent of employees in the UK and North America were attached to service industries. Services have certain characteristics that differentiate them from manufactured goods. Service providers, unlike goods providers, are in direct contact with the customer throughout the delivery of the service. Goods manufacturers rely on service providers (e.g. retailers) to fulfil the direct contact role. For this reason the interface between the service provider's staff and the customer is crucial to the success of the business. Unless these employees are motivated, they will be unable to motivate customers. This approach, which recognizes staff as vital assets that deliver value, is variously called *internal marketing* or *internal partnerships* (Egan, 2001) and has gained in importance with the increased popularity of *relationship marketing*.

The employee public may have many subdivisions, and it is seldom satisfactory to rely on a single staff newspaper to cover the whole workforce. Some typical subdivisions may be:

- Management and executives, branch managers.
- Section leaders and foremen.
- Office workers.
- Factory workers.
- Field sales force.
- Transport workers.
- Overseas staff.
- Part-time staff.

An airline is a good example of an employer with a great mixture of staff on the ground, in the air, at the home base and at overseas locations. On the other hand, a local building company will have all its staff concentrated on one site. It also depends on whether a large organization is structured vertically or horizontally. A horizontal structure may have developed as a result of amalgamations and mergers across different businesses at the same point in the supply chain. An example of this may be a retail organization with a number of different businesses (e.g. Kingfisher). A vertically integrated company alternatively is an empire of complementary interests covering some or all parts of a supply chain (e.g. resources, supplies, manufacturing and distribution). Unilever is typical of this type of company. There are also conglomerates, such as BAT, which own businesses of unrelated interests operating independently, and there are also consortiums of companies who may co-operate in a major venture.

These complicated structures may create considerable communications problems. An obvious place to begin is at the recruitment and training stage, to which public relations can contribute valuable induction material such as literature, video cassettes, CD-ROMs, etc., with the effort being sustained by house journals and other regular forms of communication. If there is a complete mixture of technologies and jobs, as with vertical amalgamations and conglomerates, each unit may have to be treated separately yet given a certain unity.

Suppliers of goods and services

A range of suppliers of goods and services will come to mind for particular organizations. Communications with these publics may be achieved through an external house journal, company visits, seminars, videos and other public relations media (including the Internet), but special efforts may be necessary in some cases. For instance, a chemical company handling dangerous chemicals would be wise to keep doctors, hospitals, ambulance and fire brigades, and the police aware of special hazards.

The maintenance of good relations with suppliers and services is one that can be easily overlooked. Remembering to put them on the mailing list of the house journal, inviting them to social occasions, seminars and works visits, sending them copies of the annual report and accounts may be very useful ways of keeping them involved. By listing them among the important 'publics', new communication tasks and difficulties may be highlighted. How does one communicate effectively with the Chief Constable, the hospital surgeon, the water company, and even one's advertising agent and public relations consultant? These are all part of the total communications of an organization.

Financial markets

Public and private companies depend on the money market being well informed about their history, performance and prospects. A favourable or unfavourable market will affect the take-up of new share issues and the maintenance of share prices. Investors may be relying on growth in the share price over time and any sudden or consistent fall may generate a takeover. The financial market begins with one's local bank manager, and extends through building societies and insurance companies to shareholders and investors, and those who advise them. At the top end of this market are investment analysts, stockbrokers, merchant banks and institutional buyers of large blocks of shares, such as insurance companies, unit trusts and pension funds.

Financial and corporate PR has become a very important part of many company's public relations programmes, and this has led to the development of a number of specialist financial public relations consultancies. The 'Big Bang' (the popular name given to revolutionary new trading systems introduced in the City of London), and the deregulation of share dealing and worldwide 24-hour trading, have imposed new demands on financial public relations, such as the Stock Exchange ban on embargoed news releases to avoid insider-trader scandals (see Chapter 24).

Distributors

This is a very broad group and different organizations will obviously have different channels of distribution and will use those distributors best suited to their business. For manufacturers and/or service providers, this may include brokers, wholesalers, cash and carry warehouses, department stores, supermarkets and value chain stores, neighbourhood shops, own shops and/or concessions, appointed dealers or agents, franchisees, clubs, hotels and holiday centres, direct response marketers (e.g. mail order, telemarketing, etc.), catalogue or Internet retailers, exporters and overseas importers, and doubtless many more.

Distributor relations is an aspect of public relations and marketing support which no manufacturer or service provider can afford to neglect, yet such neglect has been the cause of a number of product or service failures. Distributors are unlikely to sell a new product in which they have no confidence, no matter how beguiling the trade terms or how massive the advertising launch. Travel agents are unlikely to recommend a holiday without background information and confidence in the tour company. They have their own customer relations to consider. Educating the market must not be overlooked, especially in such areas as consumer durables, hi-tech goods and services.

Customers

The customer is the final arbiter of a company's success. Where this customer is another company, this is known as business-to-business (B2B) marketing. Where the final customer is a private individual, this is known as business-to-consumer (B2C) marketing. In the past few years the boundaries between these terms have become more blurred, with the development of 'buying clubs' and 'communities of interest' (e.g. the Harley Owner's Group).

Some products (and services) are never known to the final consumer, and the public relations operation is allied to the 'back-selling' operation of encouraging a supplier to adopt or continue to use a product/service. Some services may be from a group of suppliers but are 'bundled' under a particular brand. Thus, travel companies such as Thomas Cook may offer the services of hotel and or local coach operators, as well as its own services, in a 'package'. On the other hand, some parts suppliers have become well known to the public (e.g. Intel) and the pressure to include them in an offering may come from the customer. The consumer grouping can be broken down into numerous demographic subdivisions of sex, age, marital status, geographical location and so on, which makes it possible for them to be reached by more specialized or local media.

The target of PR communication may not be the current customer but the potential customer of the future. These might, for example, be current holders of children's accounts. Many banks and building societies operate special accounts and keep in regular contact (through newsletters, birthday cards, etc.) with these account beneficiaries, although the actual customers are (usually) the parents or guardians.

Opinion leaders or formers

When presented with uncertainties, it is not uncommon to turn to friends and trusted people for advice. These can be any people who, whether well or ill informed, may express opinions and influence people because of their actual or apparent authority. They are what Center and Jackson (2003) call 'intervening publics', in that they carry a message to the primary publics. Opinion leaders or opinion formers may well be ignorant, hostile or prejudiced, but certainly not apathetic. Alternatively, they could be knowledgeable, well disposed or at least tolerant. Their attitudes can be dangerous or helpful, according to the extent of their perceived knowledge and understanding. Opinion leaders or formers may be grouped under such headings as:

- Parents, teachers, academics, doctors, clergy.
- Politicians, community group leaders, trade union officials.
- Civil servants and local government officers, officials of quangos.
- Commentators, presenters.
- Journalists and authors, radio and TV personalities.
- Authorities on specialized subjects, who may write, lecture or broadcast.
- Advisory services and information bureaus.
- Officials of societies, institutions, trade associations and professional bodies.

These influential people can be very important in a public relations programme. They may have to be dealt with on a face-to-face basis, through the medium of the spoken word, at private meetings or over lunch. Alternatively, groups of them may be invited on a visit, tour or to a reception.

There is not only debate about who is an opinion leader, but also about the source of their opinions, and this has a bearing on the purpose of media communication. In 1948, the Americans Lazarsfeld, Berelson and Gaudel explained their concept of 'flow of influence'. They theorized that there was a two-step flow of communications, claiming that ideas often flow *from* radio and print to the opinion leaders, and from them to the less active sections of the population. The implication of this in public relations terms is that, since opinion leaders are often dispersed among the population, and it is difficult to identify and isolate them, the best way to influence *them* is by informing the media that reaches them. This work has been considerably added to by numerous authors, in particular Rogers (1995). He saw mass adoption, or diffusion through a population, as a communications process 'in which the message content that is exchanged is concerned with a new idea. The essence of the diffusion process is the information exchange through which one individual communicates a new idea to one or several others.' This additional 'step' in the communications process, i.e. 'interpersonal communication' between members of the population, or *'word of mouth'* (WOM), is normally outside the direct control of the organization, but not necessarily outside its influence (Cox and Spickett-Jones, 1999). It is this influence that PR practitioners seek to exert.

Other publics

Many of the relationships discussed above could be considered as traditional. In the past decade, a number of other relationship types have grown in importance or emerged into the business environment. As Doyle (1995) has noted, '... the paradox of business in the future is that to be a successful international competitor the firm also has to be a committed and trusted co-operator'. An organization's external relationships can be seen to have a vertical and horizontal dimension (Palmer, 2000). Vertical relationships are those previously discussed who represent those that integrate all or part of the supply chain through component suppliers, manufacturers and intermediaries. Horizontal relationships are represented by organizations that are at the same point (but not necessarily from the same place) in the channel of distribution (including competitors), who seek to co-operate and collaborate for mutual benefit. They may or may not be from the same point in the chain or even the same industry. An example of the latter is Handbag.com, the Internet 'magazine', which was a joint venture between publishers Hollinger Telegraph and Boots (the chemists). An example of the former are the alliances between international airlines in the OneWorld and Star alliance groups.

The above classification of the various publics is obviously simplistic and subject to considerable overlap. Other ways of classifying publics have alternatively been proposed. In the 1970s, James Grunig, an American professor, developed the 'situational theory of publics' to assist the developing and targeting of messages to the various publics (Harrison, 2000). His classification consisted of:

- those who are active on all issues;
- those who are apathetic;
- single-issue publics (active only in their special area of interest);
- hot-issue publics.

This defines publics not by descriptive category but by activity. Publics are more likely to be active when the people who constitute these publics perceive that what 'an organization does *involves them (level of involvement)*, that the consequences of what the organization does is a *problem (problem recognition)* and that they are not *constrained* from doing something about the problem *(constraint recognition)*. If none of these conditions fits a group of people, these people constitute a "non-public"' (Hunt and Grunig, 1994). Useful definitions of publics, according to Cutlip et al. (1994), go beyond demographics or psychographics to include relevant indicators of common recognition of mutual interests and situational variables that tie certain individuals, but not others, to specific situations or issues.

Evidently, the works involved in establishing these categories are more complex than those suggested earlier, although these may be important in the development of, for example, a political campaign. Center and Jackson (2003) have proposed their own classification (briefly mentioned in the previous section). This is:

- Primary publics – comprising those who can or cannot do what you want or need done.
- Intervening publics – specific groups who carry a message to the primary publics (see opinion leaders/formers).
- Special publics – either 'inward special publics' where the primary objective is to service your own members (e.g. trade associations) or 'outward special publics' servicing people rather than organizations (e.g. charities).

Again, the grey areas between these two groupings indicate that the classifications of an organization's publics is never straightforward.

Chapter 9

Media selection

LEARNING OBJECTIVES

After reading this chapter you will be able to:

■ explain the tasks a PRO or PR agency performs in relation to the media;
■ understand the importance of targeted media;
■ recognize the benefits associated with establishing good media relationships;
■ recognize that media scope and operations are changing, introducing new problems for the PR practitioner.

Introduction

According to Center and Jackson (2003), the PR practitioner serves two masters. The first is their employer and the second is the public interest. The media,[1] they suggest, often stands between the two. Although this has an element of hyperbole, it puts the importance of the media to the PR practitioner into perspective. Indeed, the terms 'media relations' and 'public relations' are often used interchangeably (Theaker, 2001). A thorough understanding of communication media is therefore one of the most important assets a PR practitioner can possess.

It should be recognized that not all public relations media are addressed to the mass public. Effective public relations may rely on addressing messages to small groups, or face-to-face communication with

[1] Although media is plural (singular: medium), we often use it as a collective noun in the singular. In this chapter it is used in both forms as appears most appropriate.

individuals, or on the use of videotapes and CD-ROMs. There are micro-
as well as macro-media. According to Hunt and Grunig (1994, p. 41):

> Many practitioners consider the media to be *the* publics for their organi-
> zation or believe that media coverage automatically means that they have
> *reached* and *influenced* a large audience. Nothing could be further from the
> truth. The media are conduits to strategic publics of organizations. But
> there are other conduits as well — such as face-to-face communications
> or specialist publications.

To reach certain groups or individuals the media may have to be specially created, and may include audio and video cassettes, slides, notice
boards, internal and external house journals, private exhibitions, seminars and conferences, educational literature, books and sponsorships. In
developing countries (see Chapter 20), media may have to be mobile,
and innovators and folk media (oramedia), ranging from puppet shows
to village gong men, may be required. Throughout the developing or
industrialized world, media may have to be chosen that contends with
problems of distance, isolated rural communities, illiteracy, multiplicity
of languages and dialects, and multi-ethnic and multi-religious societies.
For these groups a 'one-message-fits-all' approach is not appropriate.

In the macro-media sector there is considerable debate as to what
constitutes media. Smith (2002) suggests that some marketing managers
and agency media people consider 'media' as including all communication tools (for example, sponsorship, point-of-sale material, etc.) as well
as mainstream media such as television, cinema, radio and the press.
Even buildings, they would point out, can convey a message (literally
and figuratively) about the organization. The mass media are, however,
the major channels to the public and the ones most familiar to practitioners (Hunt and Grunig, 1994). Although the PRO or PR agency
would and should consider media outside of the ordinary, macro-
media, environment (for example, so-called *'ambient media'*[2]), this
chapter concentrates on the more traditional outlets.

Media development

The media scene is constantly changing, with new media such as
cable/satellite and digital television and the Internet providing new

---

[2] Ambient media is the use of unusual settings (e.g. projections onto the side of the
Houses of Parliament) to convey a message. It may be summed up by suggesting that
the uniqueness of the location induces a 'wow factor' about it. By definition, once it
becomes popular it is no longer ambient media!

opportunities, while the impact of new high-technology printing and international satellite transmission is rapidly changing the press world. In particular, the advent of 24-hour news programmes (BBC News 24, Sky News, CNN, etc.) has increased the demand for more news, and a heightened focus on the commercial and non-commercial sectors as never before. The proliferation of media has led, according to Gulker (quoted in Theaker, 2001), to 'a perpetual global slow-news day'. To the PRO and PR agency this provides both opportunities and dangers.

Media mix

Unlike advertising, we do not buy space or air time (except for a corporate advertising campaign), but the mistake should not be made of thinking that no cost is involved. With advertising there is a known cost. For example, a column square centimetre in the *Sun* and *Financial Times* costs approximately £205 and £190 respectively, whereas a full page, four-colour, advertisement in either paper is in excess of £45 000 (Smith, 2002). Once an advertisement is accepted the advertiser has guaranteed placement. In PR, media are also the vehicles of communication but the public relations costs lie in the time spent in working with media and the materials (e.g. postage, etc.) used. The guarantee of placement, however, does not exist. Even if a press release generates coverage it does not mean that coverage will be ultimately favourable. In this regard, public relations practitioners are in the hands of the media. On the positive side, journalistic copy is more likely to have an influence than advertising and can be targeted at media (such as those run by the BBC) who do not normally accept commercial advertising.

Media tasks

Black (1995) suggests the PRO or PR agency have a number of tasks to perform in relation to the media. These are:

- To source information on media and maintain up-to-date files/subscribe to media information services.
- To co-ordinate advance editorial schedules of relevant print (and electronic) media, radio and television.
- To maintain continually updated information on key contacts in the media through personal liaison.

- To maintain personal contacts with relevant editors and programme producers.
- To research and compile files/databases on specialist freelance contacts in relevant fields.
- To keep abreast of new channels of communication and to evaluate their relevance for public relations practitioners.
- To be aware of all useful reference material on the media and ensure you are always up to date with new media and developments.

The media is a powerful influence in our society and most others world-wide. It does, however, have its limitations. Center and Jackson (2003) report that research suggests:

- Media influence is cumulative and long term. A single news item is unlikely to change attitudes or behaviour.
- The main power of the media is to make us aware of products, services, companies and ideas. By itself, awareness rarely moves people to action or changes their opinion.
- The media concentrates on reporting bad news because people prefer (by a factor reported by Center and Jackson to be 7:1) to hear about bad news than good.

Advertorials

Advertorials might be regarded as a hybrid between an advertisement and a genuinely newsworthy press release. It describes a situation where advertising space is sold in a magazine or other publication but, as part of the package, product or service endorsement features are run purporting to be genuine news articles. Advertorials include: advertisements for a single brand disguised as an editorial; features mentioning or recommending brand names; special features or '*adgets*' where advertising is sold with accompanying editorial copy (Brierley, 2002). It is what Jefkins (1994) describes as 'a joint conspiracy between unprofessional consultants and inexperienced journalists'. To counter this misuse of journalistic privilege, rules have been introduced to combat misuse of this practice. 'Reader advertisements', written in journalistic style and set to resemble editorial copy, must be distinguished by the words 'Advertisement' or 'Advertiser's Announcement' (which tends to nullify the editorial effect), in compliance with the British Code of Advertising Practice. The rules so far as journalists are concerned are set out in the Chartered Institute of Journalists Code of Conduct. This requires every member to subscribe to the code that states that it is unacceptable to permit:

> The writing or altering of editorial copy at the request of an advertiser or news feature pictures at the request of an advertiser or in exchange for advertising or any other consideration, or offering to do so, except for use in clearly marked advertising pages or supplements.

Whether all journalists follow this code is, however, a debatable point.

Targeting the media

A weakness with some public relations students (perhaps, more generally, marketing students) and even senior practitioners is to generalize about the media instead of referring to a specific medium. Even the expression 'tabloid' is a generality, no longer describing the 'gutter press' but rather most newspapers, as broadsheets are now rare. We do not send stories to ITV (Independent Television Network – still the largest commercial network), as it is not yet a single national television organization but a series of regional companies.[3] National news on Independent Television (and many independent radio stations) is managed and presented by yet another organization (ITN – Independent Television News). Indeed, as the media (especially television, radio and other electronic communications) channels proliferate, it is likely that they will specialize further by region or lifestyle. Already there are a host of television channels (currently over 200 in the UK) aimed at specialist segments catering for such groups as gardeners, food junkies, football fans, do-it-yourself fanatics and children, to name but a few. Radio now caters for every kind of music from classical to rap, as well as sports and news channels. Press releases sent untargeted to the 'nationals' (as nationally distributed newspapers were known) are equally ineffective, as within each newspaper (or magazines, TV and radio stations) there are sections, features, columns and programmes all controlled by individuals. Britain is rich in press media, and throughout the country there are nearly 100 regional dailies (mostly evenings), a few Sundays, thousands of local weeklies (paid for and free), plus various categories of local magazines. Scotland, Wales and Northern Ireland can be regarded as having their own national press. Even most 'nationals' now have regional variations (e.g. the *Daily Mirror*, *Daily Record* and *Irish Daily Mirror*), whose content largely relates to that

---

[3] Although the independent regional broadcaster is slowly disappearing as ITV companies are now permitted to merge, regional coverage of news and current affairs is likely to remain part of ITV's charter requirements.

market. The ultimate in segmentation is the US *Farmer's Journal*, which produces 1000 different editions each month targeted at 1000 different types of farmer. The result is more segmented media that gives both PR practitioners and advertisers the opportunity to target their messages more effectively (Smith, 2002).

It is important, therefore, for the PRO to keep lists of the appropriate media (and sections therein) as those most likely to be of interest. Effectiveness can only be achieved if it is conveying the right message via the right media to the right audience. Today's communicators are confronted with a paradox; multiplying channels of communication permit a sharper focus of messages but greatly increase the competition for audiences' attention (Cutlip et al., 1994).

Media analysis

Media opportunities need to be analysed, therefore, in order to know to whom or to where material should be sent or contact made. It is therefore important that the public relations practitioner should be as familiar as possible with the wealth of media available and know how to incorporate it in his or her media mix. A broad knowledge of titles, contents and locations can be developed with the aid of directories such as *Contact (The Press and Public Relations Handbook)* or *BRAD (British Rates & Data)*. Although technological developments have reduced set-up time considerably, most publications have deadlines that may be hours, days or weeks ahead of the publication date. Television programmes are often recorded months before they are aired. Modern newspapers, printed around the country by strategically located contract printers, print their first editions before midnight. Although 'hot news' may cause a change of headline and some movement of articles, most features remain unchanged. According to Jefkins (1994), the PR practitioner 'who knows the media best will win the greatest coverage'.

Media relationships

Media relations occupy a central position in PR because the media serve as 'gatekeepers' who control the information that flows to the publics (Hunt and Grunig, 1994). Whilst it is largely tactical in nature, in practice good media relations can contribute to longer-term strategic objectives such as (Theaker, 2001):

- improving company or brand image;
- higher and better media profile;

- changing the attitudes of target audiences;
- improving relationships with the community;
- increasing market share;
- influencing government policy at local, national and international levels;
- improving communication with investors and their advisers;
- improving industrial relations.

The relationship between the public relations professional and the media largely depends on that practitioner providing newspeople with information they consider 'of public interest' (Center and Jackson, 2003). The first challenge, therefore, is 'is it newsworthy?' The content of press releases will be covered elsewhere (see Chapter 14). The second challenge is presenting it in a format that is likely to be accepted. No longer is a reasonably acceptable news release 'subbed by hand' (sub-edited into a format for publication). Instead, it is keyed onto the computer screen, often without further editing. Despite this, the standard advice on writing media releases (i.e double-spaced, wide margins, etc.) is a leftover from the days when journalists received hard copy through the post, marked it up and sent it to a typesetter (Theaker, 2001). In the paperless newsroom, the most popular methods for transmission of press releases includes e-mail as well as mail or fax. This in itself has its advantages and disadvantages. It is now very easy to dispatch a press release to a very wide circulation list. On the down side, not only does this discourage targeting, but the resultant flood of e-mails hitting the media makes it more difficult to get your news noticed. This leads to the third challenge of developing media relationships.

The job of the PRO is to build open and trusting relationships with reporters and editors so that they keep the media channels open to your publics (Hunt and Grunig, 1994). One benefit of co-operating with the media on a long-term basis is that the stories they cover are more likely to be accurate and sympathetic (Black, 1995). There is always an element of *quid pro quo* with the media. They are hungry for news and the PR practitioner is in a position to provide it. Although mutually beneficial, the relationship remains an adversarial one as journalists and PR practitioners are not in the same business nor do they have the same communication goals (Cutlip et al., 1994). The PRO can, however, help to close the gap. Continuous pumping out of untargeted, irrelevant and uninteresting press releases is unlikely to endear the organization to a wide range of media. According to research undertaken by Theaker (2001), the biggest problems with most media releases are that they are irrelevant or not newsworthy. Instead, the PRO should target the most important and relevant media for the fulfilment of its objectives.

It is also important to be proactive rather than reactive. If the only media contact is when the organization has a problem, it will become known as a problem company. Although it is harder to place 'good news', this should be celebrated as and when it occurs. If bad times come there is then the cushion of previous good performances to set against it. Making research available to the media is another way of developing relationships. Interesting consumer or business research findings find their way into a broad range of newspapers and periodicals. To become known as the 'point of reference' for information in any given situation or to be able to supply an 'expert' for comment can make you very valuable to particular media. Training of potential spokespersons in the finer (and trickier) points of interviewing is beneficial and is now compulsory in larger organizations and political parties. Part of being proactive is being prepared and planning for the unpredictable. What will the organization's reaction be to a number of crisis situations? Having a plan for every situation is frequently suggested (see below), although considerably easier said than done. After all, NATO planners, during the Cold War, believed they had planned for every eventuality. As it turned out the fall of communism was not one of them.

Media guidelines

By way of summary, Center and Jackson (2003) have produced a number of media relations guidelines that are widely followed:

- Start with a sound working knowledge of the methods and the technology involved in gathering potential news, evaluating it, processing it editorially, and putting it into the best format and mode for newsprint, magazine, broadcast and electronic media. Be able to fit into the process.
- Be sure that the company has a designated spokesperson available at short notice.
- Have spokespeople be as candid as possible in response to inquiries within the limits of competitive and or national security and of compassionate consideration.
- Play the percentages. In a long successful partnership take instances of bad news in your stride, together with a record of good news coverage achieved.
- Continuously educate and train employees on how to handle themselves when in contact with the news media.
- Generate good news situations as a track record to offset instances of undesired news. Do not simply wait defensively for bad news.
- Advocate the organization's views on public issues among the organization's natural constituencies and in the news media receptive of them.

● Expect the unexpected and be prepared for it. In particular, have a crisis or disaster plan for every foreseeable circumstance.

Box 9.1 outlines how PROs can achieve better coverage through the media, highlighting the often antagonistic relationship between the two.

Box 9.1 **Case outlining PRO/media relations**

PR TECHNIQUE: Pitching news stories to the media – allies and not enemies

Jo Bowman, *PR Week*, Asia, 23 August 2002

The often fraught relationship between PROs and journalists can be overcome by following a few basic rules. The relationship between journalists and PR practitioners is not usually a happy one. There is mutual distrust, neither has a good word for the other, yet they are forced to work together. PROs complain of being besieged by demanding journalists who are only interested in 'bad' news, and journalists complain that PROs are a barrier to the truth, miss deadlines, and are often difficult and inflexible as well. Stephen Cole, a veteran television journalist who now runs Click Online on BBC World, says the root of the problem is a lack of training in the PR industry in effective media relations. 'It seems that anybody with a vague idea of media studies can become a PRO, and there are very few PROs who know a great deal about journalism,' he says. 'They often go into it as a sort of accident. A lot of PR consultancies seem to hire good-looking young things and suddenly they're an "account executive". In 30 years of journalism I've come across a handful (of really good practitioners).'

Journalists say they like PROs who are quick, courteous and are aware of the pressures that reporters work under – most importantly, tight deadlines. They say PROs calling with a story should make sure that it really is a story and is relevant to the journalist's target market. Then, think about whether the journalist is likely to have time to chat. 'The most infuriating thing about many PR people is their apparent lack of the basic knowledge of how a newspaper works,' says Niall Fraser, associate news editor of the *South China Morning Post*, in Hong Kong. 'A phone call in the early evening of a hectic news day is the last thing a busy desk needs, especially when the event you are punting is a week away. It's always best to make that call early the day before an event, to get a better hearing.'

Similarly, it will not be a popular caller who phones a TV newsroom 15 minutes before the nightly news, or tries to speak to a radio journalist when they're about to go on air. Fraser says that no matter how worthy you believe your story is, if a journalist rejects it you should leave it at that.

Box 9.1   *(Continued)*

You won't change anyone's mind, but you may well become a pest. 'Newsdesks should know a story the first time it calls, so badgering a news editor for days on end about a press conference on something like a quick-dry paint is a waste of time,' he says. When it is the journalist who makes first contact, Cole says PROs need to overcome their 'paranoia' that the reporter is out to rubbish their company, and try to help rather than hinder. 'Some companies shoot themselves in the foot – they don't need journalists to do it for them,' he says. 'I've had a couple of obstructive PROs who say "no, you can't talk to him because he can't talk about that". That's like a red rag to a bull, and the first question I always put is the one they tell me I can't ask. Often you get a good answer, because half the time these guys want to talk, and they're not fools, they're senior managers, people who've made their way up the ladder and are very intelligent. They're not going to say stupid things.'

Journalists in different media need different things. Cliff Bale, station assignment editor at Radio Television Hong Kong (RTHK) Radio 3, says a quiet place for interviews is vital for radio reporters. 'If it's a lunch speech you don't want glasses clinking and you don't want an environment that's boomy, it sounds like you're in a toilet.' Print journalists always want to know whether to bring a 'snapper' (photographer). 'Three people sitting at a desk behind some microphones, or men in suits shaking hands, simply won't do. More imagination and a willingness to adapt to news and photo-desk requests is required,' says Fraser. TV crews need time to set up and the freedom to find the shots they need. Journalists working in all media say you should always choose your company's best speaker to be inter-viewed, not the person with the biggest pay packet. 'We need someone who can come on and make their points very succinctly and in a simple manner,' says Bale. Cole says: 'Media training can work, but you can't turn base metal into gold in a few sessions with a media trainer.' But it's not all complaints. Cole says the PR staff at computer firm Dell, for instance, were 'brilliant'. 'The information I was presented with was what I was looking for – not a great sheaf of PR claptrap,' he says. Dell's in-house corporate communications officer also suggested a good outdoor location – rather than an office – for the interview. 'We were being orchestrated, we were being arranged, but very positively,' Cole says. Fraser says excellent PR operators exist 'but are thin on the ground'. He believes the best ones are always available, never ask for written questions in advance and answer queries quickly. Cole's advice to PROs dealing with the media is: 'Know what you're selling and sell that. Don't try to be all things to all people, and be completely honest, always. You'll always be found out if you're not,' he adds.

Box 9.1 **(Continued)**

Technique tips

- Be enthusiastic – if you believe in what you're promoting, you're more likely to get other people interested in it.
- Have something newsworthy to give a journalist, and if they turn it down, don't badger them on the phone or send reams of follow-up e-mails. 'That's a mistake, because you won't take them seriously again,' Cole says. 'And they don't seem to realize you can press the delete button the same as you can put a press release in the bin.'
- Put some humour into press releases. 'Humour sells, big time,' says Cole. 'Inject a bit of fun into PR.'
- Call a spade a spade, or a 'staff dining facility' a canteen. Cole says: 'I would ban all jargon from PR and just make the message clear.'
- Choose your company's best spokesperson, not the boss with the longest title.
- Watch the clock – keep journalists' deadlines in mind and respond to inquiries quickly. Also remember that camera crews need time to set up equipment and get all the shots they want.
- Give a crew freedom to move around. The camera can't lie, and often helps a company project a positive public image.
- Choose an informal situation for interviews to put your spokesman at ease; a formal interview can be quite daunting.

Source: © Haymarket Publishing Services Ltd., 1995–2002, reproduced with kind permission

Chapter 10

Budgeting

LEARNING OBJECTIVES

After reading this chapter you will be able to:

■ recognize the importance of budgeting to the PRO/PR consultant;
■ explain the different types of budget that exist;
■ draw up a departmental and event budget.

Costing and controlling costs

Budgeting is not only a means of estimating costs and subsequently controlling them, it also identifies work to be done, enabling the timetable and the critical path analysis, as noted in Chapter 5, to be drawn up. A budget is similar to the shopping list that a householder prepares before going shopping, reminding the shopper of what to buy, which in turn is controlled by the amount of money that they have available in cash or on credit.

Budgets can be drawn up in many different ways. According to Smith (2002), the following are the most common forms of *scientific* (using objective formulae) and *heuristic* (more subjective and largely trial and error) budget setting approaches used in marketing communications planning today:

Scientific

● *Objective and tactics* – based on a review of the objectives and a summary of the strategy and subsequent tactics required to achieve them. This is sometimes called the 'ideal' or 'task' approach.
● *Modelling* – uses a variety of econometric and simulation techniques to model how various budget levels may affect performance.

- *Payback period* – the time taken for an integrated marketing communications campaign to pay back the costs (or budget).
- *Profit optimization* – argues that the investment in marketing communications is continued as long as the marginal revenue exceeds the marginal cost (i.e. as long as every £1.00 invested has a return of more than £1.00).

Heuristic

- *Percentage of turnover* – uses a simple calculation of a fixed percentage of either past or anticipated turnover.
- *Competitive parity* – uses the competition and their relative spend as a yardstick.
- *Affordable* – based on using all available monies after costs are deducted from required profits.
- *Arbitrary* – where senior management arbitrate between the different views of the marketing team.

Although the assumption is made that all budgeting decisions are based upon rationality, this is rarely wholly the case. Company tradition, poor trading results or even gut feeling are often the basis for decision making. It is also important to note that the PR budget should be part of a co-ordinated marketing communications budget that will be affected by other communication activities. With this in mind, the following represents those factors relevant to the PRO or PR consultant.

PR budgeting

The three principal public relations costs are time, materials and expenses. Until the volume of available time is agreed, the materials or expenses associated with the employment of that time cannot be assessed. Thus, time is often the key to public relations budgeting.

Time

Time represents the person-hours involved in carrying out the PR objectives. This can be looked at in two ways:

1. The amount of time it will take to carry out a particular task (such as editing a house journal, handling a news release or organizing an event).

2. The amount of time that is represented by a PRO's or other staff's salaries or a consultant's fee, where the value of the time is translated into an hourly or daily rate.

Internally, a *time bank* can be allocated to the tasks in the programme, whether this is for a total year or on an event-by-event basis. If this fails to agree with the estimated person-hours for the programme, it will be necessary to do one of the following three things:

1. Make cuts in the proposed campaign.
2. Engage extra staff.
3. Augment the in-house staff with freelance and/or consultancy services.

A more complicated calculation is required to arrive at the consultant's hourly rate, because this rate has to recover the costs of running the business and producing a profitable return for the company. The consultant's hourly rate will take into consideration salaries and all overheads, such as light, heat, air-conditioning, rent, rates and so on, plus a percentage desired as profit margin. There are various methods used by consultancies, with some basing the hourly rate on the salaries of the account executive and his or her team, with others working out hourly rates (salary plus on-cost) for every member of the consultancy staff so that their work is both estimated and charged out according to its usage.

The client can only expect what he or she pays for, and if the consultant exceeds the paid-for workload this is done at his or her own loss unless a percentage underage/overage (e.g. ± 10 per cent) or supplementary fee is agreed. It is essential, therefore, to calculate time and its allocation, otherwise it is impossible to plan what is to be done. In the case of salaries it is a matter of how best the time of the in-house PRO can be spent, and in the case of the consultancy fee it is a matter of how much work the client can expect for the money.

Materials

Materials consist of all goods which have to be purchased on the client's or company's behalf. Stationery, postage, photographs, print, CD-ROMs, disks, slides, videotapes, cassettes, exhibits and displays come under this heading. The consultant has to be careful to recover all such costs, otherwise they will come out of profits. Internally, the need to control costs is also of major importance. Unless there are very expensive items such as house journals or documentary films, material costs will make up only a small proportion of the total budget.

If there is a mark-up on materials purchased by the consultancy, it should be specifically agreed with the client in the original contract. A mark-up is different from commission and is an *extra* cost. When a client uses an advertising agency under the traditional commission system,[1] the agency buys space or air time at a discount (e.g. 15 per cent) and this (plus other expenses) represents the agency fee.[2] A PR consultancy has no commission income but may have *mark-up* income. If the consultant is doing a labour-intensive job for a client, expenditure on materials and income derived from percentages should be minimal. These minimal costs could cover such things as the printing of news release headings, photography, stationery, postage and so on, which would provide little mark-up income compared with the major cost of time represented by the fee.

Expenses

These are the costs of fares, taxis, hotel expenses and hospitality, and will also include catering, transportation and other costs for press events. Again, this should not be a large item in the budget, in spite of the myths that generally circulate regarding public relations entertainment.

Examples of PR budgets

In this section three kinds of budget will be demonstrated. The first is the kind that the consultant often includes in a proposition to a client. The second is a budget for a press reception. The third is an estimate of the cost of running a public relations department.

1. Public relations consultancy budget

This calls for a little preliminary explanation. It differs from an advertising appropriation because no services are covered by commission on media purchases. All time has to be paid for, including talking to the client. You

---

[1] Advertising commission is not as prevalent as in the past and is increasingly replaced by a fixed fee, with any media commissions being refunded to the client.

[2] The inclusion of this fee *above-the-line* (i.e. before expenses) is why advertising is referred to in this way, whilst other marketing communication expenditure (e.g. PR) is known as *below-the-line* expenditure.

12 progress meetings	12	x		00 hrs@ Rate =	£0000.00
Public relations coverage of exhibition	1	x		00 hrs@ Rate =	£0000.00
News releases	25	x		00 hrs@ Rate =	£0,000.00
Organizing 3 seminars	3	x		00 hrs@ Rate =	£0,000.00
Press visit to showroom	1	x		00 hrs@ Rate =	£0,000.00
3 photographic sessions	3	x		00 hrs@ Rate =	£0,000.00
Editing, designing, quarterly house journal	4	x		00 hrs@ Rate =	£0,000.00
General information services				00 hrs@ Rate =	£0,000.00
Contingency 10%					£0,000.00
				Subtotal	£0,000.00
Estimated material costs				News releases	£0,000.00
				Photography	£0,000.00
				Printing	£0,000.00
				Postage, stationery	£0,000.00
				Press cuttings	£0,000.00
Expenses				Travelling expenses	£0,000.00
				Transportation	£0,000.00
				Seminars	£0,000.00
Contingency 10%					£0,000.00
				Total	£0,000.00

Figure 10.1 PR consultancy budget.

Source: Jefkins (1994)

will notice that progress meetings and regular monthly meetings are chargeable, whether held on the client's or the consultant's premises. The calculations should be interpreted as the number of items multiplied by the number of hours multiplied by the hourly rate (see Figure 10.1). As the hourly rate varies and as the budget may not necessarily be in sterling, noughts are used in the following.

2. Budget for a press reception

This is a useful standard budget because press receptions are common public relations exercises. It is, however, easy to forget items, make mistakes and miscalculate. A press reception may seem such a familiar event that the PRO may be tempted to be careless. Too much may be left to others, especially the caterers, and unexpectedly high bills may be incurred. The practitioner must watch out for others in the organization introducing their own last-minute and sometimes overgenerous changes, and/or of company staff who are apt to stay behind after the guests have gone and so run up unnecessary bills!

Journalists or freelance writers are seldom there purely for their own entertainment purposes, but there are always exceptions. It is also possible to control the volume of drinks consumed by guests, for instance, by never having a waiter walking around with a tray of drinks unless

Printed invitation cards, reply cards, white envelopes		£000.00
Postage on invitations (and pre-paid replies)		£000.00
Telephone/e-mail: checking names on invitation list, following up non-replies		£000.00
Hire of room		£000.00
Hire of projector or VCR, TV set, PC/laptop		£000.00
Hire of sound systems		£000.00
Drinks: 3 drinks (average)	@ Rate per head	£000.00
00 buffets	@ Rate per head	£000.00
00 coffees	@ Rate per head	£000.00
Gratuities		£000.00
00 press kit wallets		£000.00
00 news releases, copies of speech		£000.00
Displays, signage, stands, etc.		£000.00
Photography and prints		£000.00
Order forms for photographs		£000.00
Visitors' book		£000.00
Samples/gifts/souvenirs for guests		£000.00
Lapel badges		£000.00
Artwork (for tent cards, displays, notices, etc.)		£000.00
Taxi fares transporting materials, staff, etc.		£000.00
Special effects: costume hire, decorations, musicians, lighting, etc.		£000.00
Incidentals		£000.00
Contingency fund		£000.00
	Total	£000.00

Figure 10.2 Event budget.

Source: Jefkins (1994)

this is the easiest way of serving a large party. If the event is merely one of those old-fashioned cocktail parties where people stand around, and eventually someone makes a speech, the drinks will flow because there is nothing better to do. But if there is an organized programme, and for most of the time journalists are seated, listening or watching, there is less time for drinking.

Figure 10.2 is an example of a budget of materials for a specific occasion. The time involved in preparation (spread over weeks) and running the event could make a total of at least three days, i.e. 21 hours, although the press reception itself occupies only two hours.

3. Budget for a public relations department

In-house public relations departments will vary in size and duties according to the type of organization. The example budget shown here (see Figure 10.3) is designed to show a comprehensive range of activities. It can be adapted for use as required. It covers everything included in the consultancy budget except profit. Overheads are identified instead of being calculated in the hourly rate. The variety of activities is likely to be greater than that of a consultancy budget because we are now dealing with full-time staff and not a share of a consultancy team. The work will also entail internal as well as external public relations

Salaries: PRO and other staff	£00,000.00
Overheads: rent, rates, lighting, etc.	£00,000.00
Depreciation: furniture and equipment	£00,000.00
Insurances: car, all risks on equipment, travel, pensions, health	£00,000.00
Press events: materials, catering, hire/rental charges	£00,000.00
Visual aids: production, distribution etc.	£00,000.00
News releases: preparation and distribution	£00,000.00
Press cutting service, television, radio, Internet monitoring services	£00,000.00
Feature articles: preparation and publication	£00,000.00
Information service: staff and equipping	£00,000.00
House journals: editing and production	£00,000.00
Educational literature: creation, printing and production	£00,000.00
Sponsorship: awards and coverage, hospitality	£00,000.00
Seminars: materials, catering, hire/rental charges	£00,000.00
Photography: shooting, prints/files	£00,000.00
Vehicles	£00,000.00
Equipment: camera, television, tape recorder, computers, copier, scanner, etc.	£00,000.00
Stationery: letterheadings, news release headings, etc.	£00,000.00
Telephone, fax	£00,000.00
Postage	£00,000.00
Travelling expenses: car expenses, taxis, rail/air fares, hotels, hospitality, etc.	£00,000.00
Contingency	£00,000.00
Total	£00,000.00

Figure 10.3 PR department budget.

Source: Jefkins (1994)

responsibilities. It is assumed that the in-house department is self-sufficient and no consultancy services are used.

It will be seen that several of the above figures are totals and require detailed individual budgets, an example of which has already been demonstrated in the budget for a press reception. Budgets can be produced in conjunction with D-Day charts or a critical path analysis chart. Some additional costs should be considered overall. These could include professional fees (e.g. PRCA, IPR) and training, including the maintenance of a library and sponsorship for courses and examinations. The library should not only be for staff training purposes, but should include the many excellent trade directories.

The proper planning of programmes, forecasting of results and budgeting of costs is the sort of accountable professionalism that will enhance the PRO's reputation. Budgets are designed to bring out the real responsibilities of public relations. Based on experience, the public relations practitioner will know roughly what most things cost (in time or money or both), so that even in a meeting or during an interview he or she should be able to produce a tentative budget at short notice. This can always be confirmed afterwards with a more accurate calculation based on real figures.

Budgeting is a primary management function of public relations that requires capabilities in time and money management. Both the PRO and the public relations consultant need to be good estimators, who not only know how to obtain and compile figures, but are also cost-conscious. In addition, they need to be aware of *all* the items that need to be costed. It is an attitude of mind and an ability that should figure strongly in the practitioner's job specification.

Chapter 11

Implementation and control

LEARNING OBJECTIVES

After reading this chapter you will be able to:

- distinguish the important factors to consider in the implementation of a PR programme;
- explain the principal means of evaluating the success of a PR campaign;
- recognize the importance of research in the evaluation and control process.

Implementation

When the problems are defined, objectives set, publics prioritized and the strategic plan approved, the implementation of the plan commences. Typically, an action plan may be drawn up and presented in the form of a 'D-Day planning timetable' (see Chapter 5) or a Gantt chart, an example of which is illustrated in Figure 11.1.

An important check is whether or not there are sufficient resources available to carry out the plan. As previously discussed (see Chapter 10), the resources required can be put under three headings:

- Time.
- Materials.
- Expenses.

Date	01/03	02/03	03/03	04/03	05/03
Book appropriate room	▓				
Advise speakers/assts arrangements		▓			
Invite reporters			▓		
Arrange refreshments			▓		
Prepare press kits			▓		
Brief speakers/assistants				▓	
Double-check arrangements				▓	
Hold press conference					▓

Figure 11.1 Gantt chart for a press conference.

Even if you are confident that everything has been considered, a series of 'what if' questions might be drawn up to identify potential problems arising. For example:

- *What if* the new product launch falls behind schedule?
- *What if* the headquarters move is abandoned?
- *What if* the guest speaker cancels at the last minute?

We cannot plan for every eventuality (it would be far too expensive), but anything that might be regarded as a reasonable possibility should be considered.

Assessing results

According to Hunt and Grunig (1994, p. 19), a PR programme that is managed strategically should not 'end when the technicians have executed the programme. Instead the objective of the programme should be measured before and after the programme to determine if change has occurred.' In his address to the IRR Congress in October 1998, MORI Director Peter Hutton (quoted in Theaker, 2001) stated:

> Evaluation is a sensible part of any PR programme ... There must come a point when you have to ask 'What effect has my PR spend had?' and 'How do I know?' ... There are many different ways of evaluating the success of a PR event or campaign. The most useful, however, will be part of a well executed PR initiative with clearly defined measures of success, which relate back to equally defined corporate and communications objectives.

Methodology

There are three main ways of evaluating the results of public relations programmes:

- By observation and experience.
- By feedback and its assessment.
- By research.

Observation and experience

Measurable objectives (see Chapter 8) will be seen to be achieved or not achieved. This is clearly the easiest and most inexpensive form of assessment. The following are some typical examples of objective setting:

- The PRO may wish to stem a trend in staff turnover, particularly if money is spent on training staff only to lose them to rival employers. The objective, therefore, may be to reduce staff turnover by 20 per cent. The public relations programme may be designed to better inform employees about company policies, performance and prospects, with a particular concentration on the benefits (e.g. pensions) of staying with the company for a longer time. If staff turnover (i.e. measured by average time in post per employee, or percentage of staff employed in the last three years) is reduced this *may* be a measure of the programme's success.
- If the objective is to improve the calibre of staff employed (perhaps as measured by relevant experience or qualifications), has a campaign to educate prospective recruits produced the desired result?
- If the company has a poor reputation locally, resulting in a bad local press, public criticism, letters of complaint and poor response to vacancy advertisements, has this situation been turned round as a result of a public relations programme to achieve a more deserved image? Is the company now respected locally? A *measurable* reduction in complaints would give an answer.
- As a result of improved communications with the financial media, has a new share or rights issue been successful, or has the stock market price been improved? Has a takeover bid been averted?
- Are distributors better disposed towards the company, stocking lines, permitting displays, receiving salespeople more favourably, as a result of a trade relations campaign? Are distributors better able to inform customers about the company's products?
- Have industrial relations improved (measured perhaps in a lower number of days lost to industrial action or lower number of days of absence per employee) as a result of better management/employee communications?

Of course, too much should not be claimed for public relations and in making such assessments it is always sensible to consider whether or not other factors have influenced the result. Economic, political and other market forces may affect the situation. It would be unwise to claim that public relations had been totally responsible for improved trade relations if one's principal rival had declined in popularity, for instance! Measurable objectives that can be correlated with PR activity do, however, provide empirical evaluation of a campaign.

Feedback and its assessment

Since public relations is a two-way process, and the PRO provides the eyes, ears and voice of the organization, part of the public relations task is to initiate and receive a constant inflow of information. This may arrive in many forms, both internally and externally. It may take the form of complaints, ideas, suggestions, reports and recommendations, or it may consist of press cuttings, monitored broadcast materials, books containing comments on the organization, parliamentary reports, independent research survey reports and so forth. Some of this may have been inspired by the practitioner, but much of it will be outside his or her direct control. Some of it may be provoked for good or ill by other people in the organization.

One of the practitioner's jobs will be to examine such feedback, and perhaps comment on it and report to those whom it concerns within the organization. He or she may have to act on it by correcting false reports or making sure that people such as journalists and broadcasters are better informed the next time that they deal with the subject. It is often poor policy to 'keep a low profile'; indeed, this can be worse than making no comment at all. Negative public relations is sometimes advocated when organizations are in trouble, but there is the adage that 'the best form of defence is attack'.

Media evaluation, according to the Association of Media Evaluation Companies (quoted in Theaker, 2001), is 'the systematic appraisal of a company's reputation, products or services, or those of its competitors, as measured by the presence in the media'. Much of this evaluation (often called a 'clippings service') is carried out by media evaluation specialists. Media evaluation of this type has long had its critics who, because of its formulaic nature, doubt its validity. Despite its detractors, Hunt and Grunig (1994) note that:

> If we define the objective of press relations as 'getting the proper message on the media agenda' then the clippings service isn't such a bad idea. The clippings show how frequently and in what context the organization has appeared on the media agenda.

Jefkins (1994) suggests that there are five ways of evaluating such media coverage. These include: monitoring; assessing readership; assessing picture usage; share of voice; and reader responses. These are considered in further detail below.

Monitoring

Monitoring those papers, magazines or programmes that have covered a story. What is the quality of the coverage? This can be important. Were they influential media? Half a column inch in a multimillion circulation women's weekly magazine could be much more valuable than a page in a small circulation business monthly. A story in the *Sun* newspaper could be more valuable than one in the *Financial Times*, and vice versa according to the type of story. The volume of coverage could be immaterial compared with the quality of coverage. An example of a value scale, where a weighting is given to different newspapers, is shown in Figure 11.2.

The ratings would obviously be different for different organizations. The quality of the coverage can also be measured by the tone of the reporting. What did they say and how did they say it? There can also be a recognizable difference or improvement in tone between past and present coverage.

Assessing readership

The potential readership or audience can also be evaluated by multiplying each appearance of the story by the published circulation or readership figure of each journal or, in the case of broadcasting, by the published audience figures. If a story appeared in journals with estimated readerships of 400 000, 600 000, 1 million and 4 million, then 6 million people had the opportunity of seeing or reading the story. This is called an OTS (opportunities to see) rating and is illustrated in Figure 11.3.

Publication	Rating	Story 1	Story 2	Story 3
Daily Blower	4	✓		
Daily Sizzle	2		✓	
Sunday Scandal	2		✓	✓
Sunday Bore	4	✓		✓
Weekly Gloom	4	✓		
Weekly Hope	2		✓	✓
	Score	12	6	8

Figure 11.2 Value scale.
Source: adapted from Jefkins (1994)

Picture usage

Picture usage can also be counted, and this may be a good indication of which publications should be offered pictures and which not. With the advent of digital photography, the cost involved with supplying photographs has been substantially reduced. There is, however, always the cost of the photographer to bear in mind. If pictures are not being used, why go to the expense of producing them?

Share of voice

Share of voice refers to the number of publications, broadcast media, etc. that covered the story. It is often used as a comparison to the company's competitive rivals.

Response

The news item may have advised people to contact a freephone number or e-mail address. In this case the level of response can be a measure of success. Product placement in, for example, television shows such as the BBC *Food Programme* can generate a huge measurable response.

Research

Marketing research techniques can be used when the objective of the programme is to effect a change or improvement in awareness, attitude or image. It is important to determine the base percentage of awareness or attitude initially, when the appreciation of the situation study or the image study was undertaken before planning the programme (see Chapter 6). This baseline attitude, for example, can then be compared with those after a PR programme to determine whether or not there has been a change in a particular public's attitude towards the company's image.

Suppose, in the case of an attitude study or opinion poll, it had been found that only 5 per cent of respondents had heard of the organization,

Publication	Date	Circulation	Total
Daily Blower	29 August	400 000	
Daily Sizzle	31 August	600 000	
Sunday Scandal	4 September	1 000 000	
Sunday Bore	4 September	4 000 000	6 000 000

Figure 11.3   OTS rating scale.

Source: Adapted from Jefkins (1994)

or knew what it did, or liked what it did, and the objective of the pro-gramme was to increase this figure to 20 per cent. A post-programme survey would reveal the degree to which this had been achieved. Similarly, with an image study, the effectiveness of the programme in achieving a more accurate image would be revealed by a later survey to measure what changes had been brought about. These methods were described in Chapter 6 as means of appreciating the company's current situation. Tangible quantitative results can be recorded because this type of *longitudinal research* measures changes in trends over time, and this can be represented in the form of graphs, bar charts or pie charts.

It would seem to be a waste of money to commission public relations without knowing what it is expected to achieve, and not caring whether it achieves it or not. Yet it is not uncommon for companies to spend an insufficient sum on non-specific public relations activity and then com-plain that it has not done anything. That expenditure should be suffi-cient to cover the essential research, and should be enough to cover a programme capable of achieving the results that, it is hoped, the final research will show have been achieved. The message is, of course, that if you want tangible results it is essential to have tangible, measurable, objectives. If an architect designs a building he expects the finished structure to represent his plans. Similarly, public relations programmes should set out to achieve definite results that at the end of the pro-gramme are capable of evaluation.

From this, it follows that public relations is most likely to succeed when management understands what public relations can do, and when management knows what it wants it to do. When the PRO or consultant is properly briefed, he or she can plan to operate effectively. Unsuccessful (and intangible) programmes result from practitioners who put forward proposals that are not aimed at satisfying client or management expectations.

The Macro Model

So far we have discussed evaluation of the effects or results of a public relations programme in relation to its objectives. This has been based on observation, experience or scientific research. This presupposes that the campaign was conducted efficiently, but in the event of a poor result the efficiency of the campaign could be subjected to a post-mortem. Of course, the campaign was as recommended and approved, but we have only to look at the quality and distribution of the average news release to see that, operationally, a good many programmes are conducted with little skill or experience.

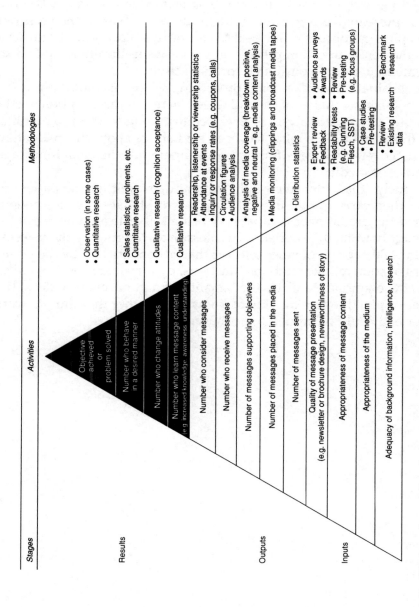

Figure 11.4 Evaluation of a public relations programme: the Macro Model.

Source: MacNamara (1992). Reproduced with the permission of IPRA Ltd

The Australian public relations consultant and author Jim MacNamara, chairman of the MACRO Communication Group, has evolved a different approach to public relations evaluation, which he aptly calls the Macro Model of Public Relations Evaluation (Figure 11.4). This was described in the IPRA journal, *International Public Relations* (MacNamara, 1992). The model is presented as a pyramid with inputs at the base. It then sets out various physical outputs, and peaks with results. Each activity forms a step in the communication process and is very specifically identified so that evaluation can be considered for that activity.

Thus, evaluation is an ongoing procedure, a form of continuous quality control using a cluster of technologies. There is no assumption of efficiency but a critical analysis of every contribution to the programme. While this is not unlike what has been said above about the evaluation of media coverage, it calls for earlier evaluation of the actual message and choice of media.

Obviously, it is better to cure the patient than wait for the patient to die and then carry out an inquest. The Macro Model is ideal in intent, provided the practitioner is capable of being self-critical. It does call for a thoroughly trained, experienced professional. Judging by the uselessness of the 80 per cent of news releases that editors discard, by the pointlessness of some public relations functions, by the amateurishness of so many house journals, and by the banality of a good many videos, the number of practitioners capable of knowing whether their inputs were good or bad could be argued to be minimal.

Planning a public relations campaign, with Marie Owens, Director of Communications, Middlesex University

Marie Owens is Director of Communication at Middlesex University, where she has responsibility for media and alumni relations, advertising, print and web publication and event management, as well as advising and leading projects as a senior communications and public relations expert. Before moving to higher education, Marie spent 17 years at the British Library, working in a number of public relations roles: press officer, newsletter and publications editor and, for the four years 1988–1992 as National Preservation Officer, when she worked nationally and internationally to raise awareness of the need for the best security and preservation practices in libraries and found herself in front of cameras and microphones, rather than in the background! Her last six years at the British Library were as Head of Corporate Communications. In this post she played a key role in the communication of, and opening of, the Library's new building at St Pancras in London. Marie cut her PR teeth in her first job – as marketing secretary at Puffin (Penguin Books), where she was encouraged, between typing and administration, to find time to write copy, help with author tours and understand that excellent information that arrived too late was not excellent!

Interviewer: Can you give me an insight into a typical day for a PR manager?

Marie: Nearly all PR managers are first and foremost that – managers. So a large part of the day is managing the team and the projects. I would expect at least half of the day to be about ongoing projects and advising on issues that are coming in hour by hour. A lot of time is spent talking with my team or with other colleagues working on various University initiatives. A good bit of time is spent making or encouraging connections: we're dealing with Web, print, media and alumni relations, advertising. A lot overlaps so we have to keep in good touch to stand a chance of having integrated marketing communications. There's a great sense of achievement when it all comes together – the ad campaign, the press work, the presentations, the communication with stakeholders.

Interviewer: What do you think are the major changes that have taken place in PR over the last 30 years?

Marie: I think on the plus side public relations has joined the heart of the organization. PR was very definitely an add-on. Even 15 years ago there was a little office that dealt with writing press releases and maybe arranging events. That's what most people thought of as public relations. They were the last in the chain of knowledge. Nobody consulted them about anything and no-one ever asked their opinion. We've come a long way. Most good organizations now do consider public relations implications at the very heart of their policy and that is a tremendous step forward.

One sad aspect: 10 years ago the first person people like me spoke to in a crisis was another PR expert, often in an agency. Now we talk to our lawyers. I think in all my early years of work I only spoke to a lawyer once or twice. Now I must speak to a lawyer several times a year. Life – and reputations – have inevitably become more legalistic. The stakes seem higher. Another positive, though, is the recognition in most organizations of the importance of leadership, the importance of good communication (and, of course, the essential linkages between the two). It's no coincidence that Richard Branson is still the most quoted, the most high profile, the most trusted (by the public) businessman, because he is an absolutely superb communicator and he approaches everything in communication terms.

Interviewer: Are there any other major changes?

Marie: The disciplines have become more integrated. Nobody is just about public relations anymore, just about press relations, just about marketing. You have to work within all those disciplines and make sense of them all. I think that is where a lot of organizations are still failing. We don't always recognize the difference between those disciplines and we don't always have the right expertise on board. I think at the moment most universities are good at PR but they are not brilliant at marketing. The Holy Grail is of integrated marketing and integrated communications. Of course, the public relations profession is in many ways the most difficult one to work within – because every aspect of what we do is dependent on human interaction. There are less rules to depend on.

Interviewer: That is an interesting point you have just made. What you seem to be saying is there is more room for personality in the communications discipline than others?

Marie: There is certainly that but there is also more room for difficulty, isn't there? It seems to me that public relations is really on the edge of what can go very, very right or very, very wrong. We're dealing with human things – intuition, willingness to listen and communicate back.

Interviewer: Can you give me some idea of how this uncertainty affects planning a campaign?

Marie: I think there are number of things about planning. Probably people like me would say that most of what we do does not really feel like planning – more like a day-to-day continuous corporate reputation task. Behind all the small and big decisions is your grasp of where your organization needs to be – how it needs to be perceived.

Interviewer: There have been a number of changes in the industry. How do you think that has influenced the way you set objectives when you are planning?

Marie: The key thing, and I think this probably applies to all professionals in all areas now, is the struggle with and for resources. Most public relations work is quite heavy on resources. So inevitably the job is about how to do it better, smarter, with less resource. That is a major change. You never used to have to think in those terms. There are good sides to such constraints: I heard a charity the other day saying that when you literally have £100 in the bank it doesn't half focus the mind on who to send the press release to!

Interviewer: One of the things you have mentioned is the Internet. How has that changed the way you disseminate the message?

Marie: I don't think that higher education is anywhere near yet the force it *will* be on the Internet. We are fine on the basics of information.

We have award-winning websites. But we've not really begun to segment markets and use truly two-way communication. The Internet has increased the speed of reaction and need and changed the way we communicate. We have to remember, though, that you need other media too. I still have lots of stakeholders who are not Internet enfranchised.

Interviewer: How would you say PR will change in the future?

Marie: I think it will develop more. It is developing. I think it will become more and more important. I'm sure we'll see more reliance on PR because it is still the thing that makes most sense. It can reach out to people as individuals and it is the personal that people want.

And lobbying. If you think what is achieved by large companies, by large businesses behind the scenes, talking directly to legislators, talking directly to the people of influence. That way to communicate is going to be more and more relevant.

Interviewer: So you are all for lobbying then?

Marie: For all its bad press a couple of years ago, lobbying will never go away. You have to achieve influence where decisions are made.

Interviewer: What about defining your publics?

Marie: That's the really clever bit, of course, and what we all still get wrong so often. I was thinking recently about the night they opened the Millennium Dome. The fact that the people for whom it went *most* wrong on that night (when few got to where they were meant to be) – the journalists – were the very people whose good opinion the organiz-ers needed most. It was announced recently that Imperial College and University College London would merge. The staff scuppered the deal very quickly and very effectively. There was seemingly no work at all to communicate or persuade. We've all forgotten about our colleagues at one time or another – and learned better!

Interviewer: What would you say are the major aspects in relation to budgeting? How does this relate to the objectives that you set and the planning process?

Marie: Obviously, there are real costs for large campaigns and you have to fight for those budgets and manage them. Most of the budgeting and planning is often about resources other than money – usually time. I don't think many of us lose sleep about bringing off something that money can buy – those skills are well honed. But how you achieve the impossible with nothing – that's the draining stuff!

Interviewer: One of the things I would like to ask you is who is your PR hero?

Marie: I feel very strongly that you shouldn't know who people like me are. We should be invisible. Certainly, we should not be in front of television cameras. We definitely should not be more known than our bosses! I want to commend people like Richard Branson [Chairman of the Virgin Group], chief executives who may have been made great by a director of communications. You cannot deny the achievements of Alastair Campbell [Chief Press Secretary to Prime Minister Tony Blair]. He has rewritten the rulebook and, as part of a dedicated and commit- ted team, won the final prize through outstanding communication. What he did he did well and he held it together pretty successfully for a long time. New Labour between 1992 and 1997 will go down in his- tory as the greatest communication coup ever. I was thinking recently about that moment that they won. Even in that incredible moment of victory, when asked what the key objective was, they got it right (though Campbell broke every rule in the government information officer book in saying it) – to win a second term. That sort of discipline is awe-inspiring.

Interviewer: You are the second person to mention [Alastair] Campbell.

Marie: Well, he's a genius. Love him or hate him.

Interviewer: This book is about contemporary PR practice. Can you define contemporary PR practice for me? So contemporary PR practice is ...

Marie: It has to be about getting the business objectives realized through communication. That may always have been the point, but it seems to me beyond question now. My job is to help make a major impact on the business objectives by the best, right, appropriate communications, within and outwith the organization.

Interviewer: Can you summarize some of the problems associated with implementing and controlling a contemporary PR campaign?

Marie: Often, the key problem is people losing their nerve. When we're doing something brave we're all robust at the beginning. You have to keep people – all the people – steady and remember what the plan was.

Interviewer: I think you are onto something immensely difficult here and that is that in order for a campaign to be effective it has to be innovative and if it is innovative it is new and different, and there is no experience associated with trying that sort of thing out. How do you know that [a campaign] is innovative and not barking mad?

Marie: What you do develop after years and years is instinct. You reach a level of good instinct and a bank of experience to call on. I would be very surprised to meet a fantastic PR practitioner who is very young. It seems a contradiction in terms.

Interviewer: Thanks.

Part 3

Managing Media Relations

The role of the press officer

The press officer

The PRO or consultancy account executive may have to be his or her own press officer, although in a large organization the public relations department often has one or more specialist press or information officers. Some organizations have only a press officer and not a full-time PRO. In diverse organizations there may be several press officers each covering specialist parts of the business. Much depends on the industry and size and type of business as to the extent of the press work. The press office, whatever its size or specialization, is there to act positively, or proactively, on behalf of the organization and this means taking the initiative in contacting the media rather than simply reacting to calls (Harrison, 2000).

Press officer or media relations manager?

The name 'press officer' may appear rather old-fashioned, since this person now has to deal with radio, TV and electronic media as well as the press. Some organizations, such as local authorities, have already adopted the title media officer or media relations manager. In general, however, the titles media officer or media relations officer have never caught on across the industry as a whole and press officer, despite its inherent inaccuracy, seems to be holding its own.

The press officer may or may not be an ex-journalist, but he or she does need to be able to write a news release in a form that resembles a newspaper report. Unfortunately, very few news releases received by editors measure up to that elementary criterion (see Chapter 14). It is also necessary for the press officer to understand how the media operate, and how to work with journalists. According to Harrison (2000), the ability to produce and transmit properly written and targeted news releases and the kind of temperament to get on well with journalists is crucial. There have been some very famous press officers, like Sir Bernard Ingham, Prime Minister Margaret Thatcher's press officer and, more recently, Alastair Campbell, who fulfilled a similar role at 10 Downing Street before and during the first and second parliaments of the Labour government elected in 1997.

Responsibilities of the press officer

As for public relations generally the press (or media relations) officer needs to be both proactive and reactive. They are there to act positively on behalf of the organization and this should include taking the initiative in initiating and maintaining contact with the media rather than simply waiting for them to call (Harrison, 2000). The press officer, therefore, has two primary responsibilities:

- to initiate media coverage;
- to supply information on demand by the media.

To do this, a two-way relationship has to be created so that the press officer is welcomed, accepted and respected, and the media come to him or her and find them helpful, sympathetic and efficient. This level of *entente cordial* is not, as has been noted in Chapter 9, always possible. It is, however, the press officer's responsibility to supply material that will help the media produce publications and programmes of interest and value to readers, listeners or viewers. In so doing, he or she will achieve maximum coverage and so help satisfy employers' or clients' objectives.

This is very different from issuing stories that management wants to have published irrespective of whether the stories are genuinely newsworthy.

Initiating media coverage

To initiate media coverage, the press officer must first have a good (i.e. newsworthy) story and then know where it is likely to be published. Familiarity with the editorial requirements for information, illustrated by way of pictures, photo-opportunities, soundbites and video/CD ROMs clips is crucial. Editors and programme makers sometimes complain that PROs fail to determine what their particular needs are. It is a mistake to send any story to every possible publication in the vague hope that it may get published. Rather, the fewest necessary publishable stories are sent to only those publications most likely to print them. The objective is not sending out the news releases but getting the story printed. It is definitely not joining the estimated 126 million press releases (out of 130 million) that get thrown into editors' bins every year (Smith, 2002). This means that the newsworthiness of a story has to be evaluated, and the most appropriate media have to be selected. In some ways this has become somewhat easier, as more recent media developments have seen more and more publications, television channels and websites offering highly segmented, specialist subject matter for particular audiences.

In order to develop a 'newsworthy story' the press officer needs good lines of internal communication so as to encourage a flow of news from people in the organization. This is not easy because other people may not recognize the newsworthiness of their work, or they may think that the project that is of great interest to them is of equal interest to others. If, however, these lines of communication are well established, the press officer has access to people who do have newsworthy information. The press officer cannot work in isolation but has to know what is going on and where news can be found.

In the other direction, the press officer has to study and know the media (or media agencies) that are most appropriate to the organization so that opportunities can be spotted for media coverage. It is towards these publications, journalists, features, columnists or programme personnel that efforts should be concentrated. This will also entail understanding production requirements so that the supply of public relations material can be timed to arrive when it is needed. National agencies (e.g. the Press Association) may also be a major conduit for news. Local and specialist agencies may also offer coverage if the company's newsworthiness appeals to them. News organizations will often plan special features ahead and will make these known to potential contributors (and advertisers). The publication *Advance* enables companies to plan news releases by listing those topics that have been pre-planned and covered by particular media. Often, the media need advance notice to ensure coverage of a particular event. The newsdesk will often have diaries of events enabling them to plan coverage on a particular day. There is equally no point in irritating an editor by sending him a good story that is hours, days, weeks or months too late for publication or transmission.

Freelance journalists can also be extremely useful, particularly if they are regarded as experts in their field. There is a danger of what might be called 'rogue journalists' who adopt dubious techniques and can hide behind the anonymity offered by their freelance status. Editorial risk can be reduced with the help of organizations (e.g. Echo Research) that compile lists of journalists who have written articles on a particular organization or their products and services, or on any particular issues (Smith, 2002).

Information on demand

The press officer should make it known that he or she is the source of information about the organization, products or services, and this can be done in the following ways:

1. When initially appointed (either in-house or consultancy), appropriate editors and journalists should be notified that he or she is available as a source of information on a subject or subjects. In some cases it can be suggested that when articles are being written about the subject(s) that a technical expert is available to contribute or check for accuracy.
2. An entry can be placed in the News Contact Directory in *UK Press Gazette*.
3. An entry can be placed in the *Hollis Press and Public Relations Annual*, which will also give editors direct online database access.
4. It is common for a consultancy to operate a named information bureau (e.g. The British Bacon Bureau) for their clients that, again, are usually listed in the publications mentioned above.

Organizations that are constantly in the news will receive numerous press enquiries, usually by telephone. The press officer should make sure that he or she has a good library of up-to-date information and digital photographs so there can be a quick, accurate and reliable response. If the answer to an enquiry is not known, he or she should promise to find out and phone back without delay. Servicing the media is a major part of the job, and one which can create good or bad relations with journalists. If the press officer is obliging, this can produce future enquiries, and there are times when only that organization is approached and reported because the service is respected and sought. It is interesting to notice in the press and on radio and TV that when a certain subject is in the news it is usually the same organizations whose spokespeople are quoted. In the retailing field, Richard Hyams of Verdict Research is often quoted as an expert observer. When social trends are discussed, Robert Worcester of MORI is a frequent contributor. Richard Branson is such a good (and willing) publicist that he is called upon to comment on many an occasion. Not every company can call upon such expert publicists, although there are usually some staff who are authoritative, knowledgeable and able enough to talk to the media. If a good rapport can be built up between the media and the sources of information within the company, these individuals may be called upon to contribute regularly.

The very fact that a company is called upon as a 'specialist' commentator helps establish the public's trust in an organization and develop the prestige of the 'brand' long term. It is important to remember that editorial coverage has a higher credibility than advertising. Smith (2002) suggests that editorial coverage has three times the credibility of advertising. It may prove useful if an organization is lobbying (see Chapter 29) for particular legislation or support to develop their arguments as specialist commentators.

Advantages and disadvantages

There are a number of advantages and disadvantages associated with the position of press officer. These are outlined below:

Advantages
- The press officer often possesses or has access to information of interest and value to readers that is unknown to, or unobtainable by, journalists.
- The press officer has the time to check the facts before supplying them to the media. The result of this is that the information can be trusted. This is important because media personnel work at great speed and, with so little time to check information, errors often appear in the editorial columns.
- If the press officer is a member of the IPR, he or she has a duty of accuracy under the Code of Professional Conduct (see Appendix 1). This requires that false or misleading information is not disseminated.
- The press officer is often in a position to help journalists to interview important people in the organization, and may be able to encourage

or advise an organizational leader to give an interview when this person might otherwise be reluctant to do so.

Disadvantages
● The press officer may be the victim of demands from the organization to issue stories that are either lacking in news value, or poor in quality and presentation. In some organizations, a number of people may have to approve a story before it is released, often resulting in an unpublishable version that may also have missed the deadlines. Editors will blame the press officer for poor stories that bear his or her name.
● The press officer may not have the status to assert his or her professional authority.
● The media may distrust the press officer as a biased communicator.
● The press officer may become the buffer between the media and management, particularly in crisis situations.

Keeping abreast of developments

The press officer has to understand the changes that are taking place in the media, and to adapt techniques accordingly. The increase in the use of direct input and computerization, and the greater use of digital photography, plus shorter lead times between editing and printing, all mean that he or she must be alert to the new demands of high technology. Online direct transmission of public relations stories to editorial computer terminals has arrived. The day of the paper news release distributed by post, or even by hand, has, in all but a few situations, passed. These developments may mean that it is easier for press officers (and indeed others in the organization) to submit press releases. There will, however, still be no place for the typical unpublishable news release. This actually makes more demands on press officers to ensure the professionalism of their copy.

Chapter 13

Writing reports and proposals

LEARNING OBJECTIVES

After reading this chapter you will be able to:

- recognize the importance of well-written reports and proposals;
- understand the formats of different types of reports;
- recognize the importance of research in the reporting process.

Why reports and propositions are necessary

Reports and propositions are necessary in order to spell out what action the PRO or consultant recommends. Reporting is a tool management understands and appreciates as it shows logical, responsible thinking. Even in an age of multimedia presentations, written reports are used extensively to summarize existing activity and research, and to propose future action. Armed with a written scheme and calculated costs, the practitioner is in a strong position to argue his or her case. A proposition should never be made unless you have researched the subject thoroughly and can back up your arguments with facts and figures.

A written report or proposition needs to be set out in an acceptable and readily understandable fashion. It should be written in an objective, factual style and, as such, is usually styled in the 'third person'. The information should be presented in a logical sequence and be comprehensible to anyone reading it at any time. The report should be preceded by the *brief* – a statement of the purpose, scope and limitations of the report.

In order to understand the report, it is necessary for the reader to understand the brief. The reader will also require a *summary* (normally called an *executive summary*) that gives a concise and actionable overview of the proposals. Although this *executive summary* will be the last part of the report to be completed, convention calls for it to be placed at the beginning of the report. This gives the reader the opportunity to take on board the main considerations without having to read the report in full.

An important aspect of report writing is to bear in mind who will read the report and when. This will affect both the construction and content of the report. For example:

- The reader is likely to be busy and have to read many documents. The report therefore has to be concise yet comprehensive and include an *executive summary*.
- It may have to be dealt with at a board or committee meeting where it was not possible to study it in detail beforehand. The reader therefore needs to be able to find his or her way about the report in the midst of a discussion.
- The report should be capable of easy reference and understanding by anyone reading it now or in the future.
- Those reading it may not have detailed knowledge of the subject. It should not contain too much jargon and any essential terms should be explained, if necessary, in a glossary.

The above remarks emphasize that writing a report or proposition is very different from copywriting advertisements, preparing news releases or developing feature articles, all of which have their special literary styles. The skilled communicator has to be able to change writing styles according to the job at hand.

The report also has to sell the proposals you may wish to make. Three aspects are therefore essential to the preparation of these documents:

- Adequate research.
- Concise, yet persuasive, writing.
- Methodical layout of information.

It is your responsibility, not your reader's, to see that you make sense of your material. It is therefore important to organize the report in such a way that will best relay your message. Listed below are the outlines for two reports, first (Figure 13.1) an internal report to management, second (Figure 13.2) a business proposition from a consultant (or any other outside service) to a potential client. A good consultant should automatically produce such a report, although extremes do occur: some consultants are poor business people and think a letter is sufficient, while others indulge in showmanship and dress up propositions in over-complicated ways. It is good practice for PROs to utilize reports as part of their management of campaigns.

The plan for a consultancy proposition (Figure 13.2) may be slightly different because (a) the client has to be convinced of the consultant's

Title page	Ensure that this is short, precise and to the point, so that it illustrates the content of the report.
Contents	This is a list of the chapters or sections in the same sequence as they occur in the report, giving chapter or section headings and page numbers.
Executive summary	A summary of the contents of a report that enables the reader to clearly understand the main points (including conclusions and recommendations) without having to read the whole document. It should only contain information covered in the main body and it should be short (perhaps no more than one sheet of A4 or 200–400 words).
The brief	(i.e. the purpose, extent and limitations of the study.)
Methodology	If there has been research, a statement of the methods used. If a questionnaire has been used, this should be reproduced in the appendices.
Main body	The main elements of the report, including secondary (desk-based) and primary (e.g. survey) research.
Conclusions	These are based on secondary and primary research. They should be concise, drawing together your findings and summarizing the points in the main body of the report. Do not introduce any new material at this point.
Recommendations	(Including plan of action and budget where necessary.

Figure 13.1 Internal report.

Title page	Stating for whom and by whom the document has been prepared.
Contents	Giving chapter or section headings and page numbers.
Executive summary	(Including findings or proposals.)
The brief	As instructed by the client.
Experience statement	Setting out the consultant's relevant experience with other clients.
Personnel	Details/background of those individuals working on the project.
Situation	As researched by the consultant.
Recommendations	Outline of the consultant's plan of action.
Budget	Detailing costs and method/timing of payments.
Brag list	List of past and present clients.
Appendices	Where relevant.

Figure 13.2 Consultancy proposal.

ability to perform, and (b) the client has to understand how the costs are arrived at and how the consultant will be remunerated. This proposition may well have to compete with other propositions. The budgetary content of reports was an item discussed in Chapter 10.

The production of the report should be neat and orderly, but not flamboyant. All pages should be numbered and a contents list or index is essential. The document should be presented in a convenient form, size (normally A4 in the UK), printed on one side of the paper only, and bound in stiff covers with perhaps a slide, spiral or comb (wire or plastic) binding. Thus, the report will be easy to read and easy to keep flat and clean.

It is necessary that both the internal report and the consultancy proposition be explicit. They should imply preliminary research, analysis of the situation, and a logical plan with detailed costings. The reader of the proposals should be able to understand exactly what is being presented, and that this can lead to the necessary considerations and discussions, resulting in rejection, amendments or acceptance. After this, there should be no misunderstandings between management and PRO, or between client and consultancy. From a public relations point of view, it is an exercise in responsible, professional management.

Any plan has to be flexible as public relations officers and consultants are often confronted by the unexpected. There has to be a plan in the first place to guide the general direction of the PR effort. Such reporting inspires the confidence of management, and status and respect for the PRO or consultancy will stem from this businesslike beginning. Written proposals, as demonstrated in both examples given above, represent potential solutions to problems. Being objective, they must lead to results that can be evaluated by observation, experience or research.

Public relations management, like other forms of management, has as much to do with the acceptance of constraints and priorities as it does with opportunities. It is sometimes thought that this elementary discipline does not apply to PR. Yet in this profession, perhaps more than others, it is the art of the possible and reporting the vehicle by which these ideas are given form.

Chapter 14

Writing press releases

LEARNING OBJECTIVES

After reading this chapter you will be able to:

■ understand the reasons behind the high failure rate of press releases;
■ recognize those factors that make a good press release;
■ understand the importance of maintaining a series of specialist databases.

Writing press releases

In a study of 200 members of the Public Relations Society of America (PRSA), 90 per cent of professionals said basic news-writing was the most important course required by the PR student, even ahead of a basic introduction to PR course (Hunt and Grunig, 1994). In Britain it is common to speak of editors filling their large plastic dustbins with 70–80 per cent of the releases they receive each day. Jefkins (1994) quoted a survey of managing editors at 123 daily newspapers where only 9.2 per cent of all news releases received from public relations sources were used. According to Smith (2002), the situation is now even worse, with only 4 million out of 130 million releases in the UK being acted upon; a staggering 97 per cent failure rate. A major reason for rejection was said to be a lack of local or regional tie-in (Jefkins, 1994). Other reasons given for non-use were that the press release contained too much advertising, that they were too long and cumbersome, and, in many cases, they arrived too late to be useful. Jefkins quotes three editors, the first of whom stated that 'too many PR people don't know the difference between news and advertising'. Another suggested that in many releases 'it looks like the copy was written to impress bosses and not necessarily for print'. The third advised that 'PR people should target their material more selectively and try to write more for individual papers'.

Research by Theaker (2001) shows similar reasons for rejection. Her research suggested that press release problems experienced by journalists include the following, outlined in order of importance (the survey allowed for multiple responses and so the total adds up to more than 100 per cent):

- Irrelevance (quoted by 66 per cent of journalists).
- Not newsworthy (65 per cent).
- Over branded (32 per cent).
- Badly written (25 per cent).
- Boring (25 per cent).
- Wrongly addressed (4 per cent).

Relevance and newsworthiness therefore seem to be the central requirements for any press release. As long ago as 1906, the American public relations consultant Ivy Ledbetter Lee established the criteria that public relations material should be *of interest and value* to the reader, but sadly the public relations world has often ignored these principles the world over. Jefkins (1994) put the blame on the industry, agents and upper levels of management when he wrote:

> There is a wilful, obstinate belief by too many people in the public relations world that nothing has to be learned about writing news releases. This is intensified by the fact that managing directors, marketing and advertising managers, advertising agents and other press relations amateurs think that not only can they write (or rewrite) news releases, but that they have the right to be published. The result is not only the adversarial situation between media and public relations, but a senseless waste of time and money.

Writing a good news release

There is nothing difficult about writing news releases, except that it is different from other forms of writing. The easiest way to learn how to write a news release is to read the news columns of a newspaper. There is usually one common style that anyone can replicate. According to Hunt and Grunig (1994), good release writing is clear, concise, correct and complete. They explain each of these as follows:

- *Clear* writing presents ideas logically and explains terms that may be unfamiliar.
- *Concise* writing takes the shortest path to understanding.

- *Correct* writing follows the rules of spelling, grammar and syntax, and is accurate.
- *Complete* writing such that it does not leave the reader 'unsatisfied and uncertain' about the subject matter.

What is news?

William Randolph Hearst, one-time American newspaper tycoon, once defined news as being *'what someone, somewhere doesn't want you to print – all the rest is advertising'*. The press of the world seems to have adopted that advice wholeheartedly in its attitude to much public relations material.

News depends a lot on the bias of the editor, the journalist or the particular publication. Bias towards local, national and/or international news; bias towards socio-economic status; bias regarding depth of coverage; bias towards a political party or stance and, certainly, many more. If a news release is to be successful, it needs to supply original information of interest and value to initially the staff and ultimately the readers of the journals to which it is sent. News does not necessarily have to be 'new' if it has not previously been made known, but it must not be stale news in the sense that it is obviously dated. One definition of news is that it is information that the reader has not read before.

Care needs to be taken with use of the word 'recent'. How recent is recent? This depends on how often a publication is published. A monthly magazine may print a story about an event which happened after the previous issue was published, but a daily will not print a story about something which happened the day before yesterday. A weekly local newspaper printed on Thursday and sold on Friday is usually unable to report Thursday night's events, and will not hold such news for the following week's issue. Even so, if the item is sufficiently important, special efforts may be made, although it is the exception rather than the rule that may call for some very tight production scheduling.

Credibility

One quality that distinguishes publishable public relations news material in the eyes of editors is its credibility. Credibility can take time to build up but can be destroyed very quickly indeed. If an editor suspects that a story is a cover-up or an attempt to put the best face on things, he or she may well expose this effort to hoodwink the media and the public. Unfortunately, there are many releases which are blatant attempts to pretend things are what they are not. Whatever the biases of the various media or journalists, a news release should be seen to be impartial and factual if it is to be credible. According to Jefkins (1994), 'to be acceptable a news release has to be like a piece of plain wood which others can cut, shape, polish, paint or use as they wish'. Facts, without comment or bias have greater credibility than those that are opinionated and obviously full of self-praise. Many releases of this latter sort are rejected simply because they are 'over-the-top'. An aim that should be borne in mind is to supply a news release that is publishable as it stands, because the journalist would have written it the same way given the same facts.

Local government PROs have a running battle with the media. The media believe that town hall news is little more than propaganda, while the elected representatives and local government officers believe that they are either misrepresented or inadequately covered by the media. In some cases, local authorities publish their own civic newspapers in order, as they see it, to get a fair and adequate press. Local political parties too often complain about the lack of coverage they achieve in local newspapers. The sitting Member of Parliament (MP) or Member of the European Parliament (MEP) may have an advantage in this respect, but most local parties deliver their own leaflets to ensure that their viewpoint gets across.

Language and vocabulary

It is a 'simple fact that people cannot be persuaded to accept an idea unless they understand it – and that clear writing is the key to understanding' (Hunt and Grunig, 1994). It does not matter what sort of story it is – whether it is destined for the *Sun* or the *Financial Times*, *Heating and Ventilating Review* or *The Lancet* – short words, short sentences and short paragraphs are preferable. If there are unavoidable long technical words, they should be explained as simply and clearly as possible. Short words mean that more can be said in the space. Short words will not be broken in narrow columns. Short sentences, providing they are not too abrupt, give the effect of urgency, and short paragraphs with their indentations help to speed the flow of reading and the ease of understanding. According to Hunt and Grunrig (1994), the dilemma PR writers face every time they sit down behind a keyboard is 'simplicity *versus* completeness'. Simplicity is vital. 'Faced with thousands of worthy stories competing for attention each day, editors and readers alike distil it down to bite-sized chunks.'

This is not to say that to avoid the monotony of repeated use a different and perhaps longer word should not be used, but the news release does have a space problem. Longer words are better for articles and books, which benefit from a rich vocabulary, a more literary style and more reading time. Short words, sentences and paragraphs not only help the story to fit scarce space, but result in less sub-editing, less rewriting and less opportunity for editorial staff to get things wrong. It is very hard to alter a sentence that is so tight and precise that there is no better way of writing it. Space *is* limited. A newspaper may have 48 pages, but a particular news release may be appropriate to only one section, page or even column. However good it is, it has to compete with other stories to be included. That is why, as we shall see, the opening paragraph is all important. It needs to grab the attention of the reader and, indeed, may be all that the editor can spare space to print.

The writer also needs to beware of generalizations that may be acceptable in more emotive and less explicit advertisement copy. It should be explained why a product is 'economical in use', 'handy', 'easy to make', 'compact', 'lightweight', 'money-saving', 'generous' or 'convenient'. The facts, the details, must be stated in such a way that the attributes are implied. Similarly, vague expressions such as the longest, tallest, shortest, biggest, smallest or cheapest should be supported by facts and not left open to challenge. One also has to be very careful about stating that anything is 'the first'. Are you sure about this claim? Editors dislike receiving contradictions and having to print disclaimers. They may also add the derogatory phrase 'claimed to be' to cover themselves, which can reduce the impact of the release.

Writing the release

Journalists tend to follow the 'news story rule' when writing a story. This rule highlights the Five Ws: who, what, when, where and why.

- *Who*   is the story about?
            else is involved?
- *What*   has happened?
            are the consequences?
- *When*   did it happen?
- *Where* did it happen?
- *Why*   did it happen?

A news release differs from this slightly, if only that it is seldom a personal story. For *who* it is best to substitute the subject. But the subject may not be the *who*, and the organization or the product may replace the individual. Moreover, the subject is more likely to be what the organization has done or the product/service can achieve, so that *what* displaces the journalist's *who*. We shall return to this again because the subject of the story is so important.

Although this chapter provides a number of pointers to good press release writing, there are no hard and fast rules. As Hunt and Grunig (1994) note:

> PR writing is doing its job when the audience never stops to think 'this is good PR writing'.

The importance of the opening paragraph

The above guidelines emphasized the importance of the subject and the opening paragraph, the two features that can make or break the news release. The subject matter should immediately establish interest. A manager's logical presentation may be to first list the facts that led to a decision, but news reporters want to know the decision. The first paragraph should fully summarize the content of the release. After all, if space is at a premium, this may be all that is printed.

The release should always be written as if addressing the reader of the newspaper or journal. It should be written in such a way as to capture their attention as they passively scan the publication in question. A problem with many releases is that they are not addressed to the reader, but to the editor. They begin with flowery expressions such as 'We are pleased to announce', while others are written like letters with salutations (e.g. 'Dear sir' or 'To whom it may concern'). Pronouns should be avoided: the editor is not going to use 'we' or 'you' in a news article. The public relations writer, according to Hunt and Grunig (1994):

> works anonymously. PR writing must stand on its own merits, divorced from the identity of the author.

It is worth repeating that the easiest way to learn how to write news releases is to read news stories in current newspapers or journals. It will be found that in every story in every paper two aspects characterize good press reports:

● the *subject* is stated in the first few words; *and*
● the outline of the story is given in the *opening paragraph*.

There are no teasers, no clever introductions in a news story. Unlike a novel, the whole story is given away right at the beginning. The rest of the report substantiates and adds substance to that story. In theory, if one reads the opening paragraph of a typical newspaper report, one would have a complete digest of that newspaper's news. Yet it is rare to find the subject of a news release in the first three paragraphs of a press release, perhaps not even on the first page. The mistake is often made of starting with the company name, which is rarely the subject of the story.

Four things are likely to result from the production of a good, professional press release:

1. An editor can see at a glance what the story is about. As he or she goes through the daily press releases, each one only has a few seconds to make an impact.
2. If there is little space, *at least* the opening paragraph may get printed. If it is a good, interesting summary you have considerably more chance of success.
3. If a longer story is printed it will be capable of being cut *from the bottom up*, as can occur when a story is printed at length in an early edition when news may be scarce – and then cut in each succeeding edition until perhaps only the first paragraph remains in the final edition. This can happen in evening newspapers, the first edition appearing early in the day, and the final edition appearing when people are going home from work.
4. If the story is written as the editor or his journalists would have written it, there is no point in him or her changing it. Editors are busy people. On some publications (e.g. trade magazines) they have no assistants to rewrite stories and may well print the ones that provide them with the least work. Why should they burrow through three pages of terrible prose to find the 30 or 40 words they have space to print?

It may not always be appreciated that editors are receiving material from many sources, of which public relations is but one. Stories will be coming in from staff reporters, special correspondents and numerous news agencies. The organizational press release has to compete with all these sources for space.

Style

Whole books have been written about PR writing styles, but in general terms *simplicity* means shorter sentences and paragraphs. Capitalization should be avoided as well as complex words or phrases. Above all, you should know your audience; write to the style of the target publication and avoid the one-size-fits-all approach. Do not be afraid to ask others for their comments or to rewrite releases to make them more reader-friendly. As Cutlip et al. (1994) note: 'make the news easy to read'.

Seven-point news release model

The discussion so far leads logically to the adoption of the seven-point checklist developed by Jefkins (1994) to provide (a) a checklist when researching story material, (b) a plot for the release and (c) a means of checking that nothing vital has been omitted.

The SOLAADS seven-point model

1. Subject – what is the story about?
2. Organization – what is the name of the organization?
3. Location – what is the location of the organization?
4. Advantages – what is new, special, beneficial about the product or service?
5. Applications – how or by whom can the product or service be used or enjoyed?
6. Details – what are the specifications or details of colours, prices, sizes and so on?
7. Source – if this is different from location.

This is not a plan for seven paragraphs. The subject, organization and location will fall into the first paragraph, together with highlights of the story. Thus, we have an opening paragraph that summarizes the entire story and can stand alone if necessary. The story is substantiated by paragraphs that concentrate on certain types of information. Finally, it is a good idea to close with words such as: 'The ABC lawnmower is made and marketed by the XYZ Company Ltd, Anytown, Anyshire', together with contact details, should the publication require follow-up.

In this fast-moving technological world, you should keep an eye on changing technology and the revised requirements developing from them. Standard advice on writing media releases (double-spaced lines, wide margins, etc.) is a descendant from the days when journalists received hard copy through the post, marked it up and sent it off to the typesetter for it to be made-up and printed (Theaker, 2001). Technology (e-mails, digital photography, etc.) has and is changing the face of journalism.

Different kinds of release

So far we have concentrated on the publishable release, as it is the most typical. There are, however, other types of release, not all of which are intended for immediate publication. There are six discernible types of news release. These are:

- The publishable release.
- The background story.

- The technical story with summary.
- The summary of a report, speech or document.
- The extended picture caption.
- The brief announcement.

The publishable release

This is as previously described.

The background story

This is a story that is not intended for immediate publication, but is issued as background information so that journalists are kept well informed and have the facts on file when they are writing about the subject. This kind of release can be especially useful for a long-term project such as a civil engineering job or the development of a new source of energy. Organizations that are constantly in the news, such as utilities, oil companies, airlines and new technology developers, will issue regular background stories. Some firms consider it helpful to distinguish between news for immediate publication and background material by having separate release headings printed with the distinctive words NEWS FROM... and INFORMATION FROM..., followed by the company name and logo.

The technical story with summary

Ideally, a release should be confined to one sheet of paper, but some subjects warrant longer and very technical accounts. In such cases it is helpful to the editor if the main story is preceded by a brief summary. To identify the summary it may be boxed.

The summary of a report, speech or document

The objective here is to bring out the important or new features of something lengthy that is being sent to the media. Journalists may not have time to read the whole speech, document or volume, and even if they did they may not know how to make comparisons or evaluations. The accompanying release can pull out the most newsworthy and relevant stories. This may guide the journalist to read for him or herself what is most interesting; it may provoke questions; it may attract the journalist's interest when otherwise the material would have been ignored. In the case of an advance copy of a speech, the opening para-graph technique already discussed is applicable.

The extended picture caption

When the picture is the real news item, a longer-than-usual explanatory caption can replace the news release. The old adage that a picture is worth a thousand words can be tested with interesting and stimulating photography.

The brief announcement

There is sometimes a mistaken idea that the submission of a press story is an opportunity to tell the editor as much as possible. Some releases read like confessions. On some occasions – if the sender has studied the media – they should not exceed one sentence or possibly a paragraph. This brevity will make them publishable and unalterable. One example is the change of address: some publications run a change of address column in which the essential facts are stated and no more. Another example is the 'new appointment' story. Most publications say no more than that Mr X has left one company to join another, the job he is taking up and maybe his age, or it may be a promotion within the same organization. Usually, many such items are published in the same 'New Appointments' feature. There may or may not be a portrait or portraits. Only a very few newspapers, e.g. *The Times* and the *Financial Times*, regularly print appointment stories; trade, technical and professional journals print very brief accounts, e.g. the cryptic items in *Campaign*, although somewhat longer stories may appear in some journals. Only the local newspaper will perhaps print a short biography if the person is sufficiently important or interesting, yet day after day editors of countless newspapers receive three-page life stories, complete with portraits, about hundreds of people who have been appointed or promoted.

This is a favourite area of public relations activity. Hours of research and interviewing can be spent to produce an approved biog-raphy, and money can be spent on special photography when in fact no more than a sentence or paragraph, and probably no picture, is required. Moreover, the expectations of the person involved can be built up out of all proportion to the coverage that is really attainable from the start.

For further press information please contact

Mike Brown on 020 8411 6761   For immediate release: 24 September, 2002

PREGNANCY RATES WELL ABOVE NATIONAL AVERAGE

The teenage conception rate in Camden and Islington is considerably higher than the national average.

Middlesex University Professor Colin Francome has analysed government figures for 2000, the latest year that figures are available, which show that in this health area there were 82 pregnancies per thousand teenagers compared with the national average of 62

This was also higher than London as a whole, which on 77 pregnancies per thousand teenagers has the highest figures in the country.

Figures for Barnet, Enfield and Haringey are 74 pregnancies per thousand teenagers, while Lambeth, Southwark and Lewisham have the highest teenage pregnancy rate in London with 114 per thousand.

"Some of these pregnancies may be desired and occur within stable relationships or marriage," says Professor Francome. "However many of them will be unwelcome. Just over three in five of these conceptions led to maternity and the rest ended in abortion."

Professor Francome adds: "Nationally, for single women who became pregnant in 2000, 40 per cent led to a maternity outside marriage registered by both parents, and a further 16 per cent led to a maternity outside marriage registered by the mother alone. Only two per cent led to a maternity within marriage. The other 42 per cent led to an abortion."

end

INVESTOR IN PEOPLE

THE QUEEN'S
ANNIVERSARY PRIZES
FOR HIGHER AND FURTHER EDUCATION
1998 & 2000

Figure 14.1 Middlesex Press Release: Pregnancy rates well above average, 24 September 2002. Reproduced with the permission of Middlesex University Press Office.

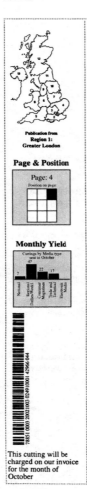

Romeike Limited
Hale House, 290–296 Green Lanes, London, N13 5TP, UK
Freephone: 0800 289543, *Telephone:* +44 20 8882 0155, *Fax:* +44 20 8882 6716
info@romeike.com   www.romeike.com

Media	Look	Order
Camden Chronicle	**Monitoring the web?**	2491 0001
Date: 03/10/2002	Get instant, unlimited	Mid Univ
Type: General Consumer	and validated links from	
Frequency: 52/Per year	just £70.00 per month	3
Circulation: 46,884		
MediaDisk Ref: 72A-240.110	Call 0800 289 543	
	for more information.	

Mrs T Kelly
Middlesex University
Press Office
Trent Park
Bramley Road
London
N14 4YZ

3   IKI3

Prof in plea for action over teen pregnancies

A LEADING professor is alarmed by Camden and Islington's high teenage pregnancy rates and says better relationship information is needed for young people.

Professor Colin Francombe, an expert at Middlesex University, analysed government figures for 2000, the latest year statistics were available.

There were 82 pregnancies per thousands girls in the two boroughs – which meant 800 teenagers became pregnant that year – compared with a national average of 62 and a London average of 77.

Professor Francome said: "Some of these pregnancies may be desired and occur within stable relationships or marriage. However, many of them will be unwelcome. Just over three in five of these conceptions led to maternity and the rest ended in abortion.

"Inner city figures tend to be higher anyway. There are pockets of poverty and poor housing.

"A lot of young teenagers I spoke to complain about the quality of information. They say they don't get very good information on forming relationships. We need to be giving them more help on this."

Camden Primary Care Trust aims to cut Camden's under-18 conception rates by half by 2010.

The borough has already acknowledged the importance relationship information plays in preventing young pregnancies – in its Teenage Pregnancy Strategy and Action Plan, launched earlier this year, it pledged to reduce pregnancies through improved sex and relationships education.

Figure 14.2 *Camden Chronicle:* Prof in plea for action over teen pregnancies, 3 October 2002. Article supplied courtesy of the *Camden Chronicle.*

Example of a press release

Figure 14.1 provides an example of a press release issued by Middlesex University Press Office. The subsequent press article generated by that press release is shown in Figure 14.2. This an example of how, following the issue of the press release, the story was reported in the *Camden Chronicle*.

Mailing lists[1]

The finest news release is useless if it is sent to the wrong media, or if it is sent to the right media at the wrong time. It is necessary to know your media – what they print, who their readers are, how they are printed, how often they are published, when they are printed and their latest date for copy. This means that, for each story, a new mailing list has to be compiled, otherwise editors will be annoyed because they have been sent stories that are irrelevant or ill-timed.

The public relations practitioner can become professional at mailing list compilation if he or she uses the many resources available. *Benn's Media Directory* and *PR Planner* provide much of what needs to be known. The development of database software tools makes this even easier than in the past. An experienced PRO, who has a thorough understanding of the media relevant to the story, should be able to use this knowledge to create a targeted mailing list.

One of the biggest faults with mailings is that too many releases are sent to too many untargeted publications. The point is that standard mailing lists, to which new titles are constantly added and defunct ones are never removed, are unprofessional. Each story requires its own carefully selected list so that the hit rate is maximized. Not only are costs reduced, but you reduce the risk of boring or annoying an editor with a constant stream of untargeted releases such that, when the day finally comes around when you do present him or her with a relevant, newsworthy article, it is likely to be missed. When compiling mailing lists, it is necessary to restrict titles to those publications that:

1. *Are likely to print the story*. If publications are studied it will be found that some newspapers or magazines regularly, irregularly or never carry your type of story or any kind of public relations story. For example, what is the editor of *Exchange and Mart* (a second-hand car advertisers' magazine) supposed to do with a news release? Therefore, it is a waste of time and money sending releases where they are unwanted

---

[1] This is rapidly becoming an out-of-date term with the advent of e-communications, but is used here as a general term covering all types of transmission.

and unwelcome – yet it is not unusual for releases to be sent to 'all nationals' or 'all women's magazines' or all 'local weeklies'. Editors expect PROs to know what kinds of story they print.

2. *Have time to print the story.* It is pointless sending a release to a publication that has been made up or printed already. Mailings have to be timed correctly and sometimes staggered. When is the publishing date? How long before do stories need to be in to stand a chance of making that edition? In the case of a daily it could be hours, but a weekly will need the story four to seven days in advance and a monthly even longer.

These two factors are vital, and with such understanding of editorial and publishing requirements it will be sensible to *eliminate* from the list those titles which are useless if immediate publication is desired. Some stories may be timeless, but few publications will carry forward a dated story. It is also worth investigating what are the journalists' preferred methods of receiving press releases. Despite the advances in electronic mail, Theaker (2001) notes that some journalists and editors prefer more basic technologies. In her research she outlines the following preferred methods of contact (more than one choice was permitted and therefore the total adds up to more than 100 per cent):

Mail	48 per cent
Fax	46 per cent
E-mail	15 per cent
Telephone	8 per cent
Other	1 per cent

There is little doubt that the percentage preferring or requiring electronic delivery will increase as journalists utilize more and more new technologies and, perhaps, under the pressure of cost restraints. Nevertheless, at the time of her research, mail and fax formatted press releases continued to predominate, probably because they are quicker to read and dispose of, if necessary.

News agencies

Several kinds of news agencies exist. The Press Association (PA) supplies the UK press with home news, and newspapers subscribe to this service. News releases sent to the PA should not exceed 100 words. Reuters supply and distribute international news. There are also news agencies that specialize in the reporting of news and the supplying of features to the press.

Chapter 15

Writing feature articles

LEARNING OBJECTIVES

After reading this chapter you will be able to:

- understand the means by which feature articles are promoted or commissioned;
- prepare a feature article;
- understand how effective articles are written and the style considerations that need to be made.

Exclusive signed feature articles

An article is not a long news release, but an entirely different literary form with its own special characteristics, uses and values. Here, we are concerned with the article written exclusively for one publication. It cannot be reproduced elsewhere without permission. One can, of course, rewrite the article, presenting the same basic information differently and with fresh examples to suit other journals, but each paraphrased article will be an exclusive. When the same article is supplied to more than one publication, this is called a syndicated article. Sometimes permission may be obtained from an editor to publish an article elsewhere, such as in a foreign journal. Whereas a news release is given broadcast distribution, could be printed at any time, may not be printed at all, and could be cut or rewritten, the article will be written for a particular issue of one journal and, if well produced, is unlikely to be seriously edited.

An article can have permanent value in at least three ways: magazines especially are often retained in binders or libraries; articles are often kept as part of the literature on the subject; reprints can be made for future use as direct mail shots, enclosures with correspondence, or as give-away material in showrooms or on exhibition stands. An article can have a long working life, and the initial cost may be easily recouped. A magazine readership is often substantially larger than its circulation. In addition to those commissioned, articles may also be initiated by offering them to editors, or by suggesting them at press receptions, or in other ways.

An article can be authoritative, especially if the author is an expert on the subject, and it can be very informative and well illustrated. Over the years, newspapers (e.g. the *Daily Mail*) have often published articles on the budget, written by the Chancellor of the Exchequer. Colour photographs may be possible, but they are unlikely to be printed with news releases. An article will be more costly to produce than a news release because time has to be spent on obtaining permission to write about the subject if others are involved, negotiating publication with editors, researching the material, writing the article and checking the draft with those who have supplied information. This cost (it may be a number of days work in all) has to be set against the article's long-term influence rather than against the achievement of one single press cutting. When producing the budget, the public relations manager or consultant should be careful to calculate this time element if feature articles are to be included in the year's programme. How many articles are to be produced and what demand for articles should be anticipated?

Marketing considerations

When an article is first suggested, there are a number of considerations that an editor must decide upon. If the writer has past experience of writing feature articles for that particular publication or for other publications, then reputation will be an important influence. If this is a first time request then other factors will often predominate.

In considering the type of article, there must firstly be an *idea, theme* or *subject*, not just a bare description. It could be how someone used a bank loan to make a fortune, how a new invention overcame a problem, why a new holiday resort is different from any other, how a dangerous task was made safe or how a new bridge has changed traffic patterns. It is this *idea* that is going to convince an editor that the article should be written and published. Secondly, it must be possible to have *access* to the information, which usually means getting permission from owners, contractors, customers or whoever may be involved. Several organizations and individuals may have to be approached. It must not be assumed that everyone will agree with the article being written, and only those with full responsibility for giving approval should be approached. It is both courteous and helpful to make initial approaches through the PROs of the various organizations, who can then assist the writer.

Negotiating with editors

Once the idea and the permissions are settled, the next step is to negotiate with the editor of the selected publication. The article should not be written speculatively and sent to an editor because (a) we do not know whether he or she will print it, (b) we do not know what he or she wants, and (c) we do not know how many words he or she wants. The article should be written as instructed by the editor. 'Instructed' means taking note of how the editor wants the article. That is whether the tone is light-hearted or serious, human interest or not, highly technical or non-technical, and so on. Even a serious subject can be lightened up with anecdotes, but this should not be undertaken where the subject matter is very serious, such as a national disaster, for instance.

There is also the question of *who* will write the article. The PRO or other PR staff may not be the most appropriate source, although they may wish to have some guiding influence over the article. Public relations articles may therefore be written by many different people, including some of the following:

- *The editor or a staff writer.*   Large circulation publications may not accept articles from outsiders, and will prefer to be provided with the idea and with facilities for visits and interviews. They have their own staff writers. The initiator of the idea will then make the necessary arrangements, probably accompanying the staff writer and perhaps arranging for photography. This has advantages and disadvantages. The article will have the independent authority of the bylined staff writer, but control may be lost over *what* is written and *how* the article is written. It can look better and less biased if the publisher has produced the article himself, but the piece can be inaccurate or biased by the writer's point of view.
- *A contributor.*   The article could be written by a contributor, as when a professional writer supplies a regular feature to a journal. A lot of business magazine writers do this. The PRO may be able to provide an idea and facilities to such a contributor.
- *The PRO.*   In this case the article could be written by the in-house PRO or by a consultant, or a freelance writer could be engaged, or someone within the organization might be the author.

- A *'ghost writer'*. A fourth possibility is that the PRO, consultant or a freelance writer could 'ghost write' the article for a VIP, such as the managing director.

There are therefore many ways in which public relations articles can be produced, and if they are fully exploited much valuable media coverage can be obtained, often of a volume, quality and authority far more significant than is possible with news releases. But it does take time, and has to be worked at professionally.

How to propose a public relations article

The closer the relationship with the decision maker and/or the better the requirements are known, the more likely it is that a proposal will be accepted. However, a good proposal does improve the chances. The *proposition* should present the idea, state that permission has been obtained to cover the subject and conduct the necessary research, and say that if the editor likes the idea will he or she please state:

- The number of words required.
- Any special treatment required, such as human interest, technical, non-technical.
- If illustrations are required, what kind and what number, and whether black and white or colour.
- The date of the issue in which the article will appear.
- The copy date or deadline for delivery of the article.

If the article proposal is accepted and the PRO (or another) is commissioned to write it, the article must be supplied on the agreed date. There will be no fee for the article, and in any case it would be unethical for the PRO to be paid twice, once by the employer or client and again by the publisher. It is wise to promise the editor that commercial references will be kept to a minimum, but the editor will probably safeguard him or herself by agreeing to publish 'subject to sight of the copy'. It is up to the writer to supply a publishable article. This means that, as with a news release, the information must be factual. It has to be a legitimate feature article that merits publication, and not be an advertisement.

How to write feature articles

Bad articles result from having too little to write about. A well-researched, readable article results from having to select from a wealth of information. The following checklist developed by Jefkins (1994) is useful for developing the article.

Seven-point checklist for feature articles

1. Opening paragraph.
2. The problem or previous situation.
3. The search for a solution or improvement.
4. The solution or improvement.
5. The results achieved.
6. Closing paragraph.
7. Check draft with sources of information.

This checklist is useful for writing a case-study article that enhances the current situation or experience by contrasting it with an inferior situation or experience in the past. Such *before* and *after* treatment gives a dramatic quality to an article. It may also suit a technical or trade journal. Other media (e.g. most business magazines) may require a less formal, more chatty style. As with press releases it is worth reading through the magazine's or newspaper's feature articles before deciding on the style and before submission.

The topping and tailing of the article can be done after the heart of the article has been composed, and ideas for these paragraphs may spring from the central material. Once again, the importance of the first paragraph in catching the attention of the reader should not be underestimated. Unlike a press release, however, it should not give the game away but should lead the reader into the body of the article by means of an irresistible statement, question or perhaps an intriguing quotation.

The article draft should then be submitted to *all* those who gave information or have the authority to approve its publication. This is a professional courtesy, which also acts as insurance. One owes it to all concerned, including the editor, that the facts are correct. It may be wise to draw attention to statements, figures and spellings that should be checked. Since a publication date is usually involved, there must be a deadline for the return of the approved or amended draft. If there is any risk of delay it is a sensible precaution to state quite emphatically that the draft will be assumed to be correct unless returned by a certain date. This date should be early enough for the writer to supply the editor with a final version. Even then, it pays to telephone if the draft has not been returned.

This checking with sources cannot be stressed enough. It is very easy, during an interview, for people to make statements 'off the top of their head' that can turn out to be incorrect. Such errors need to be detected before publication, otherwise there could be embarrassment all round.

Other types of article

The seven-point outline above is very useful when contrasting a new situation with that of the past. However, there are obviously occasions when this format does not apply. If you are discussing new roses for the garden, recipes for Christmas fare, or the attractions of a holiday resort, there will be a more general flow of information throughout the article. Another style might be to base the article on an interview with questions and answers. Another kind of article could be a paper presented at a conference by a company speaker, which could be edited to form an article with the speaker as named author. Such an article could interest the editor of a trade, technical or professional magazine, and should be negotiated in advance of the event.

Syndicated articles

Feature articles need not be exclusive and may be *syndicated*. In other words, supplied to, and published in, more than one publication. This is possible provided care is taken to see that the article does not appear in rival journals. Articles should not be sent out in broadcast fashion like news releases. Unsolicited articles may be rejected and the possibility of offering them elsewhere will be lost. The most practical procedure is to send a synopsis of the article to a selection of publications that do not have competing circulations (e.g. evening newspapers or free newspapers published at least 50 miles apart), and then, upon acceptance, to supply the article together with any requested illustrations.

Some companies undertake overseas distribution of articles, with translations as required, and with their long association with foreign editors such companies often achieve excellent international coverage. Syndicated articles are popular in the holiday and travel industry, often written by well-known travel writers, and they are usually aimed at the holiday features that appear in the regional press in January and February. The syndicated article usually succeeds best with products and services which are of interest to a large number of readers.

Writing style

This chapter began by emphasizing that an article is not a long news release. While it should follow the same rules of presentation as the news release and as set out in the next chapter, it is written quite differently. A principal difference is that, although the first paragraph must capture the attention of the reader, the story is not given away in the first paragraph, which is essential to the writing of a news release. The writing style is also different for a feature article. Whereas the news release should be a disciplined factual account that can often be confined to a single sheet of paper, the author of an article can use a more imaginative style and a richer vocabulary, although he or she should avoid exuberant and technical language, and avoid turning the article into a long advertisement. He or she still has to be factual, but the information can be presented more attractively. For instance, he or she could make observations, use reminiscences, or quote from interviews with people or from other acknowledged published work. According to Hunt and Grunig (1994, pp. 71–2), feature article style:

> calls for luring the reader with a catchy lead, then relating the information in a tone that is more casual and light than one would expect in a straight news story. 'Human interest' material including informal quotes, illustrative passages, and sometimes even the first-person approach to telling the story are all permissible when the topic and the communication channel make the feature style appropriate.

There may be a temptation to make frequent references to the company or the product or brand name, but care must be taken not to overexpose brands. Names can be used when no other word would be suitable. Even so, it is often best to make very discreet commercial references, restricting them to the byline, photo captions, or perhaps just one sentence.

Authorship

One of the advantages of the article over a news release is that it can carry the author's name. If the author is an expert on the subject, or it is ghost written in the name of someone important, this can give the article authenticity and authority. It would be silly to use an obviously commercial person as author if that tended to make the article look like an advertisement. In some cases, however, it may pay to employ a well-known author to write the article.

Event management

Hospitality

PR departments are normally responsible for all types of company events, particularly where this includes some form of hospitality. Public relations has obtained a clichéd image of too much wining and dining, although there is a fine balance between being hospitable and being ostentatious. There is perceived to be a difference between hospitality that seeks to unduly influence the recipient and that which is simple courtesy. In reality, however, the line between the two is considerably blurred. If there is to be, for example, the launch of a new product range, a party where the press are invited would be welcomed and expected.

Press events

In this chapter, we shall consider six kinds of public relations press functions and events:

1. The press conference.
2. The press reception.
3. The facility visit.
4. The open day.
5. The press lunch.
6. The exhibition press visit.

The press conference

This may be a regular event or one that is called at short notice. Its purpose is to give information to the media and to receive and answer questions. It will be a comparatively simple and informal occasion, and hospitality is normally minimal (i.e. tea, coffee). It may be held in the boardroom or conference room, or at a hotel, and if called at short notice there will be no printed invitation cards. The term 'press conference' should not be confused with the more elaborate 'press reception', although some people use the terms interchangeably. Press conferences are held at relatively short notice because, normally, something unexpected has happened and a press statement is necessary, or a currently newsworthy person offers themselves for interview.

During national and local elections political parties may hold regular press conferences (sometimes daily). In a general election these are often used to attempt to set that day's policy agenda as established by the party campaign organizers, although such attempts are not always successful. In non-election times, regular press conferences may be held by heads of government, ministers and opposition spokespersons to keep the media informed on an ongoing basis. Although, as one broadcaster stated, 'if something happens on the economy and I don't get the Chancellor on my programme, it's my head on the block, if the shadow chancellor doesn't get on the programme it's their head on the block' (Boulton, 1999). So, it's much easier for the incumbent party to get their ideas aired than the opposition, simply because the governing party's policies have a direct impact upon people's lives. Sometimes a minister will advise the media 'off the record' or from a 'non-attributable source'. Based on such official 'leaks', journalists may refer the story as originating from 'a usually reliable source', 'a source close to the department' or other such phrase.[1] During a period of crisis a government (e.g. the Falklands War and the Hutton Enquiry) or a company (e.g. Perrier, Pepsi-Cola) may hold daily briefings to inform and reassure the public through the media.

The press reception

This is a more planned and sociable occasion than a press conference. The planning may begin some months in advance, and it will be as thoroughly organized as a wedding reception, complete with venue, invitations, catering, speeches and presentations. It will mean drawing up a targeted 'hit list' of journalists geared to the subject matter and follow-up of invitations to further encourage attendance. It calls for a timetabled programme of activities that may include an audio-visual presentation, product demonstrations and/or speeches. An organizer of a press reception should consider that presenters invariably talk for too long and need managing accordingly. A good 'rule of thumb' is that audiences get bored after about 20 minutes. If it is that important that the talking should go on longer a break should be introduced. It is also wise, where you are using presenters from other organizations, that you see what material they are presenting to ensure that it fits with your own, especially where your organization is the lead organizer.

A press reception must have an adequate purpose and a good story to justify good attendance by the right people (i.e. those media most likely to deliver our message to our target publics). An uninteresting storyline is likely to attract the wrong people (e.g. juniors sent by editors who think the event unimportant) or no one at all. Press reception organizers often invite clients whose needs differ from those of the journalist. If practical, a separate presentation geared to clients should be considered.

The facility visit

This may be a press trip to a site, a factory or new premises; it could be a flight on a new aircraft or a voyage on a new vessel; it might be an official opening; it could be an overseas visit, an exhibition (see Chapter 22) or a new holiday attraction. One way or another, it usually means taking a person or a group of people by some form of transport

---

[1] This lobby system may or may not last. There are already signs that the system is breaking down, as more journalists are seen to be breaking the lobby rules of confidence.

to the location of the visit. If people are travelling from a variety of places they may have to make their own way. At least a day is usually involved, but overnight stops may be necessary. A great deal of organization is required. Because you are expecting journalists to sacrifice their time, a facility visit has to be worthwhile in terms of it being newsworthy. Journalists are unlikely to respond if they have to travel 500 miles to see a jam factory that is no different from the one near their home town. They will, however, be delighted to go behind the scenes of something unusual or unfamiliar. Such visits should not depend on complicated arrangements that could be wrecked by the weather or transport difficulties.

The open day

This is an opportunity for the press to make a visit and see what goes on in an organization, although there may be nothing 'new' to be seen. Such a visit could be to a factory, college, hospital, mine, town hall, airport, charity home and usually somewhere where the press do not normally have general access. There may or may not be a direct story (although it is more likely to attract journalists if there is such an angle). It is often more of a goodwill effort to familiarize the media with a particular place and what happens there. This may provide background knowledge that may help them when news stories are being processed. Planning is still necessary, and any management and employees likely to be involved should be aware of the visit. British Nuclear Fuels Limited (BNFL) runs open days at Sellafield, its nuclear reprocessing plant in Cumbria, where the press is regularly invited in an attempt to improve the general public's image of what may be perceived as a dirty, polluting industry.

The press lunch (or breakfast or supper)

This is a variation on the press reception where individual journalists, or groups of journalists, may be given lunch, breakfast or supper depending on the timing of the event. This type of event can be a pleasant way for journalists to meet the personalities within an organization, to get to know them informally, and so discuss topics of mutual interest. It can be helpful in creating understanding between management and journalists. There may or (more normally) may not be formal speeches, nor may there be an immediate story (although again a good newsworthy story helps).

The exhibition press visit

This can take several forms: an open invitation to journalists to visit the stand for demonstrations, or a press reception on the stand itself or else-where in the exhibition facility. The same criteria apply to exhibition press visits as with other events: the better the story, the more likely the press are to be interested in attending and the sharper the presentation, the better the likelihood of favourable coverage.

Planning considerations

Planning and executing a press event is an exercise in good management, whether by the in-house PRO or the consultant. Control is necessary at every stage of the planning, budgeting, purchasing, stage-managing and control phases of the event. Otherwise it may become a disappointing waste of time and money. A lot of people's valuable time is likely to be invested on both sides.

The purpose

Is the event justified? Is it worth the cost to the organization and the time of the guests or would a news release be sufficient? Afterwards, consideration should be given as to whether or not it fulfilled the PR objectives, what tangible coverage was received and if it is worth repeat-ing in the future? These are very important questions given the direct and hidden costs (e.g. staff time) involved. It is good practice to review each and every event, before and after, on such a basis.

Date and time of day

Whilst the chairman may think it convenient to hold a press reception at 6 p.m. on a Friday evening, journalists might well prefer it at 11 a.m. on a Tuesday morning. In this situation, if you want a success-ful event, then the wishes of the latter should hold sway. The event should be held when it suits the press, otherwise there is likely to be a poor turnout, little coverage and possibly a heavy bill for a wasted effort.

There are three main rules for the choice of date and time, and none of them are easy to apply satisfactorily. The first is to avoid *clashing* with a major event or another press function. You can check the social calendar for major events (e.g. Wimbledon fortnight, the Chelsea Flower Show). You can ring PR colleagues or the press and ask if they have heard of anything else on the same day. However well you check there are likely to be occasions when clashes occur; it is usually a question of which event is deemed to be more important by the journalists you are targeting your invitations at.

The second rule relates to choosing a day that satisfies copy requirements. Although modern technology has sped up the process, the day of the week is still important. The end of the week is poor for daily newspapers, and too late for some magazines. The week in the month is important for monthly magazines that may go to press before the middle of the month. However, many of the large-circulation women's magazines still need the story a number of months in advance. That is why receptions for Christmas gifts are held in July/August, ones for central heating in April/May, and those for summer holidays (January editions) in September/October. To publish stories coinciding with the March Ideal Home Exhibition, for example, the press reception needs to be held in November. Again, you will be unable to satisfy everyone, but try to accommodate your targeted media in particular.

A third rule relates to the time of day events are held. Traditional advice suggests that it is best if the proceedings begin in mid-morning and close with a buffet lunch from about 11.30 a.m. to 1.30 p.m., although the availability of 24-hour news media makes this less crucial than previously. As a very general rule, early in the day, early in the week and early in the month will suit the requirements of most publishers.

Venue

The convenience of the guests is a first consideration, rather than the glamour of the venue. A major city centre location should easily be reached on foot, by public transport or by taxi. Remember that journalists may have more than one reception to attend. In smaller towns and cities it may be more important that there are good car-parking facilities, if guests are coming from the surrounding district. Consideration should be given to laying on transport to, but especially from, more isolated events, especially when they include a champagne reception, for instance. The venue should have good conference facilities, ranging from catering to audio-visual equipment. It should have rooms large enough to accommodate the anticipated audience but not so large that even if everyone turns up it looks half empty.

Programme

A timed programme should be drawn up when the event is being planned. If it is a facility visit, the timetable should include the assembly time of the party at the station or airport, coach pick-up point, and return time. Precise timings may be involved. How early, for example, should the party be collected in order to reach the venue in time to make a tour or see demonstrations before and/or after lunch? This may determine the form of transportation, perhaps require the provision of breakfast. It may be necessary for the PRO or consultant to go over the route and tour and time the various stages – on foot, by car and so on, allowing, for example, for the time it takes to get a certain number of people on and off coaches and from point to point during the day. Some flexibility needs to be built into the schedule, but not so much that guests are left hanging around with nothing to do. The maximum number of people to be accepted may be determined by the size of a coach, aircraft, demonstration theatre or luncheon room. With most visits there is usually some factor that limits the size of the party.

Guest list and invitations

People are normally more receptive to invitations if they are person-ally invited by name. This may mean taking the trouble to telephone around and check names. Not even the best contact directories are always fully up to date. If the guest list is large enough, a printed invi-tation is better than a letter. The invitation should state exactly what the event is about, not vaguely invite people to a reception or visit. A timetable can be printed on the back of the card with details of the event's location. To ensure prompt acceptances or refusals, there should be some means of reply (reply card or telephone number), not merely an RSVP note at the foot of the card. An important rule when seeking the maximum number of replies is to make responding as easy as possible.

Rehearsals

Events need to occur without any hitches and, while a timetable provides the basis for a well-organized event, it pays to time each stage (speeches, demonstrations, video, presentations, etc.) and to rehearse wherever possible. Build in enough flexibility as possible, but not so much that guests are left hanging around with nothing to do. Speeches and presentations should be kept as short as is practical. Overlong speeches or a long and seemingly endless procession of presenters challenges the most attentive of audiences.

Press material

The media should be supplied with press packs containing only the minimum of material necessary to develop a story. A news release, copy of a speech, a photograph and, on a visit, an itinerary should be sufficient. PROs should avoid the mistake of providing guests with over-stuffed packs filled with irrelevant items. Remember, the guests may be standing, eating, drinking, or walking round the site or premises. They will not enjoy having to carry around a weighty press kit. If there is a lot of useful information it may be better to supply it when the guests leave or offer to forward it to them by post. Many an unwelcome press kit has been found dumped after the event!

Final thought

Event hospitality is often seen, rightly or wrongly, as part of the public relations' information dissemination process. The image that the event portrays (welcoming, mechanical, efficient, disorganized, etc.) will have a direct effect on how guests perceive the organization regardless of the reality. The onus is on the PRO to present the organization in the most favourable (and realistic) light.

Chapter 17

Broadcasting public relations and funded television programmes

LEARNING OBJECTIVES

After reading this chapter you will be able to:

■ establish the importance of broadcasting to public relations;
■ spell out those important factors requiring consideration when working with television or radio broadcasters;
■ identify those areas of broadcasting where PR opportunities exist.

Broadcast PR

There is a lot more to broadcasting than sending news releases to Independent Television News, Independent Radio News, Sky News or the BBC news services. Merely putting the broadcasting services on the mailing list is likely to be ineffectual, if only because the story will probably arrive too late to be usable. Air time on both radio and television is divided into numerous programme slots, not unlike the pages and features of newspapers and magazines. In the past, the news was a small part of any particular broadcaster's output. With the advent of 24-hour news television (e.g. BBC News 24, ITN, CNN, Sky News) and radio (e.g. NewsTalk), dedicated news coverage has increased substantially, although perhaps not as a percentage of overall programme transmission.

Although, in the past, broadcasting theorists (and regulators) suggested that channels should combine information, education and entertainment, the tendency was for broad entertainment to predominate, even to some extent in the educational and news programmes. This was because, as with popular newspapers such as the *Daily Mirror* and the *Sun*, the limited number of radio and television stations catered for the mass public, which has a preference for entertainment. This is a statement of fact, not cynicism. Even with the advent of satellite, cable and digital television, the majority of combined channel output is entertainment of one sort or another. What has changed is that the breadth of stations allows for niche viewing. This tendency is promoted by the growing number of households with two or more television and radio sets, and the increasing use of video/CD-ROM/DVD and now Internet recording. Real Networks' webstreaming technology allows the user to view film and video footage on the Internet. It also offers numerous news channels displaying footage as individual five- or ten-minute stories on subjects such as IT news, for instance. Individual channel audiences may be smaller but they are more targeted than previously.

Television

Despite the proliferation of stations, the traditional broadcasters in the UK, i.e. the BBC and Independent Television companies (ITV), still hold over 58 per cent of total viewing (see Table 17.1), although this is much reduced from the time when they represented the entire output (see Table 17.2). With British terrestrial television audiences still numbering millions, most public relations material for television still has to be of interest and value to a very large number of viewers. Much of the company news that would suit certain sections of the press, special interest columns or features even in the popular press (e.g. City Page) has to be directed to selected broadcasters such as BBC News 24 or Sky News, who have specialist programmes covering the business sector.

It can be a valuable public relations exercise if programmes, presenters, producers, scriptwriters and research assistants are diligently selected,

Table 17.1 All UK channels audience share, 1 December 2002

Week ending 1 December 2002 (BARB)	Average weekly viewing (hours/ person)	Share of total viewing (%)	Share of total reach (% daily)	Share of total reach (% weekly)
All/any TV	**26:48**	**100.0**	**76.1**	**92.6**
BBC1	4:58	18.5	50.8	84.8
BBC2	1:56	7.2	31.1	72.4
Total BBC1/BBC2	**6:54**	**25.7**	**57.2**	**87.5**
ITV	5:11	19.3	48.1	82.1
Channel 4/S4C	2:12	8.2	32.3	71.9
Five	1:21	5.0	20.2	56.9
Total/comm. terr. TV	**8:43**	**32.5**	**59.6**	**87.7**
Total terrestrial	**15:38**	**58.3**	**68.7**	**90.5**
Sky 1	0:54	3.4	13.9	41.5
Sky News	0:13	0.8	4.5	14.5
Sky Cinema	0:03	0.2	1.0	5.3
Sky Cinema 2	0:02	0.1	0.8	4.2
Sky MovieMax	0:05	0.3	1.6	7.8
Sky MovieMax 2	0:04	0.2	1.2	6.3
Sky MovieMax 3	0:03	0.2	1.1	5.5
Sky Moviemax 4	0:03	0.2	0.8	4.4
Sky MovieMax 5	0:02	0.1	1.0	5.7
Sky Premier	0:14	0.9	3.3	15.1
Sky Premier 2	0:05	0.3	1.4	7.6
Sky Premier 3	0:04	0.2	1.3	7.1
Sky Premier 4	0:05	0.3	1.4	7.7
Sky Premier Widescreen	0:04	0.2	1.3	7.0
All Sky Movies	**0:54**	**3.4**	**10.0**	**27.9**
Sky Sports 1	0:30	1.9	5.7	20.8
Sky Sports 2	0:09	0.6	2.3	9.3
Sky Sports 3	0:03	0.2	1.0	4.1
Sky Sports News	0:08	0.5	3.7	12.1
Sky Premiership Plus	0:02	0.1	0.3	2.2
Sky Sports Extra	0:02	0.1	0.7	4.0
All Sky Sports	**0:53**	**3.3**	**9.8**	**27.8**
Sky Travel	0:01	0.1	0.8	4.1
Sky Travel 2	0:01	0.1	0.4	2.3
Sky Box Office	n/a	n/a	n/a	n/a
Total Sky	**2:58**	**11.1**	**28.9**	**62.7**
Animal Planet	0:04	0.2	1.1	5.1
Animal Planet +1	0:01	0.1	0.5	2.5
At The Races	0:02	0.1	0.6	1.9
BBC Choice (now BBC3)	0:07	0.4	3.1	13.6

Table 17.1 (*Continued*)

Week ending 1 December 2002 (BARB)	Average weekly viewing (hours/ person)	Share of total viewing (%)	Share of total reach (% daily)	Share of total reach (% weekly)
BBC Knowledge	n/a	n/a	n/a	n/a
BBC 4	0:02	0.1	0.8	4.6
BBC News 24	0:09	0.6	3.6	12.2
Bid Up TV	0:04	0.2	1.1	3.7
Boomerang	0:09	0.6	2.3	8.8
Bravo	0:10	0.6	4.5	18.1
Carlton Cinema	n/a	n/a	n/a	n/a
Cartoon Network	0:10	0.6	2.9	10.0
Cartoon Network Plus	0:02	0.1	1.2	5.4
CBBC	0:02	0.1	1.0	4.6
CBEEBIES	0:22	1.4	4.3	11.3
Challenge TV	0:07	0.4	2.8	10.6
Channel Health	0:01	0.1	0.6	3.0
Chart Show TV	0:01	0.1	0.7	3.9
CNBC	*	*	0.1	0.8
CNX	0:02	0.1	0.9	3.6
Discovery	0:08	0.5	2.5	10.3
Discovery +1	0:03	0.2	1.3	6.6
Discovery Civilizations	0:01	0.1	0.6	3.0
Discovery Health	0:02	0.1	1.0	5.0
Discovery Kids	*	*	0.2	0.8
Discovery Sci-Trek	0:03	0.2	0.9	4.5
Discovery Travel and Adventure	0:01	0.1	0.5	2.7
Discovery Wings	0:01	0.1	0.4	1.9
Disney Channel	0:09	0.6	2.2	9.5
Disney Channel +1	0:04	0.2	1.4	5.9
Playhouse Disney	0:02	0.1	0.7	3.0
Toon Disney	0:04	0.2	1.4	5.1
E4	0:21	1.3	6.6	23.0
Einstein	n/a	n/a	n/a	n/a
Eurosport	0:04	0.2	1.6	7.2
Eurosport News	*	*	0.2	0.9
Extreme Sports Channel	*	*	0.3	1.4
Fashion TV	0:01	0.1	0.5	1.9
Film Four	*	*	0.1	0.5
Film Four +1	*	*	*	0.3
Film Four Extreme	*	*	0.1	0.3
Film Four World	*	*	*	0.1
Fox Kids	0:04	0.2	1.3	4.9
Fox Kids +1	0:02	0.1	1.1	4.8
Granada Men and Motors	0:04	0.2	2.7	11.6

Table 17.1 (*Continued*)

Week ending 1 December 2002 (BARB)	Average weekly viewing (hours/ person)	Share of total viewing (%)	Share of total reach (% daily)	Share of total reach (% weekly)
Granada Plus	0:14	0.9	3.3	11.9
Hallmark	0:10	0.6	2.2	7.6
The History Channel	0:04	0.2	1.2	5.4
History +1	0:02	0.1	0.7	3.2
Home and Leisure	0:07	0.4	2.7	10.3
Home and Leisure +1	0:02	0.1	1.2	5.2
ITN News	0:07	0.4	2.6	13.2
ITV Sport	n/a	n/a	n/a	n/a
ITV Sport Select	n/a	n/a	n/a	n/a
ITV2	0:26	1.6	8.2	32.8
Kerrang	0:02	0.1	1.5	6.3
Kiss TV	0:02	0.1	2.1	9.7
Living	0:14	0.9	5.3	20.8
Living TV +1	0:05	0.3	2.1	10.0
Magic TV	0:04	0.2	2.0	8.8
Motors TV	0:01	0.1	0.6	2.8
MTV	0:03	0.2	2.6	12.2
MTV2	0:01	0.1	1.1	5.0
MTV Base	0:02	0.1	1.4	6.5
MTV Dance	0:01	0.1	0.9	4.8
MTV Hits	0:05	0.3	2.9	12.1
National Geographic	0:02	0.1	1.0	5.1
National Geographic +1	0:01	0.1	0.6	3.2
National GeographicAdv. One	0:01	0.1	0.4	2.5
Nickelodeon	0:11	0.7	3.3	11.0
Nick Replay	0:04	0.2	1.7	7.3
Nick Junior	0:07	0.4	1.7	4.7
Nick Toons	0:03	0.2	1.4	5.7
Paramount	0:10	0.6	3.6	13.8
Q Channel	0:01	0.1	1.5	7.1
Reality TV	0:05	0.3	2.0	7.5
Sci-Fi	0:09	0.6	2.7	10.7
Smash Hits	0:04	0.2	2.6	11.5
Tara	n/a	n/a	n/a	n/a
The Biography Channel	0:02	0.1	0.8	3.7
The Box	0:05	0.3	3.1	13.3
The Dating Channel	n/a	n/a	n/a	n/a
The Hits	0:03	0.2	1.6	7.1
TMF	0:01	0.1	0.5	1.5
The Travel Channel	0:01	0.1	0.4	2.0
Trouble	0:06	0.4	2.1	7.6

Table 17.1 (*Continued*)

Week ending 1 December 2002 (BARB)	Average weekly viewing (hours/ person)	Share of total viewing (%)	Share of total reach (% daily)	Share of total reach (% weekly)
Turner Classic Movies	0:06	0.4	1.9	8.4
UK Drama	0:02	0.1	0.5	3.0
UK Food	0:03	0.2	1.0	3.8
UK Gold	0:26	1.6	6.8	25.3
UK Gold +1	0:05	0.3	2.0	9.7
UK Gold 2	0:03	0.2	1.4	6.8
UK History	0:05	0.3	1.6	6.1
UK Horizons	0:04	0.2	1.7	7.6
UK Horizons +1	0:02	0.1	0.8	4.3
UK Play	n/a	n/a	n/a	n/a
UK Style	0:13	0.8	4.1	14.7
UK Style +1	0:02	0.1	0.8	4.1
VH-1	0:03	0.2	1.8	9.4
VH-1 Classic	0:02	0.1	1.4	7.2
Total of all other channels	**0:58**	**3.6**	**12.8**	**38.0**
Total non-terrestrial channels	**11:10**	**41.7**	**57.8**	**84.8**

*Means not zero but less than smallest number shown.
Totals may not add exactly due to rounding errors.

Source: BARB (2002). Reproduced with permission of Broadcasters' Audience Research Board Ltd. (BARB)

and if approaches are timed correctly. For example, a businessperson might appear on *Question Time*, a topic might have a place in *EastEnders* or *Coronation Street*, an export order success story could suit a regional or even national news bulletin, or a holiday subject might be welcomed by one of the holiday programmes on BBC or ITV or the numerous (and growing number of) travel channels.

However, involvement in television programmes can be very time-consuming, with many hours taken up for a few moments of screen time. There is a need to weigh up the advantages of the programme's relevance and audience size with the brevity of the broadcast. Before getting involved in television, the PRO should consider whether he or she really has the time to spare compared with the value of the coverage. Television can be a temptation and a disappointment. It is a visual medium that invites critical viewing if the subject or personality is not attractive on a small screen in private homes. Some well-known personalities have suffered adverse publicity because they have come over badly on television. The viewing public does tend to look at, rather than listen to, television,

Table 17.2 Percentage share of audience, 1981–2000

	BBC1	BBC2	ITV (incl. GMTV)	Channel 4	Channel 5	Others (incl. sat./cable)
1981	39.0	12.0	49.0	–	–	–
1982	38.0	12.0	50.0	–	–	–
1983	37.0	11.0	48.0	4.0	–	–
1984	36.0	11.0	48.0	6.0	–	–
1985	36.0	11.0	46.0	7.0	–	–
1986	37.0	11.0	44.0	8.0	–	–
1987	38.0	12.0	42.0	8.0	–	–
1988	38.0	11.0	42.0	9.0	–	–
1989	39.0	11.0	42.0	9.0	–	–
1990	37.0	10.0	44.0	9.0	–	–
1991	34.0	10.0	42.0	10.0	–	4.0
1992	34.0	10.0	41.0	10.0	–	5.0
1993	33.0	10.0	40.0	11.0	–	6.0
1994	32.0	11.0	39.0	11.0	–	7.0
1995	32.0	11.0	37.0	11.0	–	9.0
1996	33.5	11.5	35.1	10.7	–	10.1
1997	30.8	11.6	32.9	10.6	2.3	11.8
1998	29.5	11.3	31.7	10.3	4.3	12.9
1999	28.4	10.8	31.2	10.3	5.4	14.0
2000	27.2	10.8	29.3	10.5	5.7	16.6

Source: BARB (date). Reproduced with permission of Broadcasters' Audience Research Board Ltd. (BARB)

whereas with the radio it is the attractiveness of the voice that matters. The most famous example of this phenomenon is described in Box 17.1.

It pays to study the programmes printed in the *What's on TV, TV Quick, Radio Times, TV Times* and other listings magazines (or similar magazines in other countries) to see which programmes are being broadcast, and to note the names of presenters, editors and producers. There is no cast-iron rule about this, but for different programmes one may have to deal with the producer, the editor, the presenter or the researcher. If in doubt, it is best to contact the producer in the first instance, setting out the proposition in a letter or a telephone conversation with postal/e-mail confirmation. It has also to be remembered that while programmes may be networked to a national or partially national audience, they may originate from a regional ITV station, a regional BBC facility or (in a growing number of instances) from independent production companies such as Hat Trick or Channel X. The low-cost airline, easyJet, managed to considerably raise awareness of its service at Stansted airport, and the

Box 17.1 **Kennedy versus Nixon**

In the 1960 United States Presidential Election the two candidates, Richard Nixon and John Kennedy, were due to take part in a debate that was to be covered on both radio and television. Nixon arrived at the studio looking tired and drawn, having been unwell on the previous day, but refused any make-up. This did not, however, affect his speaking voice. Polls taken after the broadcast showed significantly more radio listeners suggested that Nixon had come out on top. Television viewers, however, came out considerably in favour of Kennedy.

difficulties associated with delivering such a low-cost service, when a documentary series entitled *Airline* was broadcast in 2001/02.

A major justification for increased PR input into television is the perceived reduction in the power of television advertising. The proliferation of new media (e.g. VCR, DVD, CD-ROM) in particular has changed viewers' (and to a lesser extent listeners') habits. Most noticeably, viewers are now 'zapping' (i.e. changing channels temporarily or permanently to avoid advertising) or 'zipping' (i.e. recording programmes and fast-forwarding through commercial breaks) more than ever before. To address this problem, major advertisers are switching to programme sponsorship (previously prohibited in the UK but long used in the US television industry). An argument can be made that sponsorship (although financially supported) has closer links to PR as part of the integrated marketing communications (IMC) mix. Such sponsoring companies (e.g. Cadbury's sponsorship of *Coronation Street*) make full use their connection in PR events and in their website activity (see Chapter 27 for more details on sponsorship). Satellite and cable also offer interactive television facilities that can only develop further in the future as more subscribers choose these formats (see Table 17.3).

Further considerations: TV broadcasting and PR

Because of the nature of television, it is important when developing your TV PR strategy to consider the following factors:

1. Some programmes are live or are produced only a few days before transmission. For example, BBC Television's *Watchdog* is a combination of pre-taped material and studio performance. If a programme is live it is important to be very well briefed and prepared.
2. Other programmes, such as a holiday series, may have been filmed months in advance (usually during that resort's peak season). Any direct

Table 17.3 Satellite and cable development, 1992–2002

	Satelite	Cable	Total
January 1992	1 893 000	409 000	2 302 000
January 1993	2 387 000	625 000	3 012 000
January 1994	2 754 000	744 000	3 498 000
January 1995	3 060 000	973 000	4 033 000
January 1996	3 542 000	1 399 000	4 941 000
January 1997	3 804 000	1 845 000	5 649 000
January 1998	4 117 000	2 471 000	6 588 000
January 1999	4 114 000	2 911 000	7 126 000
January 2000	4 196 000	3 352 000	7 618 000
January 2001	5 450 000	3 490 000	9 010 000
January 2002 (at Dec 01)	6 389 000	3 819 000	10 278 000

Source: www.barb.co.uk (2003). Reproduced with permission of
Broadcasters' Audience Research Board Ltd. (BARB)

participation may have to wait until the following season. It is, however, possible to get an item onto the following week's show if you know the transmission schedule (available from most listings magazines).

3. Sometimes material may be recorded for a particular magazine programme but may not immediately be used. You may even be told 'it's going on tonight' only to find it is held over to a future programme. Be careful that you do not demand that the producer should have used your material. It is his or her prerogative to use the material as they see fit.

4. Television can be not only time-consuming but exasperating. In the process of editing an interview it may be broken up and other pieces, perhaps from other interviews, inserted. This can, potentially, give an entirely different meaning from what was discussed in the separate interviews!

5. The public relations practitioner needs to understand the technical demands of the medium. While it is simple and quick to record a quick, 'off the cuff', television interview, anything more substantial may require planning, the use of equipment, proper lighting, sometimes many people, and probably a budget allocation to undertake the job. This implies, therefore, that the concept has to be marketed and sold to the production company, facilities must be provided, and a lot of co-operation will be required in providing scenes or venues, or people for interview. It is unlike inviting a group of journalists to a press reception or on a press visit as there is a need to devote time to a television crew, and to do so on a day convenient to their schedule, and for however long it may take to set up, script, rehearse and shoot the story.

6. If videotapes, or digital footage, are supplied to a television company, and they contain any material that is not the copyright of the owner, this must be declared as reproduction fees may have to be paid. The television company will demand details of copyright ownership.

The public relations practitioner has to be aware of the pitfalls and peculiarities of television production, as it may prove to be used as a device to amuse rather than inform audiences. Inspired controversy based on innocent interviews is a form of entertainment. The wise practitioner may therefore find it a matter of responsibility towards clients or employers to advise them against participation in some television programmes. This may require considerable tact, since some people may be anxious to appear, if only to impress their friends. Vanity can prove costly.

Opportunities for public relations coverage on television

News bulletins

There are basically three types of TV news bulletins. There are national news broadcasts (e.g. BBC or ITN news), which report major national and international news, and regional broadcasts (e.g. BBC London News), which often follow the networked news. To these intermittent services must be added the 'rolling news' services of BBC News 24, Sky News, ITN and CNN. To obtain national coverage on current terrestrial stations is rare. Local news broadcasters are usually more amenable, particularly if the 'newsworthy story' is of significant regional interest. Rolling news broadcasters may be the hungriest for news either for bulletins or special segments (e.g. business sections).

Magazine programmes

As these programmes are regularly broadcast (up to five, six or seven days a week), they are open to suggestions for material that is both topical and of interest to their particular audience (e.g. farmers, gardeners, motorists, businesspeople).

Chat shows, discussion panels, interviews

Opportunities exist for participation in such shows by interesting personalities, particularly if their subject matter is topical. Two things are essential for live interviews: that the interviewee must be articulate and must know his or her subject, to be capable of responding instantaneously, authoritatively and sincerely to any question. Poor performances reflect badly on the individual, their company and the broadcaster. To keep poor performances to a minimum many companies, political parties and even University faculties now offer staff 'media training'.

Serials

It may be possible to introduce a public interest subject into a fictional programme if it can be made relevant to the characters or storyline. A number of topics such as this appear in 'soaps'[1] if they are relevant to the storyline. Charitable and other cause-related organizations have put forward ideas that have been adopted and promoted as storylines as diverse as the promotion of The Royal Agricultural Show (*The Archers*, BBC Radio 4) to penal reform (*EastEnders*, BBC1).

Series

These appear regularly at certain times during the year. Gardening, travel, wildlife and cooking are amongst the more popular. As noted previously, the series may have been filmed months in advance and any direct participation may have to wait until the following season. More short-term opportunities may exist if a particular topic is to be covered and the PRO is aware of the transmission schedule (available from most listings magazines). In addition to the traditional series, there is a growing number of 'reality television' programmes. Some companies have wholeheartedly co-operated with such series (e.g. easyJet), although there is always a danger of such co-operation backfiring if the company is seen in a bad light.

Current affairs programmes

Current affairs programmes (e.g. *Panorama*) may require co-operation in covering a subject or may be interested in a proposed topic. In general, however, such programmes tend towards exposure of wrongdoing rather than general interest subject matter. Sometimes they seek to

---

[1] The common name for continuously running serials (e.g. *Coronation Street*, *EastEnders*, etc.). The name originates in the USA, where the first such series were generally sponsored by soap companies.

reveal something detrimental to an organization. That organization has to make a decision about whether to co-operate or to withhold information. The major problem is that investigative programmes are more intent on dramatic entertainment than, necessarily, a fair treatment of the subject.

Archival material

This consists of ready-made profile or promotional clips that can be inserted into programmes to give background effects or information – for example, a factory complex, production line or financial trading floor.

Library shots

Action films are often shot in studios, and outside scenes are borrowed or hired from libraries. Famous landmarks and geographical scenes are typical examples. Many airlines make available shots of their aircraft taking off, in flight or landing.

Documentary videos

Some commercially produced documentaries (sometimes initially produced for internal consumption) may be of sufficient interest to be shown in their entirety. Known in the USA as a 'video news release' (VNR), it has been used extensively in that market in, for example, political campaigns or book reviews (Cutlip et al., 1994). Clips may be taken from videos for use in programmes, usually with acknowledgement.

Stills

Colour photographs can be useful for news stories, being televised to coincide with the release of an associated (hopefully, good news) story.

Properties and product placement

Many products have to be used in television films and series. They can be supplied to property rooms, and so used on sets, or they may be supplied for use on location. It is noticeable that major automobile company products are often used in both American and British detective series, and sometimes credited in the subtitles. The James Bond series of films have always had a large element of product placement, particularly as regards cars (Aston Martin and, more recently, BMW). The supply of products for use in films, plays and television programmes is called 'product placement' (see Chapter 27), and there are firms that specialize in getting products placed in the media. Another name for this is 'presence advertising', which really means making payment for using products as 'props' (i.e. properties). Theatre programmes often credit companies that have contributed props such as clothes or furniture. For many international film companies there is now substantial money to be made in charging fees for product placement. This is not permitted on British TV (although cinema product placement is another matter), but many firms (through their agents) endeavour to supply props for various programmes. *Coronation Street*, for example, abounds in such props on the sets for the Rover's Return public house and the local shops.

Prizes for give-away and contest shows

These are usually purchased by the programme makers and are unlikely to be identified in the UK (to avoid the charge of advertising), although many may benefit from easy recognition.

Radio versus television

Before listing the opportunities for radio coverage it is useful to compare radio and television. The following are five differences between the two media:

1. Radio is not confined as is television to indoor audiences. Radio is generally available to more people, in more places (e.g. the car, at work, etc.) at more times than television.
2. Television requires the attention of immobile viewers. This does not usually apply to radio, which can be listened to whilst driving or working, although this does have an effect on how information is processed (see Chapter 2).
3. Radio is less complex than television. A radio programme can be produced at short notice. Television programmes usually require considerable advance preparation.
4. Although there is a growing number of niche television channels, radio has the capacity to be highly localized and niche market

(e.g. age, culture, taste) specific, albeit that many of these stations are heavily biased towards audiences interested in music.

5. Television transmits images whereas radio challenges the listener to develop their own image of the actors and presenters. This self-created image can be very powerful.

With these differences in mind, and remembering that radio does not have television's realism and entertainment value or vision, colour and movement, let us now consider how to use the radio as a public relations medium.

Opportunities for PR coverage on radio

News bulletins

There are national, regional and local radio stations, so that different news stories will interest different radio stations. There is great competition for radio audiences and stations are eager to cover local stories of interest to their listeners.

Taped interviews

Interviews can be produced in one of two ways. The station may commission an interview, either at the studio or with a reporter outside the studio, or the taped interview can be produced by a public relations source and supplied to radio stations. The latter is done more often than listeners realize, which shows that the public relations material was broadcast on its merits. No commercial reference is normally made during the interview, but the identity of the company or product is usually mentioned in the announcer's introduction and close. Sometimes the identity will be obvious if the interview is about, say, a public event, a new entertainment or a new book. Or it could be a trade organization or professional body giving advice with the message more important than the source (e.g. financial advice).

Studio interviews, discussions, talks

Being an audio medium, programmes based on talk and the human voice are characteristic of radio. Interesting voices, conversationalists, commentators or subjects suitable for a talk or discussion are all ideal for radio.

The phone-in

The phone-in produces listener participation and offers opportunities to call-in a public relations message if it is an appropriate and genuine contribution to the programme. Alternatively, phone-in programmes frequently seek 'expert' contributors, perhaps commenting on the calls as they come in.

Serials and series

There are possibilities for including public relations messages in radio serials, as has happened a number of times on Radio 4's *The Archers*, provided they are of interest and value to large numbers of listeners. In spite of television and local radio, *The Archers* has many millions of dedicated listeners. It is interesting to note that this programme was created specifically to offer advice to UK farmers. Even today, charities and other voluntary organizations have made good use of this radio 'soap' to advise the public on matters of health and safety.

Getting the company known to broadcasters

Even with a very large PR department it can be difficult to monitor what is to be broadcast and when. One alternative is to let the media do the job for you. Advising media groups of the type of help that you can give them, together perhaps with a list of potential expert contributors, may lead to substantial coverage over time. If a PR department can grow a reputation as professional contributors, the organization will be asked over and over again for help, thus gaining valuable exposure.

Chapter 18

Photographs, captions and printing

LEARNING OBJECTIVES

After reading this chapter you will be able to:

■ understand the importance of photography in creating a newsworthy story;
■ recognize the need for comprehensive captioning and referencing and the requirements of the Copyright Act;
■ exhibit a broad knowledge of the production and other processes involved with printing.

Photographs and captions

Editors frequently complain about the poor quality of public relations pictures. The reason why public relations pictures are sometimes poor is rarely the quality of photograph. Professional photographers can be employed who should ensure the quality of the final product. Even in-house photography quality has improved immeasurably with the introduction of less complex, more user-friendly, photographic equipment. The usual reason for complaint is that the practitioner does not fully appreciate one or more of the following important aspects:

1. How to create a story with pictures.
2. The sort of pictures editors want.
3. How to work with a photographer.

Without this appreciation it is inevitable that the practitioner will fail to make the best use of photography and, subsequently, will disappoint editors. It is therefore a managerial responsibility to see that public relations staff are proficient in the use of photography and in the briefing of photographers. It helps immeasurably if the practitioner can use a camera, and with modern SLR cameras and, more recently, digital technology, it is not difficult to take good pictures. The secret is not in what button to press but to know how to compose a picture. With this knowledge you (or your photographer) can create a story with a camera just as one does on a word processor.

Telling a story pictorially

A public relations picture should convey a message, not be a mere record. Sometimes the message is subtle (for example, daffodils representing a Spring fashion collection), at other times it is more explicit (for example, a Save-the-Children appeal). Pictures are easier to read than words: they take less effort and give the eye freer movement (Smith, 2002). Human interest may improve a picture, provided it is relevant and helps to explain the subject. A travel company, to highlight a brochure launch, may, for example, use a family evidently enjoying themselves. Sometimes the association is tenuous. Barely clad female models, used in the past to illustrate products as diverse as fridge-freezers and industrial diggers, are not as obvious today. Although sex may still sell, this form of blatant association is now likely to attract ridicule rather than praise.

In many ways the more basic the product or service, the more thought has to go into a photographic composition. A brick looks better if a bricklayer is laying it, a sewing machine is better demonstrated by a dressmaker using it. If it is a lorry, give it a load, show the crane working, have the fork-lift truck lifting things. Have the bus driving along a well-known street, the weighing machine weighing a parcel, and the singer clutching a microphone.

People in pictures should be concentrating on what they are doing, but not so hard that it makes the photograph overly serious (unless of course that is the objective). If the size of the subject is difficult to judge, the message is made clearer if, say, a tiny object is held in the palm of a hand, or a human being is seen standing beside something very large. A lot of public relations pictures could be made interesting and publishable if the people in the photograph were used properly. They do not have to be professional models although, in certain circumstances (e.g. a fashion clothing), a model's training and knowledge may prove valuable.

Movement is another device for giving pictures interest and realism. An aircraft in the air looks more interesting than one on the ground, while a static object such as a building looks better if someone is walking up the steps, or passing through the entrance. Action can thus be real or induced. Three-dimensional effects give a picture depth. It is more interesting to see three sides of an item than a frontal shot. This applies to many subjects. Do not face the subject head-on: stand to one side and take it at an angle, whether it is a portrait, a piece of machinery, a ship or a loaf of bread. It is sometimes more dramatic to photograph a part rather than the whole. A section of a building can look more impressive than if you tried to get the whole building in the picture. The cricketer at the wicket, with the wicket-keeper crouched behind him, can make a better picture than a bird's eye view of the match in progress.

What do editors want?

Editors want pictures that enhance the page and flatter their ability to please their readers (Jefkins, 1994). Most of the public relations pictures they receive do neither. They also want pictures that reproduce well according to the printing process they use, which today usually means a digital format.

A caption should provide the information from which the editor may create his own description. This may be attached physically for a print or electronically for a digital image. The caption will remain with the picture to explain the picture and identify the source. It should be remembered that a photograph may be stored in a picture library long after the news release that accompanied it originally has been discarded. Even when captions are fixed to pictures it is extraordinary how often the senders forget to include their name, address, telephone number and/or e-mail address.

Care has to be taken to observe the requirements of the Copyright, Designs and Patents Act 1988. (For a summary of the act, visit http://www.copyrightservice.co.uk. A full copy of the act with amendments can be found at http://www.swarb.co.uk/acts/1988Copy DesPatAct.) Under this act, the photographer owns the copyright of the prints as well as the negatives, unless the work is produced as part of employment when, normally, the copyright belongs to the person/organization that hired that individual. The Computer Programs Regulations 1992 extended the rules to include computer programs and images. When the public relations practitioner commissions photography, he or she (or his or her organization) does not own the copyright unless there is a written assignment of the copyright. The act also gives the creators of any copyright work the right to control the ways in which material may be used. In many cases, the photographer will also have the right to be identified as the creator and to object to distortions and mutilations of his or her work (UKCS, 2003). This could relate to something as simple as retouching or amending a design or photograph. The public relations practitioner may be tempted to use photographs and other images from newspapers, agencies or, increasingly, the Internet. They must remember that copyright will be held by other people and that it may be necessary to pay them reproduction fees and/or print acknowledgements. These pictures cannot be distributed to illustrate a public relations story if the copyright does not belong to the practitioner or that authority has not been sought to reproduce it.

In April 2001, the European Union ministers gave final approval to harmonize copyright and 'related rights' across the Community (Directive 2001/29/EC can be found in full at http://eurorights.org/ eudmca/CopyrightDirective.html). The Directive places particular emphasis on media products and services, including those delivered online and by the Internet. The new rules, according to EU Commissioner Frits Bolkestein, bring 'European copyright rules into the digital age'. In effect, the Directive extended copyright to the Internet.

Distribution

Digital photography has begun to revolutionize the cost of producing and duplicating in-house photography. In an earlier edition, Jefkins (1994) correctly exhorted against avoiding wasteful distribution of pictures based on the cost of prints. Digital photography means that prints can now be kept to a minimum. Although cost is less of a consideration than in the past, the maxim that states 'pictures should be sent only to those publications likely to print them' still rings true.

Editors are normally inundated with pictures they cannot and will not use, and advances in technology are as likely as not to increase the flow. In such cases, editors will soon learn to ignore photographs from sources who continue to send then untargeted releases. On the other hand, if a picture supports and augments a publishable, newsworthy story for that publication, it is highly likely to get printed.

Working with the photographer

In many situations the PRO will want to use a photographer who will use his or her experience of lighting and composing a picture to produce a professional result. The photographer is not, however, an expert in *your* particular business. They should not be left to their own devices. The photographer cannot produce pictures that convey the right message unless the practitioner is clear in his or her mind what is wanted and instructs the photographer accordingly. The photographer is not a mind-reader. It is useless sending a photographer to take pictures unless he or she has been thoroughly briefed. In an ideal world, the practitioner should accompany the photographer, help to set up pictures, and even look in the viewfinder to see if the right picture has been composed.

Working with the printer

Even in this digital age, printed materials are of very great importance to the PR practitioner. Whether this is for presentation packs, folders, brochures, leaflets or signage, the PRO relies on the co-operation of a printer to carry out the work professionally.

Printing is a craft on its own, but one that is rapidly changing with the introduction of computerized technology. While the practitioner does not need to have expert knowledge of printing, it can increase his or her efficiency if he or she has a working knowledge of printing processes and techniques, and can work intelligently with printers. Moreover, as a manager he or she is a buyer. Quotations cannot be invited, compared, understood and accepted if the practitioner wholly lacks some technical knowledge.

There are three aspects to working with a printer:

1. A broad understanding of the different processes, so that the best process can be used for the job and suitable material can be supplied for printing by that process.
2. An understanding of production time schedules, so that a print job can be delivered by the desired date.
3. An understanding of proofreading and correction.

Print processes

Details of the various printing processes are beyond the scope of this text. PR practitioners are not so much interested in the minute technical detail rather than the eventual outcome. Many years ago, most magazines were printed by letterpress, then photogravure took over for large-circulation magazines such as the women's press and the Sunday newspaper colour magazines. In more recent years, many such magazines have been printed by web offset-litho. Similarly, while silk-screen printing was confined to short runs of rather crude posters, the process has become sophisticated with photographic reproduction, long runs and specialities such as printing vandal-proof posters on vinyl. Bus-side and other large posters can be printed by silk-screen (or simply screen) printing. Today, the principal costs are the quality of finish (determined by the paper/card quality, print and finish) and the quantity involved. On this last point, considerable savings can often be made by negotiating to fit conveniently into the printer's print-runs. For example, it is frequently considerably less expensive to print four leaflets in one run than the total cost of each produced separately. When producing specialist material such as folders or tri-fold leaflets (perhaps for a product launch), bear in mind standard sizing. The cost of producing a new cutting die for a special pack can be prohibitively expensive.

Working closely with your printer can produce advantages over time. There will always be the temptation to shop around for the cheapest package (indeed, in some organizations tendering is compulsory), but this may be detrimental in the longer term. Printing has gone through a revolution from craftsmen printers who were artists in metal, to keyboard operators and paste-up artists (more than likely computer generated), whose attitude to print is as different as that of horse-carriage drivers and motorists to transport. What cannot be mechanized, however, is creativity and it is in this regard that the PRO's influence can be most important.

Print production

Despite the advances in printing technology there is still normally a production delay between initial preparation and delivery of the finished product. The customer may want delivery by a certain date. The printer will say he can deliver by an agreed date provided a time schedule is followed. This is a discipline that must be followed, otherwise delays will result in rushed work and/or increased costs. Production has to be planned to cope with the different stages of different jobs for different customers. A print schedule may look something like the following:

Copy to printer	1 April
Proofs from printer	14 April
Corrected proofs to printer	21 April
Revised proofs from printer	28 April
Corrected revised proofs to printer	5 May
Delivery by printer	19 May

The use of software compatible with the printer (e.g. Quark Express) may help eliminate at least one of the printing proof revisions, as it enables the PRO to prepare mock-ups prior to submission to the printer. Whereas it may constrict the proofing, it should not replace it. To avoid costly work, it is wise to heed the printer's instructions on making corrections, and to understand at which stage further corrections should not be made.

Correcting proofs

Two things should be remembered about correcting proofs. Firstly, it is generally too late at this stage to start rewriting copy. However, if serious amendments are vital, they should be made in such a way that the length of the column or page is not exceeded, otherwise subsequent columns and pages will have to be altered to take in the overflow of extra material. When deleting and replacing copy, the new copy should consist of approximately the same number of characters. This is not, however, quite as crucial a feature as when the old, inelastic metal type was used. The modern software program can expand or condense type to fill more space or accept more copy, but only within certain parameters, without changing the overall layout.

Secondly, the corrections should be made clearly so that the printer can understand what is required. If you are using compatible software, changes may be made direct onto the file before returning this to the printer. If, as is still generally the case, manual corrections are made, they should not be scribbled all over the proof, but confined to the margins and the proper correction signs used. Proof correction signs have been changed in recent years to conform with international requirements. The long-used *stet* (meaning 'let it stand' when something has been deleted in error) has, for example, now been replaced by a tick in a circle. The current correction signs are shown in Figure 18.1.

The following advice may be helpful when correcting proofs:

- When manually correcting proofs, the author's corrections (i.e. changes introduced by the author or customer) should be made in black or blue. They may be chargeable!
- Corrections of printer's errors should be in red. (If the printer has read the proof he will make his own corrections in green.)
- Mentally divide the work with a vertical line down the middle, placing corrections on the left-hand half in the left-hand margin and those on the right-hand half in the right-hand margin.
- Read syllable by syllable slowly.
- Check headings, as errors here are frequently missed.

Instruction	Textual Mark	Marginal Mark
Correction is concluded	None	/
Leave unchanged	- - - - - - - - - under character to remain	✓
Push down risen spacing material	Encircle blemish	⊥
Insert in text the matter indicated in the margin	ʎ	New matter followed by ʎ
Insert additional matter identified by a letter in a diamond	ʎ	ʎ Followed by for example ⟨A⟩
Delete	/ through character(s) or ⊢——————⊣ through word(s) to be deleted	♂
Delete and close up	⌐/⌐ through character or ⊂————⊃ through character e.g. character character	♂
Substitute character or substitute part of one or more word(s)	/ through character or ⊢——————⊣ through word(s)	New character or new word(s)
Wrong fount. Replace by character(s) of correct fount	Encircle character(s) to be changed	⊗
Change damaged character(s)	Encircle character(s) to be changed	✕
Set in or change to italic	——— under character(s) to be set or changed	⊔⊔

Figure 18.1 Proof correction signs. Reproduced by permission of the British Printing Industries Federation.

Instruction	Textual Mark	Marginal Mark
Set in or change to capital letters	▬▬▬▬ under character(s) to be set or changed	═══
Set in or change to small capital letters	▬▬▬ under character(s) to be set or changed	══
Set in or change to capital letters for initial letters and small capital letters for the rest of the words	═══ under initial letters and ▬▬▬▬ under rest of word(s)	═══
Set in or change to bold type	∿∿∿∿∿ under character(s) to be set or changed	⌒⌒
Change capital letters to lower case letters	Encircle character(s) to be changed	╪
Change italic to upright type	Encircle character to be changed	⨆
Invert type	Encircle character(s) to be inverted	↺
Substitute or insert full stop or decimal point	/ through character or ⋏ where required	⊙
Substitute or insert semi-colon	/ through character or ⋏ where required	;
Substitute or insert comma	/ through character or ⋏ where required	,

Figure 18.1 (*Continued*)

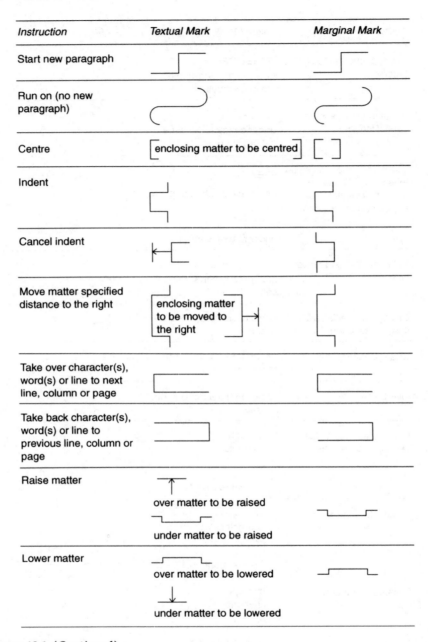

Instruction	Textual Mark	Marginal Mark
Start new paragraph		
Run on (no new paragraph)		
Centre	enclosing matter to be centred	
Indent		
Cancel indent		
Move matter specified distance to the right	enclosing matter to be moved to the right	
Take over character(s), word(s) or line to next line, column or page		
Take back character(s), word(s) or line to previous line, column or page		
Raise matter	over matter to be raised / under matter to be raised	
Lower matter	over matter to be lowered / under matter to be lowered	

Figure 18.1 (*Continued*)

Instruction	Textual Mark	Marginal Mark
Correct horizontal alignment	Single line above and below misaligned matter e.g. $mi_s{}_a{}^{li}g_n{}_e d$	‾‾‾‾‾ ‾‾‾‾‾
Close up. Delete space between characters or words	linking ⁀ characters	⁀
Insert space between characters	❘ between characters affected	Y
Insert space between words	between words ⋎ affected	⋎
Reduce space between characters	❘ between characters affected	⋏
Reduce space between words	between words ⋏ affected	⋏
Make space appear equal between characters or words	between characters or words affected ❘	⋎⋏

Figure 18.1 (*Continued*)

- Check the spelling of all names, especially those with alternative spellings such as Allan, Alan, Alain and Allen, Ann or Anne, Sidney and Sydney, or Davis and Davies.
- Check figures, especially when there are noughts involved.
- It is particularly important to double-check telephone numbers and e-mail addresses.
- Look up dates. It is easy to transfer dates from one year to another, or even look at the wrong year's calendar in a diary.
- Check prices. Have they changed? Is the currency correct?
- Watch out for transpositions of dates, such as 2030 for 2003.
- Check captions below illustrations. Are they accurate? If numbered, are these correct?

- Look out for blank spaces where copy has run short. Can you fill it, perhaps by introducing a subheading? In proofs based on computerized typesetting, watch out for long space gaps in lines, or wrongly broken words at the ends of lines. If an item is italicized, make sure that the typesetter has returned to roman where the italics should end.
- Look out for 'widows and orphans' (a widow is the last line of a paragraph printed by itself at the top of a page. An orphan is the first line of a paragraph printed by itself at the bottom of a page).
- Watch out for words like 'of' and 'or', which are commonly mistyped in original copy (or file) or misread by typesetters, and 'i's' and 'e's', which can result in 'blind' instead of 'blend'. One of the most difficult things about proofreading is spotting an error that could make sense because it forms a normal word, as in the last example. It also fools most spell-check programs used to scan the proof. Typesetters using computer software are apt not to worry about errors because they are so easy to correct, but the customer has to find them!

Finally, never be afraid to invite other people to check proofs, especially strangers to the copy, who may well find errors that are overlooked by readers who are so familiar with the copy that they tend to read into it what they expect to find there.

Managing media relations, with Sir Bernard Ingham, Bernard Ingham Communications

Sir Bernard Ingham is an Associate Professor at Middlesex University Business School and was formerly employed as Chief Press Secretary to Prime Minister Margaret Thatcher from 1979 until 1990. He has considerable experience in journalism and is currently running his own communications consultancy. He has written frequently for the national press on government communications. He is author of *Kill the Messenger* (HarperCollins, 1991), *The Wages of Spin* (John Murray, 2003) and the forthcoming *Kill the Messenger ... Again* (Politicos, 2003).

Interviewer: Sir Bernard, what I would like to talk about today is media relations and specifically what it was like in the past, what it is like today and how it has changed.

Sir Bernard: What I think you should first understand is that journalists of my generation had an entirely different upbringing. They were brought up to be accurate – and I mean dead accurate – fair and balanced, and to produce stories which were complete in themselves. There was very little nastiness around. I'm not saying there wasn't nastiness in the nationals. There was and always has been. There wasn't of course any television then. But in provinces, where the vast majority of journalists were, things were a little different. You've only got to read the *Kemsley Manual of Journalism*, which came out about 50 years ago, to realize how lofty a view Lord Kemsley himself took of journalism, how high minded was his approach.

The further you get from your readers in terms of proximity the more journalists try to get away with and the more in fact they do get away with. But in my time as a journalist the trade was driven by a certain ethic. We also had a certain view of 'rights' which journalists are forever demanding these days. I was brought up on a little local weekly in West Yorkshire never ever to assume any rights over and above those of any ordinary member of the public. We might be given privileges like a seat in the Council Chamber because that would be public service reporting, or a seat in the stand at the local soccer match because of our publicity, but we knew we had no rights and didn't demand any. What's more, our editors didn't want any rights because they feared that if they got them they might incur responsibilities they couldn't discharge. So there was a fairly moral base to journalism.

This made for very interesting relations with government information officers, as I discovered when I became one in 1967. But the point was that you could have a relationship as a press officer with that kind of journalist. Their retribution would have been very severe if they thought they had been lied to or misled or used. You had to be pretty open and transparent with them, and you would have been in pretty deep trouble if they thought you were using them.

If you refused to play or, for example, asked them not to use something they had gleaned, you had to convince them that you had a good reason or that some very serious consequences would result if they broke a story. If you had been caught lying to them, your credibility would have been lost. And if you had tried to lean on an editor or threaten him, then retribution would have been very swift. They would not take that at all. They were very hot on their independence. Now that sort of attitude continued during the 1950s and 1960s, but don't get me wrong: everything in the garden wasn't lovely. After all, we got a Press Council (forerunner of the Press Complaints Commission) in the early 1950s because of media excess – among other things, glamorizing crime. But the real problem lay in the snazzier national dailies and Sundays.

Then we came to the 1970s and it's not surprising that things should change. The 1960s were the years of radical change and not surprisingly the media was caught up in it. One of the symptoms of change was the BBC's satirical *That Was The Week That Was*, with David Frost and Gerald Kaufman among the performers. That contributed to an atmosphere of falling respect for institutions and individuals until precious little was left. Some would say that society became less hypocritical and humbuggy and more open. But reticence and respect disappeared down the plug hole. And with them went standards, a certain restraint and decency. What remained was nastier. And the media have continued to get nastier and the power of television has increased. And TV is very seductive to politicians who crave publicity.

I came into all this as a government press officer in 1967, having previously consumed the services of press officers, some of whom were helpful and some like a brick wall. But even in 1967 you could have a relationship with journalists, though it was becoming more difficult and was to become increasingly difficult as my career continued. The media have always had a high opinion of themselves, but we began to experience their growing conceit, their increasing sense of power and their increasing intrusion into private life. Not surprisingly, the Press Complaints Commission instituted more stringent definitions of privacy in the wake of Princess Diana's death – in which the media had a part whether they like it or not.

John Major, poor chap, caught the full blast of rampant journalism and it became increasingly difficult for him to manage relations with them. This brings me to the prime responsibility of the head of any public relations organization or press office: it is to manage relations with the media. That is what he is there for – to stop things going off the rails, as they can easily do. I lasted over 11 years as Prime Minister's press secretary, but it was a pretty close run thing in 1986, when you recall the Great Lobby Revolt that never was – when *The Guardian*, *The Independent* and *The Scotsman* tried to break up the lobby by withdrawing from my briefings, but not the lobby, and reporting on the record what they could pick up second hand from my unattributable lobby briefings. Nonetheless, I managed to survive for 11 years as a press secretary and we ended mostly on more or less good terms. Indeed, I attended a number of media parties in my honour when I retired on Mrs Thatcher's resignation in 1990 and the Communist *Morning Star* paid me a handsome tribute by saying that I had not discriminated against anybody.

Now, given the difficulties over intrusion, of nastiness, of increasing scepticism shading into cynicism over the whole process of government, I must admit that politicians have done nothing to help themselves. It is frankly difficult to be condemnatory of the media. They reflect what is going on and politicians have given them far too many openings.

How did it work out on the ground? In a curious way you find yourself caught between two moralities. First, there was the one I was brought up with which was reflected in the Civil Service press officers' code. And then there were the methods, attitudes and increasing cynicism of the media. Just to rehearse the main elements of the Civil Service ethos: first of all, 'You shall not lie'. By that I mean 'You shall not know-ingly lie'. I have to put in that qualification because it is very difficult at times to know what the truth is. You are very dependent on your informants but that teaches you, just as it teaches a journalist, to be very careful about your information and to check it. When I was dubious about things, I just did not perform in the authoritative way they per-haps expected me to. I would preface my guidance with the words 'So I am told' or 'I'm still checking' or 'I'm told this is the position' or what-ever – which just put that distance between me and my informants and their information.

People realized that I was being careful and that they should be care-ful too. So, thou shall not lie. That does not mean to say that you can tell the whole truth or indeed perhaps should tell the whole truth even if you are confident that you know it. If, for example, a journalist asks a narrow question, you give them a narrow answer. There is a big argu-ment as to whether you should give them a broad answer, but you know what they are like. You know that frequently they are fishing and that they are out to cause mischief and trouble. It may be, of course, that by answering only narrowly you might be storing up trouble for the future. On the other hand, you can say to them honestly that you gave them a straightforward answer to their straightforward question. It wasn't the full answer, but I don't habitually give you the full answer – and some-times I can't give you a full answer. But what you don't do is mislead.

The second thing is that you don't have favourites. If you are a ser-vant of the taxpayer you can't have favourites. You have to serve every-body equally in the dissemination of basic news. You give it out at a formally constituted meeting of the lobby or to the Press Association, which would make everyone privy to the information at exactly the same time. What you did when people rang you up to try to build on the story would inevitably depend on their record of reliability or unre-liability. You certainly could not take journalists at face value. But this is part of managing the media. You have to know their track record. Do they let you down? Sooner or later even the most reliable journalists may let you down for the simple reason they are under pressure because they are in a highly competitive business. It follows that if you don't have favourites in the dissemination of basic news you don't leak. And most certainly don't leak in the way that this government has systemat-ically leaked every announcement before formal publication to useful idiots, as Marx described 'poodles'.

Fourthly, and I made this an absolute article of faith – you do not challenge and try to browbeat people if they come up with comments on decisions or actions that do not please your political master or mistress. In a free society, people have a right to their opinions. You can only attack people when they have got their facts wrong or formed opinions based on 'mis-fact'. Therefore, I never ever challenge people's opinions. I might not have agreed with them, but they were entitled to them. By the same token I did not try to influence where a story came in the pecking order of news. If you have a free society, then a free media are entitled to decide what to lead on. I never argued with them before the event, though I might raise my eyebrows at their news values later. It was up to them to decide.

You may rightly conclude, because I was not a political appointee, that I had a much more relaxed approach to the media. I had. But so had my boss, Margaret Thatcher; we were much more relaxed than the current government have been. But we were operating under a different regime at a different time. 1997 was a complete watershed where Labour imported an entirely opportunistic, politically motivated creed into the management of media and the dissemination of information. They offended every known tenet that I had been brought up with. And all that I can say is: 'Look where it has got them.' Their approach has served this government very badly and has effectively destroyed this government's reputation for reliability and credibility inside three years.

That, I think, is my potted summary of how it was and now is and what's changed.

Interviewer: What would you say are the principles of good media relations?

Sir Bernard: Know your subject. Establish a reputation for accuracy, reliability, speed and access and integrity. I think you are nowhere if you don't have a reputation. The media don't have much of a reputation so I think a communicator should retain the moral high ground. You are in a much stronger position if you do so. Reliability, accuracy, being there when you are needed, speed, obviously an appreciation of what the media needs, a refusal to play games and a determination to establish a long-term reputation and maintain it. You either are a credible informant or an incredible informant. The tragedy of this government is that it has a lot of incredible informants.

Interviewer: One of the topics from the book is crisis management. I would like to talk to you a little about that. What approaches do you think one should adopt in crisis situations?

Sir Bernard: I do not think crises can be divorced from your everyday work. It is in the day-to-day relationships with journalists that you establish your reputation as a press officer. There is no point in assuming that if you don't have a reputation as a result of day-to-day work that you can serve your organization well when it has a crisis. Good crisis management stems from years of relationships with journalists who feel they have a voice at court, as it were; who feel they have a chap there who understands what they require. He may not always deliver – the more sensible journalists recognize that – but he is a chap with a track record and will help, if he possibly can. That is the first point.

The second point turns on what authority the spokesman has in the organization, which is another facet of reputation. His authority is crucial in a crisis. If you have some authority you can, to a degree, control the strategy adopted by the organization. If you are not in control, what happens is that, because all organizations are appalling bureaucracies (which by definition are secretive and not open), the amateurs, the silly naive amateurs, take over. They believe they can keep things under wraps, believe they can get away with playing for time, with half-truths, utterly oblivious of the consequences if they are found out. The result is that the organization behaves just as the government did in the property dealing crisis involving Cherie Blair and just as it has done in every crisis since the beginning – from [Formula 1 boss] Ecclestone to the Hinduja brothers and Mittal. It all comes out in dribs and drabs. In a crisis you need a professional, competent, credible, reputable press officer in on the discussions and controlling the strategy. If you don't have one, then it soon shows. The objective must be to act decisively as soon as you know the facts – and get the facts in the round over to the media. Otherwise, you are not in control. You may not always be in control even if you have done all that because the media may twist things. You can deal with their twisting things you have been open about. But you can't deal with them twisting things you have tried to keep quiet because you start with an immense disadvantage. I must say that this philosophy is not very often adopted. But in my view the crucial relationship in handling a crisis is that between the boss and his head PR man. It is what sorts out the wheat from the chaff.

Interviewer: This is a different type of question. Who would you say is doing a good job of managing media relations?

Sir Bernard: You mean today? The difficulty with this question is that the people who are managing them best are by definition unsung. They are not having crises. They are having a steady relationship. The short answer is that I don't know. You will not know until you see how they handle a crisis. The one thing that is absolutely clear to me is that you can't rely on even such well-provisioned giants as Shell handling a crisis, bearing in mind its Brent Spar problem. I can't honestly say they handled that very well. The problems of measuring good handling are very complex. Probably the best press officer you have is the one you put on to the most difficult stories, which he kills because of his credibility and his deployment of the facts. But no-one knows how well you managed that one – and you don't want them to know either.

Interviewer: Where did you get some of your inspiration from?

Sir Bernard: I was brought up with some of the pioneers who were age-ing by 1967. People like Sir Fife Clark, Don Bickerton, Henry James [at No. 10], Peter Brown [Department of Social Security] and Charles Birdsall [Department of Employment]. All these people had been there in the Government Information Service for a very long time. They gave off the kind of philosophy that I have talked about. I think they gave me a very good start in life because of the way they conducted their affairs. They were also operating in an entirely different atmosphere then – when press officers had to fight for their place in the sun. But they were seen as people of calibre and personality, and I sought to continue to uphold their ethic. There are, of course, entirely different kinds of people employed as press officers. I recall in the seminars I conduct chief information officers who never wrote anything – well certainly no more than half a side of A4. Yet they were really up to date because they were *par excellence* news gatherers who patrolled and trawled their department to find out what was going on. Others were writers – and I was one of these – who, quite apart from newsgathering and reading papers, sought, if you like, to win on paper and I think if you can express things on paper with clarity and get it down first you are a long way ahead of the game when it comes to controlling the briefing line. But press officers come in all shapes and sizes and inclinations, and all have their merits. I was lucky to work with those who laid the founda-tions for the Government Information Service. The public relations industry is certainly very worried about the current ethos of media management.

Interviewer: A final question if I may. Lobbying: how do you think lobbying has changed over the last 20 or 30 years?

Sir Bernard: It has become institutionalized. Previously, organizations such as Chambers of Commerce, the CBI [Confederation of British Industry] and major institutions had their relationships with govern-ment in frankly a more corporatist state and put their concerns directly to government. But now, with the rise of NGOs [non-governmental organizations] and pressure groups and under, I suppose, American influence and European influence and the increasing intrusion of gov-ernment into our lives, we find every organization, every charity, every pressure group in the business of lobbying. Pressure groups are a very interesting development in the way they have made a beeline for the media, especially in the environmental area. Indeed, many of these pressure groups have become creatures of the media. They put on a show. At any rate, lobbying is now an institutionalized sport, but it seems to work more through special advisers than ministers or MPs under Blair's centralized regime. So many people are now at it that I regard lobbying as a Tower of Babel; it may be self-defeating unless you have a very serious point with serious implications for votes at the next election. They will sit up and take notice then.

I can't honestly say things have improved. The implication today seems to be it's who you know rather than the strength of your argument that really matters – or that it's the stunt you can pull with some so-called 'celebrity' that impresses people rather than the intrinsic worth of your case. Perhaps all you can do is shout and resort to celebrities and stunts if your arguments wouldn't convince a kindergarten.

Interviewer: Thank you, Sir Bernard.

Chapter links

Chapter 12 – The role of the press officer
Chapter 26 – Crisis management
Chapter 29 – Public relations in political context

Part 4

Communication Media

Chapter 19

The press and broadcast sources

LEARNING OBJECTIVES

At the end of this chapter you will be able to:

- understand the workings of the UK and overseas press;
- outline the important advantages and disadvantages of television as a PR medium;
- recognize the value of radio as a potential PR medium.

The press

The press in the UK and around the world is still an important mass medium. British public relations is remarkably lucky in having access to thousands of publications, including the relative novelty (until more recently) of a national press. For most of the twentieth century, few industrialized countries had the benefit of a centralized national press, but rather suffered a fragmented localized press. The reason for this is largely historical and geographical. London has been the British capital for many hundreds of years. Other countries have had various capitals, or they are either federations of former kingdoms and the old capitals remain as press centres (e.g. Italy), or there have been partitions and new capitals (e.g. Korea). It may also be a question of distance, as in Australia and the USA, which has resulted in city-based rather than nation-based newspapers. The exceptions in the USA are *USA Today*, a relative newcomer, and the *Wall Street Journal*.

The press is one of the most versatile and resilient of all mass communications media. Sophisticated electronic media has, despite some predictions, not destroyed the press in industrial countries. Indeed, the press has embraced the new media and almost all have associated websites with updated news and views.

Special merits and characteristics of the press

Depth of information

Publications can provide information in greater depth than transient broadcasting media. The extent of this will depend on the class of the newspaper, ranging from a brief account in a popular tabloid to more elaborate coverage in the business press or in magazines devoted to the subject.

Portability

A newspaper can be read anywhere; about the home or office, while travelling, sitting out of doors, over a meal, while waiting somewhere, and at times and in places beyond the reach of much electronic media.[1] Newspapers and magazines are portable and can be carried almost anywhere, or they may be supplied at the reading point, such as in a waiting room or reception area.

Extended life

Publications often have an extended life because they are kept in binders supplied by some magazines, or back numbers may be looked up in libraries, or because copies are passed on to other people. This is proved by the number of enquiries and orders which advertisers receive weeks, months and even years after publication. For some, this extended life is deliberate, as with the *Radio Times*, *TV Times* and other listings magazines that are published about four days in advance, are referred to daily after that, and so survive for at least ten days.

---

[1] WAP technology has yet to take hold of the popular imagination and may never do, if it is superseded by more effective technologies.

New types of newspapers and magazines

With the development of new printing presses we have seen better typography and half-tone photographic reproduction, while colour pictures have become common in both national and regional newspapers. Generally, the quality of printing has improved, and we see this especially in the glossier, more colourful magazines printed by web offset-litho, taking advantage of better quality paper, richer pigmented inks, finer half-tone screens and computerized photo-typesetting. The growth and popularity of the magazines supplied with weekend newspapers has seen the arrival of new titles, and with their ready-made readerships they have been attractive to both advertisers and readers at the expense of the traditional large-circulation consumer weeklies, especially women's magazines.

The downside

There are fewer home-delivered newspapers than in the past. Many younger people never buy a newspaper. The number of dailies and Sunday tiles has stagnated over the past 20 years. The habit of buying an evening paper on the way home has diminished. There is (currently) only one London evening newspaper (*Evening Standard*). Its former rival, the *Evening News*, once used to boast the highest evening newspaper sales in the world.

Newspapers (as opposed to magazines) can have short lives, and a morning paper may survive no more than a commuter's journey to work. Consequently, one has to be wary of the large circulation and readership figures claimed for them. It is worth remembering at this stage that the circulation is the net average sales over a period, usually six months. That means that there can be days or weeks when sales are below or above the average. Readership is a very different thing. It is not a strictly counted and audited figure, but an estimated figure of primary and secondary readership based on an interviewed sample, and it takes into consideration that people other than the original purchaser may also read the publication. It is therefore important to interpret figures carefully. A business newspaper like the *Financial Times* could have a small circulation but, because of pass-round, reception room and library readership, it has a high readership figure.

Another potential problem with circulation figures is that not every section of a paper is likely to be read by every reader. Those who read the sports pages may never read the city pages and vice versa. In calculating 'opportunities to see' readership figures for press cuttings, it may be necessary to estimate the *proportion* of a readership figure that will actually read the *part* of the publication from which the cutting was clipped. As an example of this, a reading and noting test showed that the most read feature in the *Financial Times* was not the financial news but the digest of general news on the front page. Similarly, we should not be deluded by the multimillion circulation and readerships claimed for popular tabloids. A story in the *Sun* may be hardly noticed, whereas the same story in *The Times* could be much more carefully studied, yet the former's sales are ten times those of the latter.

Bias

Most newspapers and magazines have their particular bias so that either they do not print certain stories or, if they do, they may distort them to take account of their particular viewpoint. You only have to look at the headlines and/or the editorials in the *Daily Mail* compared to the *Daily Mirror* or *The Guardian* as opposed to the *Daily Telegraph*. There is rarely objective reporting in the press, and it is often true that a good, factual news release from a professional public relations source is more impartial than the average newspaper report. *The Guardian* and *The Observer*, for instance, have been known to adopt an attitude of mock intellectualism and parody public relations events or stories, whereas the *Financial Times* welcomes and uses public relations material. In sending news stories to the press, it is wise to understand the peculiar traits of those publications.

Editorial bias has to be understood and accepted. It may derive from political, religious, class, ethnic or simply proprietarily attitudes. Rarely do these attitudes change,[2] unless there is a major change in ownership.[3] Bias can be observed by studying the way different newspapers treat the same story, and it has to be reckoned with when sending releases to the press or inviting journalists to press receptions. Some papers may be best omitted from media and invitation lists. It is not only public relations people who are responsible for the adversarial situation.

Unreliability of reporting

Newspapers, especially, can be unreliable in their reporting, either because of the speed with which they are produced or because journalists cannot be expected to know everything about a particular subject, and they cannot know for certain whether the stories they receive are either

---

[2] The major exception to this was the *Sun* newspaper's switch from supporting the Conseravives to supporting Labour in advance of the 1997 General Election.
[3] Arguably, the *Daily Express* newspaper has been the most recent example.

true or accurate. Unfortunately, readers are apt to believe what they read in the papers on the optimistic assumption that it would not be printed if it were not true. As the oft-quoted maxim states, 'mud sticks'.

Behind this sort of controversy lies the illusion of the freedom of the press, and the idea that the press is a democratic fourth estate. Far from the public relations world attempting to manipulate the press, it is more often nearly the case of the press exploiting public relations opportunities. However, to be realistic and to avoid being too contentious, the publishers are entitled to print what is most likely to sell papers, whether it be a law report in *The Times*, a knitting pattern in *Woman's Weekly* or a model's vital statistics in the *Sun*. In public relations terms, this means that stories are most likely to be printed if editors consider them, in the words of Ivy Ledbetter Lee (quoted in Jefkins, 1994), to be of *interest and value* to their particular readers. The PRO, in submitting press material, has to reconcile him or herself to the facts of life about a commercially owned press and the peculiarities of democracy in a free enterprise society which may not always work in his or her favour.

Location and distribution

Britain has both a national and a regional or local press. London, having been the capital for centuries, also became the country's press centre when good road and rail communications and a more urbanized population made it economic to produce national newspapers. The first popular national daily was Northcliffe's ha'penny *Daily Mail* of 1896. Overseas visitors are sometimes puzzled to find local weekly newspapers in Britain which have circulations as large as their national newspapers, and to be even more bewildered by the presence of free newspapers with circulations of maybe 100 000 copies weekly. There are about 850 free newspapers! The volume of the British press is phenomenal, and it is not therefore surprising that press relations forms such an important part of public relations.

If we take round figures, the circulations of the London-based British national dailies were roughly as shown in Table 19.1 in 2001 (the 1992 estimated circulation figures are shown for comparison).

Circulation figures are issued every six months, and result from publishers returning audited figures for the number of copies printed, given away and actually sold to the Audit Bureau of Circulations (ABC), which certifies the average net sale for over 2000 publications per week. Readership figures result from interviewing members of the public to discover which publications they read, and the demographic details (e.g. age, sex, occupation, etc.) of those readers. One is an arithmetic calculation, the other is the result of a national readership survey of 28 000

Table 19.1 Circulation of major UK newspapers

	2002/3*	1992
Sun	3 576 406	3 500 000
Daily Mirror	2 088 469	2 800 000
Daily Express	980 646	1 500 000
Daily Mail	2 452 051	1 700 000
Daily Star	784 654	800 000
Daily Telegraph	960 442	1 000 000
The Guardian	404 551	400 000
The Independent	221 962	380 000
The Times	682 446	380 000
Financial Times	715 000	290 000

* September 2002 to February 2003.
Source: adapted from www.abc.org.uk and Jefkins (1994)

households conducted by an independent research company on behalf of National Readership Surveys (NRS). Freesheets or local newspapers use the VFD (Verified Free Distribution) system.

NRS represents the publishers, advertising agencies and advertisers through their trade associations, and is thus a tripartite body servicing all sides of the industry. While it operates primarily in the interests of advertising, the findings published in the National Readership Surveys are valuable when evaluating media and public relations coverage. Thus, NRS is also independent compared to surveys that are occasionally conducted by individual publishers.

Readership figures are still classified according to the social grades A, B, C1, C2, D and E, although there has been pressure to upgrade these classifications. These NRS social class definitions represent employment as distinct from socio-economic grades based on income. The latter are still not used widely in Britain.

NRS social grades

Social grades in Britain may be described briefly as follows:

A	Upper middle class	Higher managerial, administrative or professional
B	Middle class	Intermediate managerial, administrative or professional
C1	Lower middle class	Supervisory or clerical, and junior managerial

C2	Skilled working class	Skilled working class
D	Working class	Semi-skilled and unskilled manual workers
E	Those at lowest level	Pensioners, casual workers, those on subsistence or dependent on social security

The British mass market thus consists of about three-quarters of the population, the readership of popular newspapers and the audience for peak viewing television. In a seemingly class-conscious country such as Britain, the national newspapers can be ranked against social grades, roughly as follows:

A	*The Times, Financial Times*
B	*Daily Telegraph, The Guardian, The Independent*
C1	*Daily Express, Daily Mail*
C2, D, E	*Sun, Daily Mirror, Daily Star, Daily Sport*

Types of publication

Daily morning newspapers

Daily morning newspapers are usually published six times a week, that is, except on Sunday in Christian countries (or Friday or Saturday where other religions predominate). However, new technologies have brought about some changes over the past few decades:

- Direct-input computerized editing and new printing technologies are enabling later copy times and dates.
- Locally printed editions, using facsimile and satellite services, are leading to editions being printed simultaneously at strategically situated printers. In the USA, *USA Today* was the first American daily, being printed at 53 US locations and also in Europe and Asia.
- Some newspapers, such as the *Financial Times*, have achieved international circulations by sending copy by satellite to printers in distant parts of the world. The *International Herald Tribune* is another printed simultaneously in Paris, London, Hong Kong, Singapore and other cities round the world.
- Most London newspapers have moved from Fleet Street, the traditional home of newpapers, to modern offset-litho printing works located in East London, or they print at strategically located contract printers outside London.

Regional or city daily morning newspapers

Outside Britain, it is common for morning newspapers to circulate within certain population areas, with perhaps a fringe circulation penetrating further afield. Even world-famous titles such as the *Washington Post*, the *Sydney Morning Herald* and *Il Messaggero di Roma* are generally restricted to their city of origin. In Britain, there are long-established regional morning papers that compete with the nationals, although they tend traditionally to have a more middle-class or business readership. Some of the best-known regional newspapers are the *Liverpool Daily Post*, the *Birmingham Post* and the *Yorkshire Post*.

In addition to the English regional mornings, there are similar papers published in Scotland, Wales and Northern Ireland, which really have their own national press, again in competition with the London nationals. There are the *Glasgow Herald* and *The Scotsman* in Scotland, the *Western Mail* in Wales, and the *Belfast Telegraph* in Northern Ireland. In the Republic of Ireland, Irish nationals such as the *Irish Times*, *Irish Independent* and *The Examiner* compete with the UK nationals printed in Dublin or Belfast.

Interesting variations occur in other countries. The popular German *Bild* (which is more sensationalist than the British *Sun*) has a huge multimillion circulation made up of local editions published in several German cities. In the USA, there are chains of newspapers which appear under separate city titles, but contain some standard material which is syndicated nationally to all newspapers.

Local weekly (or bi-weekly) newspapers

Britain's weekly newspapers tend to fall into three groups: (a) those published in the suburbs of cities like London, Glasgow and Manchester; (b) town weeklies; and (c) regional series or county newspapers. In Britain, most towns, and even suburbs of the largest cities, have their own weekly newspapers. In Greater London there are big circulation weeklies, and a number of groups like the *Croydon Advertiser* and *Kentish Times* with separate editions carrying the titles of nearby towns or boroughs. The *Croydon Advertiser* group includes papers covering many surrounding districts. Particularly popular around London, these periodicals can be the source of very local news. They include papers such as the *South London Press* or the *Hendon Times*. These local papers include many that are distributed free to householders (e.g. the *Dulwich & Streatham Guardian*).

Evening newspapers

This is a rather ambiguous description, because so-called 'evening' newspapers often have early editions appearing in the morning, follow-up sports editions and lunchtime editions until the main city edition appears as people are going home from work. Publishers may publish up to ten editions during the day. The London evening newspaper, the *Evening Standard*, has a fringe circulation up to 50 miles from London, but within 40 miles of the capital, and in most of the large cities of England, Scotland, Wales and Northern Ireland there are regional evening newspapers. While the number of regional titles has shrunk from the days when several cities including London had two if not three evening newspapers, there are still around 100 dailies published outside London, most of them evening papers.

Examples range from the *Liverpool Echo* to the *Brighton Evening Argus*, which is close enough to London to have to compete with the *Evening Standard*. These newspapers cover many popular topics and can be valuable for public relations purposes. While circulation figures are quite large, most evening newspapers show a falling circulation. This is partly due to the impact of the increase in free newspapers.

Sunday newspapers

The majority of British Sunday newspapers are national, but there are a few regional ones, and there are 'national' Sundays in Scotland and Northern Ireland.

A similar social grading breakdown can be made with Sunday newspapers, except that the 'heavies' do not correspond with *The Times* and the *Financial Times*, and they have larger middle-class circulations. The breakdown is as follows:

A, B	*Sunday Times, The Observer, Sunday Telegraph, The Independent on Sunday*
C1	*Sunday Express, Mail on Sunday*
C2, D, E	*News of the World, Sunday People, Sunday Mirror, Sunday Sport*

The English regional Sunday newspapers are the Birmingham *Sunday Mercury*, the Newcastle-upon-Tyne *Sunday Sun* and the Plymouth *Sunday Independent*. Scotland has its Glasgow *Sunday Mail* and *Sunday Post*, while Northern Ireland has its *Sunday News* and *Sunday World*, which also circulates in parts of the Irish Republic.

Magazines

In industrialized countries there may be hundreds of titles. These can be divided into various categories:

- *Consumer magazines.* Covering popular subjects, many of these magazines have large circulations of hundreds of thousands, frequently more than a million. Sometimes called 'specialist' magazines, they cover every possible interest, such as food, sports, hobbies, gardening, politics, religion, travel, fashion, motoring, house-buying and many other topics. They are called consumer magazines because they are bought by members of the general public and sold by newsagents. A visit to a High Street newsagent or to a bookstall at a large railway station will give a good idea of the range of interests catered for. Most are printed in colour. One of the most successful and interesting groups of consumer magazines, in which there are today many subgroups, is that of the women's press. Traditional titles such as *The Lady* (1885) and *Woman's Weekly* (1911) compete with newcomers *OK!* and *Hello!*
- *Listings magazines.* These include the *Radio Times, TV Times, TV Quick* and *What's On TV.* They contain large editorial sections devoted to broadcast entertainment.
- *In-flight magazines.* A specialized group of magazines that offer opportunities for public relations articles of interest to travellers and tourists are the in-flight magazines to be found in the passenger seat pockets of nearly every airline.
- *Trade, technical and professional magazines.* Trade magazines are published for the benefit of a business readership, whether they are aimed at distributors such as wholesalers, retailers, agents, brokers; technicians such as electricians, builders, engineers and other craftsmen; professionals such as lawyers, doctors, architects, teachers and others. If the subject is very specialized, the national (or perhaps international) circulation will be small. There are exceptions, such as those British and American journals (e.g. *Lancet*) that are so authoritative that they are widely read abroad. Such journals often incorporate 'International' in their titles, e.g. *Coffee and Cocoa International, International Drinks Bulletin*, and *Conferences, Exhibitions and Incentives International.* The British Medical Association earns considerable income from the international sale of its medical journals.

These are all very useful publications for public relations purposes, but the size of circulation, coverage of the trade, industry or profession, and consequently their impact and influence, may depend on the method of distribution. This may also influence the type of material carried, i.e. mostly news or mostly feature articles. Do readers *subscribe* to it, which could mean that the circulation is not large since it is dependent on payment? Is it *mailed to members* of an organization? If so, the circulation will depend on the size of the membership, but it would mean an official and regular distribution. Or does it have a *controlled circulation* – that is, mailed free of charge to a combination of selected readers and those who have requested copies? Most of the circulation of *PR Week* is of this order. Controlled circulation figures can be impressive, meaning good penetration of the subject area. The public relations practitioner also needs to be aware of the very different content of journals with similar titles.

- *Directories, year books, annuals, diaries.* In some of these annual publications entries are free, in others they are paid for, while in all cases charges are made for more prominent or more displayed entries. Absence from such publications, or inadequate information, can be very bad public relations, giving the impression that an organization is of too little consequence to be listed. It is therefore a managerial responsibility on the part of either the in-house PRO or the consultant to see that an organization is properly listed wherever possible. Certain yearbooks and diaries give advice to readers, and it will be in the public relations practitioner's interest to make sure that such published advice is correct, up to date or refers to the company's products or services if this is permissible.

A problem when compiling mailing lists is that the titles themselves may not define the nature of the journals or their readership, and unless this is known (or can be found from the various directories, e.g. BRADs), it is very easy to send stories to the wrong publications. This is not only a waste but it can irritate editors, who will expect their journals to be better known to the PRO. Standard mailing lists are rarely satisfactory (unless the same publications are relevant every time), and it is best to compile tailor-made lists for each occasion (see Chapter 14).

How to know the press

Some tips on developing a greater knowledge of the press are the following:

- Study newspapers and magazines at first hand as often as possible. They change infrequently. Look at them in libraries. Browse through copies in newsagents' shops, or at railway or airport news-stands. This is easy and can be a valuable and informative habit.
- Read the profiles on publications in *Benn's Media Directory* or *BRADs* (*British Rates & Data*).

- Make use of the media lists supplied by the *PR Handbook*.
- Keep up to date with news of new publications and publishing plans as announced in *UK Press Gazette*.
- Talk as often as possible to editors and journalists, at events such as press receptions, on the phone or whenever you meet. Always ask them what they want and when they want it.

Press relations has to be worked at, and it often calls for selectivity. It is wiser to send a story to one journal and get 100 per cent coverage than to broadcast it hopefully to 100 journals, get only one cutting, and achieve only 1 per cent coverage!

Broadcasting

How broadcasting media differ from the press

Broadcasting media are very different from the press, and television and radio have their special advantages and disadvantages. They do have one thing in common, which is that they are transient unless recorded on video, DVD, CD or audiotape. Unlike printed messages, it is difficult to retain broadcast messages. They usually have to be absorbed at the time of transmission, and one has to be satisfied with instant impact, and to remember that the message may, as a result, be misunderstood or forgotten.

These electronic media can, however, be extremely valuable when the public relations manager or consultant is planning public relations programmes, if they are understood and used properly, especially as audiences may well exceed the readerships of newspapers or magazines. Although the surfeit of new terrestrial, cable, satellite and digital channels in Britain has lowered the audience for individual channels (see Chapter 19), a networked television programme may have an audience of perhaps 10 million viewers. For example, more than 14 million people watched Martin Bashir's documentary on Michael Jackson on ITV1 on 3 February 2003.

Television

It is difficult to generalize about television because there are different systems in operation around the world. In the USA there are many commercial television stations in each city, whereas in Britain there is the national BBC (non-commercial) and regional commercial stations and Good Morning TV (known as ITV) plus Channel 4 and 5. The satellite revolution has seen the introduction of many new channels (see Table 17.2) covering many niche markets. Digital broadcasting has led to the recent introduction of BBC3 (formally BBC Choice), BBC4 (formally BBC Knowledge), ITV2 and E4. BBC and Independent Television (the ITV Network) also have some regional programmes. The programmes may be on BBC1 and 2 or ITV and may also be broadcast partly or wholly nationally or even at different times or on different days.

In Singapore there are programmes in English, Indian and Chinese, but in Indonesia they are entirely in the national languange. The expressions 'commercial' and 'sponsored' television have different meanings in some countries. Until relatively recently, commercial television in Britain meant that a company such as Granada would be responsible for the programmes, and would sell advertising time usually in two-minute slots. In the USA there is a long tradition of sponsorship that has only recently been introduced in the UK. Cadbury, for example, sponsor *Coronation Street*, whilst Stella Artois sponsor Channel 4 films. In Nigeria there is also both brief commercials and whole programmes (mainly sports such as major and often international football or athletics) sponsored by companies such as Coca-Cola, Cadbury's or Guinness, with interpolated commercials. The time allotted to sponsorship credits in the UK is very brief, but creative firms such as Media Dimensions have exploited the opportunities very cleverly.

A number of musical programmes have been made in association with the BBC, including the Young Musician of the Year competition sponsored on BBC TV by Lloyds Bank, who also sponsor fashion shows seen on BBC TV. Meanwhile, BSkyB has sponsored the Cricket World Cup and Premier League football.

Sponsorships on commercial radio are common, but are more localized because there are so many ILR stations. There are a number of national shows (e.g. Pepsi Charts), but these are in the minority. Both commercial radio and TV sponsorships are strictly controlled by the separate sponsorship codes of the Radio Authority and the Independent Television Commission. Primarily, this kind of sponsorship is a form of advertising, as distinct from the kind of sponsorship described in Chapter 27. This latter type of sponsorship could be for advertising, marketing or public relations, but it seeks media coverage on its merits and this coverage will be at the discretion of the media. For instance, a company may sponsor a football strip, as Vodafone do at Manchester United, and viewers of a match in which the team is playing, both at the ground and on TV, will be aware of Vodafone sponsorship. Similarly, when the results of various cricket and football matches are broadcast, the sponsor's name will be given, e.g. Barclaycard Premiership. So, too, with horse-racing, whether it be the Whitbread Gold Cup or the Vodafone Derby. Games, races or results will be broadcast independently by the TV and radio stations, and no payment will have been made for this air time. One of the most amusing sponsorships was Specsavers opticians sponsoring of Scottish Premier referees!

However, while the new kind of broadcasting sponsorships may be undertaken for advertising purposes, and they have proved to be very economical, they do nevertheless have a certain public relations content. This occurs in two ways. It can be very appropriate to associate a product with a characteristic programme, and it can also be a good thing to associate a product with a programme which is well liked, so that the product shares in this goodwill. It is significant, for instance, that the three characters Rumpole, Maigret and Inspector Morse all enjoy a drink, and their sponsors are all drinks firms. They are also, all three, distinguished and well-liked programmes. Matching the product to the character, the programme to the social grade of the viewer is important and beneficial.

While the convention of a balance between entertainment, information and education may be the ideal, the tendency is for television to lean towards popular entertainment, especially with the competition between stations for viewers.

Characteristics of television

- Programmes are watched mostly in the home or other social settings, but may also be seen in schools and workplaces such as offices.
- While not as captive as a cinema audience, the television audience has to view the programmes in a particular place, and remain seated. The viewer cannot (generally[4]) be mobile like a radio listener.
- The blend of sound, movement, colour and realism is its greatest asset.
- It is a *visual* medium. Viewers do tend to watch rather than listen to television. This means that people such as a company chairman or other representative of an organization should be visually interesting. This can be through the way they dress, but more especially how they look physically. Television tends to caricature people, highlighting their oddities. This can be critical and can demolish even famous people if they do not come over well. Very few politicians are successful on the small screen. The PRO should be careful not to rush the chief executive on to television, unless this person looks *interesting* and is sufficiently *articulate* to hold his or her own with an interviewer! Television familiarization courses can be attended, prospective interviewees being trained in interview techniques under studio conditions.
- An important aspect of television has been its ability to introduce new interests to viewers, who take them up actively and want to know

---

[4] In-car television is not widespread. There are other exceptions, such as in coaches and trains.

more about them. This leads to a demand for information in more detailed and permanent form, such as new magazines, new newspaper features and new books.

- It is possible to record and play back programmes, to show one's own programmes with video cassettes, and to call up teletext or digital information, always provided that the viewer has the necessary equipment.

Disadvantages of television

- Facilities, such as a factory or office background, are often requested and an organization can go to a lot of trouble without gaining much, if any, credit for it. If such premises are used, it is best if they are recognizable by viewers.
- Television can be very time-consuming, both in the negotiations and in the actual shooting. Many hours may be spent on rehearsal and shooting to produce a few minutes of scene time. However, that has to be weighed against the size of the audience.
- If an organization is asked to provide someone for a programme made up of several interviews, the edited version may be disconcerting when it is found that bits of interviews have been paired with bits from other interviews to produce a controversial juxtapositioning not apparent during the original shooting.
- Television can be a wasteful medium, not only of the PRO's or the organization's time, but of audiences. Is the audience of relevance for the public relations message?

There may be times when it is wise to reject approaches from television producers who are concerned only with exploiting an organization or a personality for programme purposes. No company or individual is obliged to accept an invitation to be interviewed! The negative and even damaging effects of television appearances have to be considered. On the other side of the coin, non-appearance may create its own perceptions!

Radio

Perhaps the feature that makes radio different from all other mass media, and of special interest to the public relations practitioner, is that it can often be an instantaneous medium. Immediate announcements can be made on the radio. This immediacy has been valuable in ending a war (Morocco), calming the effects of a coup (Nigeria) and stopping a riot (Singapore). In Britain, the state of the share market, traffic conditions and road diversions, the cancelling of trains, the arrival times of aircraft, sports results, requests for information by the police, and exchange rates for those going abroad are typical examples of instant news and information provided by radio. Local radio (both BBC and ILR) have greatly increased this service, and much of it is derived from public relations sources or is a form of public relations. Digital radio is currently in its infancy, but it can be expected that there will soon be commercial rivals to the BBC's Radio 1X, 5Extra, 6 and 7.

Characteristics

- In contrast to the visual nature of television, radio has the intimacy of the human voice, and therefore requires voices that please the ear. The history of radio is one of famous (or infamous) voices. For example, Franklin Delano Roosevelt, Sir Winston Churchill, J. B. Priestley, Richard Dimbleby or, more recently, presenters such as Chris Tarrant or Zoe Ball.
- Not unlike a newspaper, radio can be portable (either as a player such as a Walkman or as a service on a Nokia mobile telephone). Many sets may exist in one household, or a portable set can be carried from room to room. Vehicles are nearly all fitted with radios; they are often installed in public places – for example, a hospital – where headphones may be used without disturbing others in hospital beds. Radio can be listened to while doing many jobs in factories, on building sites, or while making deliveries. It is often used as background in eating establishments around the country.
- Many listeners may tune in at particular times during the day. There are the breakfast-time listeners who want to check the time and traffic, the commuters, people at work, the businesspeople driving in their cars, the homecoming motorists, and younger people who often listen at night. The radio audience differs from the television audience, with its peak hours during the middle evening. Consequently, the PRO can reach particular radio audiences if the material is properly timed for certain programmes.
- Radio has long been an effective way of reaching people of different ethnic groups and languages in developing countries, including large numbers of people who cannot read, through either personal or public radios. It is easier and more practical to produce a radio programme in several languages, or to broadcast locally in the appropriate language, than to publish vernacular newspapers which people may or may not be able to read. With the relaxation of barriers to broadcasting, many ethnic groups have set up their own services (e.g. Turkish Radio). The BBC has also recently launched Radio 1X aimed at a black music audience and Asian Network.
- Many people around the world listen in to overseas programmes transmitted by the BBC World Service, Voice of America and others.

The British World Service in English has programmes which discuss new British products and achievements, and this can be useful to PROs interested in international public relations. Many people in Singapore, for instance, listen to the British World Service throughout the day. It broadcasts 18 news bulletins every 24 hours. The BBC External Services also broadcasts foreign-language programmes. Some people in Third World countries are critical, however, of foreign broadcasts, regarding them as propaganda from foreign cultures.

- In Britain, the local radio stations of the BBC and Independent Radio usually cover a smaller area than the regional television stations, which makes them ideal for local information such as traffic and public transport announcements. Community radio may become an even more localized form of broadcasting. Some organizations (e.g. hospitals) and large showgrounds (e.g. Frankfurt Messe) have their own radio stations in a narrowly defined area.

Chapter 20

Public relations in developing countries

LEARNING OBJECTIVES

At the end of this chapter you will be able to:

■ explain how cultural differences impact upon the media;
■ describe how media structure differs in developing countries;
■ outline some important methods of communicating in these countries.

Introduction

This chapter is not an exhaustive guide to media in developing countries. To do this topic justice would require a separate book of considerable size. The chapter is written from the perspective that whilst American media and the media of Western European countries are different, they are more similar in their characteristics than the media of developing countries outside of the large cities. This chapter aims to inform about differences in media in developing countries and how this affects some aspects of PR activity since many of these countries, in Africa, Asia, the Middle East, Eastern Europe and Latin America, will become major markets in the new millennium (Sriramesh and Vercic, 2001).

Towards the end of the twentieth century, the world was less clearly divided into the first world (North America, Western Europe, Japan and Australasia), the second world (communist states including the

Soviet Union, China and North Korea) and the third world (underdeveloped or developing countries in Africa, Asia Pacific, the Indian subcontinent). With the collapse of the Soviet Union in 1990 came the collapse of the Berlin wall, partitioning East and West Germany, the end of Soviet hegemony in the Balkans and the resultant war, and the Soviet Union's military withdrawal from Afghanistan. There have been many other effects throughout the world based on these after-effects. In Russia, sources of media have increased considerably since the policies of 'perestroika' and 'glasnost', first developed by President Gorbachev, brought down the Soviet Union and its communist ideology. Nevertheless, PR professionals in Western companies like Coca-Cola spend much of their time communicating with intrusive bureaucratic governments and their employees rather than journalists and consumers (Guth, 1998).

In China, too, the number of advertising agencies has drastically increased from virtual non-existence in the early 1980s to many tens of thousands by the mid-1990s (Fan and Pfitzenmaier, 2002). Media structures within countries are affected by the nature of the political system. The above introduction, outlining the Russian scenario, was intended to convey this notion. The independent mass media flourishes under democratic systems but has tended to stagnate and die under communist or theocratic rule. Mass media systems are subject to the nature and structure of regulation, based as they are on political objectives. There are differing degrees of restrictions on media and paid advertising in different countries. The nature of what the press is allowed to report is also subject to national cultures (and authoritarian regimes!).

A good example of the difficulties of adapting PR techniques to different cultures is probably best exemplified in China. Networking in America, whilst often derided by those most adept at it, is nevertheless a relatively open process. In China, the equivalent, *Guanxi*, is very different. Whereas networking in the US tends to be public, in China it is more private and secretive. Discussions will take place in closed environments rather than in open ones. Whilst a Chinese person may claim they have *Guanxi* (namely, good interpersonal contacts), it is not usually possible to verify this except through trial and error. Whilst US PR mainly uses mass media, *Guanxi*, by definition, operates as an interpersonal medium. Finally, whilst *Guanxi* operates through the development of friendly relationships and ties (perhaps what we might call cronyism in the UK), in the US, negotiations are usually more principle-centred. So, we can see a very different culture in operation. Clearly, this style of communication can drastically affect how PR techniques are conducted. Organizing an event would require a very different process in Shanghai as compared to New York or London.

Western companies developing sponsorship programmes in China have tended to target sport, music and arts events because of huge growth in these sectors. Music, particularly, allows young Chinese people freedom to express themselves and so is often linked with fashion, products and lifestyle marketing approaches (Fan and Pfitzenmaier, 2002).

There are three ways of looking at public relations media in developing countries. First, there is the dearth of Western-style mass media; secondly, there are the limitations of the existing mass media; and thirdly, there are the problems, special needs and special techniques of communicating with illiterate people and those, often remotely located, of different ethnic groups, languages, dialects, religions and lifestyles. These are problems that confront the PRO working in a developing country, or the PRO of an organization that exports to, or operates in, these countries. Nevertheless, PR professionals do operate in these countries and lifestyles are changing as fast as these countries' economies can develop.

Dearth of Western-style mass media

The number and circulation of newspapers, the number of television sets and computers, and number of Internet-connected computers, the number and kind of television viewers, the nature of mobile telephony, and the number of radios and listeners will depend on the following factors:

1. *The degree of literacy.* This depends on the primary education system on the one hand and adult literacy education on the other.
2. *The sophistication of the economy.* This will influence the size of the market, the justification for advertising and the ability for media to be commercially viable. There are several ways of looking at this. A country may depend on a particular crop or mineral, e.g. sugar, cocoa, copper or rubber. If there is a slump in the world market for that product, the country's economy will suffer. A net exporter may become a net importer so that restrictions will be placed on imports. In some countries, a large number of people may be outside the cash economy (e.g. China) because they are subsistence workers who sell little or no surplus produce.
3. *The popularity of television.* Community viewing in developing countries has popularized television, but programmes are often shown in the evening, and since it is usually not the custom for women to go out at night, audiences are limited to men. Young people are also likely to be excluded. In the Taliban-controlled Afghanistan of the late 1990s/early 2000s, cinemas were closed down and music was banned.
4. *The quality of broadcast material.* Programme material is usually of poor quality. Videotape is expensive, studios have limited

capacity and equipment, newsreading and acting experience are meagre, outside broadcasts are rare and foreign programmes may be too expensive or even restricted by import controls. The poor quality of programmes also deters some people from watching television.

5. *The viability of television.* The quality of programmes in independent television markets can be influenced by the lack of advertising revenue if the market economy is limited or depressed. In markets where television is largely state controlled, the only PR activity undertaken may be government propaganda.

Consequently, television in developing countries may not be the most effective medium for disseminating a company's messages to its publics. However, where a company wishes to communicate with the countries' more elite citizens, television may well be the perfect medium.

The importance of radio

There is a common belief that radio provides the more effective communications medium in developing countries because it can so easily penetrate distances, and one does not have to be able to read and write to listen to broadcasts. This is an over simplification because radio also suffers from its own limitations. In large countries with large rural populations containing a variety of ethnic groups, radio stations may transmit from remote and distant centres, and be considered unrelated to local interests. Radio might lack credibility as a result. This fact may not be realized by the broadcasting authority. In Namibia, the radio has been used to some extent for electioneering purposes, since the tribes of Northern Namibia make use of it. However, it can be costly in this country because the tribes speak in different dialects and different versions of a news broadcast, for instance, would need to be made. It is not always satisfactory to provide multi-language programmes radio because there may be too many languages. In addition, if the programmes are broadcast from one station, only a short portion of the day can be devoted to each language, with the result that speakers of other languages are deprived of broadcasts. In this context, radio becomes a more limited medium.

Although large numbers of people are believed to possess radio receivers, a surprising number of sets do not work. This might be because developing countries suffer from being sold imported technical products that cannot be serviced or repaired. For example, Kuwait could not use its British-made tanks during the Iraqi invasion in the early 1990s because many of the tanks had broken down and the Kuwaiti government had not ordered the spare parts necessary. They are often considered too expensive to be replaced. Batteries are often expensive and radios fall into disuse because people cannot afford to buy new batteries. Equally, electricity may not be available, meaning that receivers cannot be used. More recently, this problem has been somewhat lessened with the invention of the clockwork radio. This problem may well recede over time, as the possession of wind-up radios becomes more commonplace.

These problems do not generally confront broadcasting in industrialized countries. Yet, in spite of all these difficulties, radio can penetrate the large populations of developing countries. All sorts of people may enjoy radio for companionship and entertainment. In some countries with large land masses, and neighbouring countries nearby, foreign radio programmes may be preferred if they provide desired programmes, e.g. popular music. Box or rediffusion radio is cheap and popular, and may be available in public places such as cafés. Illiterate peoples, beyond the reach of newspapers, can listen to the radio. Thus, radio audiences are likely to be far larger than newspaper readerships. Radio has been shown to command authority in situations of emergency or national importance. Examples include times of war, political upheavals or environmental disasters. In countries of vast distances, radio has also been successful for educational purposes, with lessons being broadcast that can be listened to by individuals, listening groups or classes of students. This has proved to be very successful in Indonesia.

Other mass media

How else can people be reached on a broad scale in multi-ethnic, multi-language, multi-religious societies? One successful technique is through the use of pictures and diagrams. These can inform without the need for words. Visual messages can be applied to give-away leaflets (useful in villages) or on posters where sites exist in or near towns. Posters can also be displayed on public transport, which may travel about the country. The poster method showing, say, parents and two children has spread the idea of planned parenthood in many parts of the world, especially in Asia. In a similar way, cartoon drawings can be used to explain many things to illiterate people. Even so, there are problems and the artist needs to beware of the literal meanings people may place on pictures. Different peoples attach different meanings to different symbols.

Folk, traditional and other localized media

For centuries, people have communicated with one another, although in the past only scholars and scribes used written or drawn symbols. Many of these simple forms of communication are still practised. Even in Britain, the town crier survives, and in villages in West Africa the *gong man* or court messenger still proclaims the news in the morning and evening, acting as the communication medium between the local ruler and his people. It may be necessary to have public relations messages conveyed in this way in order to give them credibility and to reach people who are outside the orbit of Western-style mass media. A detailed study of village and rural communication techniques, termed *oramedia* because it is mainly oral or conveyed by sound, has been carried out (Ugboajah, 1985).

Literacy is not only to do with reading and writing. There can be both *visual* and *oral* literacy. So-called illiterate people often possess visual literacy superior to that of Westerners. Similarly, in West Africa, for example, one finds illiterate street-traders who act as postmen between villagers and their friends and relatives in town, carrying elaborate messages word perfect in their minds. These forms of communication should not be overlooked when communicating with people in developing countries. Market gossip becomes critical in this context. In Iran, public relations is centred most in bazaars. The *'bazaaris'* (business-people) might distribute their wares to the needy on public religious holidays, for instance (Kamalipour and Rad, 1997). Today, we would call this a corporate social responsibility programme! In developing countries with small farms and surplus produce, or local craftsmen with wares to sell, the market provides a meeting place where news is shared. Consequently, market gossip becomes an important medium for spreading information.

Public relations activity in Iran encompasses designing bulletins and posters, writing news releases, administrative activities, organizing public affairs campaigns, and producing audio–visual material. It hasn't yet got to developing sophisticated PR initiatives based on opinion polling, although such market research is developing slowly (Kamalipour and Rad, 1997).

Open-air events

Open-air events are more common in warm climates and they appeal to the gregarious instinct of people who have little entertainment. It may be an exhibition or agricultural show, or a mobile demonstration or mobile cinema that tours villages where newspapers are unknown and radio sets may be rare or radio has little impact. A crowd will gather to watch a film shown on a screen erected on the roof of a Land Rover. These may be called van cinemas and the terms mobile or static may be used to distinguish between the visiting and the permanent city cinema (covered or drive-in). But the audience figures and effectiveness of mobile cinema may be subject to doubt. They can also be infrequent regardless of whether or not they are corporate or public service information films. The films may also be too long; they may not retain the concentration of the audience. Equally, they may be too sophisticated and contain unfamiliar subjects. An eight-minute video might well be long enough, after which attention is likely to wander. A film shown to unsophisticated audiences should avoid using scenes or objects that are *foreign* to limited local knowledge and experience. People in a land-locked country may have never seen the sea, while those in tropical countries will be unfamiliar with snow.

Very few Western-style documentaries are suitable for such audiences. The sight of a skyscraper to people used to living in mud huts, for example, may arouse howls of derision, disbelief or terror. When Western firms make videos to show to people in developing countries, they should remember that the content needs to be credible to people with very different lifestyles and experiences.

Gregarious people living in simple surroundings often welcome entertainment when it comes to their village. The van may bring videos, and song and dance teams may accompany it. There may be more local forms of communication such as the village theatre that can be used to dramatize a message, an approach that could be used for bringing new ideas to villagers. Thus, it becomes education through entertainment. A puppet show can be very effective when there are linguistic problems, as messages can be mimed. This is a medium that has been used for public relations purposes in Africa and Asia. In Malaysia and Indonesia, wire puppets and shadow puppets are used.

Chapter 21

Video, DVD, CD-ROM and the Internet

LEARNING OBJECTIVES

After reading this chapter you will be able to:

- understand the PR advantages of video and DVD;
- recognize the potential of CD-ROMs for PR purposes;
- establish the advantages and potential disadvantages of the Internet as a communications medium.

Introduction

As noted in Chapter 9, public relations departments are rarely concerned with the 'general public' *per se*, but with a range of communities made up of individuals or groups with some particular interest or some other connection. Video and, more recently, DVD, CD-ROM and the Internet, are media that can be adapted to target important publics as distinct from commercial or mass media. Usually, such media are created to reach special, private, identified and sometimes small audiences. In public relations we are not only concerned with mass communications, rather it is often necessary to reach separate publics or groups of people – for example, families involved in a relocation project, who cannot be addressed broadly and impersonally through the mass media. The intent is not to reap immediate monetary return, but rather to develop favourable ideas, motivations, attitudes or behaviour in viewing audiences (Cutlip et al., 1994). It is therefore very much a public relations responsibility to produce and use videos and new media, or for the consultancy account executive to be able to advise clients on their applications.

Video

Video, since its general introduction in the 1970s, has become a very important PR tool used in a variety of different ways. Videos can be used internally for training or motivational purposes or externally for information or promotion. Video cassettes are portable and video players widely available across the globe (although UK-made videos require adaptation for North America and the Far East, who work on a 400-line, as opposed to 650-line, television format). Being compact, the video cassette is easy to store, carry or dispatch, and if shown on a TV set it is ideal for a small audience, including showing in the home. Business offices and conference venues are, more often than not, equipped with VCRs.

Three basic considerations apply to the use of video. They are: (1) purpose and audience; (2) production; and (3) use and distribution.

I. Purpose

A series of questions can help establish if video is the best medium to use in a particular situation. Why is the video being made? To whom do we wish to show the video? What communications problem is it designed to resolve? Is video (particularly given the development of new media) the best medium for the purpose?

2. Production

The production format will again be largely decided through answers to the questions above. There are a wide range of techniques, including the use of stills or slides, documentary or question style, or animation. It might use external locations, studio locations, live or dubbed sound, professional actors or members of staff, and original or hired music. To these basic film techniques can be added specialities such as computer-generated creative effects, introduced at the post-production stage.

One elementary aspect of production that can easily get out of hand is length. Far too many videos are too long, and either there should be fewer scenes or there should be sharper editing. Some of the best public relations videos are shorter than 20 minutes. When a video stretches to 30 minutes it is usually 10 minutes longer than viewer interest can be sustained. Unfortunately, there is a temptation to cram in too much, diluting attention and interest, provoking boredom and obscuring the message.

Two important aspects of production should not be overlooked: the spoken commentary (with or without a visual commentator) and the musical accompaniment. If it heightens the interest and is not a distraction, the commentator may be a well-known personality such as a TV newsreader or an actor or actress. Characteristic music that fits the mood of the video and does not intrude can make a significant contribution. It is not necessary to compose special music, and all types of popular and classical music tracks can be hired from music libraries.

3. Use and distribution

The ability to produce videos relatively inexpensively in large or small quantities for distribution makes video versatile and flexible. Videotapes can be sent easily through the post or by other carriers, and are frequently used by organizations (e.g. travel companies) to promote their products and services. Videos have even been distributed country-wide, in place of a traditional printed manifesto, by the Referendum Party in the 1997 British General Election.

Video sequences can now be distributed via the Internet although, currently, the play-back quality and length is limited. Any individual or organization with an Internet connection can download video player software, free of charge (upgrades from the basic player are chargeable), from Realplayer.com. That is sufficient for most current video offerings. As technology develops and broadband services become more available, the more the quality will improve, shortening the download time and lengthening the video extracts.

There is a wide range of companies available who will develop videos (and other new media) on behalf of organizations. Silver Products Ltd., for example, produce finished products in various formats (VHS Video, CD-ROM and DVD). They also enable video streaming (downloading) by hosting and maintaining client's corporate videos on their site (for further details visit http://www.silver-productions.co.uk).

Types and uses of video

Videos have a great many uses. They can be made for specific and sometimes short-term use, such as for an exhibition, conference, road show or relocation project, or longer term – for example, as part of a training library. Some of the more usual uses are outlined below.

- *Video house journal*. Although this form of video may have enjoyed its heyday (particularly with the introduction of the Internet), the video house journal still has its value for some organizations – for example, those with staff working in many locations at home or abroad, or where there are mergers and acquisitions and an inflow of new employers to a group. It is, perhaps, interesting to note that empirical evidence suggests that video house journals (or, indeed, their new media equivalents) seem to be less popular than the printed employee newspaper or magazine.
- *Documentary*. This is the narrative type of video which tells the story of the organization, or some side of its work. A construction company might film a project, a brewer could animate the brewing process, or an airline might make a video about new aircraft. Such videos could have a variety of uses and could be shown to potential clients, at press receptions, on exhibition stands, in showrooms or to groups of visitors. This is the kind of video that tempts sponsors to produce it at too great a length, and sharper editing would improve them. Few subjects merit more than 20 minutes screen time.
- *Recruitment*. Video is often used to demonstrate to potential employees the work conducted by the organization, whether it is a bank, a retail store or other industry. This video may be offered to school/college/university careers officers, shown at careers evenings and/or offered on free loan to youth organizations. Many universities and colleges also produce recruitment videos for use at open days or for distribution to schools and other organizations.
- *Induction*. Videos can be especially useful as induction material for new recruits, explaining what the organization does and who is responsible for what.
- *Training and continuous development*. Regular video releases can be a relatively inexpensive way of training and updating employees, particularly if the organization operates from diverse locations – for example, a multiple retailer. The Body Shop was a notable pioneer of video, with the company distributing these weekly to all its shops and franchises worldwide (Harrison, 2000). In hazardous industries, especially where it is imperative to wear protective clothing, a dramatic video can be made to illustrate the need for compliance.
- *Relocation*. Many videos have been made for this purpose, and they need not exceed 8–10 minutes in length. By showing the new premises and location, the shopping, entertainment, sports, educational and medical facilities, and concluding with a brief message from the managing director, members of staff may be attracted to move.

As a portable medium it means that families can be involved more closely in the decision making.

- *Annual reports and accounts*. There may be several reasons for making a video detailing the performance of the company. It may be used to report to employees in locations at home and overseas, or to show to financial consultants or shareholders who cannot attend the annual general meeting. For employees, the video could take the form of an interview (with or without a celebrity interviewer) with the managing director or other officers.
- *Marketing education*. The objective is to explain how a product or service works, and such videos can be screened in the home, in shop windows or in showrooms, on exhibition stands, or supplied on loan to clubs and societies.
- *Show reels (or video pitches)*. A form of market education, show reels can be made by service companies such as advertising agencies to demonstrate their work when pitching to potential clients.
- *Corporate identity*. When a corporate identity scheme has been created, including logo, typography, colour scheme, livery, dress and so on, its correct application can be demonstrated in a video that supplements a style and layout book.
- *For visitors*. Organizations who entertain groups of visitors frequently use videos to explain their activities, especially when certain processes (e.g. glass blowing or brewing) cannot be entirely viewed during a tour.

The video news release (VNR)

The video news release has been described as the modern day equivalent of the press release. This innovation has caught on slowly in the UK, but has become increasingly important as an ever-growing number of television companies, including the news services, find that their budgets limit their ability to cover outdoor events. The genuine professionally produced video news release kit can often secure coverage that would not otherwise occur. In the USA, VNRs have been common for several years, and in some areas, such as pharmaceuticals, there have been abuses of the 'free advertising' kind. Consequently, in late 1992, a special committee of the Public Relations Service Council (PRSC) established a Code of Good Practice for Video News Releases to affirm standards of accuracy and good practice in the PR industry.

Video news releases are, in practice, quite different from paper news releases. Before shooting anything, negotiations are conducted with broadcasters to see whether they will take VNR material on a stated subject. The VNR itself is a kit of pictures that the broadcaster can combine to provide a visual report with his or her spoken newscast or commentary. VNRs may be used in three ways. The first is as live pictorial news material for news bulletins. An example, quoted by Shimp (2000), is Hershey, the American confectionary company, who introduced their new Hershey 'Kisses with Almond' by dropping a six-foot, 500-pound replica covered in gold sequins and foil from a building in New York's Times Square. The event was videoed by their PR company, who distributed tapes to network TV stations. For less than $100 000, the launch received favourable exposure to millions of Americans. Other uses for VNRs include as live pictorial material for documentary and public affairs programmes and as archival or library picture material for future news or documentary programmes. A good example of the use of the latter is that even when the news story is a bad one (e.g. factory lay-offs), the positive images in the VNR (e.g. robotics in a motor car factory) can help soften the negative effect on the company's image. Jefkins (1994) uses the example of Abbey National's use of VNRs. Typical items in the Abbey National VNR kit are shots of types of houses, for sale boards, interviews on mortgages, and people using cash dispensers. The broadcaster can pick what he wants to use from the kit. In essence, it is what the broadcaster might have shot himself, but left to their own devices the broadcaster may choose to promote a competitor!

DVD (Digital Video Disc)

DVDs have become a popular format amongst both businesses and consumers. In effect, their purpose, production and distribution are the same as for videos discussed previously. DVD, however, has a number of distinct advantages, not least its capacity to hold great amounts of data. The DVD storage capacity is 4.7 gigabytes or over seven times that of a Compact Disc (CD), which is 680 megabytes. This enables DVD to produce not only higher resolution pictures than VHS,[1] but also:

- different presentation formats (e.g. widescreen);
- different language commentaries;
- additional background material;
- easy, quick and cheap distribution.

---

[1] DVDs use up to 720 horizontal line resolution using MPEG-2 compression compared with 650 (UK) or 400 (US) lines with VHS video.

CD-ROM (Compact Disc – Read Only Memory)

CD-ROMs are used for retrieval of text or data to a VDU screen and are normally used in association with personal computers (PCs). For those PC users with machines capable of providing video and audio presentations and who have CD-ROM drives (in effect, all computers produced in the past few years), they can be used to access information or act as a database for various software functions (e.g. Yellow Pages). They can also be used interactively with the Internet. CD-ROMs are used extensively because they are relatively inexpensive to mass produce yet hold considerable data. Examples of uses for CD-ROMs include university prospectuses, city guides, software demonstrations and much more.

Internet

The Internet and WorldWide Web (WWW) are terms that are frequently used interchangeably, although strictly speaking the WWW is the graphical, user-friendly end of the Internet that came to the fore in the mid-1990s.[2] It would not be too much of a claim to say that the Internet, and subsequently the WorldWide Web, have revolutionized business communication. It is a relatively inexpensive way to accumulate or distribute data to and from around the globe. There are a number of different Internet tools that are valuable to the PRO or public relations consultant.

E-mail

Electronic mail (or e-mail) was the first commercial use of the Internet and remains its most popular function. It has two significant advantages over so-called 'snail mail'. The first is its speed; an e-mail can arrive within seconds of transmission. The other is cost, where it is estimated that 10 000 individuals can be contacted for the price of one letter (Prabhaker, 2000). In many instances, e-mail has become the preferred distribution medium for press releases, with the added advantage that the mailing can also carry a number of electronic attachments. Buena Vista International, for example, launched the film *Starship Trooper* with a digital press kit. There is always, however, a downside. E-mail has, according to Dann and Dann (2001), a fundamental flaw. Its ease of

---

[2] For more technical descriptions of the differences see, for example, Dann and Dann (2001).

access has enabled it to be hijacked by unscrupulous individuals. The end result has been to create an environment where Spam (unsolicited electronic mail) is rampant and where even solicited mail (or opt-ins) is feeling a backlash.

Websites

The website has become a major communication point between organizations and their publics and, as such, is of considerable importance to the PRO. Unfortunately, in many companies it is the sinister sounding 'web-master' who controls content rather than the marketers and/or PRO. As a result, many websites are highly user-unfriendly and frequently out of date. Effective websites require careful design in both form and function (Smith, 2002). Form is the way that the site looks; function means its interactivity, integration, navigation and structure. It must help contribute to the communication objectives and, in particular, satisfy the need for information (recognized or unrecognized) by that organization's publics.

The WWW is, however, a passive medium and it is no good having the most effective site in the world if no one visits it. The classic dilemma is whether to put more resources into the website or generating traffic to visit it (e.g. advertising, web links/banners, press releases). A growing number of organizations are sponsoring websites of sporting or community-based organizations. In 1997, IBM paid $1 million to be sole sponsor of the US National League Superbowl.com website, which generated over 8 million hits (Shimp, 2000).

On the downside, the Web has become the medium of choice for those organizations and individuals who wish to attack a company. Such high-profile businesses as Shell, McDonald's and Nike have all had to contend with attacks from militant hackers.

Intranet

The importance of internal communications has been known for some time and the Internet offers the company a means of communication with employees around the globe. If internal communications are normally through a site with protected access, as is today normally the case, then it is an *intranet* site as opposed to the externally available *Internet* site. According to Center and Jackson (2003), the advantage of Internet/intranet technology, in relation to internal marketing, is that it shortens the communication cycle. It is a convenient way to give and get feedback, store and retrieve information, and enables people on different floors, different time zones and different continents to have immediate access to working documents.

On the downside, empirical evidence suggests the electronic journal is not as popular as the paper-based one and that employees are beginning to suffer from information overload. According to one PR chief executive (quoted in Center and Jackson, 2003), the Internet is 'speed without analysis, data without wise interpretation'.

Chapter 22

Seminars, conferences and exhibitions

LEARNING OBJECTIVES

By the end of this chapter you will be able to:

■ outline the role the PRO plays in organizing conferences and exhibitions;
■ describe some important considerations when planning a conference;
■ explain the common reasons for exhibiting at a trade fair;
■ outline how PR techniques can be used to support an exhibition;
■ outline some different forms of PR exhibition.

Introduction

This chapter outlines how the public relations function is involved in organizing conferences, exhibiting at trade fairs and, when it is appropriate, organizing seminars. There is a brief discussion of the role of public relations as conducted by the exhibition organizers themselves (as distinct from those attending the exhibition). The chapter outlines the use of PR exhibitions and their various forms.

The PRO's role

Organizing seminars, conferences and exhibitions (of short or long duration) calls for managerial skills in planning, budgeting, organizing and directing. Examples of such events might include sales conferences, break-out seminars linked with exhibitions, the annual general meeting (AGM) or investor relations meetings (see Chapter 24) in the event of a merger or takeover bid. Internal meetings, perhaps to discuss changes in mission, vision or values, or local community meetings (for example, for a football club, a university or an airport) will usually be organized by the PR department, or corporate communications department, as it is now often known. The exhibition has become increasingly popular for business development purposes, with companies set to spend more on this medium over the next few years (Vence, 2002).

The PRO's role might incorporate organizing a product demonstration, the co-ordination of press activities, the co-ordination of photography, audio-visuals and Internet websites, and the generation of publicity, all of which help to generate audiences for conferences and exhibitions. For a sales conference, he or she may have to produce a video, CD-ROM or an Internet webcast to demonstrate new products or selling propositions. If the company and the size of attendance is sufficient to justify the cost, the video, CD-ROM or webcast can be given extra dramatic or humorous impact by the casting of well-known TV personalities.

Such events differ in length of duration depending on how many people need to be consulted and when they can make themselves available for such meetings. Meticulous planning is important, since forgetting the smallest detail can often have a big impact upon how an event is evaluated. For example, if your organization held a conference in a local football club's banqueting and conference facilities (where other events are also being held), it is important to provide proper directions for delegates in order to ensure that they arrive at the appropriate place. This is a small detail (since they could ask at reception anyway), but if delegates continually have to ask the way to a room, they may begin to wonder why they bothered coming to the conference in the first place!

A key factor for success in organizing conferences and exhibitions is to establish a good relationship with those people at the venue who will be responsible for your arrangements. This could include the venue manager, banqueting manager, food and beverage manager, head waiter, receptionist, electrician, and often the car park attendant. Ensuring car parking facilities are available is particularly important if you intend to hold your event in a remote location. Nevertheless, even if you don't, it is very likely that most people will travel using their cars. They should be greeted on entrance, and good practice is to present them with a registration pack and a badge, so that other delegates can ascertain where they are from and what they are called. The registration pack will contain different things depending on what the event seeks to do (e.g. sales conference, investor relations meeting or trade exhibition) and who the delegate is (e.g. press packs would be handed out to journalists). It is very easy to assume that delegates will know where your location is, but this could prove fatal when trying to recruit delegates. They should always be provided with a map and possible travel directions.

The value of exhibiting or running a conference can be greatly enhanced if full advantage is taken of the many public relations opportunities created by these events. The PRO can support exhibitions and conferences by:

- Helping to secure pre-event and post-event publicity to increase the number of visitors to events and maximize repeat attendees for the following years. Recruitment to exhibitions and conferences is typically undertaken using personal invitations by (e-)mail and telephone, advertisements in newspapers and magazines, and through direct mail to prospective attendees (see Herbig et al., 1998).
- Contacting those newspapers and magazines interested in publishing previews of the event.
- Providing relevant spokespersons for interviews with press, radio or television journalists should they be required.
- Advising the Department of Trade and Industry in advance, where a product has export potential, as they may be interested in issuing overseas news stories, filming the exhibit or taping a radio interview through the Central Office of Information.

Conferences

It might be useful at this stage to describe what a conference is before we proceed. A conference typically consists of a large audience with platform speakers. Usually, conferences are designed to bring people from a company or industry together to discuss and debate issues relevant to that company or industry. So, a company may have a conference of its senior managers for the purpose of determining what the company's ten-year strategy should be. At the conference, top management might propose various missions and conference delegates discuss them in break-out seminars. Platform speakers might outline what each of the missions are in further detail and summarize the break-out discussions after they have taken place. Conferences are also frequently organized at the industry level for the purposes of sharing industry best practice and know-how. Such conferences are often designed to incorporate speeches from well-known industry spokespeople and networking events designed to encourage the development of relationships across companies within the same industry.

Conferences typically last for between one and three days, but the vast majority tend to be only a day. They are often held midweek, but are sometimes held over a weekend (as academic conferences often are). It may or may not be residential. Delegates may pay an attendance fee, or admission may be free of charge. Accommodation may be paid for by the sponsors or by the delegates and the delegates may be either recruited (thereby paying for themselves) or invited free of charge. There are clearly many variations on how the attendance will be achieved and how the costs are met. The events may be so valuable to participants that they will be willing to contribute to the cost, while another event may succeed only if people are invited on a non-payment basis. Providing free delegate places can cause ethical problems – for example, where a pharmaceutical company pays all the expenses of doctors who are invited to a conference about a new drug treatment. The pharmaceutical company could be criticized afterwards for bribing doctors to attend. There is no reason why participants should not pay to attend. There is also the danger that if the sponsor provides too much hospitality at the event, it may provoke suspicion that it is only a publicity stunt for the organizers, or the sponsors, rather than a serious endeavour. Usually, people place more value and credence on something for which they have to pay.

There is also the question of whether or not the delegates can afford to pay. A conference for doctoral students may be poorly attended if the organizing university is unwilling to provide some paid expenses for students to attend. Funds to cover delegate fee discounts can be provided through sponsorship (see Chapter 27). In order to secure sponsorship for your conference, it is important to find those organizations whose objectives tie in with the objectives of your conference.

At a conference, the most important element is to have an interesting programme with high-quality speakers, supported by appropriate videos, DVD or CD-ROM presentations, satellite link-ups or other audio-visual aids. The speakers should be experts where possible (i.e. designers, technicians, scientists) rather than marketing or sales personnel, since if it is the latter and the subject of the conference is not sales or marketing, they are less likely to be perceived as good speakers. It is often useful to bring in external speakers who are both well known and familiar with the subject. There are various important considerations when organizing a conference. These are outlined in further detail next.

Special considerations

1. *The date.* A day and time should be chosen which does not clash with another event of interest to prospective participants. So the World

Cup matches or Wimbledon tennis finals should be avoided, for instance. The date should be organized sufficiently far ahead to permit proper planning, and so that invitations may be sent out (or announcements may be published) in sufficient time for people to make arrangements to attend. Conference planning should usually start when the previous conference ends. Typically, for a one-off event, planning might start from three to six months prior to the event date. The event typically should be announced between four and six weeks in advance. The length of notice really depends on the time delegates need to get permission to attend. With international events, the time needed to obtain visas and currency and make flight and hotel arrangements may increase the notice period so that, for overseas visitors, up to six months notice is often required.

2. *The venue.* A conference should be held at a venue which is (a) well equipped for conferences, (b) attractive in itself or in an attractive location, and (c) easily accessible by road, rail, sea or air, with good car parking facilities. Again, if foreign delegates are likely to attend, the venue might be located near an international airport, as the NEC (National Exhibition Centre) is in Birmingham and the G-MEX complex in Manchester. Often, the venue can be a hotel, which offers both excellent sleeping accommodation and commercial facilities. The Novotel, Jury's and Hilton Hotels in major UK cities frequently provide such facilities. It is also important to ensure that the main hall, where the speakers' platform is held, has good acoustics and that a screen (if one is used) is capable of being viewed even at the back of the auditorium.

3. *Recreational activities.* People cannot be expected to sit endlessly in a hall listening to speeches, so it is wise to include some recreation or entertainment. According to the type of audience, venue and time of year, social activities could include a coach tour, boat trip, murder mystery dinner, or a visit to local tourist spots. It might even be necessary to arrange activities for delegates' partners, especially when organizing an international conference.

Planning a conference

When planning a timetable for a conference there are certain fixed times that dictate where sessions should be positioned. So, generally, people expect to start a conference between 09.00 and 10.00. They expect to have lunch between 12.00 and 14.00, and they usually expect to finish between 16.00 and 18.00. Most delegates would expect there to be a 15- or 30-minute break approximately halfway through the morning for coffee (or tea) and about halfway through the afternoon for tea (or coffee).

A typical day's programme is outlined in Figure 22.1. Note that there are usually four speaker's sessions in a day, two in the morning and two in the afternoon.

So, in the various sessions, the conference organizers can determine whether they want speeches, presentations, workshops or some combination of these activities. When organizing a conference, it is very important that someone checks to ensure that the various sessions and breaks finish and start when they are supposed to. Whilst Figure 22.1 exemplifies a conference where the sessions are organized in series (i.e. one after another), there is nothing to stop the organizers from holding a number of sessions at the same time (see Figure 22.2).

Time	Activity
09.00–9.30	Delegate registration
09.30	First session
11.00–11.30	Coffee
11.30	Second session
13.00–14.00	Lunch
14.00	Third session
15.00–15.30	Tea
15.30	Fourth session
16.30	Close

Figure 22.1 Typical skeleton outline for a conference event (organized in series).

Time	Activity
09.00–9.30	Delegate registration
09.30	Session A
11.00–11.30	Coffee
11.30	Sessions B, C and D
13.00–14.00	Lunch
14.00	Sessions E and F
15.00–15.30	Tea
15.30	Session G
16.30	Close

Figure 22.2 Typical skeleton outline for a conference event (organized in parallel).

The traditional conference format, where rows of seated staff are subjected to 'death by powerpoint' (i.e. slide after slide), sits uncomfortably with many companies trying to portray a more futuristic image. Barclays Bank converted Wembley Conference Centre into an airport lounge to convey the notion of the organization embarking on a journey (Goddard, 1999).

The organization of a conference requires considerable planning. In addition to the organization of the speeches and break-out sessions, PROs may have to organize flights for guest speakers, dinners, after-dinner entertainment, hotel accommodation, conference packs and promotional activity. Table 22.1 outlines a hypothetical plan for a conference expecting to produce a small profit by recruiting 100 delegates to a three-day event requiring guest speakers from overseas. The plan is written so that costs and profit (i.e. income − costs) can be determined for the potential scenarios of recruiting 50 and 75 delegates instead of 100. At this conference, delegates will also attend a champagne reception at the start of the conference. Besides the main costs (e.g. organizing committee costs, catering, conference packs, delegate social costs and promotional expenses), the plan also includes income from potential sponsors and from the delegates themselves in the form of a delegate fee. In this example, there are actually two delegate fees illustrated, one at a reduced rate and the other a full rate fee. At many conferences, there is usually a discount offered to those companies who book their places early, who are involved in the organization of the conference or who are members of a particular professional body. In the above case, conference places have been offered at a 60 per cent discount.

Sponsors might be encouraged to pay for individual aspects of the event – for instance, a champagne reception in the above example. Sponsorship packages can be designed to include, but not be limited to, the following benefits:

- Sponsor's name and logo associated with the words 'Conference Sponsor' on the front cover of any printed Announcements, the invitation to Register and Conference Programme/free full page advertisement on back page of the Conference Programme (sponsor to supply camera ready artwork).
- Sponsor's name and logo associated with the words 'Conference Sponsor' on the conference website and link to sponsor's website/display of sponsor company name and logo on-screen at the beginning and end of every plenary session.
- Prominent sign or banner at a highly visible location in each conference venue, e.g. the entrance to the venue or in the registration area.
- Complimentary exhibition space at the Conference Centre and the opportunity to extend this at a discounted rate to be agreed with a preferential choice of exhibition space location.

Table 22.1 Typical conference financial plan

Conference financial plan (All cost figures in thousands of pounds)	50 delegates	75 delegates	100 delegates
Full cost (100% registration fee)	39	64	89
Reduced cost (60% discount registration)	7	7	7
No cost	4	4	4
Costs	£	£	£
Organizing committee			
Flights/organizing committee	1000	1000	1000
Accommodation/organizing committee	500	500	500
Dinner + room	150	150	150
Trains	36	36	36
Catering			
Dinner (£25 per person)	1250	1875	2500
Meals/lunch and tea breaks	5000	7500	10000
Venue Hire	0	0	0
Champagne reception £25 per person	1250	1875	2500
Conference packs			
CD-ROM conference papers	3000	4500	6000
Conference bags, etc.	1000	1500	2000
Printing, programme details, fliers, etc.	400	400	400
Coach hire (£100 per hire)	800	1000	1000
Temporary staff at conference	200	300	300
Temporary admin. staff	120	120	120
Social for delegates			
Entertainment	2000	2000	2000
PA system	1000	1000	1000
Promotional expenses			
Advertising	1000	1000	1000
Total costs	18706	24756	30506
Income			
Delegate fees (average £300)	11700	19200	26700
Delegate fees (reduced £140)	980	980	980
Sponsorship	6000	6000	6000
Total income	18680	26180	33680
Income−Costs	−26	1424	3174

- Two full complimentary conference registrations (excluding hotel accomodation).
- Insertion of approved promotional materials in the conference bag/opportunity to supply gifts to delegates (at the organizer's discretion), e.g. conference bags/pads/pens.

- Use of conference name in your promotional literature and releases.
- The organization name may feature in approved conference press releases/access to and use of conference photography for promotional purposes.
- First choice in sponsoring other elements of the conference, including main social events.

Seminars

A seminar is a smaller gathering. It is shorter than a conference and will be confined to an evening, half a day or at most a whole day. A large conference venue will not be required, and a medium-sized public room at a hotel or a lecture room at a professional institution or university will usually be adequate. Whereas in a conference with a large audience it will be more orderly to confine questions to question time, it is easier and often desirable during a seminar to permit people to participate at any time and for the speaker to encourage discussions rather than deliver a set speech. Evening receptions, common with financial planning and investment seminars, are often more informal. A group of clients may be invited to listen to a talk and perhaps attend a video show on company premises or in a hotel room. The hospitality may range from wine to a private bar and a light buffet. The financial services industry frequently adopts this modest but effective technique, as do automobile distributors. It lends itself to organizations with local branches or showrooms. The host and speaker is usually the local manager. The main challenge is to target specific groups, encourage them to attend and offer the collective group information that addresses individual concerns (Chambers, 1999). This, of course, is difficult to do, but the task is made easier if the content of the seminar is customized for the audience by asking them what kinds of information they require after recruitment and before the seminar. Increasingly, exhibitors at major trade fairs are scaling back their stands and spending more on seminars and hospitality (Gander, 2002).

Exhibitions

What is an exhibition? Exhibitions are events where companies or individuals (exhibitors) place products, services or works (exhibits) on show for an appropriate audience either for the purposes of selling those exhibits or in order to allow the audience to appreciate them – for instance, for their aesthetic value. Typically, in the business context, exhibitions take the form of trade fairs, where companies purchase stands at an appropriate exhibition centre. It is important that the PRO is aware of the company's participation in exhibitions, since he or she will need to co-operate with those persons responsible for their organization. This is particularly important since there are numerous public relations opportunities to be exploited over the many weeks or months before, during and after an exhibition.

Why would a company wish to attend an exhibition? Blythe (1999) outlines the following top ten reasons, determined from a recent survey:

1. To meet new customers.
2. To launch new products.
3. To take sales orders.
4. To interact with existing customers.
5. To enhance the company image.
6. General market research.
7. To meet new distributors.
8. To keep up with the competition.
9. To get information on the competition.
10. To interact with existing distributors.

When Blythe asked those organizations that exhibited regularly (i.e. more than six times per year) why they exhibited, the top three answers were to meet new customers, take sales orders and to launch new products. Exhibitions can be an important part of a company's yearly calendar – for instance, the Harrogate International Toy Fair for toy retailers, importers and manufacturers; the Birmingham Gift Fair for the gift industries; and the Munich Book Fair for publishers, agents, book retailers and wholesalers, and authors.

Exhibitions are not in themselves a public relations medium, except on special occasions when a stand is used for public relations rather than selling purposes (e.g. a police exhibit shown at a press conference). The PRO's role at an exhibition is not simply to hand out press kits to journalists (especially since there might be limited interest from this public). A good example of a successful, effective event was when Kraft Foods exhibited its Carte Noire coffee brand at the three-day Vive La France exhibition by Café Carte Noire just inside the exhibition entrance. French waiters served guests with coffee, leaflets and money-off coupons, and other exhibition participants with 12 000 coffee sachet samples (Anon., 2002b). Another example of an innovative event was when The Russell Organization (TRO) organized a product launch for Mini UK for 800 distributors and corporate buyers. The exhibition took place over five days, with four groups of 44 people attending ride and drive exercises and workshops, games and competitions. In order to maintain a less traditional, more immersive, experiential event, TRO provided a 'hostile, monochrome' before mini-ownership environment and a warm, colourful after mini-ownership environment within the exhibition (Anon., 2002c).

Exhibition promoters' public relations

Although this chapter has so far discussed conferences and exhibitions from the perspective of the company organizing a conference or attending an exhibition, exhibition organizers also employ public relations specialists in their own right. The PRO employed by the promoters or sponsors of the exhibition have a special type of public relations job to do. The efforts of the promoter are three-sided: he or she has to inform prospective exhibitors, then prospective visitors before and during the show, and finally achieve follow-up coverage. Moreover, much exhibition public relations is continuous, following on from one event to the next. The coverage for one helps to recruit attendees and exhibitors for the next exhibition.

Large exhibition promoters have a permanent team of PROs who work on a number of projects. Smaller exhibitions may employ consultants, and sponsoring organizations, such as trade associations, often employ their regular PRO to service their events. The exhibition PRO may be involved in the following tasks:

- The organization of public relations activities such as a press reception and issue of news releases to announce a forthcoming exhibition.
- Co-operation with organizations which circulate information about exhibitions (e.g. *Eventline* and *Exhibition Bulletin* in the UK).
- Co-operation with government agencies such as the Department of Trade and Industry, who circulate information abroad, although note that government agencies frequently have different objectives when exhibiting overseas compared with commercial companies (Seringhaus and Rosson, 1998).
- Seeking advance information from exhibitors.
- Distributing advance information, including translated versions to the overseas press.
- Negotiating, writing and publishing feature articles prior to the show.
- Co-operating with arrangements for the official opening.
- Organizing the press day and media coverage of the official opening, and managing it on the day.
- Preparing the press room, displaying news releases on tables or in racks, and displaying photographs and captions on panels.

- Obtaining maximum coverage of the official opening in the press and on radio and television, as this can produce important publicity at the beginning of the show and so attract visitors.
- Maintaining the press room throughout the exhibition, assisting journalists with information, sometimes arranging to send material to their offices, and providing hospitality as required.
- Producing an end-of-exhibition report on exhibitors' or visitors' comments.
- Monitoring and announcing attendance figures and post-show evaluation.

Public relations exhibitions

Here we refer to the use of the exhibition as yet another private or created public relations medium, with or without a large audience. They may be portable or permanent. The various kinds include portable exhibitions, permanent exhibitions, mobile exhibitions and virtual exhibitions.

- *Portable exhibitions.* These may be designed and constructed so that they can be taken apart and transported to a venue. They may be working models, or sets of panels or frames, forming mini-exhibitions which can be assembled at a conference, or in hotel rooms, public libraries, schools, theatre foyers, department stores, shop windows or other suitable locations.
- *Permanent exhibitions.* These are usually on company premises. A permanent exhibition is ideal for an organization which regularly receives groups of visitors. The Wedgwood Company, which produces fine pottery, has turned its factory into a permanent exhibition, The Wedgwood Story, incorporating various elements of the manufacturing process at its site in Barlastone, near Stoke-on-Trent in the UK. Permanent exhibits can also be mounted at trade centres in overseas markets or in regional trade centres, e.g. in London or provincial cities such as Manchester.
- *Mobile exhibitions.* Great ingenuity has been applied to the touring exhibition, which can take a compact show from place to place by road, rail, sea and even air. The types of mobile exhibition are diverse, ranging from a caravan to a train (which could stop in a bay at a local station) to a floating exhibition (e.g. Japanese trade ships). There are also custom-built exhibition vehicles and converted double-decker buses. The latter has often been used by political parties in the UK as 'battlebuses' designed to take the campaign team up and down the country at election times. These mobile events can combine

audio-visual presentations and demonstrations. Mobile exhibitions using road vehicles are frequently set up in market squares, car parks, school playgrounds, hotel yards or at agricultural shows.

- *Virtual exhibitions.* These events recreate the look and feel of a conventional exhibition without the need for attendees to be physically present at a specific location or time. They are cheaper than their physical counterparts and enable companies to offer their products, services or works to an audience on a permanent basis. Virtual exhibitions are particularly popular with museums and other artistic organizations. Recent advances in streaming audio technology, synchronized with webcast video images, allow delegates to enroll at their convenience, take part in discussion forums, and download press packs and other material (Bird, 2000).

Chapter 23

House journals and public relations literature

LEARNING OBJECTIVES

After reading this chapter you will be able to:

- recognize the importance of house journals to internal and external communications;
- understand the uses to which different types of house journal can be put;
- discuss and analyse the different techniques used in successful PR literature.

House journals

The house journal is one of the oldest forms of public relations, with the Americans being pioneers of this medium. As early as the 1840s, Charles Dickens referred to a publication for New England cotton workers. *The Lowell Offering* (1842), I.M. Singer & Co.'s *Gazette* (1855) and the Travelers Insurance Companies' *Protector* (1865) were all produced for the first time around this period. In Britain, Lever Brothers (now part of Unilever) and the Manchester Co-operative both launched a house journal towards the end of the nineteenth century.

House journals have been given a variety of names, such as newletters, employee newspapers and company newspapers, but, in effect, they carry out the same function. House journals are private publications and are therefore discussed separately from the commercial press. Over the years they have tended to change from pulpits for employers to preach from to supporting more open forms of management–employee relations. According to Harrison (2000, p. 130):

> The typical house journal of the past, an all-purpose affair with lots of photographs of men in suits, giving messages that your organization is a great one to work for, is now more or less moribund.

House journal types

There are also two distinct kinds of house journal: *internals* for staff and *externals* for outside publics. The two are distinct and should not be expected to serve the dual purpose of serving, for example, employees and customers. House publications are not confined to the world of commerce and industry, even if house journal editors have, in the past, been given the curious title of 'industrial editors'. In fact, private magazines and newspapers are published by almost every kind of organization, whether it is in the public or private sector, commercial or not-for-profit.

There are basically five types of house journals. Although some of these previously printed publications have converted in whole or part to electronic media, it is not so much the medium but the message that is important, and which medium best suits the function of reaching the target publics.

1. *The sales bulletin* is a regular communication, perhaps weekly, between a sales manager and sales representatives in the field.
2. *The newsletter* is a digest of news for busy readers, e.g. management, technicians. The term *newsletter* is sometimes used to describe printed house journals in general. Membership organizations such as the Chartered Institute of Marketing (CIM), British Franchise Association and others use this as the principal conduit to their membership. In recent years there has been a considerable switch from printed to e-mail newsletters.
3. *The magazine*, which typically contains feature articles and pictures and may be published at monthly or quarterly intervals. It is usually A4 size.
4. *The tabloid newspaper*, which resembles a popular newspaper and contains mostly news items, short articles and illustrations, and may be published weekly, fortnightly, monthly or every two months.
5. *The wall newspaper* is a useful form of staff communication, where the staff are contained in one location such as a factory, department store or hospital.

These are general descriptions. In very large organizations all five may exist, addressed to different types of reader. While the tabloid newspaper format is popular, there is now a tendency for a number to adopt A4 size magazine format.

Externals are likely to use a magazine format, since they are more educational and informative, less full of news items, personal stories and gossip, but some follow the tabloid format. Many organizational publications (e.g. CIM's *Marketing Business*) may be outsourced to professional business magazine companies (e.g. Communications Team), who may also generate revenue through advertising.

Why publish a house journal?

Such a publication could be one of the media used by the public relations manager in order to carry out a planned public relations programme that, importantly, includes internal relations. In other words, the house journal should be a meaningful agent of public relations management. As Dawn Jones of Shandwick International notes: 'truly successful internal communications turn organizations into intelligent organisms which learn and grow' (quoted in Theaker, 2001, p. 134). Harrison (2000) notes that BP, with 62 000 employees in 70 countries, have an enormous internal communications challenge. The BP Exploration division publishes *BPXpress* in four editions from four separate locations annually. It is significant that, although all kinds of innovations (including new media) have been introduced into internal communications, the printed house journal has survived as the most effective medium.

In the past, the house journal provided the means by which a paternal management could preach to the staff, and there are still some journals that are produced that way. A good house journal should be published because management have things to communicate to employees and in order to generate feedback. This is particularly important where there are staff scattered between different locations, or where mergers and acquisitions are occurring and old and new staff need to know each other. Staff may also want to communicate with one another, or let off steam about problems in the workplace. When reasons such as these are considered, the house journal becomes an important instrument in the process of management–employee relations.

How should a journal be edited?

How independent can or should a house journal editor be? To some extent this depends on the status and authority of the editor. Is editing the house journal someone's part-time job, or is the editor a specialist professional? In other organizations it is the culture and climate of the business that sets the standard.

In some organizations there is an editorial board or committee. In others the chief executive officer has to approve all material before it is printed. In others, possibly a minority, the editor is completely independent.

House journal techniques

There are special considerations concerning the publishing, editing, production and distribution of house journals that are best discussed under the following separate headings.

Readership

The sponsor and the editor of a house journal should be absolutely clear about who are the readership of the publication. Technicians will want to read about the technicalities of products; factory workers will enjoy reading about themselves and their companions; sales representatives will appreciate a journal that informs them about the company and helps them to sell. It is difficult for a journal to be all things to all people, hence the need for separate publications to cater for the different interests of different people. This is not always appreciated, and too many journals attempt to appeal to too wide a readership.

Frequency

For reasons of cost or the workload of the editorial team, it may be decided to publish a journal only every so often. There should not, however, be too large a gap between issues, otherwise the sense of regularity and continuity will be lost. Readers should look forward to the next issue, and it should appear on a regular day such as the first of the month. Frequency may also be determined by the need to publish news as soon as possible or because of the shelf-life of a feature article. Another factor that affects frequency is the number of copies required to reach all readers. The latter concern has driven many house journals onto the Internet, especially where they are having difficulty maintaining readership.

Title

Just as the naming of a company or the branding of a product is a form of communication which creates distinctiveness and character, so the title of a house journal establishes the image of the publication. If it is a newspaper, it may be a good idea to incorporate a typical newspaper name like 'Times', 'News', 'Express' or 'Mail' into the title, while if it is a magazine, a typical name such as 'Review' may be used; or a very distinctive title may be invented such as *The Black Dragon* if perhaps that is part of a trade mark. The title should be a permanent one, which makes it all the more important to decide on a good name.

Distribution

There is no point in going to a lot of trouble to produce a fine journal, only to let it suffer from ineffective distribution. If an organization has many branches or locations, and bulk supplies are sent to each address, there should be a systematic distribution to individual readers. If employees are merely expected to pick up copies from a central point, even from an automatic newsvendor, they may not bother and copies will be wasted. Similarly, if copies are handed out at the workbench they may be discarded on the floor. Although this may be costly in terms of wrappers, envelopes and postage, and the mailing list must be kept up to date, the best method is to post copies to home addresses. Employees can then read the journal at their leisure, and it may also interest their families.

Advertisements

The inclusion of advertisements can help to make a journal look more realistic and may be of value to readers. Three types of advertisement may be included: (a) those inserted by the organization about its own products or services or, perhaps, *situations vacant*; (b) outside commercial advertisements if the circulation makes the journal a good advertising medium; (c) readers' sales and wants advertisements. The latter can be a reader service, adding to reader interest, and can be inserted free of charge.

Contributors

There should be a planned supply of editorial material, with the editor planning future articles agreed with the various contributors. Roving divisional correspondents can be appointed with the responsibility for collecting news and submitting regular reports. The editor should also organize the taking of photographs of newsworthy events. It may also be necessary to commission features from professional writers, while the PROs of other organizations may offer house journals free articles.

Production

House journals call for a combination of writing, print design and print buying skills. A very amateur-looking journal can result if there is weakness in one of these areas. Some editors are principally journalists, who have little or no design or print knowledge, and rely on a printer to convert copy into a journal. The result can be disappointing. At the other extreme, there are sponsors who appreciate these deficiencies and appoint an expert house journal consultancy to produce a professional journal.

Some large public relations consultants have specially staffed and equipped desktop publishing (DTP) units that produce first class house journals in both electronic and paper-based form. Modern software makes DTP considerably easier than in the past and well within the scope of many organizations. With others, the reporting, commissioning and editing is handled in-house, and a consultancy is used for design and production. Some organizations may give everything to a consultancy, including collection and writing of editorial material.

Regarding production quality, the mistake is sometimes made of using a paper which is either too highly finished or of too heavy a weight, and this looks incongruous in a web-offset-printed tabloid newspaper. Credibility is vital: a house journal should look like a normal commercial journal, not be too prestigious or resemble sales literature. Jefkins (1994) reported that the editor of *Ford News* goes so far as to say it must be as good as the popular tabloids read daily by Ford employees, even though *Ford News* is published fortnightly. Again, care should be taken not to have a journal designed by a studio that is so design conscious that legibility is sacrificed.

Externals

Most of the above remarks also apply to externals, except that the policy, readership and contents must concern readers outside the organization. Externals should not normally be aimed at a targeted readership. It should fit into the public relations programme as a private medium directed at a defined public for a precise purpose. These chosen publics could be:

1. *The trade*. Distributors can be educated about a company and its products, with advice on business matters and how to display, demonstrate or sell the products.
2. *Users*. Specifiers, formulators, designers and others can be shown how to use products such as materials, components or ingredients.
3. *Professionals*. Products and services of interest to professionals can be described and explained, ranging from products they may recommend or use to services they may buy.
4. *Patrons*. The in-flight magazine is a good example, as are the journals supplied to hotel guests. Added to these are the tourist journals provided by tourist information organizations, which may also be found in hotels.
5. *Customer magazines*. These are journals issued to customers and clients, typical sponsors being hotels, insurance companies, motor car manufacturers and retailers.
6. *Opinion leaders*. Some journals of a wider appeal are distributed to those who express opinions about the organization and need to be kept informed.

The circulation list may include the editors of relevant trade, technical and professional journals, with the invitation to reproduce features free of charge in their own publications.

The changing nature of media, with Richard Quest, CNN

Richard Quest is British, holds an LLB (Hons) degree in Law from Leeds University and was called to the Bar. He began his career in journalism as a BBC news trainee in 1985 before later joining the BBC Financial Section in 1987, when he reported from London and New York on the stock market crash. He was subsequently appointed as a news correspondent and then moved to New York as the BBC's North America business correspondent in 1989. Richard has covered virtually all major business news stories across radio and television in the past decade, monitoring the ups and downs of the dollar and pound and the highs and lows of the stock market. Richard joined CNN in 2000 as co-anchor of CNN's twice-daily business programme *Business International*. He is now the anchor of CNN's daily business show *Business Central* and co-anchor of *BizNews*, a rolling four-hour live morning news and European business breakfast programme.

Interviewer: Can you give me an insight into the nature of how media has changed over the last 20 years and how firms are changing their corporate communications?

Richard: Well, most of my time has been spent in the US. I spent 10 years working there. If I go back to when I started as a financial reporter in 1987, it was simply that the press release came and you

went and covered the story. It was not nearly as sophisticated then as it is now. If you attempted to put pressure on the companies it was without success. In Britain there were only a few major PR companies who did all the financial PR. What has happened is the advent of more news networks. When I started, we worked on the *Financial World Tonight* and that would typically be one round of company results. It was a fine programme on Radio Four but it was typically a run round of company results that would lead into the company chairman. Depending on how well you had done your research about the company you would start off the interview with 'Chairman, you must be very pleased with these results'. There was one question you could always have asked and that was 'Chairman, what were the factors that influenced this set of results?' and 'Chairman, how would you explain these results to your shareholders?', and he would answer the question for you. We were more concerned with the minutiae of the company results and the Chairman than the overall sector and how the company had performed within it. Since then, things have become much more complex. We have become more sophisticated in our coverage; with more coverage and more programmes, it has become easier for the PR companies to get their people on air. From the PR companies' point of view it is probably easier to get some sort of coverage for their story.

Interviewer: Do you think there has been a change in the quality of information?

Richard: Well, yes and no. There is a fundamental mistake that PR companies make. There is the PR that comes with the umpteenth press release about a minor development in a corporation. I will try to give you an example. A company announces a revamp of its software to enable users to monitor such and such. You look at this sort of thing every day and you think, this is boring! Not that it is inherently boring but they have pitched it to the wrong people. An organization like CNN is not interested in that. Then you have the PR where there is an interesting development: a new product for an obesity problem or a big company announcing a new strategic direction. There you will get good coverage. Or a product recall announcement and then you have crisis management. That is where the PR companies earn their money and there are very few of them that do very good crisis management.

Interviewer: What sort of press releases would you be interested in? How should a decent press release be constructed in order for you to be interested in broadcasting some aspect of it?

Richard: That is missing the point. That assumes we will be interested to start with. Intel announcing that its Pentium widget will work a bit faster than the one that it has on the market is of no interest to a large broadcaster. Ford announcing closures, or a new revamp of its Ford Mustang, or that it has come up with toughened glass that will never break is of interest to the mass market. PR people cannot understand the difference. We are so bound by the rules, and have integrity, so we don't just give companies gratuitous plugs. We will use that as a reason to talk about the sector, the industry, the developments and we will want to talk to the top person, the chairman, the CEO, and usually no-one else. I will give you a good example. We had the CEO in. Then for the entire two minutes of the interview every answer plugged the product. It was about a computer anti-virus product. So I tried to wind the interview up with the problem generally of computer viruses and then the person said 'Ah, if you had had this product' and then I put another question and he came back with 'But if you had had this product', and I finally lost my temper with him on air. I said: 'Alright, you have had your two minutes, you have mentioned your product five times and now I am going to mention all your competitors' names.' I said to the PR person afterwards: 'You have abused our trust.' That is the understanding there has to be between the PR company and the broadcaster. We will let them get the name of their company on and we will let them mention their product, but they are not here to do an advert. If they want to do an advert, then they have to pay for advertising.

I had another one of these recently. I started the interview. The company was a brewery. They had announced their results and I suddenly got a note from the producer saying: 'I have just been called by the PR person saying you must not ask about this particular subject.' So in the interview I asked about this particular subject. I had told the CEO before the interview about it because there is nothing worse than a bad interview and he had answered it and we carried on. Afterwards I rang the PR guy up and said: 'How dare you telephone my producer and tell us what to ask and what not to ask.' I said: 'First of all, the announcement was in the news, this was not speculation. I would have looked an absolute fool if I hadn't asked about this.' As soon as he realized that the Anchor [TV news presenter] himself had telephoned, not some assistant, he said 'No, no, I was only doing this because the client asked us to make sure we were not asked about this particular subject' and I said 'Well, you were not doing your job were you, because you should have turned round to your client and said we can't do this, or it's obvious he is going to ask about this, he has to ask about this, so I suggest you start working on an answer when he does ask this.'

That is the biggest problem with PR companies. They are pusillani-mous when dealing with their clients because their clients pay their bills, but they should tell their clients that they should have a strategy for dealing with awkward questions before they are asked. Too many PR companies do not take a strong enough line with their clients. The best ones are those who are absolutely blunt with their clients and say: 'CNN is going to ask us this. We may not like it but we had better have an answer when they do ask it.' The best PR people are those that put the fear of God into the broadcaster. They do that by saying: 'Well, you can ask about that but I can tell you now you will not get a very good answer!' What I found is that when I have been warned not to ask a CEO about something I tend to say to the CEO beforehand: 'Well, obviously I am going to have to ask you about this because it will look as if we are ignoring the obvious.' The PR people are so concerned about being on message. The really sophisticated PR people are the airline companies, they are really the top of the range. They will do it on their terms.

Interviewer: Can you give you two or three major differences that have occurred in the last 20 years?

Richard: PR has become more ubiquitous. At the top end it has become much more complex, but the sheer amount of it means that there is a lot more rubbish out there. There is a lot more indiscriminate punting of stories without the proper realization that certain media will not be interested. PR people always want to hold the tiger by the tail and they are always surprised when the tiger bites.

Interviewer: To be fair, Richard, how would you know that a broadcaster would be interested in your particular event?

Richard: Well, that is where your experience comes in. That is the art. From the PR's point of view they want their announcement in the broadcast media but the broadcast media have a higher threshold of interest than the smaller press organizations. For example, De Beers Diamonds are opening their first shop and selling the diamonds under their own name. That's interesting, and one that the mass media might be interested in. I had on the programme this morning, Ray Webster, the Chief Executive of easyJet; he had results out but the peg was to talk about the whole industry and he did.

I would say the big change has been the sheer explosion in public relations work. We are the victims, and we are also the culprits because, as we have increased the amount of air time available – like Radio Five Live, more programmes on Radio Four, CNN, Sky – so we have led the PR people to believe it is a lot easier to get on our air waves.

Interviewer: Has there been a decrease in the amount of advertising booked as a result?

Richard: No, I don't think there has. You can never guarantee that you are going to get coverage. There has been a huge decrease in the amount of advertising due to the recession, but that's another subject. I think it is the lack of sophistication amongst the bulk of it which we have encouraged. Consequently, when they try to get stories onto our main flagship programmes, like my morning news programme, they seem almost offended or surprised when we don't want to do it. We may have done the story three months ago but we did it in a news item or an art show and when you are now talking about doing it on the main evening news the pressure is different.

   I once remember being told by a PR person, who I had a very good relationship with, when I rang them up about a story: 'Its not one for you Richard, it's not big enough.' I said: 'Fine, I won't waste any more of your time.'

Interviewer: Would you say you got the vast majority of your financial information from a relatively small number of sources?

Richard: Well there are two types of financial information. There is one that comes from breaking news, that comes from the wires, and/or from announcements from the companies, press releases, product warnings, things they have to give to the stock exchange, and the second is feature ideas. Feature ideas come from PR companies. They pitch a feature idea and you look at it and think it's either a good one or a bad one. What could be a bad one on a Tuesday could be a brilliant one on a Friday because you may be short on a Friday. So, you think it will have to do because there is nothing else around. The other thing is once we have decided to do it the PR company should just let us get on with it. If they try to manage the story it will fail. Once you have let the lion in you have to let it get on with eating the meal. That's not to say you give it free rein, and the best PR companies will make it quite clear that you will be able to do this but you will not be able to do that, so there are expectations.

Interviewer: Let's discuss crisis management. How would you characterize good and bad crisis management?

Richard: Microsoft during their trial in the US on anti-trust charges conducted excellent crisis management because they kept their side of the story out there. Admittedly, they were fighting tooth and nail so the company was very aggressive to start with, but they never let their side down, they were constantly bombarding the media with interviewees, their side of the story.

A disastrous crisis management [campaign] was Coca-Cola in Belgium – that was truly awful. Coca-Cola recently announced another Coke [Vanilla]. We were invited to do the story. I had to say to the PR guy, obviously we are going to have to ask about when you brought out a new coke in the 1980s and it was the biggest PR disaster you ever had. He said: 'Yes, we are ready for that one, we are well prepared for that question and answer.' Remember the health scandal in Belgium when a batch of Coca-Cola was found to be contaminated a couple of years ago? They ignored it for ages and made an appalling PR fist of it and then had to rescue it by doing interviews left, right and centre.

Ford and Firestone Tyres – that was dreadful crisis management. The Lockerbie bombing incident when a plane exploded over Scotland was a particularly bad example of crisis management by Pan Am. A good example of minor crisis management was when Concorde lost a bit of its rear rudder. I called British Airways, who explained that a Concorde pilot will be available for interview next to the Concorde model in the lobby at BA headquarters and that I should be there at one o'clock. The Concorde pilot was a perfect interviewee, nothing you can say will throw him and the story was spun the BA way.

When it comes to disasters most of us will allow companies a bit of leeway. The chairman who comes on the phone when the ship is sinking and says, 'Well, I don't know enough but I can tell you there will be a full investigation' and you keep pumping away and you say 'But why has this happened?' and he says 'I can't tell you at the moment, we are investigating.' That's fine, he has told us his point of view. Remember Townsend Thoresen, the North Sea ferry operator, they went out of business as a result of an incident where the ferry sank because the bow doors of the ferry had been left open. Their PR was so bad.

Interviewer: If you have a situation where people have actually been negligent, the facts speak for themselves, don't they?

Richard: They do, but the actual facts don't come out until later. Until then, you have the opportunity to put the best face on it. Now if you have 200 deaths, it is impossible to do that. Banks are notoriously bad at PR.

Interviewer: There is a standard response which seems to come out these days when a crisis occurs, which is: 'We are very sorry for what has happened, we are looking into it and there will be a full report.' Is that sufficient?

Richard: Well, it may not be sufficient but it's all you'll get.

Interviewer: Can you give me some examples of how PR has changed?

Richard: Going back to 1987, when I started in financial journalism, you would never be allowed to be in the Stock Exchange in London. The Stock Exchange had a press office but it wasn't very good. Now the Stock Exchange has a city media centre which is used by every international broadcaster for their business coverage out of London.

The PR company will go to the Stock Exchange and one after the other the broadcasters will do satellite media tours or 'gangbang' interviews using fixed cameras. So the interviewee stands there and all you do is connect your earpiece by phone, everybody takes the same pictures and everybody gets a five-minute slot with the interviewee. Microsoft did that during the trial. They would put up their legal counsel again and again and everybody would have a five-minute window.

Interviewer: I remember a broadcast journalist, when talking about video news releases, saying that most network broadcasters were not interested in using them from political parties. Do you think things have changed?

Richard: Well, maybe not from political parties, but with companies you've got to. You have two types of VNR. A company will give you a VNR of all its products, its manufacturing process, its bottling plant, for instance. That is company-provided video and we all use it. We don't like it, we were against it in some cases, but the reality is you can't film everything. Major companies often provide an annual VNR. The second VNR concerns news events: the launch of a car or the opening of a building. Again, the rules are quite specific. You can use it but you must make it clear that the company has provided the material. So you will name the company that has provided the material.

A lot of corporations are failed by their PR companies where the VNR has soundbites within it, provided by the company, and there we have an absolute ban on it. The exception made was with Microsoft. Microsoft did a VNR following a judgement and they had a soundbite by Bill Gates. There is an almost total prohibition on using soundbites from the participants because they can't be tested by your own questioning.

Interviewer: Let us discuss the Royals. Give me some idea about how they have improved their communications.

Richard: The Golden Jubilee is a classic example. They made spokespersons available. There were press conferences held at the palace, there were meetings held at the palace openly and on the record, and we were allowed to film in the palace gardens. This was very different from the past.

Interviewer: How?

Richard: Well, if you asked questions the palace did not want to answer they would say: 'We don't want to talk about that. That is a private matter.' There is somebody now who will entertain the questions, they will not just say 'no comment'. They will say 'That is a private matter and we don't want to comment on that', but there is a difference. It is a difference of style. In the olden days, it was: 'How dare you ask the question?' Now, they are saying: 'We accept your right to ask the question but we are still not talking about it.' That may not produce results in the most sensitive of cases. So although we may not get more information, the threshold upon which they will comment goes up. It's sometimes like a war zone. There is so much off-the-record briefing.

Interviewer: It looks as if they are courting the press now, have you felt that?

Richard: Absolutely. They provide websites and facilities. Once we were outside Buckingham Palace and we asked for the lights to be switched on and they agreed to put the lights on at a particular time.

Interviewer: We'll end there. Thank you.

Chapter links

Chapter 17 – Broadcast public relations and funded television programmes
Chapter 19 – The press and broadcast sources
Chapter 26 – Crisis management

Part 5

Specialist Public Relations Areas

Chapter 24

Financial public relations

LEARNING OBJECTIVES

At the end of this chapter you will be able to:

- define financial public relations;
- outline the nature of financial public relations;
- describe the main techniques used in financial public relations and investor relations;
- outline the importance of the Regulatory News Service to UK LSE-listed companies.

The industry

Some public relations managers and consultants may be active in financial public relations on a day-to-day basis, because that is the nature of their own or their client's business. Other in-house public relations managers may use financial public relations rarely, and the public relations consultants who handle financial public relations will usually be specialists. According to Blackhurst (2000), anyone can become a financial PR professional, although there are usually three entry streams: (1) ex-senior financial journalists; (2) former bankers and brokers; and (3) the fresh university graduate. Table 24.1 illustrates the nature of change in the financial PR market between 1999 and 2001. The table shows increasing revenues within the industry by Lanson Communications, Hill & Knowlton, Fishburn Hedges and Weber Shandwick Worldwide. Takeover battles and flotations, particularly in the dotcom sector,

Table 24.1 Top ten financial PR firms (UK, 1999–2001)

Market position 2001 (1999)	Company name	Revenue 2001 (£)	Revenue increase (1999–2001, %)
1 (2)	Lanson Communications	5 340 000	154
2 (3)	Hill & Knowlton	4 213 000	127
3 (4)	Fishburn Hedges	2 492 000	89
4 (7)	Weber Shandwick Worldwide	2 477 000	167
5 (–)	Penrose Financial	2 342 000	n/a*
6 (5)	GCI UK/APCO UK	1 763 000	73
7 (–)	Polhill Communications	1 681 000	n/a*
8 (6)	College Hill	1 537 000	66
9 (–)	Golin/Harris International	1 461 000	n/a*
10 (8)	Consolidated Communications Management	1 236 000	91

* Not in top ten by revenue, 1999; therefore, revenue increase figures not provided

Source: derived from Anon. (1999a) and Gofton (2001)

fuelled the demand for the services of financial PR consultants. The UK government also introduced ISAs (individual savings accounts) as the principal consumer tax-free saving device, as a replacement for PEPs (personal equity plans) and TESSAs (tax exempt special savings accounts) (Anon., 2000a). Gofton (2001) expected the market to slow and then decline when share offerings, mergers and acquisitions activity dipped in the US, and the knock-on effects were subsequently felt in London. Whilst the classic city type of PR did dip, financial services PR continued unabated in 2002 (Anon., 2002d).

Those PR professionals working for banks, insurance companies, building societies, unit trusts, the London Stock Exchange (LSE), stock-brokers and other financial service operators have become very active following deregulation in the mid-1980s in the UK. Nevertheless, limited and public limited companies also need to communicate with shareholders, institutional buyers, city editors and investment analysts for various reasons.

Institutional buyers are regular buyers of shares because they have an inflow of funds, which need to be invested, e.g. insurance companies, pension funds and unit trusts. They employ their own public relations professionals, but they are also the targets of public relations communications from those whose shares they buy. Thus, we can distinguish between two types of public relations: the first is aimed at financial publics (e.g. regulatory agencies, banks, rating agencies, venture capitalists) by organizations. This is the traditional financial or 'City' PR. The other type of public relations is aimed at investors, e.g. by financial services companies selling investment products, and by companies seeking to raise equity or sell debt. The latter form of public relations is known as investor relations.

City editors, the editors of the business or financial section of newspapers, are not to be confused with the news editors of newspapers. Usually, the more up-market the newspaper, the more extensive the coverage of City news. These editors have their offices located in the City, rather than wherever the newspaper has its main editorial offices. They ensure an in-depth coverage of business issues. Their audience might be investment analysts, pension and unit trust fund managers, bankers, insurers, company operations and finance directors, and others interested in financial news. Investment analysts are particularly important, since they prepare reports on those public limited companies listed on the Stock Exchange. They set market expectations by making recommendations regarding their investment prospects (e.g. suggesting that investors buy, hold or sell). The accuracy of their reports often depends on the information they receive from public relations sources. Companies have a duty to ensure that their shareholders understand their financial position at all times. Cantwell (2000) argues that companies often underestimate the importance of their relationship with rating agencies (e.g. Dun & Bradstreet and Standard & Poor). A company's financial position can be badly affected by a downgrading in credit rating as banks consider loans riskier and charge higher interest rates. British Telecom (and other telecommunications companies) found this out to their cost. BT's rating was downgraded after their debt soared above £30 billion in 2001 after unchecked purchasing of overseas telecom interests, the purchase of European third generation mobile licences (which may never realize their costs) and the costs associated with infrastructure development in their various markets. Only after selling many of their overseas interests, refocusing on their mission to become a European provider of broadband voice and data services, and sacking and installing new senior management, has BT begun to climb the slow road back to recovery.

An in-house PRO's normal responsibility for financial public relations may not extend beyond shareholder relations and preparations of the annual report and accounts and AGM, unless there is a share issue, rights issue or a takeover situation when a specialist financial public relations consultant would probably be engaged. Investor relations become particularly important, since shareholders have voting rights and can attend company meetings or issue proxies with voting instructions. They have to be kept informed of issues that may affect the risk of their investment. So it is important not only to send interim and annual reports and accounts, but other communiqués as the need arises. In the modern post-privatization era of share ownership, shareholders may well be employees and customers. Since shareholders may be tempted to sell during a takeover bid, loyalty can be crucial. Some companies have a large number of shareholders other than institutions and speculative buyers who merely seek to take a profit by buying cheap and selling dear. Maintaining their loyalty is a much more difficult task. An important part of management–employee relations, whether or not employees are shareholders, consists of keeping staff aware of the company's financial performance. This can be done through explanations of the annual report and accounts in the printed house journal, or the video house journal, or via webcasting services on an investor relations section of the company's website. Some companies produce audio-visuals in which a well-known TV personality interviews the CEO and the accounts are explained.

The ownership of shares has been greatly widened by the privatization of previously public industries (e.g. telecommunications, electricity, gas, water, airlines) and deregulation in financial services markets. Moreover, the availability of share registers has already made millions of people subject to direct mailings from firms selling financial services. In the past, such lists were used for direct marketing purposes, but companies are now required to ask potential members of a mailing list if they wish to be added to it if the potential buyer wants to receive such information. The whole financial market has been extended. The protection of the corporate image and integrity of reputable sellers of financial services comes to the fore in such a situation. There have been numerous major financial crises since the mid-1980s, e.g. the Maxwell Pension Fund scandal, the collapse of the Bank of Credit and Commerce International (BCCI), the collapse of Barings Bank and the fall of Enron. Public relations will be crucial in rebuilding stakeholder trust, particularly where fraud (e.g. BCCI, Barings) and supervisory negligence (e.g. by auditors or regulators) were to blame for the crisis in the first place.

Why financial public relations is different

Financial public relations was originally defined by the Public Relations Society of America in 1963, but recently amended in 1988, as 'that area of public relations which relates to the dissemination of information that affects the understanding of stockholders [shareholders] and investors generally concerning the financial position and prospects of a company, and includes among its objectives the improvement of relations between corporations and their stockholders' (PRSA, 2002). The above definition outlines the importance of ensuring that shareholders understand a company's financial position. This is one of the reasons why financial PR differs from other forms of public relations. The product with which it deals is a very sensitive one. Share prices are notoriously fragile. Mergers and acquisitions, new product development, and diversification can all affect a company's share price. Depending on how wise the market views the strategy to be, the share price may rise or fall substantially.

Unlike other forms of public relations, where PR professionals relish maximum media coverage, in financial PR this could very easily generate overconfidence in the market. If analyst expectations are dashed, and they subsequently advise their clients of the company's true position, the company could face large-scale selling of its shares, lowering demand, the share price and ultimately the market capitalization of the company. Large falls in share prices could make the company a target in a takeover bid as the company's market capitalization (i.e. the value placed on the company by the stock market) drops. Equally, however, large rises in share prices, perhaps created by inflated earnings, can increase a firm's market capitalization. This makes it better able to compete in the market. It could subsequently become a predator in a takeover struggle for a smaller company by using its own overvalued shares as currency for the purchase.

Inflation of earnings, and the subsequent inability of auditors to pick up the discrepancies, has created outrage in the financial markets in the early 2000s. Examples of such companies include Enron, AOL Time Warner and WorldCom. Shares in the world's largest media company, AOL Time Warner, plunged when it was revealed that an investigation was being undertaken into its accounting practices. US financial regulators began investigating allegations that it inflated the advertising revenue for its America Online division: the division that originally took over Time Warner. The company's share price dropped by as much as 21 per cent on Wall Street after chief executive, Richard Parsons, revealed the inquiry (Sky News, 2002a). In the same year, WorldCom was also reported to have inflated its profits – by £2.5 billion! The eventual disclosure sparked panic selling as investors sought to reduce their risk exposure. The company, worth some £110 billion in 1999, has now filed for bankruptcy (Sky News, 2002b). Shareholders that didn't sell sufficiently quickly will have seen their investments plummet.

The Public Relations Society of America's guidelines on conducting financial PR state that 'under no circumstances shall members participate in any activity designed to mislead or manipulate the price of a company's securities' (PRSA, 2002). The information disseminated should be accurate, clear and understandable. This is important for reasons of compliance, e.g. in the UK, the London Stock Exchange regulates share dealings. In the above examples (Enron, AOL Time Warner and WorldCom), the US Securities Exchange Commission would be the regulatory authority. However, the market itself, a system that operates in a delicate equilibrium, will not tolerate the uncertainty created by an act of dishonesty. Shareholders within it will move to minimize their exposure and reduce their risk immediately.

Information should be released in a timely manner to avoid the possibility of any use of the information by an insider or third party, criminal offences in most markets around the world. Releasing information at the appropriate time is fundamental. Ill-timed statements by Marconi regarding profits warnings and management departures led to a considerable decline in its share price (Cowlett, 2001a) and subsequent de-listing on NASDAQ, the American exchange for high-technology stock.

Financial PRs have a duty to correct rumours, and false or misleading information, in connection with their company's or client's stock or business position if they are affecting investors' attitudes and behaviour. There is a subtle difference between creating overconfidence, which produces a bull market, and creating confidence in a company to stabilize its shares at a realistic price.

Frank, informative one-to-one relationships with city journalists, institutional investors, investment analysts and credit rating agency professionals are fundamental. They may be more productive than a flow of news releases to the business newspapers. The PRO should be aware that instantaneous means of communication and trading exist. Electronic trading systems, online information facilities and global information systems have now replaced the frenetic trading and shouting matches that used to occur on the trading floors of isolated stock exchanges and bourses around the world. In the information age, trading is facilitated by the latest information from the likes of the printers of the *Financial Times, International Herald Tribune*, the *Wall Street Journal* and *The Economist*. Reuters and Bloomberg supply real-time financial information regarding money and capital markets, equities and stock markets, and commodities, usually updated every 15 minutes, on a global scale.

The London Stock Exchange

In the UK, most financial PR is conducted in relation to shares traded on the London Stock Exchange (LSE) and particularly shares in the FTSE 100 (the top 100 UK companies by market capitalization). There are, of course, other important exchanges, both in the UK (e.g. London International Financial Futures Exchange – LIFFE) and abroad (e.g. the New York Stock Exchange and the German stock exchange in

Frankfurt), but this chapter will focus on the LSE for the purposes of describing how financial public relations works, and its communication vehicle, the Regulatory News Service.

Regulatory News Service

The Regulatory News Service (RNS) is the leading publisher of regulatory news announcements submitted by listed companies in compliance with their obligations to the London Stock Exchange. The RNS is designed to ensure that these announcements, which have a material effect on market activity and the prices of securities, are validated and communicated promptly to the market. Typical announcements can include year-end and half-year results, boardroom moves, takeover situations, major contracts, directors' dealings and shareholder benefits (LSE, 2002a). The RNS allows texts of announcements to be submitted directly (the Direct Input Provider Service) in HTML, by diskette, in hard copy or by fax. The RNS has distribution agreements with numerous major financial services' information publishing houses (e.g. Bloomberg, Reuters, Lexis-Nexis, Infoshare Europe, Durlacher, Thomson, Cazenove, Dow Jones & Co., E-Trade UK and many others). The result is that it is able to reach over 250 000 trading screens and press desks (LSE, 2002b) with over 170 000 announcements per year (LSE, 2002c). The RNS also provides services to distribute non-regulatory announcements, video and audio content through a webcasting service, a key stakeholder targeted distribution service, and a website-based service that allows a company to monitor its own and competitors' RNS announcements.

Investor relations

With many millions of shareholders, largely as a result of privatizations, increasing deregulation and globalization, a new kind of shareholder relations has developed. Aside from institutional shareholders, private shareholders may no longer be sophisticated finance professionals (if indeed they ever were). They are more likely to be interested in the qualitative side of a company (i.e. its business positioning and its corporate strategy) than the quantitative side (e.g. its profit and loss account and balance sheet). Good relations with shareholders make good business sense. As the shareholder franchise has widened it is increasingly likely to include consumers. Thus, a BP shareholder can be encouraged to buy BP petrol, whilst an Egg shareholder is probably more likely to be persuaded to take out a personal loan. Investor relations activity typically includes dissemination of the annual reports and accounts and organization of the annual general meeting (AGM), and communication of statements (e.g. the company's corporate strategy). Typically, a comprehensive website might also be developed.

Annual reports and accounts and the AGM

The public relations manager is usually responsible for the writing, designing, printing and to some extent the distribution of the annual report and accounts, as well as the organization of the annual general meeting (AGM). In relation to the annual reports and accounts, most analysts would say that content was more important than style. The annual accounts and report should be clear, accurate and understandable. The design of the accounts and annual report should be distinctive. They are usually characteristic of the company, but the objective of the exercise is to make it readable and understandable. The design, typography and general presentation should ensure simplicity, readability and legibility. In many reports, the text is too long and would benefit from judicious editing. The chairman's report should not be a personal soapbox. It should provide an overview of the leadership of the company, the difficulties the company faces and the obstacles it has overcome. Sometimes the type is too small, it is printed in a light colour on a tinted paper, the paragraphs are too long, or there are no subheadings to break up vast sections of copy. So attention should be given to readers' needs. Writers should pay particular attention to the presentation of figures in the accounts, ensuring that they can be easily understood.

It is important to design the annual report by first considering those publics it will be aimed at. Some reports may appear to be aimed at pleasing the vanity of their management, more than the needs of their financial publics. It is important to remember that these publications are communication tools. Institutional and private shareholders, financial journalists, investment analysts, distributors, potential investors, employees, and many other groups of people might all read these documents. Copies might be placed on exhibition stands, particularly at international trade fairs. Annual reports often act as company ambassadors. They might well be the first port of call for those wishing to find out more about a listed company. Does the annual report and accounts have a place in the media list for reaching selected publics, as part of the public relations plan, particularly financial stakeholders? Can a special public relations exercise be built around the annual report itself, not withstanding the annual general meeting of shareholders? The annual general meeting is probably less well attended now than it has been in the past. As a result of the availability of annual reports and accounts on the Internet, AGMs have increasingly become a focus for pressure groups targeting financial journalists with negative messages about the company (LSE, 2002d). Suggestions to generate loyalty amongst shareholders, particularly private shareholders, include holding prize draws, making company announcements at the AGM, and holding company visits for institutional shareholders and analysts at the same time (LSE, 2002d).

Analysts' briefings, institutional meetings and company visits

Financial PR personnel also set up briefings with analysts where a number of key issues will be addressed, particularly the long-term future of the company and the direction it intends on taking. They will expect a company to disclose as much information as possible (without breaking the rules on disclosure). Generally, they may well ask specific questions about investment in, or disposal of, individual business units or product lines. The role of analysts becomes particularly important when a company is due to float on the stock exchange. Since the company has no previous trading history, and since the company wants to raise as much money on the equity market as possible, their financial PR professional needs to ensure that analysts value their company at the top end of what management consider to be an acceptable share price, whilst also ensuring that its share offer is still oversubscribed (i.e. all the shares are sold at the highest price). This is sometimes a delicate balancing act. Where companies do not feel they are sufficiently valued, they may withdraw their offer. Most of the flotations pertaining to privatized companies in the 1980s were many times oversubscribed, particularly in the first instances (e.g. British Telecom, British Gas), as the government didn't really appreciate how much these companies were worth. Later privatizations offered the public much less long-term value (e.g. Railtrack).

Institutional meetings will also need to be organized by the financial PR. Institutional shareholders usually own the vast majority of a company's shares and are often the majority owners of a business. Institutional owners should be kept abreast of important events or factors affecting the company. One-to-one meetings should be organized by the financial PR with a company's financial director and chairperson. This gives institutional shareholders the opportunity to weigh up the management of the company they have invested in. The financial PR will receive the institutional shareholders views on the company, which may well be useful feedback on how the company should be run.

Company visits usually involve a tour of a company's facilities to enable investors to familiarize themselves with the company they have

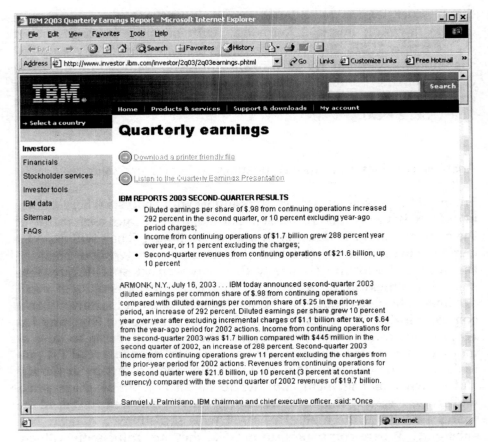

Figure 24.1 IBM's Investor Relations website. Reproduced courtesy of IBM Corporation.

Source: http://www.investor.ibm.com/investor/2q03/2q03earnings.phtml

invested in. A lunch with senior management should be organized, as well as an opportunity for investors to meet middle managers.

Websites

UK and Irish companies listed on the LSE can have their web pages directly linked to their corporate website. Their individual page on the LSE website will provide share price information (updated at 15-minute intervals), share price performance information, graphing functionality, the last five real-time regulatory news (RNS) announcements, the last five trades, and company background information (LSE, 2002e). Most companies also have their own investor relations websites incorporating the above features, but also including a news release archive, corporate brochures, prospectuses, webcast presentations from key company personnel, annual reports and accounts, company policy (e.g. corporate social responsibility) and other important shareholder information. Figure 24.1 provides an example of the IBM Investor Relations website.

Case study in brief: Glas Cymru

When the government decided to sell Welsh Water, a company providing water and sewerage services to over 3 million people, with £2 billion in debt, it did not expect a not-for-profit company, Glas Cymru, to raise the money to pay off the debt, remove shareholders and offer a value-for-money service, but that is what happened. This innovative financial PR campaign conducted by Good Relations won an IPR excellence award at the 2002 ceremony.

Its objectives were to gain city approval for the strategy and to ensure access to the financial markets. It had to contend with three major publics comprising the City, politicians and the regulator (OFWAT). It also had to illustrate its credibility in the face of rival bids with a more conventional approach to raising the funds necessary to buy the company. This was achieved by borrowing money on the more conservative bond market and by securing the support of the Welsh parliament by projecting the scheme as a 'Welsh solution'.

The PR campaign managed to secure endorsement in major national newspapers and on broadcast news channels (e.g. Today and Radio Five Live) after its announcement to bid for the franchise and subsequent analyst briefings. After conducting opinion polling among key opinion leaders, the campaign conducted further investor briefings prior to regulatory approval. Following this event, the campaign continued with analyst and media briefings outlining the benefits of the approach. The bond issue was 30 per cent oversubscribed and the Welsh Water franchise went to Glas Cymru (IPR, 2002).

Chapter 25

Internal public relations

LEARNING OBJECTIVES

At the end of this chapter you will be able to:

- describe how internal communication is linked to product and service quality;
- explain the importance of management–employee relations;
- recall the different types of communication in existence within an organization;
- outline some methods of developing downwards, sideways and upwards communication.

Importance of management–employee relations

Internal communications have advanced a long way from the management-sponsored house journals of yesteryear to well-organized systems of internal communication. There are a number of reasons for this. These include:

1. A greater requirement for companies to inform their employees about policy and financial affairs, including the annual report and accounts.
2. Increasing democratization of industry on the continental European pattern of worker directors, works councils and works committees.
3. Increasing employee ownership of company equity through privatizations, flotations, management buy-outs, share ownership schemes and performance-related pay schemes.
4. The availability of new communications technology, making it easier to organize and conduct internal communications. These new techniques

include intranet websites, video magazines, webcasts, business TV, journals, teleconferencing, mobile telephones, e-mail and SMS (short messaging service) text messaging for field personnel.

5. Increasing importance of service industries in Western economies, with particular reference to knowledge-based services, e.g. investment banking, marketing services, website design and development.

This reflects a changed industrial climate as the old industrial/manufacturing age is replaced by the new information/knowledge age. The 'them and us' attitude common in the industrial age, between bosses and workers, has diminished as the power of the unions has decreased. Management has learned how to manage, workforces are now more flexible and have been downsized. Increasingly, organizations feel that they need to adapt more quickly to change than their counterparts half a century previously. This is probably a myth. Fast-moving consumer goods firms had to cope with the new promotional opportunities that came with the mass enfranchisement of popular TV ownership. In previous centuries, major opportunities came with the development of railway networks, canal systems and, in times long gone, roads. Each change in infrastructure brought different opportunities and threats. Nevertheless, contemporary business generations have learned to cope with the uncertainty brought about by change in the environment by recognizing it for what it is.

Change management programmes, typically organized by human resource management departments, have a fundamental role to play during mergers, takeovers; mission, visioning and value programmes; and rebranding/positioning initiatives. When Lloyds and TSB, two of Britain's largest clearing banks, merged in 1999, the combined bank had to work quickly to communicate the new positioning to 77 000 staff. They did this by relying on 5000 key staff to attend a live event organized by event specialist, Carabiner, and feed back the message to the rest of the employee base (Anon., 1999b). This was conducted by these brand ambassadors, nicknamed 'pathfinders', in structured cascade sessions with 15 of their colleagues each, using a pack containing bullet point summaries, overhead transparencies, a computer disk and a video summary (Anon., 2000b). Research conducted pre- and post-event indicated loyalty and motivation had increased as a result (Anon., 1999b). This campaign won the UK Marketing Society's award for the Internal Communications category in 2000.

The role of the internal PR manager is particularly important when one considers that recent research undertaken by MORI has determined that 30 per cent of UK employees are brand neutral (not interested in their company's brand), 22 per cent are brand saboteurs (subverting the brand) and 48 per cent are brand champions (Hiscock, 2002). In branding and company visioning exercises, companies are increasingly developing workshops that allow employees to interpret and apply the company brand to their own jobs. The PR professional has an important role to play in developing understanding amongst employees of management expectations and vice versa during these periods of reorganization. A key component to change management is not just informing personnel of what needs to be done, although it is helpful when management realize what needs to be done and communicates this effectively, but listening to employees' concerns about the impact that change will have on their work and lives.

According to research undertaken by Richmond Events, in the UK, 75 per cent of companies now have a department with responsibility for internal communications. Frequently, this task rests with the marketing department (46 per cent of cases) compared with human resources (17 per cent) (Murphy, 2000). Most large companies will have an internal communications manager. He or she will be responsible for editing the house journal and any other form of communication, writing speeches for the CEO, conducting community relations, organizing incentive schemes, controlling noticeboards, and working closely with the personnel manager, the training officer and the industrial relations officer. These latter links will range from providing induction material for new staff (such as videos, webcasts and literature) to assisting labour relations by keeping employees well informed about management policy. Wise management have come to realize that many strikes could have been avoided if only they had communicated better with workers. Thus, internal PR is key to successful management.

Quality and internal relations

A focus on managing quality and internal relations was precipitated by the development of quality circles from Japan, productivity councils in Singapore, quality assurance in Britain, and just plain 'quality' in the USA. They are all expressions of a desire for perfection in product manufacturing and service industries. These techniques have since evolved into the concept of total quality management or TQM, where TQM can be defined as the involvement of all employees in continuous improvement of an organization's products and services. This approach was originally labelled a thought revolution in management, but it has sometimes also been regarded as just another management fad, like time and motion studies, operational research, and organizational development before it. There have been mixed views expressed about its usefulness. However, the general aims to emphasize customer satisfaction (internal and external) and improve quality continuously have become the top priorities of many organizations (e.g. Harley-Davidson). Rover, now MG Rover Ltd, and Rank Xerox both adopted the TQM approach for their quality control and product quality programmes, and have since adapted it for customer satisfaction programmes.

Total quality was embraced by the manufacturing industry first, but has also been taken on increasingly by service-based industries as this sector becomes an increasingly important, majority part of most Western economies in the latter part of the twentieth century. Particular quality improvement schemes include the British Standards Organization's BS5750 and the International Standards Organization's ISO9000/2. A large part of the documentation for these awards requires an organization to outline its quality improvement processes, with a particular emphasis on internal quality control procedures. Quality schemes are now commonplace in most industries and have their own peculiarities. For instance, the British beef industry introduced certification schemes to map the origin of beef produce from the farm to the supermarket (from 'gate to plate') after a ban was placed on it by the European Union in 1996, because of a suspected link between BSE-infected beef and Creutzfeldt–Jacob disease (CJD) in humans. Whilst this scheme was not initiated within specific companies, it was initiated within the beef industry supply chain in an attempt to integrate it and improve its external image. In the higher education sector, Masters in Business Administration programmes are often accredited by the Association of MBAs (AMBA). In the US, business schools are accredited by the Association to Advance Collegiate Schools of Business (AACSB). In Europe, business schools are accredited by the education standards organization, EQUIS. In all three cases, these standards have been adopted outside their original place of origin by aspirant foreign universities.

The ownership of the organization's quality control function depends on the nature of the business. It will often reside with the operations director in manufacturing companies and even some service-based businesses (e.g. banks). It may also come under the remit of the marketing director or customer services director. It is less likely to come solely under the remit of the director of communication, although it may well form part of their job description. It is more likely to form part of the job description for a PR position that focuses on internal communication, particularly in a service-based business. The human resources director also has an important role to play. Empowering employees is vital if they are to avoid strikes and reduce product defects. In many service industries (e.g. banking, professional services), operations management, human resource management, marketing and total quality management functions are interwoven in the development of service quality. A critical encounter occurs in service businesses when a customer's expectations are not met. Programmes aimed at recovering customer satisfaction after a critical encounter (e.g. a bank charges an overdraft fee for a customer that rarely overdraws and has sufficient money in another of the bank's accounts) might ultimately require input from the four functions listed above as follows:

1. Operations managers would need to redesign the bank's systems and processes for evaluating how and whether or not a customer should be charged for going overdrawn.
2. Human resource managers would need to develop training programmes for members of the bank's staff – for example, in dealing with difficult customers to ensure that they maintain a polite and informative attitude throughout a critical encounter.
3. Marketing managers should be involved in the redesign of the service to ensure that it meets with customer requirements and in subsequent promotion of the redesigned service.
4. Total quality managers would be involved in monitoring quality and developing improvements from within the organization.

Of course, these four functions are seldom clearly delineated. One function may subsume the other, e.g. the total quality management function might be performed by the operations department. This section has outlined the importance of employees in the process of continuous quality improvement in both product and service industries. However, it's one thing to recognize the importance of employees in delivering customer satisfaction, it's quite another redesigning their jobs to actually deliver it.

Employee empowerment

Empowerment was perhaps *the* buzzword of the 1990s (Webster, 2002). Of course, competent managements have been empowering employees for years. Despite this, jobs in some industries are so deskilled that employees only perform simple tasks, often as part of an unknown wider task, thereby not knowing the role they play within the value chain. Through empowerment, employees should feel that they have the authority to deal with a problem holistically as they see fit. This sounds simple, but many organizations have built-in bureaucracy to ensure that employees do not abuse their authority, if they have any. For instance, a university counsellor would not usually have the authority to change a student's course grades in the UK. They would, however, if they felt empowered, feel able to make recommendations for deferral or a resit for a particular student that merited this.

A customer service adviser for a telecommunications company should feel sufficiently empowered to waive a fee, say, for a cable TV service where the quality of the transmission was poor. Pret-à-Manger has empowered its existing shop staff by giving them the say over which job applicants get hired. Thus, prospective members of staff are required to work for a day in a Pret shop and are assessed by the existing team.

Management have slowly begun to realize that their employees, the front-line foot-soldiers in the company–customer interface, can deliver incredible customer value if they feel empowered to make decisions on behalf of the customer. Ballantyne (2000) argues that internal relationship development was fundamental in developing customer consciousness – an enhanced market orientation – amongst employees in the banking sector. He argues that the bank created a new understanding of its customers by setting up a customer service group with links to marketing and other departments. Harley-Davidson have also trained their employees to engage with their customers. Many employees have their own motorcycles and have joined and organized Harley Owner's Group (HOG) events. Their policy of 'super-customer engagement' has delivered incredible results for Harley-Davidson over the past 20 years. The basic thesis then is that a happy employee makes customers happy. But how do you determine whether or not employees are happy? And what do you do if they are not?

Internal communications audits

A number of companies today take the trouble to invite professional research units to conduct employee attitude surveys or internal communication audits to measure employee attitudes and the level of staff morale. It is often surprising how little management know about their own employees, and likewise how little employees know about the company in which they work. An independent survey guaranteeing employee confidentiality to all who are interviewed can provide some of this information. These types of surveys should not be confused with surveys conducted by management consultants, who are mainly concerned with the way a company is managed. Some of these internal audits are long standing. Rank Hovis McDougall conduct such studies approximately every three years. Cadbury-Schweppes also have such a scheme. Burson-Marsteller, the PR consultant, is well known for their conduct of both internal and external communication audits. Kitchen and Daly (2002) suggest that employees should be asked their perceptions of a variety of aspects comprising the following:

1. Internal communication.
2. Employee participation and involvement.
3. Employee loyalty and commitment.
4. Staff morale.
5. Institutional reputation.
6. Ethics.
7. Recognition of employees' contribution.
8. Alignment of corporate, department, team and individual goals.
9. Leadership.
10. Employee development opportunities.
11. Resource utilization.

By considering each of these areas, the internal PR manager can ascertain how valuable and satisfied employees feel. The internal PR manager should also be able to suggest solutions where particular problems exist. He or she should be able to institute an intranet system, for instance, if employees are not communicating well with each other. If employees do not feel involved, particularly in decision making, management could ensure their representation on senior management committees, as well as ensuring that policy is developed by incorporating a period of employee consultation in the future. Castrol, owned by BP, has commissioned Baston Greenhill Andrews, who designed a game to appeal to employees. The game encourages staff to verbalize what the brand means and think about the kind of imagery that it conveys (Bashford, 2002).

If staff loyalty is low, this may be because employees do not understand the mission or vision of the organization. In such a situation, the internal PR manager has an important role to play in cascading information down on, and in generating participation in, these initiatives. Where staff morale is low, the internal PR manager has a duty to inform senior management. It could be improved through sideways communication programmes (see next section) using house journals (see Chapter 23) and staff events (parties). If there is a particular reason for low morale – for example, bad press because of poor labour practices (as happened at Nike because of their labour practices in Asian countries) – the internal PR manager might counsel senior management to develop a clear ethics and values policy, to develop a corporate social responsibility programme, or a cause-related marketing programme, or to communicate with employees about why the company adopted the particular policy that it did, and to apologize to them if necessary. Usually, whilst both cause-related marketing programmes and corporate social responsibility programmes are intended to improve the image of the company generally, they also have the positive effect of making the organization a better place to work for its employees, since the organization is involved in charitable work. Broadly, whilst cause-related marketing programmes tie in the marketing of the organization with the marketing of a charity or not-for-profit organization, corporate social responsibility programmes generally expend resources on a particular social project with less expectation of a 'marketing return', i.e. the business objectives are often less explicit.

A staff audit will provide interesting information on how employees view the company, and how the employees think that external stakeholders will view the company. Such information provides useful input to a corporate image, identity and advertising programme (see Chapter 28). Where an organization's ethics impact upon employee productivity, internal PR staff have a dual role, working with management to develop the ethics policy and ensuring staff have input and are happy with the outcome. Cause-related marketing programmes are most likely to be successful when pre-launch communication activities are used to cement senior internal commitment to the strategy (Gray, 2001). House journals and staff competitions can both be used as devices to recognize staff involvement and participation, and are an important component of internal PR. The internal PR manager also has an important role to play in the development and communication of the organization's mission, vision and value statements, and the leadership of the organization. He or she should be able to provide an indication of how well a mission and visioning programme is being received by employees, as well as being able to design media to communicate that mission and vision with employees (e.g. Cisco uses webcasts to disseminate messages from its CEO). Williams (2002) suggests that 'if a company is serious about its ethical image, its vision, values, mission and strategy have to become part of its corporate culture, and that means selling those things to employees'. But it's *not* just about one-way communication, it's also about listening to employees.

Staff attitudes are critical input for developing the corporate values on which most organization's missions and visions are built. Internal PR also has a role to play in communicating employee benefits, such as training or redeployment or other development opportunities. Finally, internal PR managers might investigate staff attitudes towards resource utilization generally, perhaps through suggestion box schemes or intranet bulletin boards.

Internal PR techniques

Internal PR can be placed under the three headings of *upwards, sideways* and *downwards* communication (Jefkins, 1990). This incorporates employee–management relations, employee–employee relations and management–employee relations respectively.

Upwards communication

How can employees communicate with management? Moreover, how can they be encouraged to do so, because it may not have occurred to them that they should or could. They may have thought that their only means of communication with management was through their trade union shop steward, and then only when they had something to complain about. But upward communication is not only, or even, about grievances. The facility to talk to one's leaders is the ability to belong, to identify, to join in and to participate. Job satisfaction is derived from enjoying one's work and feeling fulfilled. This requires a measure of engagement by employees in their work. Some of the methods of upward communication include reader's letters, suggestion schemes, house journal articles and specialist workshops.

Readers' letters

When employee newspapers like *Ford News* print readers' letters, two things happen: (1) there is reader participation and (2) the publication contains one of the most popular features of the press. Readers' letters not only provide the opportunity for people to have their say, but they add reality and credibility to a journal. They are what people expect to find in a real newspaper or magazine. They give pleasure to hundreds, perhaps thousands, of readers who may never bother to write a letter themselves.

Suggestion schemes

The opportunity may not be exercised by everyone but the fact that anyone may propose something creates a good feeling that one's ideas are valued. The means of doing this should be conveniently located, as when boxes are fitted to corridor walls, or an intranet suggestion website, which is clearly signposted. Murphy (2000) states that the UK electrical retailer, Dixon's, developed its idea for its now well-developed and demerged ISP (Internet Service Provider), Freeserve, from an intranet site and a suggestion from a junior manager. Such schemes are even more likely to generate successful ideas when a reward is provided for ideas that help improve productivity.

House journal articles

A way of communicating upwards can be the contribution of an 'own job' article, or an interview about one's job for the house journal or video magazine. Members of staff may describe aspects of their work experience, which could be quite unknown to management. Remember, business leaders including directors have seldom grown up in the company, and they can sometimes be remote from what actually goes on in the working lives of employees. A house journal may well have a network of frequent contributors from different employees throughout the company, some of whom may be scattered throughout the country and possibly abroad.

Specialist workshops

These may be organized to develop productivity (e.g. quality groups), customer service (as recounted in the banking industry in an earlier section of this chapter) or particular aspects of company policy (e.g. corporate social responsibility). In fact, specialist committees could be organized for any number of company functions. They serve a particularly useful purpose because they make employees feel valued, especially when their recommendations are put into practice. They tend to work best when the members are volunteers.

Sideways communication

Sideways communication is appreciated in organizations where there are good relationships between members of staff and they are interested in each other's affairs. This may simply be because there is a friendly working environment, or because staff roles are mobile within the organization. Organizations with many branches or subdivisions can develop this aspect into a strength. It can make the organization more interesting to work for! Internal PR to develop sideways communications may include the house journal, staff clubs and social events, and staff news items.

Classified house journal advertisements

Usually inserted free of charge, but restricted to a certain length, a marketplace can be established in the employee newspaper providing details of items for sale or wanted items. Other examples might include available accommodation and accommodation wanted. In journals such as *Ford News*, classified ads fill a couple of pages. Like readers' letters, classified ads are very popular. They not only add to the interest of the publication and give it a realistic appearance, but they encourage reader participation and create many staff contacts.

Staff clubs and social events

Reports in the house journal, on a controlled noticeboard, perhaps on the intranet, provide further links between staff when there are staff clubs and societies covering sport, hobbies and other interests. Controlled noticeboards are usually of a standard design, with input from an authorized person only. Thus, the boards can be kept tidy and attractive, and employees know where to find different kinds of information.

The house journal, bulletin boards and the intranet can also be used to announce parties, perhaps organized by the PR department. These could be end-of-year parties or special celebrations (e.g. for having met sales targets). Sometimes, these social events could be linked to sponsorship schemes (see Chapter 27) where the sponsoring organization receives special benefits for its staff as a result. For example, as a consequence of sponsoring the Tate Modern, BT distributed tickets to employees during training events.

Staff news

Special columns in the house journal can be devoted to topics like 'On The Move', 'New Appointments', 'On Leave', 'Marriages, Births, Retirements' and 'Obituaries', so that employees can learn more about people they know. Many journals are distributed to retired staff too.

Downwards communication

A house journal should be neither a pulpit nor a platform for senior management, but there are various ways in which they can keep the staff well informed about developments, prospects and finances. A well-informed staff is likely to work more satisfactorily. Some of these methods used for downward communication include annual reports and accounts, company policy documents, appointment announcements, corporate identity and corporate advertising schemes, the house journal and cascade briefing sessions.

Annual reports and accounts

These can be explained graphically and in straightforward language in the printed house journal or visually in the video magazine or in a webcast. However, a method adopted very successfully by some companies is to produce a video in which the chairman is interviewed by a professional interviewer such as a TV presenter. Financial reports can interest a considerable number of staff now, as many employees own shares in the company for which they work (or may consider buying some), or have unit trust shares and the company is included in the portfolio, or there is a profit-sharing scheme.

Company policy documents

There is nothing worse than employees learning about the company's plans at second hand, say in the press or on TV, or as a rumour rather than as a result of timely and planned communications by the internal PR manager. It will pay to delay a public announcement until staff have been told. The PR manager, who should be aware of all company plans, may have to use an urgent form of communication rather than waiting for the next issue of the house journal. This might include intranet, e-mail or webcasting. It might equally involve a general corporate meeting, which all employees are required to attend. Cascading information in this way can be very effective.

Appointment announcements
All new managerial appointments or changes should be communicated to staff as soon as possible. The staff should always be familiar with the management structure. Reminders of this can appear in the house journal and company induction documents or audio–visual material. Meetings and visits can also be arranged, or tours of premises can be made to meet the staff. Top management personalities should not remain remote. It sends a bad message to other employees.

Corporate identity and corporate advertising
Corporate identity and advertising are covered in greater detail in Chapter 28. Here they will be described briefly. Corporate identity schemes can be particularly useful in service operations to ensure uniformity of the service offering. A corporate identity scheme is likely to include at least uniform dress, stationery, vehicle livery and a corporate logo. Whilst such schemes are often expensive, they can improve employee morale and instil pride. There have been instances where employees have rebelled against an identity scheme, as UK train operator, Connex South Central, staff did when they were forced to wear branded yellow uniforms, apparently because they were fed up with being teased by customers! (Mazur, 1999).

Before major corporate advertisement campaigns break, employees should have an opportunity to see the advertisements first. They might be reproduced in the house journal. If possible, commercials should be shown to the staff before they are released to the general public. It depends on the size, nature and location of staff as to whether or not these advance showings are possible. By being given prior knowledge of advertising campaigns, employees can see what is being done to promote the prosperity of their company.

The house journal
This medium can be useful for explaining issues to staff in a more informal way than by presenting them with reports and official company documents. The journal could incorporate interviews with the managing director or CEO on the direction of the company or on a new venture. Marks & Spencer, the UK retailing company, originally produced

two house journals: one for shop-floor staff and one for management. This created a division between the two sets of staff and the two were eventually merged in a new magazine, *On Your Marks*. Management have used the magazine to explain company policy on contentious issues – for example, the unpopular sacking of their clothing contractor, William Baird, in 1999 (Murphy, 2000). Thus, when articles are written in co-operation with management on issues that affect employees, the house journal can be a useful downward communication device. The house journal is covered in more detail in Chapter 23.

Cascade briefing sessions

These may be organized to develop customer service or vision, mission and value statements. Like specialist workshops, they could be organized for a number of reasons. The 2002 IPR Excellence award winning campaign team at SEEBOARD Energy (i.e. the former Southeast Electricity Board) used cascade briefing sessions to communicate their new customer vision and the contribution staff would make to developing this vision. These cascade sessions were themselves based on previous 'Leader's Workshops' events, where the customer vision and strategy were originally developed. In the cascade sessions, leaders presented the new customer vision to their individual teams and discussed how the vision could and would be implemented. Further workshops were organized by SEEBOARD Energy to tackle contentious issues related to the customer vision as they arose.

The above is just a sample of items that can be included in downward communication, but they give an impression of how management can be forthcoming, and can generate interest, enthusiasm and above all understanding.

Chapter 26

Crisis management

LEARNING OBJECTIVES

At the end of this chapter you will be able to:

■ outline the types of crisis that can affect organizations;
■ explain how public relations techniques are used in crisis situations;
■ recall some of the dos and don'ts of crisis management;
■ understand the importance of urgency and empathy in crisis management.

What types of crisis can affect your firm?

The best way to destroy one's reputation is to be ill-prepared for all manner of crises and fail to take a stand on appropriate issues (Hayes, 2001). 'A true crisis, if improperly managed, can destroy an organization' (Pearson, 2002). But what is a crisis? According to White and Mazur (1995), a crisis has the following characteristics:

1. A high degree of threat to life, safety, or to the existence of the organization.
2. Time pressure, meaning that decision makers have to work urgently to resolve the situation.
3. Stress is placed upon those responsible for managing the situation (as a result of the importance of the decisions being made).

Sen and Egelhoff (1991) state that crises can be caused by human error, technological faults, societal reasons (e.g. war, terrorism), natural disasters or management. They outline that the cause of the crisis is important because it determines where blame is apportioned. Examples of possible crises include executive kidnappings, product tampering, security leaks, unethical behaviour, workplace violence, employee fraud (Pearson, 2002), industrial accidents, environmental problems, investor relations, hostile takeovers, strikes, product recall and government regulatory problems.

Do you remember any of the following incidents: Bhopal, the Hillsborough stadium disaster, the Ford and Bridgestone/Firestone tyre recall, or the BSE/British beef scare? In each case, human lives were lost and the parties considered to be at fault suffered considerable damage to their reputations. In the first example, approximately 3000 people and 2000 animals died (accounts differ) when a toxic substance, methyl iso-cyanate, was released from a Union Carbide plant located in Bhopal, India. Union Carbide, as a result, was forced to downsize its operation considerably, restructure itself and get out of its profitable consumer products business (Sen and Egelhoff, 1991). In the second example, the police service came under severe criticism for allowing overcrowding at the Sheffield Wednesday football ground, where over 50 people were crushed to death. In the third example, Ford Motor Company and Firestone, a Japanese-owned, US-based tyre maker, both suffered considerable damage to their reputations, and their businesses, when tyre blow-outs, apparently precipitated by tread separation on the Firestone tyres, caused the Ford Explorer sport utility vehicle to roll over (allegedly due to poor vehicle design). In all, 175 people were killed and 700 injured in more than 1400 accidents related to tyre blow-out (Freitag, 2002). The accidents have cost the two companies billions of US dollars in recall costs, replacements and lawsuits. In the fourth example, British beef was infected when bonemeal contaminated with BSE (bovine spongiform encephalopathy) was fed to cattle, allegedly causing a debilitating brain disease when eaten by humans. In total, approximately 90 people died from the disease. As a result, the European Union announced an export ban on British beef products. The British beef industry lost more than half a billion pounds in annual export income, while it cost the UK government well over £4 billion in subsidies alone (Baines and Harris, 2000). The result is a UK and EU government that is much more likely to adopt the 'precautionary principle' on matters of food policy in the UK, bringing it into conflict with various trade bodies (Davies, 2002).

Thus, as one can see above, in crisis situations it may not be the problem *per se* that causes a critical episode, but the company's response to that problem (Stewart, 1998). The process of managing crises then becomes paramount. But what is crisis management? It has been previously defined as 'a systematic approach that engages the whole organization in efforts to avert crises that may affect the firm, and manage those that do' (Pearson, 2002). In the next section, we consider the origins of crisis management and how it should be approached.

Public relations in disaster situations

The pioneer of modern public relations, Ivy Ledbetter Lee, was called in by the American anthracite coal industry and the Pennsylvania Railroad, in 1906, to handle the media during a period defined by pit disasters and railway accidents. Lee demanded access to boardrooms to get the facts, and arranged access for the press to the scenes of disaster. He achieved fair and accurate reporting from the press despite the exaggerations and inaccuracies based on rumour and hearsay that had been published on previous occasions. This is an early example of crisis management at its best.

Today, we live in the midst of potential chemical (e.g. Bhopal), nuclear (e.g. Chernobyl, Sellafield, Three Mile Island), electronic (e.g. Y2K and computer viruses), terrorist (e.g. the Al Qaeda declaration of jihad and the bombing of the World Trade Center have precipitated a substantial increase in the cost of terrorist insurance) and activist hazards (e.g. McDonald's during the May 2001 Reclaim the Streets protests in London). It is necessary to accept that anything can happen, not merely taking precautions about the most likely. The modern public relations manager has to reckon with the unlikely. This is being realistic, not fatalistic. It is a special area of public relations calling for *management* skills in prevention, preparation and provision: the three Ps of crisis management. A key consideration in crisis management is the speed at which public relations personnel and other crisis managers must act. This problem is exacerbated by the fantastic speed of modern communication. The world may know of a disaster before the organization can manage to work out what to do. CNN, Sky News and the BBC World Service all provide global TV coverage of events, and Reuters is capable of transmitting a story to editorial terminals worldwide in less than five seconds.

Let's discuss the three Ps of crisis management – prevention, preparation and provision – and then consider different kinds of crisis situations that might occur for a particular type of organization.

Prevention

It is easy to be wise after the event and say 'if only ...'. Too often, disasters occur through poor management. They happen all the time in everyday public relations life. The causes of any disaster vary between the extremes of casual optimism and, sometimes, selfish greed. In some cases there is evidence of downright corruption. It is the public relations manager who must represent the conscience of an organization because he or she is not only the spokesperson, but also the guardian of its goodwill and reputation.

Crisis management means planning to deal with the unpredictable. It is entirely possible to plan for different eventualities. Prevention procedure should be based on trying to anticipate what could go wrong. Building two lists, one of the disasters or crises that are possible, together with a list of unlikely disasters that could occur, is one way of approaching this task. *How often is this ever done?*

Let us compile two brief hypothetical lists to demonstrate the above, taking the example of a university. Table 26.1 provides an indication of those possible and impossible events that might occur in the university environment.

At different times in different circumstances, an unlikely crisis may become distinctly possible. Who would have considered that a 'dirty

Table 26.1 Examples of possible and unlikely crises affecting a university

Possible crises	*Unlikely crises*
Could be robbed and have to suspend classes because of lack of available computer equipment	Could be occupied by demonstrators or other fanatics
Bomb scares could affect class or examination attendance	Could be forcibly privatized by the government
Someone could be held at gunpoint, or murdered, on campus by a disgruntled student or employee	Destruction could be threatened by a terrorist organization
Student could die on campus as a result of poor health and safety procedures and practices	A kidnapper could hold a victim hostage inside the university
University could be taken over by the funding council or could go bankrupt or both	A building might collapse
There could be a financial scandal (e.g. misuse of public monies)	Certain universities might be closed by the government in a Treasury budget-cutting exercise
The lecturer's union could strike, forcing all student grades to be withheld until a settlement occurs	A freak heatwave might damage telecommunications and IT equipment
Union could force a strike because of job cuts	Student records are sabotaged by an Internet hacker

bomb' (i.e. containing poison gas, bacteria or low-level nuclear material) might be placed on the New York or London subway prior to 11 September 2001?

How many of these possible or even unlikely crises have been considered by university managers? Or any other managers, in any of a myriad of other types of organizations? The problem is how to detect and even accept the unthinkable, and be prepared for its possible occurrence. Too many organizations do nothing because they sincerely believe crises are impossible or that they will 'go away'. One suspects that less than half of the above are considered at any one time, and then by whom: university vice-chancellors, the Police, the Higher Education Funding Council, local councillors, the Fire Service? And do they have an emergency plan incorporating public relations requirements? Once crisis managers have divided their crises into the above two categories, they should then arrange them into three types: those that the organization is already prepared to manage, those that it needs to prepare to manage and those that it chooses not to manage (Pearson, 2002).

One of the ways in which such emergency lists can be compiled is by running a press cuttings check on disasters, and adding new kinds of hazard to one's list as and when they are spotted. Remember the old adage: the wise learn from others' mistakes.

Much crisis communication work centres on post-crisis apologia, often considering the organization's own needs rather than those of the stakeholders. There is a strong argument for developing extensive communication channels to generate positive value positions long before the crisis occurs (Ulmer, 2001). Thus, the development of strong, positive relationships with the media, employees, suppliers and others can ensure that companies are more able to ride out a crisis when it occurs because they have developed goodwill with their main publics (see Ingham interview at the end of Part 3).

Preparation

Two things are necessary in order to be prepared for a crisis. First, there should be a basic crisis committee comprising such people as the chief executive officer, personnel manager, works manager, safety officer and public relations manager, or whomever is appropriate depending on the kind of organization. If there are several locations, each should have a representative on the committee so that the organization can go into action locally, nationally or even, perhaps, internationally. Secondly, these people should have regular contact through meetings, e-mail or teleconferencing so that procedures can be reviewed and updated, including means of *rapid* communication in the event of a disaster. For instance, media requirements are constantly changing, including access to media by online computer facilities.

One of the objectives in this planned procedure is to make sure that all members of the crisis committee have access to, or are in receipt of, the same information, are agreed on what can be said to the media and are consistently giving out the same information. This is necessary because the release of information has to be controlled, not because the organization is afraid to be frank but because there may be restrictive commitments or protocols to be observed. For instance, if people are killed, next of kin must be informed first. There may also be legal or insurance implications if liability is admitted.

Provision

The media will demand every kind of information, although they have no *right* to anything. They are in business, and for them bad news is good news that helps to sell papers and attract audiences. The organization has its own responsibilities to itself, employees, distributors, shareholders and others. So a balance is necessary, coupled with the knowledge that any crisis invites criticism, rightly or wrongly. The immediate conclusion, often drawn, is that the organization is to blame when something goes wrong, and it is unlikely to receive any sympathy. Often, the public feels hostility, prejudice and ignorance. It is the organization that may be accused of apathy and even negligence in extreme cases. The opposite and obvious danger is putting the company in a bad light by trying to cover up information that is likely to come out at a later date or trying to divert blame towards another company (e.g. Ford's attempt to blame Firestone – see later in this chapter).

It is therefore necessary to be organized regarding provision of information, and organized in order to provide it. A media statement should be written and agreed by the crisis committee as soon as possible. Ideally, the media should be assembled wherever this is feasible and given every reasonable facility. It may be necessary to be frank but blunt, and keep control of the situation.

It all depends on the public relations manager's skill to satisfy and convince the media representatives. Once he or she slips into a defensive, apologetic and therefore weak position, the media may well report negatively on the company or organization's situation. It is better for him or her to make frank, authoritative statements as far as he or she can go at the time, and promise additional facts as soon as they are available. Under no circumstances should the PRO (or others) adopt a 'no comment' attitude. If a question cannot be answered, he or she should explain why. The PRO needs to carry the media with them, and earn their respect, however fiercely and irresponsibly he or she may be badgered.

There should be an initial statement, followed by more detailed statements at press conferences or facility visits. If it is possible to lay on tours, these should be made with facilities available such as telephones, fax machines, computers and transport, so that media representatives may dispatch their stories, pictures or tapes. It's important to understand the sensitivities of the media. Usually, 'the media are looking for novelty, interesting stories that will appeal to their readers, listeners or viewers, and which are obtainable without too much expense' (Harrison, 2000). Thus, when several victims were killed and injured by a gunman in Dunblane in the UK, Harrison states that the hospital dealt with the crisis extremely well by setting up a well-equipped press room, conducting a twice-daily press conference, regular briefings, a 24-hour telephone service, and providing tea and sandwiches.

When the problem has been resolved, the media should be invited back and told what has been done and why the problem has or is being resolved, even if this is at some time in the future. The new situation may well be recognized as to the credit of the organization. Revisiting the crisis may depend on the nature of the catastrophe. There is no point in reminding people of a disaster. Much may depend on the ability of the CEO to handle the media, for such a person will carry authority and avoid criticism of a cover-up. An excellent example of this was when Rudolph Giuliani, the New York City Mayor, took charge during the World Trade Center attacks on 11 September 2001.

Those organizations that were best able to recover from the collapse of the World Trade Center after 11 September had made substantial provisions (see below). They:

- took prompt, decisive action to deal with the immediate crisis and communicated promptly and frankly with employees, customers, suppliers and the media, demonstrating compassion for the injured, frightened and bereaved at the same time;
- were prepared for an interruption to the continuity of their business (though certainly not for the collapse of their whole building);
- had strong balance sheets, positive cash flow and good cost control (Anon., 2002e).

The importance of understanding people's sensitivities, particularly those that have been involved in a crisis, is paramount. This was outlined by Pamela Porter, at Crisis Management International, whilst she was working for various corporate tenants within the World Trade Center. The tenants had mentioned that just before the attack they had been looking at downsizing. What should they do now, they asked? Porter explained that they should 'deal with what's in front of your face. Take care of your people first. After a few weeks have gone by, you can turn and look at the downsizing question again' (Fishman, 2001).

Post-11 September 2001, US oil and gas companies are redefining possible crises which might face them. Dittrick (2002) quotes a former US career naval officer: 'As opposed to thinking about keeping vandals out, now there may be [a need for] a larger strategy for targeting a facility. Industry was planning for accidents and natural disasters. Now we have to think of deliberate acts with the intent of disrupting the economy or the public safety.' Since much of the oil and gas industry infrastructure is mechanized, and some by remote access over the Internet, some members of the industry are worried about the threat of sophisticated terrorists conducting computer-based sabotage.

Coombs (1998) argues that, in a crisis management situation, there are seven crisis response strategies that a firm can adopt. These range over a continuum from defensive to accommodative.

The strategies represent approaches ranging from denying all knowledge of the causes of the problem and persecuting the accuser to issuing a full apology and taking full responsibility for the crisis (mortification). In the modern litigious world, this latter position clearly has legal ramifications. It may not always be possible to make a frank admission of responsibility because many insurance companies require that policyholders do not admit liability. Many firms deny that they are a particular cause of a problem. Firestone and Ford denied that there was a problem with the Ford Explorer's Firestone tyres initially. Companies sometimes try to play down their own responsibilities to the situation or argue that the crisis is not as bad as it might appear (*salience reduction*). These are all defensive strategies. Accommodative strategies include trying to escape the media spotlight by outlining previous good deeds or practice. Responsible firms will take corrective action to sort out the situation and make sure it never happens again. Mortification is when firms accept full responsibility for the crisis. Firms often adopt any one or a combination of these strategic approaches to solving their crisis management problem.

Dos and don'ts in crisis management

Although checklists abound of what to do, and what not to do, during crisis situations, every situation differs in its requirements. Western Union (1985) has compiled a useful list, outlined below.

Dos

- Gather all the facts and disseminate them from one central information centre.
- Speak with one voice, consistently, via designated and trained spokespeople.

- Select credible spokespeople, train them and make sure they are well informed.
- Be accessible to the media so that they will not have to go to other sources for news.
- Report your own bad news. If the media has to dig it out of you, they may decide you are guilty of creating the crisis.
- Tell your story quickly, openly and honestly to allay suspicion and rumours.
- If you can't discuss something, explain why.
- Provide sufficient evidence of statements.
- Record events as the crisis evolves, including photographs and video-tapes, so later you can present your side of the story.
- Update your crisis communications plans periodically.

Don'ts

- Say 'no comment', as it leads to speculation.
- Debate the subject.
- Attempt to assess blame; rather, address and solve the problem at hand.
- Overreact and exaggerate the situation.
- Deviate from corporate policy or agreed-upon crisis procedures.
- Make an 'off-the-record' statement; there is no such thing as 'off the record'.

Many suggest that it isn't enough to deal with the crisis as it occurs. It is imperative that every effort be made to ensure it does not happen in the first place. If it does, the organization should take full responsibility (not liability) for mitigating the circumstances. Mitroff (2001) defines this as crisis leadership and argues that it is made up of seven components:

1. Crisis prevention – work hard to determine what the likely causes of a crisis might be and how they will impact on the organization.
2. Develop crisis capabilities rather than just crisis plans – what matters is developing the process of how to communicate, not what is communicated.
3. Crisis leadership should be driven from the top down.
4. Reveal the awful truth immediately.
5. Respond to the emotional needs of your publics, not just their informational needs.
6. Conduct a post-mortem on why the crisis occurred.
7. Work hard to improve your crisis leadership procedures every year.

Crisis by criticism

Laws, codes of practice and investigative journalism can all provoke crises of confidence. Many companies have received unfortunate media coverage as a result of prosecutions under the Trade Descriptions Act, Consumer Protection Act and various labelling laws. They have ranged from misleading descriptions in holiday brochures to inadequate labelling of food products. Codes of practice such as those of the Independent Television Commission, the Radio Authority and the Institute of Public Relations (see Appendix 1), and the Public Relations Consultants Association, can lead to adverse publicity if their recommendations are breached. Offending items are widely published in the press, as are complaints to the ITC, even though TV commercials are vetted before they are screened.

Investigative journalism, especially on TV, can be very hurtful and over the years many famous firms have been pilloried for dangerous products like inflammable clothes and furniture, dangerous children's cots and pushchairs, and dubious treatments and foods have been criticized on programmes such as *That's Life*, *World in Action* and *Watchdog* in the UK.

Product recall

An ever-present crisis risk is that of product failure. It may not seem very good public relations to have to admit that a product is faulty, yet the best way to retrieve goodwill is often to admit the fault immediately, and organize the speediest possible recall so that the defect can be remedied. It is no use being timid and attempting to hide behind excuses or deal with the problem discreetly, because this will often only worsen matters. *The key to product recall is speed*. It may be quicker to place advertisements in the press than to rely on news releases being printed, and posters or showcards may be advisable at the point-of-sale. A problem with some recalls is that the fault is not always easy to trace.

A recall advertisement has to temper urgency with reassurance. Failures test the commitment of an organization's customers but, as mentioned earlier, it might not be the problem *per se* that causes a critical episode to develop, but the company's response to that problem (Stewart, 1998, p. 9). Although the fault does the manufacturer no immediate credit, what is done about it could show that it is a caring company. Indeed, there is some research evidence (Bejou and Palmer, 1998) that suggests that a satisfactory response to a problem *may* lead to greater levels of satisfaction than existed prior to the incident.

Recalls can be difficult to conduct because, while some customers can be contacted through guarantee cards and retailer's records, appliances are sold through a variety of outlets and customers may not necessarily buy for themselves. Walker (2000) argues that direct mail has an important role to play in product recalls, especially nowadays when many manufacturers have extensive customer lists. He argues that mass media may well miss the people who need to know, whereas direct mail does not. He has a good point. In the product recall case study below, the example company, a car manufacturer, would have tended to have valid details on the vast majority of its customers. Conversely, however, a supermarket with an infected food product is far less likely to be able to use this method exclusively since, at best, it will probably only have details of those customers holding loyalty cards.

Activists (e.g. animal rights groups) and terrorist organizations have provoked a double-edged crisis situation. If confectionery, baby food or some other product is impregnated with dangerous substances, or there is even a hoax to this effect, both retailers and manufacturers come under attack. The retailer, often a large supermarket chain, does not want to lose trade by appearing to stock the offending product and will clear the shelves. The manufacturer will be expected to take back perhaps millions of pounds of stock. A double crisis has to be solved. Usually, the retailer will not restock unless the manufacturer can guarantee a safe product. This may mean repackaging, or introducing a new tamper-free pack. Then the consumer has to be convinced that the product is safe. These can be costly crises, running into millions of pounds in losses. In most cases such crises have been resolved in a few days, and sales have been recovered in a few weeks or months, but it can be a terrifying situation for the manufacturer, retailer and consumer when it occurs.

Sometimes, contamination occurs by accident, but the results are usually no less devastating. For instance, in 1999, cans of Coca-Cola were ordered off Belgian supermarket shelves by the Minister of Health when children fell ill after drinking 'foul-smelling' cans of the world's most popular soft drink. The Coca-Cola Company 'failed to respond in a timely and appropriate manner'. The subsequent drop in sales, caused by the loss of consumer confidence in its products, cost Coke about $200 million (Mitroff, 2001) after it withdrew 2.5 million bottles of Coca-Cola, Coca-Cola Light, Fanta and Sprite because they were contaminated with defective carbon dioxide and/or pesticide. In total, 120 people were affected (Bell, 1999). Of these 100, all children, were hospitalized. Coke subsequently bungled the crisis management, finally offering a belated apology. Their second quarter earnings in Belgium that year dropped 21 per cent (Campbell, 1999).

Product recalls frequently affect children's products. For example, Random House had to recall 39 000 copies of its board book, *Monsters in the*

Closet, a tie-in with the movie *Monsters, Inc.* (Britton, 2002). August et al. (2001) explain that the major fast-food giants have, in the previous couple of years, recalled the Hour Glass Space Sprout and 25 million Pokemon balls (Burger King), the Tangled Treeples toy (KFC – Kentucky Fried Chicken) and the Scooter Bug (McDonald's). All these products were regarded to be possible causes of harm to children if ingested.

The Bridgestone/Firestone and Ford Explorer tyre recall: a case study

The Ford Motor Company and Firestone, its US-based tyre supplier – owned by Japanese company, Bridgestone – suffered considerable reputational damage when tyre blow-outs caused the Ford Explorer sport utility vehicle to rollover; 175 people were killed and 700 injured in more than 1400 accidents related to tyre blow-out (Freitag, 2002). A timeline for the Ford and Bridgestone/Firestone crisis is outlined in Table 26.2.

Table 26.2 A chronology of events in the Ford, Bridgestone/Firestone tyre recall

Date	Event
1990	Ford's Explorer is launched, becoming the best-selling sports utility vehicle in the US
1991	Ford puts Firestone's Wilderness tyres on Explorer
1992	First lawsuits filed against Firestone for its Ford Explorer tyres
1998	Cases of tyre failure reported in the press in Saudi Arabia
July 1999	Ford conducts tyre recall in Saudi Arabia, quietly
February 2000	Ford recalls tyres in Thailand
May 2000	Ford recalls tyres on around 30 000 explorers in Venezuela, Ecuador and Colombia. The National Highway Traffic Safety Administration (US regulator) announces it is to conduct an investigation
August 2000	Firestone and Ford announce a recall of 6.5 million tyres
September 2000	Firestone's public relations firm, Fleishmann-Hillard, quits the account without elaboration.
	Ketchum Public Relations takes over the difficult job of crisis management
February 2001	Bridgestone/Firestone reports an 80 per cent profit reduction, whilst Firestone announces losses of $510 million
May 2001	Ford announces plans to replace another 13 million Firestone tyres. Firestone announces it will no longer supply Ford vehicles

Source: based on Eisenberg and Zagorin (2000), O'Rourke (2001), Welch (2001), Freitag (2002)

Initially, the two firms tackled the media and the crisis together, but antagonism between the two firms swiftly set in and they battled to shift blame onto each other. This achieved the break-up of their 100-year-old relationship. Whilst Ford blamed the accidents on Firestone's tread separation problem, Firestone argued that if the Explorer had been designed properly, the accidents would not have been so serious. It noted that 60 per cent of the accidents reported involved tyres placed in the left rear position of the vehicle (Freitag, 2002). When Ford announced another recall of a further 13 million Firestone tyres it said might be unsafe, Firestone announced it would no longer supply Ford, costing it around 4 per cent of its $7.5 billion revenue (Welch, 2001). Nevertheless, Ford seemed to come out best in the crisis, as it shifted most of the blame onto its partner (the *responsibility avoidance strategy* outlined in an earlier section), and worked hard to both recall tyres at its own cost (*corrective action strategy*) and communicate with the various publics involved. According to O'Rourke (2001), at one point the crisis communication centre at Ford directly employed around 500 employees on the entire 11th and 12th floors of its headquarters in Michigan, USA, and indirectly employed a further 4000–5000 employees in various related activities. The Firestone safety recall notice outlined the following affected vehicles, giving the reader some indication of how a recall notice might be organized:

- Firestone P235 75R15 ATX or ATX II tyres installed on the following lights vehicles and SUVs:
  - 1991–1996 Ford Explorers;
  - 1991–1996 Rangers;
  - 1996 Mercury Mountaineers;
  - 1991–1994 Broncos;
  - 1991–1994 F150.
- Firestone P235 7R15 Wilderness AT tyres produced at the Firestone Decatur plant installed on the following vehicles:
  - 1997–2001 Ford Explorers (excludes 1999–2001 Eddie Bauer and Limited Editions);
  - 2001 Ford Explorer Trac;
  - 1997–2000 Mercury Mountaineers;
  - 1997–2000 Ford Rangers (Ford Motor Company, 2000).

General Motors has also recently announced a product recall of 1.9 million vehicles because of a potential problem in the steering column of its 1995–1997 Chevrolet Cavaliers and Pontiac Sunfires, and its 1996/1997 Buick Skylarks, Pontiac Grand Ams and Oldsmobile Achievas (Anon., 2002f). As mentioned earlier, however, car manufacturers are more likely to be able to contact their consumers by direct mail rather than having to rely solely on mass media: little consolation, of course.

Chapter 27

Sponsorship

LEARNING OBJECTIVES

At the end of this chapter you will be able to:

- outline the main types of sponsorship that exist;
- explain the characteristics of these sponsorships;
- define the relative benefits of different types of sponsorship.

Growth of sponsorship

In the past, wealthy patrons sponsored arts and social services through philanthropic acts. Composers, performers and artists depended on the patronage of the church, royalty, aristocracy and business. The latter category included people like Henry Ford and Henry Tate. The modern equivalent of this philanthropy is sponsorship, and it is now regarded more as a business investment than a philanthropic gesture. It is not, in itself, simply a corporate image-building exercise either. Sponsorships are often undertaken because they are capable of achieving significant mass media coverage. Those areas (e.g. sport, entertainment) that gain the greatest amount of regular media coverage are often the subjects of most sponsorship activity. Media coverage is sought to raise awareness of a company, product or cause, for positioning purposes, because it can be more cost-effective than traditional advertising, because it can often reach specified global markets, or simply to generate goodwill amongst important publics. Sponsorship is now a multibillion pound business, as the mass media, paradoxically, simultaneously fragments and globalizes, as marketing communications campaigns increasingly integrate, and events such as the World Cup and the Olympics, and Hollywood films appeal to global audiences.

The nature of sponsorship

Sponsorship may not be undertaken wholly for public relations purposes, but even when its primary objectives are marketing or advertising there can be an important public relations element. If we consider some of the marketing and advertising aspects first, it will be easier to detail and define the public relations content. Most of the larger sponsorships of sports are conducted because these popular events receive extensive TV, press or other media coverage, resulting in repeated naming of the sponsor by the media or by others, including supporters.

The tobacco industry is no longer permitted to advertise on radio or TV and in billboards and magazines in the UK. As a result, tobacco companies use sponsorship, mainly with arts and sports events. In Britain, tobacco companies will continue to be able to sponsor global sports events such as Formula One until 1 October 2006, although the British government has announced that legislation to outlaw tobacco sponsorship remains on its agenda (Kleinman, 2000). The British government did subsequently introduce legislation banning cigarette advertising from 14 February 2003. Marlboro, for example, is involved in sponsoring Formula One. Tobacco firms have previously supported other sports such as golf, rugby, snooker and tennis. In fact, TV coverage of Grand Prix racing had to be abandoned in France because regulations forbade coverage of tobacco sponsorships. Tobacco sponsorship is also currently prohibited in Belgium and Italy (Kleinman, 2000).

Some TV advertisers have recognized that there comes a point when further purchase of air time (i.e. commercials) is not cost-effective, and that a given expenditure on sponsorship, with its associated TV coverage, is more efficient. It can also be more economical than conventional advertising, although it works best when integrated with sales promotion, PR, corporate hospitality, advertising and online marketing initiatives. Sponsorships do not have to be costly. They can be modest, appealing perhaps to a small or more specialized audience, or they may be local ones such as supplying shoes, shirts or strip for local sports clubs, for example.

Organization of sponsorship

There are two sides to sponsorship, those seeking funds and those who wish to engage in sponsorship. They may not necessarily be sympathetic to one another. A potential sponsor may wish to support something that traditionally has had no commercial connections and may consider them undesirable. In contrast, an organization or person in need of funds may make the mistake of imagining that businesses are wealthy and therefore likely to be willing benefactors, not recognizing that commercial firms will ask what's in it for them. In between there are specialist agencies, which match would-be sponsors with appropriate beneficiaries and plan and run the whole sponsorship programme. Among some of the best-known consultancies in the UK specializing in sponsorship are Saatchi & Saatchi's The Cause Connection, Octagon Marketing, Hill & Knowlton, and M & C Saatchi Sponsorship.

Figure 27.1 provides an outline of the sponsorship process, indicating the importance of appropriately matching the sponsor and the sponsee (the sponsorship opportunity). This is often underpinned through the use of a specialist agency. When deciding which agency to use, firms might wish to consult The European Sponsorship Consultants Association (ESCA) website (http://www.sponsorship.org/start.htm). The ESCA make available two kinds of services: those for ESCA members, representing the interests of the buyers of sponsorship rights or opportunities, and those of the interests of sellers of such opportunities, i.e. event or rights owners. Prospective members of the ESCA, which was founded in 1990, have to conform to criteria with regard to financial stability, track record, numbers of staff and length of experience. They are also required in their dealings to abide by a Code of Professional Conduct

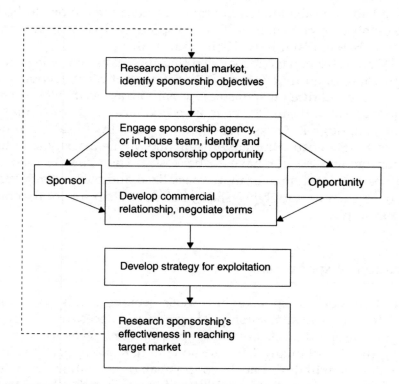

Figure 27.1 Stages in the sponsorship process.

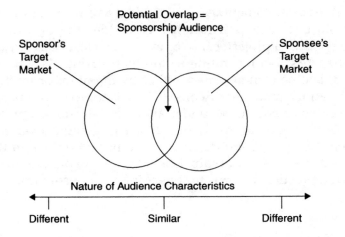

Figure 27.2 Venn diagram illustrating sponsorship audience.

designed to protect interests of their clients, the breaching of which can lead to expulsion of the member. Alternatively, companies wishing to sponsor events might use their own dedicated in-house team. Whatever approach they adopt, they should conduct research into the appropriateness of the sponsorship (before the event) and the effectiveness of the sponsorship programme (after the event). Sponsors, and sponsees for that matter, should be clear about why they are entering into a sponsorship agreement and what benefits they expect (see next section).

Figure 27.2 illustrates the importance of matching the sponsor's target market with that of the sponsee's target market. Thus, there is little point in a life insurance company supporting *Monsters, Inc.*, the children's film, because most of its viewers will be too young to appreciate the benefits of its products. There would be obvious scope for McDonald's, as they could package *Monsters, Inc.* toys into their happy meals. The diagram indicates the importance of matching the sponsor and sponsee on related characteristics. The sponsorship of Manchester United by Nike allows it to market its jointly branded Nike/Man Utd products to fans not only in the United Kingdom, but also in overseas markets such as Hong Kong and Malaysia. The potential overlap, the sponsorship audience, outlined in Figure 27.2 is the Far Eastern and UK markets for sports clothing and sports casual wear in this example.

Reasons for sponsorship

Sponsors usually have very definite reasons for spending money on sponsorship. It is rarely solely just for creating an image or purely for promotional reasons. Sometimes, it is invoked as a result of the whim of a chairperson, but such philanthropy is seldom the only reason for deciding to sponsor a project, cause or event. So, clear objectives need to be established first before indulging in sponsorship. When should a sponsorship deal be contemplated, either by intention or invitation? If the public relations manager or consultant wishes to recommend sponsorship, research needs to be undertaken to determine the potential effectiveness of it. Do the likely benefits (e.g. greater awareness and increased positive image amongst target audience) outweigh the costs (e.g. employee time, sponsorship licensing and exploitation)? Let us examine some practical reasons for engaging in sponsorship.

Corporate image and identity

By means of sponsorship, a company can make familiar its logo, house colour, typography, livery and other physical representations to intensify recognition of its corporate identity. Equally, it can promote what it stands for through different sponsorship types (see Table 27.1), hoping to ensure that it becomes associated with certain image constructs.

Audience awareness

Sponsorship offers the sponsor intensive repetition of its brand, with subtle associations to the sponsee. People tend to trust things with which they become familiar. Sponsorship may be a way of penetrating foreign markets where the name is unfamiliar. This is the reason for Vodafone's sponsorship of Manchester United Football Club, since there are large numbers of their fans in the Far East. The joint tie-up between the New York Yankees and Manchester United allows both companies to market their merchandise in the UK and USA respectively. Traditional advertising methods used to raise awareness can be slow and costly, or even illegal or impossible in some parts of the world. Sponsorship is particularly useful for generating awareness amongst its target groups because it exploits that elementary form of advertising, repetition, without the more overt inferences such as in advertising, which can sometimes offend viewers.

Employee and customer relations

Employees may well take pride in the sponsorship activities of their company and may be able to participate in them. Cornhill Insurance discovered that their support for Test Match cricket enjoyed the spin-off of being a morale booster for their staff. Sponsors of racehorses and show jumpers have taken parties of employees to events to see the horses perform, while BT have made tickets from their sponsorship of The Tate available to staff. An excellent benefit sometimes arising from sponsorship is that sponsees provide facilities to hold events either for staff or for clients. This can range from organizing parties of visitors to a staff away day at a museum, for instance, to the provision of free tickets for executive boxes at football matches, to the provision of free tickets for the theatre.

Essential considerations in sponsorship programmes

When investing in sponsorship, it is necessary to determine whether or not a proposed sponsorship merits the expenditure and promises the desired results. Sometimes the expectations are clearly defined, but they may be obscure and unlikely to be fulfilled. The prospective sponsor should choose subjects carefully, for he or she will be invited to fund many such ventures, particularly if he/she works for a large business with a track record of sponsorship! It is very easy to waste money on dubious sponsorships; they could be no better than buying advertisement space in charity programmes and magazines. The modern sponsor is rarely interested in giving money away, but is intent on receiving a return on investment. Both sides should benefit.

Media coverage

A primary consideration is where and what kind of media coverage may be expected as a result of the sponsorship. Not all media sources will credit the sponsor. It will usually be necessary to augment and reinforce the sponsor's name by some visible means that cannot be avoided or ignored. Names might be blazoned on players' or participants' clothing, or on vehicles or equipment. Racing cars usually bear the names of several co-sponsors. Additionally, stadium advertising boards may be hired in football or athletic grounds, large poster sites may be erected beside a racetrack, and banners may feature prominently at motor racing circuits. Media coverage is not limited to the actual event either. It can extend before and after an event, as occurs with much talked about events such as the Grand National steeplechase, the World Cup, and the New York and London marathons. Potential sponsors should be aware of 'ambush marketing'. According to Smith (2002, p. 463), it has been around as long as sponsorship itself. He uses the example of the 1991 Rugby World Cup. Although not one of the main sponsors of the competition, Sony sponsored the TV coverage. Later research suggested they, and not the competition's real sponsors, benefited most from the association.

The cost

The budget will usually include the cost of hiring specialist consultants to negotiate possible contracts, and to administer the sponsorship, and this can be a complex and highly skilled business. The sponsor will also need to allocate in-house staff to collaborate with the consultant. Where such work is an ongoing affair, it may be necessary to engage a sponsorship manager, as BT do, for example. This person may be totally responsible for all sponsorship work or may liaise to a larger or lesser extent with an outside consultant. Either way, there is a manpower cost to budget for.

The full extent of the cost of sponsorship has to be reckoned carefully, and a prospective sponsor should understand that costs usually exceed the initial sponsorship fee payment. There is a need to exploit association with the subject in other advertising. The initial sponsorship fee should be seen as an exploitation rights fee rather than just as an advert in its own right. The sponsor should be clear on exactly what they are getting for the sponsorship payment. Fry (2001) states that sponsors should be wary of falling TV audiences, spiralling rights fees and sponsor clutter in sports sponsorship. He argues that entertainment sponsorship is increasingly becoming attractive as an alternative because of its lack of clutter.

Provision of prize money, a trophy and other items may usually be required in sports sponsorship. There can be many add-on costs, ranging from advertising to hospitality, that the sponsor may have to meet. The sponsor should expect to spend at least the same amount of money again (as the exploitation rights fee) to exploit the association they have purchased, in related communications activity as a minimum. Larger, more experienced sponsors might well spend up to three times as much as the rights fee on exploitation activities if they are sponsoring global events. Sponsorship executives should also factor in the cost of research conducted to determine the effectiveness of the sponsorship in meeting whatever objectives were set for it.

The sponsor's participation in the event will often need to be advertised, or included in current product advertising. It may well be necessary to advertise the event itself if the sponsor is the organizer, in order to ensure attendance. When events are televised, sponsors may buy space on billboards or in TV magazines. Advertisement space may also be bought in programmes published by the promoters and sold to members of the public. Point-of-sale material may also be produced for retail outlets or public houses. Sainsbury's sponsorship of the England football team, for example, was accompanied by extensive signage in all its stores. In addition, the sponsor may feel obliged, or may wish, to provide entertainment and refreshments while the event is taking place. It could be 'a day at the races' for company guests, or lunch for the journalists in the commentators' box, be they sports writers or radio and TV commentators. This latter courtesy is often much appreciated.

Provision of clothing, equipment and supplies

Part of a sponsorship contract may be the supply of company products or services, but in what quantity, when and how often are supplies required, and when and where are they to be delivered? Considerable costs may be involved, including production, staffing, packaging, transportation, and possibly actual provision at venues at home and abroad. Executives in charge of sponsorship programmes should negotiate carefully.

Each sponsorship will have its own individual supply problems, possibly concerning clothing, working equipment, food and drinks, and manpower. Shirts for footballers, shoes for athletes, tennis rackets and cricket balls for players, golf balls for golfers, saddle-cloths for horses, overalls for mechanics, tyres for cars, all kinds of spare parts and repair and maintenance services; all manner of provisions, catering and catering services may be required. These are the sort of logistical problems that justify the use of specialist consultancies.

Research

The sponsor should seek an evaluation of how appropriate their sponsorship will be to intended audiences before the event, and how effective their sponsorship has been after the event. Firms might commission a calculation of media coverage, conducted by specialist media monitoring firms, illustrating stories in the press, on the radio and in TV coverage. Meticulous reports can be compiled of days, times and programmes of broadcast coverage, together with details of dates, media and volume of press coverage. In addition, appropriate samples may be asked questions about the extent to which they recall or recognize particular sponsors of particular events in quantitative studies. Qualitative research is also frequently used to probe the appropriateness of the sponsorship programme, usually before, but sometimes after, the event has taken place.

Types of sponsorship

Subjects for sponsorship fall into certain broad major categories, of which sport predominates. These categories are entertainment, arts, sport and social causes. The first works predominantly through sponsored broadcasts and product placement, and the second through sponsored exhibitions, artists or galleries. The third involves the sponsorship of events, teams and stadia, for instance, whilst the latter sometimes involves direct corporate donations but increasingly corporate social responsibility, community relations or cause-related marketing projects. For the purposes of this chapter, cause-related marketing is discussed further and the category described herein includes educational sponsorship projects.

Table 27.1 provides an outline of the different major sponsorship types, indicating the image constructs that might be conveyed in a sponsorship programme by the sponsor. The table also indicates the types of audiences these types of sponsorship tend to focus upon, with some market-based reasons for why these sponsorship programmes might be undertaken. For example, entertainment sponsorship is increasing in popularity because it allows firms to cut through traditional media advertising clutter, whilst sport sponsorship has allowed tobacco companies to subvert the laws banning advertising of their products.

Sport

This form of sponsorship now predominates worldwide. Sports are conducted internationally and may be supported by multinationals because of their global media coverage. For instance, Formula One Grand Prix motor racing takes place at circuits worldwide, including Suzuka in Japan, Indianapolis in the USA, Barcelona in Spain and Silverstone in the UK, and is watched by television audiences everywhere. Sponsors choose sports that are most appropriate to their own target markets, whether it be the mass market, a particular market segment, or the men's, women's or youth markets. Coca-Cola has concentrated on young people's interests such as swimming and athletics, while Cornhill Insurance chose Test Match cricket to sponsor to reach the household insurance market. Benetton, infamous for some of its controversial poster advertising, has consistently supported Formula One motor racing.

Football is now the subject of Britain's biggest sports sponsorship. During the 1993/1994 football season, the FA First Division became the FA Carling Premier League, with a four-year £12 million sponsorship

Table 27.1 Sponsorship types and characteristics

Sponsorship type	Typical association properties (image to be conveyed)	Predominant audience type	Typical audience size	Typical market-based reasons for sponsorship	Example (sponsor/ sponsee, UK)
Entertainment	Established, progressive	Particularly dependent on genre of broadcast	Mass national appeal	Market penetration, media clutter and fragmentation evasion	Npower/ITV's *The Bill*
Arts	Excellence, creativity	Exclusive, fairly specified	Niche	Niche market development, positioning	BT (British Telecom)/the Tate Gallery
Sport	Dynamism, vitality, competitive	Youth, young adult	Often large, sometimes global	International market development, positioning, circumvention of promotional bans	Vodafone/ Manchester United
Social causes	Caring, socially concerned, 'good' corporate citizen	Often community based, sometimes regional, local or international	Variable	Corporate image development, market development, repositioning	PepsiCo's Walkers Crisps/ Computers for Schools initiative

package from the parent company, Bass. The brewers had previously sponsored the Tennants Charity Shield, the Tennants Scottish Cup and the Stones Rugby League Championship. In European football generally, with the emergence of the Premier League in Britain, Serie A in Italy, Spain's Primera Liga and France's Division 1, football clubs have started to generate significant sources of sponsorship income. Such clubs include England's Manchester United, Ajax of the Netherlands, Spain's Real Madrid and France's Paris St Germain. Manchester United announced a £30 million, two-year deal with Vodafone in 2000 and a £300 million deal over 15 years with Nike to distribute Manchester United sportswear in the same year. At the heart of the Vodafone partnership is the notion that Vodafone will benefit from customer acquisition through an increased exposure to European and Far Eastern subscriber bases, and from the increased voice and data traffic that will occur from watching matches on mobile Internet platforms. Meanwhile, Manchester United gains extra revenue to purchase players and increased media exposure. Thus, when compared with the 1993/1994 Carling sponsorship, almost ten years later companies were paying almost three times as much, for half the duration, and only one team. Times certainly have changed!

The 12 sponsors of the football competition, Euro 2000, each paid £12 million for title rights including: Carlsberg, Coca-Cola, Fuji Film, Hyundai, JVC, Mastercard, McDonald's, Philips, Sony PlayStation, Procter & Gamble's Pringles division, PSINet and Sportal. They expected to reach a cumulative global audience of 7 billion people in 210 countries (Fry, 2000). In World Cup 2002, the 15 top-tier sponsors each paid soccer's ruling body, FIFA (Federation Internationale de Football Association), £25 million apiece to exploit the rights to associate with the competition (O'Sullivan, 2002). Yet there is considerable clutter within the media environment because national teams are also sponsored by companies and because some non-sponsoring companies (e.g. Nike and Pepsi) use football-themed adverts to take advantage of the event without paying for the rights (so-called ambush marketing). So, for instance, Coca-Cola is a FIFA partner and the England official soft drinks provider, whilst Pepsi ran a football-themed advert with the likes of David Beckham, Rivaldo and Petit (O'Sullivan, 2002).

Sara Lee Corporation paid $40 million to obtain sponsorship rights for the Atlanta Olympics in 1996. They spent approximately $100 million more on related advertising, marketing and promotional activities. But, being an Olympic sponsor *does* improve corporate reputation (Wally and Hurley, 1998). Spiralling sponsorship fees are unlikely to continue indefinitely. In Germany, media company Kirch has declared insolvency after falling $60 million behind with payments. In the UK, ITV Digital was put into receivership owing the Football League $260 million (Ewing and Capell, 2002).

Ambush marketing is regarded by most as an abuse of sponsorship, often associated with major events such as the Olympic Games and the World Cup, where an official paid-up sponsor has to compete with a pirate publicity seeker. FIFA, football's governing body, defines it as: 'the unauthorized association of a business or an organization with the FIFA World Cup™' (cited in Dignam and Murphy, 2002). Essentially it consists of companies or brands exploiting association with a sports event or competition through a wide range of marketing activities. It can be a grey area, as when arena or perimeter boards encircle a stadium where a sponsored event is being held, and the advertisers could be the sponsor's rivals. There can be more obvious examples when merchandise is hawked as being 'official' – a problem that faced Arsenal Football Club in the early 2000s until a successful verdict in the European Court stopped market traders from selling unauthorized Arsenal-branded merchandise. But there are other ways to associate with sports events without paying for a merchandising licence or the rights. Tango, the innovative advertiser, took the mickey out of Coca-Cola's slogan 'eat football, sleep football, drink Coca-Cola' by coining its own tongue-in-cheek slogan at France 98, 'eat pies, sleep a lot, drink Tango'. Companies have organized large sampling events as a sales promotion gimmick outside event stadia in the hopes that the cameras would catch the logos of their soft drinks! (Dignam and Murphy, 2002).

The arts

Historically, sponsorship began with the patronage of the arts by wealthy people. Today, there are sponsored orchestras, concerts, operas, ballets, theatres, recordings, art shows, museums, book awards, and many other cultural organizations and events. Many of them, such as symphony orchestras, would not survive without commercial or government support. Arts Council or National Lottery grants are often inadequate even if they are available. Today, corporate sponsorship has replaced corporate donations as the major funding vehicle for the arts (Reiss, 2000).

As with sponsorship of other activities such as education, however, there is the increasingly pressing problem of the degree of influence a sponsor might wield over the sponsee. Reiss (2000) quotes the uproar caused by Charles Saatchi's sponsorship of the 'sensation' exhibition at the Brooklyn Museum in New York City, which also happened to increase the value of the works he loaned the exhibition.

The problem with many of the arts is that they represent minority public interests. Why, it may be asked, should pop enthusiasts pay for symphony orchestras? Shakespeare's plays may be part of the national heritage, but should the citizen pay if they don't ever watch theatre productions? An example was the sponsorship of the Royal Shakespeare Company performances at Stratford-upon-Avon by Royal Insurance. Tickets were offered at only £6, but were limited to two tickets per person per day. The tickets were advertised in *The Independent*'s Saturday magazine with an application form for tickets. This sponsorship helped to enhance the reputation of Royal Insurance and raise awareness of the sponsor within the target audience.

In addition to the sponsorship of museums, galleries and orchestras, companies often sponsor book awards, such as the Booker Prize in the UK. Guinness, for example, sponsors the *Guinness Book of Records*. There are also long-established sports and motoring annuals, guides, maps, DIY guides, gardening and cookery books, to which firms such as Rothman, Shell, Michelin and the RAC (Royal Automobile Club) have lent their names. Recently, again in a case of undue sponsor influence, Fay Weldon provoked controversy by agreeing to write a novel for the luxury jewellers, Bulgari, entitled *The Bulgari Connection*! She had originally agreed to write the book, after negotiating 12 mentions of the Bulgari brand, for 750 of Bulgari's best customers before it was released to the general public (Goldman, 2001). Such product placement, whilst usual in TV shows and movies (in the US), is far less common in publishing. Perhaps she's started a trend!

Social causes

In the future, 'companies will increasingly differentiate themselves by sponsoring high-consensus social causes' (Kotler, 2000). It has become a useful way in which to build a civic, corporate persona, and builds customer and employee respect and loyalty. Tesco's Computers for Schools and Walker's Crisps' Books for Schools initiatives, tackling computer and reading literacy respectively, have had significant impact upon UK schools, with 98 per cent of schools participating (Adkins, 2000). Such activity generates consumer awareness of mainstream brands very early on in children's lives – a matter of some concern to many. Npower has also tied in with 1000 schools in a pilot scheme to develop online shops, providing schools with the resources to market them to parents and local communities (Rogers, 2002a). It seems, however, that generally it is the schools in the wealthier areas that tend to be more likely to find sponsorship, a disconcerting finding when one considers that it is the schools in the deprived areas that are likely to need the most resources (Bennett, 1999).

Till and Nowak (2000) argue that cause-related marketing can affect consumers' overall attitude toward the sponsoring company or brand, and that it can also affect their cognitive knowledge (i.e. what they know about the brand). It tends to be more effective when it is used over a longer period of time, and when communications focus predominantly on the brand and the cause. Sponsorships are more successful when sponsoring brands that are associated with fewer qualities and sponsees are not associated with other brands. The perceived fit between the sponsor and sponsee is important to the effectiveness of the sponsorship. Sponsors should test this perceived fit beforehand amongst target audiences through research programmes prior to making a decision to go ahead (see Figure 27.2). In addition, they should exploit the association using as many areas of the marketing mix as possible. According to Gifford (1999), charities and other non-profit organizations should recognize that the charitable organization's most important asset is its name, and that cause-related marketing is a business deal and therefore subject to contract. Charities, it is argued, should not undersell themselves, obtain the sponsorship fee up front, control all uses of the name and check every deal with solicitors and accountants. In addition, they should develop a policy for cause-related marketing ventures.

Bursaries, scholarships, awards, fellowships and university chairs have all previously been sponsored by commercial interests. Littlewoods, the mail-order company, have sponsored a professorship of retailing at Manchester School of Management for many years whilst Boots, the pharmacy and general household goods company, sponsor a post at Nottingham University, in the home town of their headquarters. This may contribute to the advancement of the industry, provide the sponsor with high-calibre recruits, and often be a long-lasting form of support. There are many colleges or college buildings (e.g. The SAID business school at Oxford, the Judge Institute of Management at Cambridge University, the John Molson School of Business at Concordia University in Montreal, Canada) that bear the name of their sponsor in perpetuity. There are increasing reports of undue sponsor influence, particularly in the medical research field (Raeburn, 2002). The practice of sponsorship in higher education is less prevalent in Britain but is commonplace in the United States. For example, Nike have been sponsors of Penn State University.

Entertainment

When commercial broadcasting was first permitted in Britain nearly 50 years ago, it was protected from the excesses of American broadcasting, where whole radio drama programmes were sponsored by soap and other companies, hence the genre's nickname: soap operas. In the 1980s, there was some relaxation of the rules, especially with BBC television programmes such as British Gas cathedral concerts and the Lloyds Bank Young Musician of the Year contest. The Broadcasting Act 1990 brought about fundamental changes. The Independent Television Commission (ITC) replaced the Independent Broadcasting Authority (covering both independent television and radio) with responsibility for awarding regional commercial TV franchises, and the Radio Authority responsible for awarding both local and national commercial radio franchises. Under the Act, commercial TV and radio programmes may now be sponsored, although the sponsor has no control over the programme and their products cannot be featured (product placement). Instead, in the case of ITV programmes, there may be brief commercials in trailers, at the beginning and end of programmes. These brief commercials usually last around five seconds.

Some of these sponsorships are well matched to the product – e.g. Npower, the utility company, sponsors both the ITV weather forecasts and the ITV police drama series, *The Bill* (get it?), and Cadbury's and *Coronation Street* (advertised as The Nation's Favourite). Recently, Nescafé has paid £9.5 million to sponsor Channel 4's flagship programme *Hollyoaks*, a teen soap. Nescafé has managed to land the rights to use the cast in its promotional material, effectively as celebrity endorsers. The show is particularly attractive to Nescafé, who are targeting *Hollyoaks'* 5 million, 16- to 24-year-old viewers (Rogers, 2002b). Sony has paid around £500 000 to sponsor Sky's Box Office movie service in a move to replicate the success of Stella Artois' sponsorship of the Channel 4 movie channel, FilmFour (Anon., 2002g). In the US, Sunglass Hut International has joined The Weather Channel to launch Rays Awareness 2002, in a campaign to promote eye health and safety (Dolbow, 2002a).

Is the sponsorship of television programmes a form of advertising or of public relations, or content within the programme? An example of the latter occurred when the US broadcaster NBC approached Schiefflin & Somerset, a Diageo subsidiary, asking for a brand that they could include in the dialogue of a scene in *The West Wing*, when a key character extols the virtues of a drink. S & S suggested Johnnie Walker's Blue Label and, apparently, it cost them nothing (McMains and Mack, 2001). Programme sponsorship, and indeed any sponsorship, can associate the brand with the inherent values of the programme, so that it takes on the qualities of that programme. This is distinct from advertising, although celebrities are used in much the same way in advertising, in the hopes that some of their supposed good qualities will become associated with the product being advertised (e.g. cereal advertisers and sports stars).

Nokia, Lexus, PepsiCo, Guinness, Reebok International and American Express all had products placed in the Philip K. Dick-inspired sci-fi (or future reality according to producer Steven Spielberg) flick, *Minority Report*. Nokia and Lexus are reputed to have spent $5–7 million in paid media to promote the tie-in (Friedman et al., 2002). Philips has launched a new range of James Bond-branded shaving products after its tie-in with flick *Die Another Day*, which premiered in December 2002 (Kleinman, 2002b). Previous Bond placements have included BMW's Z3 and Z8 cars. Ford Motor Company's stylish brand, the Aston Martin Vanquish, also makes an appearance in the film, and there is an associated video game, 'James Bond 007: Nightfire', created by Electronic Arts (Elkin, 2002). Ford has appointed specialist market researcher Millward Brown Precis to measure the impact of its placement (Anon., 2002h); see Chapter 11 for further details on measuring PR's effectiveness. Rockport, the shoe manufacturer, has signed a deal for a movie tie-in with *Men in Black II*. It has also produced a 30-second spot aired around the time of the film's release featuring some footage from the film, which reportedly has the Men in Black wearing Rockports (Dolbow, 2002b).

Commercial radio sponsorships take a slightly different form, with the presenter introducing the programme by declaring that it is broadcast 'in association' with a sponsor, followed by a brief statement or slogan. Sometimes these are long-running sponsorships, such as Nescafé's eight-year sponsorship of the *Network Chart Show*, between 1985 and 1993.

Other types of sponsorship

Many other events are sponsored by newspaper or magazine publishers, companies or by trade associations, professional bodies and voluntary societies. The *Daily Mail* Ideal Home Exhibition is an example of a public exhibition that has run for a great many years. Attendance at a trade exhibition may be encouraged by the issuing of free admission tickets in the sponsoring magazine to attract exhibitors to participate. A number of trade magazines sponsor exhibitions. Feats such as mountain climbs, exploratory ventures, one-woman voyages around the world, journeys to the North Pole, and other endurance tests have been part-financed through sponsorship. It may be done by a single sponsor, by a number of companies which contribute either funds or equipment and supplies, or by a publisher or TV company. In supporting these remarkable endeavours, the sponsor needs to be clear about its likely rewards. Is it purely a question of philanthropy or are media coverage and other credits expected? Sometimes the sponsor's name will be publicly associated but, equally, it is entirely possible for sponsors to be remain virtually anonymous. Sponsors of such subjects need to be aware of the scope or limitations of their support.

Chapter 28

Corporate image, identity and advertising

LEARNING OBJECTIVES

At the end of this chapter you will be able to:

- define corporate image and identity;
- illustrate the process of changing an organization's image;
- differentiate between groups of stakeholders for image campaign purposes;
- understand the importance of logos and straplines in corporate advertising campaigns.

Identity crisis or image problem?

Frequently, commentators misunderstand the difference between corporate image and corporate identity. They are very two different things, although the second should contribute positively to the first. Put very simply, the first is mental and the second is physical, or what one thinks about an organization and how one sees or identifies it respectively. Sometimes, people talk about creating, improving, polishing and projecting a positive corporate image, but this is not always possible. It is very important that public relations practitioners should understand what corporate image and identity are and how they affect a firm's corporate reputation. PROs may well need to explain to management what a corporate image actually is, commission research to identify its components amongst appropriate publics, and how corporate identity schemes and corporate advertising can contribute to its development.

A corporate image is not invented as such, but it can be influenced. Sometimes, members of an organization's publics may not know what it is, or equally they may have an incorrect or unfair idea of what it is compared with how management feel their company should be seen. Equally, where management's view of themselves and how they should be viewed is unrealistic, that can be put right through using appropriate PR techniques: public relations techniques generally (e.g. media relations), and corporate identity and corporate advertising specifically.

So a poor image problem can be principally twofold: the firm is badly perceived because it is *misunderstood*, or because it *has* a deservedly bad image. Whilst the first can be righted by means of public relations techniques, corporate image schemes and corporate advertising, the second can only be corrected by the organization itself.

Thus, corporate advertising might be used to explain a company's particular situation when they feel a particular public views them unfairly. A good example of this was when low-cost airline, EasyJet, placed adverts in the *Daily Mail* to explain that their fares were going up disproportionately because the majority shareholder, Barclays Bank, of Luton Airport had voted for increased landing charges. But the company might also decide to initiate corporate identity schemes in a bid to improve its image, to be more presentable and to be identified more clearly. Corporate identity schemes might involve renaming the company, redesigning its slogan, livery, logos and other associations.

In the situation where the company has a deservedly poor image, the public relations manager or consultant might well also be able to advise on how an image change can be brought about. It might, for instance, require staff training. Cable telephone companies in the UK have a poor reputation amongst their consumers for customer service, particularly non-payment telephone enquiries. Equally, it may require a change in company policy (e.g. strategic sourcing as a part of procurement policy). Nike and its alleged use of foreign 'sweatshop' labour is a good example of this. GlaxoSmithKline also encountered a blow to its image worldwide when it, and a number of other international drug companies, took the South African government to court for patent infringement. The cause: the Pretorian government introduced emergency legislation to allow its pharmaceutical industry to import generic versions of AIDS/HIV drugs from India and Brazil. When the South African government's cause was taken up by the likes of Medicines Sans Frontieres and the United Nations, the drug companies, fearing the potential backlash, terminated their court action and lowered their prices to tiny fractions of what they had been (Brennan and Baines, 2002). But Miller (2001) cites Erik Stern, managing director of

Stern Stewart Europe, a financial consulting outfit, who argues 'the more they [GSK] are made to look evil, the more people will question their profitability...if other countries invoke this case [to challenge GSK's patents], then its share price will be affected'. GSK had been using this very argument; that if patents weren't recognized, how could it continue to invest in R&D? It looks like GSK may well have lost this PR battle for the time being. It remains to be seen whether or not other badly affected regions of the world will also contest the anti-retroviral patents (e.g. the Caribbean countries) and the GSK brand/reputation suffers any long-term effects.

Corporate image, identity and reputation

So a corporate image is the impression of an organization held by a public based on knowledge and experience. Since everyone's knowledge and experience of an organization will be personal and will differ, the corporate image will vary between one public to another, and even within publics. The PRO's task is to increase people's knowledge and experience, uniformly, so that they have as clear and as correct an impression of the organization as is possible. It may not necessarily be a favourable impression. Use of PR techniques may not lead to love, but it could lead to understanding and tolerance between an organization and its publics. An image will go on developing in the minds of various publics, just as the character of a person develops on better acquaintance. The corporate image defines the character of the organization. The way the company is seen to behave will influence the impression people have of it.

In the world today there is great strife between some groups simply because of a lack of understanding (e.g. Protestants and Catholics in Northern Ireland, Jews and Arabs in Israel/Palestine). Such a breakdown in communication and understanding can be brought down to the commercial level, e.g. between management and employees. The lack of clear corporate images in all sorts of social, religious, political, industrial and commercial situations is frequently the cause of conflict and misunderstanding. Corporate image is defined as 'the global evaluation (comprised of a set of beliefs and feelings) a person has about an organization' (Dowling, 2001, p. 19).

Once these beliefs and feelings are recognized by a member of a particular public, individuals start to become familiar with an organization and how it goes about doing things. Eventually, members of a public develop an understanding of the company's values (for more on values, attitudes, opinions and beliefs, see Chapter 2). It is at this point that a company is said to have developed a reputation. Dowling (2001, p. 19) defines corporate reputation as 'the attributed values (such as authenticity, honesty,

**Table 28.1 Corporate ranking pharma-
ceutical industry**

Rank	Company
1	Johnson & Johnson
2	Merck
3	Pfizer
4	GSK
5	Genentech
6 =	Bayer
6 =	Eli Lilly
8	Bristol-Myers Squibb
9	Novartis
10	Aventis

Source: adapted from Resnicks (2002)

responsibility and integrity) evoked from the person's corporate image'. Table 28.1 provides the reader with an insight into how various member companies within the global pharmaceutical industry were viewed by industry analysts and senior-level executives, according to a reputation study undertaken by Rating Research.

According to Resnicks (2002), 'reputation has a lot to do with trust'. The prime drivers for developing a positive reputation in the pharmaceutical industry were 'offering innovative products and services', 'investing sufficiently in R&D' and 'effective corporate advertising, sales and marketing'. Of course, these reputation drivers will not be the same in all industries, so research is fundamental to determine what they are.

If a company is seeking to develop a more positive image amongst its publics, it might choose to do so by hiring an agency specializing in corporate identity. Corporate identity is defined as: 'the symbols and nomenclature an organization uses to identify itself to people (such as the corporate name, logo, advertising, slogan, livery, etc.)' (Dowling, 2001, p. 19). Examples of companies offering corporate identity services in the UK include Wolff Olins, Interbrand, Futurebrand and Landor Associates. Fee income for the automotive and professional service sectors in 2001 'held up well', whilst fee income for the telecoms, media and technology sectors was down considerably (Anon., 2002i).

Changing an organization's image

Some corporate images may be simple and distinct. For example, it is easier to establish a corporate image for a gas or electricity company, a hotel group or an airline because they work in one recognized industry than it is to establish a corporate image for a conglomerate or a multi-national with a diversity of businesses. For example, British Telecom has moved into a variety of high-technology services (e.g. BTOpenworld, BTIgnite, BT Exact Technologies), to complement its fixed-line telephone businesses (e.g. BT Retail, BT Wholesale). The convergence between telecommunication, media and technology companies provides such a mix of companies, and corporate cultures, and industry standards and practices are still developing and emerging. So, reputations are still being made. Image and identity are fluid and dynamic. Conversely, corporate identity should be uniform (literally!) and discontinuous. Sometimes it is necessary to accept that people may never have a comprehensive corporate image that is in line with how management perceive their company, and it is necessary to establish what may be termed an optimum image – a digest of what publics can be expected to reasonably accept. A lot of corporate image public relations work has to work in this context, attempting to unravel publics' confusions and misunderstandings.

Figure 28.1 outlines the process that should be undertaken when a firm needs to bring about an effective change in its image. The diagram clearly illustrates the difference between how a company sees itself (mirror image) and how its public sees it (its corporate image). When these two images are not realigned, managers (guided by the PRO) need to conduct a gap analysis to determine why the images are so convergent. Often, this divergence results because people view a particular organization from their own perspective rather than empathizing with

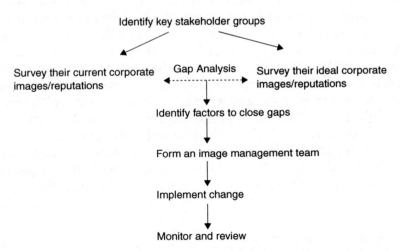

Figure 28.1 Changing an organization's image. Reprinted by permission of Oxford University Press.

Source: Dowling (2001, p. 243)

what it does, from the particular company's perspective. A good example of this was when Camelot succeeded in retaining its franchise for the British National Lottery, despite the fact that government felt its competitor, the Sir Richard Branson-inspired The People's Lottery, had a better offer (a non-profit enterprise donating more money to good causes). This was because Camelot managed to convince the courts and the media that it had been unfairly treated during the bidding process.

Figure 28.1 clearly illustrates that these images or reputations are different for different publics. This has been mentioned previously, but how should we go about determining with which groups to measure our image or reputation? Publics could range from employees, distributors and consumers to shareholders, government regulatory bodies and the media. Each may view the company quite differently according to their own considerations (e.g. employee conditions, trade discounts, quality of products, dividends, compliance issues, etc.). It is important to realize that different publics have different impressions or images of a company because of their particular association with it. The PRO needs to consider to whom the information is being directed in order to make the organization properly understood, and what information should be directed in each case.

If an organization wishes to bring about a change in its image amongst a particular group of publics, it should first conduct a stakeholder analysis exercise to identify how important different groups are to its mission and vision. Stakeholders can be usefully organized into four categories:

1. Key players with high power to affect company and industry policy (e.g. regulatory agencies for the pharmaceutical industry).
2. Those stakeholders with low power but high interest need to be kept informed (e.g. British farmers during the BSE crisis in the UK were in this category).
3. Those stakeholders with high power but low interest need to be kept informed (e.g. this category could include umbrella associations who have not yet developed a strong relationship with a particular company).
4. For those stakeholders with low power and interest, minimal effort is necessary.

Figure 28.2 illustrates how one might categorize those stakeholders of a government-funded university project, with a European Regional Development Fund (ERDF) grant, administered by a government agency (Government Office for London) to develop an advisory service for small to medium-sized enterprises (SMEs) in the fictional London Boroughs of Sedgewick and Toppelton.

	High	Power	Low
High Interest	*Key players* Government Office for London (administrators of ERDF grant) Partner commercial organizations SME customers		*Keep informed* Other development agencies (e.g. London Development Agency) Local media (press, radio, television, magazines) Other universities' departments Govt. business support agencies
Low	*Keep satisfied* London Boroughs of Sedgewick and Toppelton SME umbrella organizations Department of Trade and Industry		*Minimal effort* National media Competitors (for now!)

Figure 28.2 Stakeholder mapping for a university SME project.

Note that each of these categorizations might need to be reassessed depending on how circumstances change. In the above example, if the advisory service became well known, appropriate government departments and competitors might well start to take notice! The national media might also take more of an interest. The stakeholder analysis matrix can be used to determine with which publics image and reputation should be researched.

This image study often defines both negative and positive attitudes towards a company or organization. It is not a case, as some think, of saying this is the kind of image we want people to have, and then proceeding to impose it on people. Usually, that approach will not work if it is not congruent with the organization's past approach and current resources. Research conducted into the organization's image often uses semantic differential scale questions where the words are either uni- (e.g. friendly/not friendly) or bipolar (e.g. friendly/hostile). When bipolar words (opposites) are used, one can use a dictionary of antonyms to identify them. So, a question of the following type might be used to measure a particular public's perception of an organization:

> I would like you to consider company X's reputation. I will read out a list of image attributes and I would like you to rate company X on each item on a scale from 1 to 5, where 1 represents the positive side of the image and 5 represents the negative side. OK, giving an answer from 1 to 5, how _____ or _____ do you consider X to be?

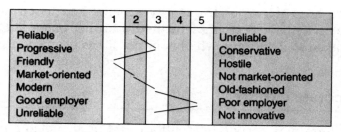

	1	2	3	4	5	
Reliable						Unreliable
Progressive						Conservative
Friendly						Hostile
Market-oriented						Not market-oriented
Modern						Old-fashioned
Good employer						Poor employer
Unreliable						Not innovative

Figure 28.3 Hypothetical image survey results.

Words such as reliable/unreliable, progressive/conservative, friendly/hostile, market-oriented/not market-oriented, modern/old-fashioned, organized/disorganized, good employer/poor employer, innovative/not innovative, and many others can be used. The results of such an exercise when averaged over the whole respondents can then be used to provide an indication of the general image profile of an organization. When the same question is asked of another public, the company might well be able to identify a significantly different perception of a company's image between the two publics. Figure 28.3 outlines how to display hypothetical answers to an image study for an organization using the above image parameters.

A good example of a situation where two publics have different perceptions is in the UK pharmaceutical industry. There is evidence (Wright and Fill, 2001) that doctors and pharmacists have different perceptions of companies in this industry. This is probably partly to do with the fact that it is doctors that generally prescribe most drugs, although changes are likely to occur and, increasingly, medicines are becoming available over the counter (OTC) as less potent versions of the prescribed medicines. Many pharmaceutical companies now accept that it is important to identify the key attributes that these two groups use to form an image of a company. Both pharmacists and doctors believed that drug effectiveness was the most important corporate image cue. Whilst *doctors* felt that GlaxoWellcome (the study was undertaken before the merger with SmithKline Beecham was completed) was the best value, *pharmacists* thought that AstraZeneca was the best value (Wright and Fill, 2001).

Once the image has been measured amongst publics, Dowling (2001) suggests that we identify factors to close image gaps between management and its organization's publics, that we formulate an image management team. The composition of this team might comprise the PRO, the chief executive or the operations director, but it really depends on what the drivers of your company's reputation are and who can affect these. The image management team might then go on to commission a corporate identity programme and/or corporate advertising. Once the advertising and/or corporate identity scheme and associated public relations activity have been implemented, a further image study should be undertaken to determine whether or not it has been successful.

The corporate identity

The need for a new corporate identity could occur when a number of organizations have been united by amalgamations, merger or acquisition, e.g. when GlaxoWellcome and SmithKline Beecham formed GSK in the early 2000s). It could also occur when the nature of an organization's activities has changed and the old identity is misleading or inadequate, e.g. the British New Labour Party after it ditched its policy to renationalize major industries. When Andersen Consulting decided to split from Arthur Andersen, and an arbitrator decided that the Andersen name should reside with Arthur Andersen, Andersen Consulting became 'Accenture'. Apparently, it took 80 days to generate, clear and announce the new name (Spaeth, 2002). In view of Arthur Andersen's problems as auditor of the bankrupt Enron, and the subsequent impact upon the image of its auditing function, the Accenture people must have been heaving sighs of relief that they lost their case. It is also likely that Ben & Jerry's will have to work particularly hard to retain its bohemian corporate identity, particularly amongst its consumer publics, after it was taken over by consumer goods giant, Unilever, in 2000 (Arnold, 2001a).

Ironically, a company may require a new corporate identity when its name has become so synonymous with a particular benefit that people cease to view its special attributes. It may be flattery when everyone refers to vacuum cleaners as 'hoovers' (except to Electrolux) or to Thermos flasks, Pyrex dishes and Sellotape, but a loss of identity has occurred with these products, which can be serious for their parent companies. A product may also be unfairly associated with inferior or rival brands, as when one orders a Coke and is served a Pepsi-Cola. Some of these names have slipped into the language. A company may go to extraordinary lengths to preserve its image and identity. A good example of this was when American toymaker, Mattel Inc., makers of the Barbie Doll, pursued MCA Records in court for trade mark infringement when Danish band Aqua released an album in 1997 with lyrics defaming Barbie as a 'blond bimbo' (Anon., 2002j). They lost their case in the Court of Appeals.

Whereas the corporate image may be relevant in different ways to different people, the corporate identity should be the same for all people who come into contact with it. Corporate identity schemes like those of Coca-Cola or Holiday Inn are similar even in their international markets, although some corporate images take on local interpretations.

For instance, the Guinness corporate identity, as expressed by the typography, the dark stout with a white head (which is often pictured in advertising) and the brown label with the harp insignia, is familiar in many countries, although in Malaysia and Indonesia the labels carry a dog or a cat respectively in addition to the harp. The Malaysian Chinese say Black Dog beer or simply Black Beer, and the Indonesians say Black Cat beer, but neither says Guinness, which is unpronounceable.

Corporate identity has a historical background. Centuries ago, a king would lead his army and identify himself by means of an emblem on his shield, such as the cross of St George or the cross of Lorraine. But since this was rather dangerous, it became the fashion for all the king's knights to wear the same emblem so as to confuse the enemy. Emblems became flags, and troops started to wear uniforms. When transportation began to develop, stagecoaches were decorated distinctively. The most splendid liveries of modern companies have been those of the world's airlines. It is very costly to paint a fleet of aircraft, especially when, as occurred with British Airways over a decade ago, a new corporate identity was introduced. Livery is one of the most effective ways of establishing corporate identity.

The creation and introduction of a corporate identity scheme can be a costly and extensive business. When there is such a scheme, everyone responsible for ordering or buying advertising, print, paintwork, decorations and furnishings is usually obliged to follow the instructions contained in a company corporate identity kit. For instance, even the corridor lampshades in a Hilton hotel conform to the Hilton corporate identity scheme, as do the serviettes on most airlines, or the chequebooks issued by banks. In a department store or supermarket there is no doubt whose shop one is in, for the corporate identity is explicit in many things visible, such as the dress of staff, price tags and shelf labelling, instore displays, store layout and carrier bags (e.g. Marks & Spencer, Tesco). Here are some of the items that may be involved in such a scheme:

- The livery of road vehicles, trains, ships, aircraft and other forms of transportation.
- All stationery including letterheadings, faxes, press releases, invoices, purchase order forms, receipts, compliment slips, business cards and tickets.
- Name displays on premises, e.g. factories, offices, shops, warehouses, depots and garages.
- Websites – intranet, extranet, Internet.
- Exhibition stands, showrooms, mobile exhibitions.
- Sales literature, price lists, catalogues, sales promotion material, house journals.

- Labels, packaging and containers.
- Instruction leaflets and service manuals.
- Uniforms, overalls, blouses, headgear, cap, pocket and lapel badges, company ties and cuff links, and corporate presents such as key rings, pens and novelties.
- Point-of-sale display material.
- Advertisements in all visible media.
- Credits on videotapes, slides, DVD and CD-ROM presentations.
- Diaries and calendars.
- Annual reports and accounts, share prospectuses and any other communications for shareholders.
- Cutlery, crockery, food packs, serviettes and menus.
- Drip mats or coasters, table-mats and tablecloths and ashtrays.

Not every item applies to every organization, but organizations that are frequently in the public eye, and operate very close to their customers (e.g. hotels, banks and airlines), will usually take up a long list of such items. The corporate identity scheme can be incorporated as new things are bought. Often, the cost of scrapping old letterheadings, faxes and memos can be considerable. Identity schemes can have a consolidating repetitive effect, with great positive psychological impact, often enhancing the morale and pride of those working within the organization. Few companies have made such remarkable efforts to establish and maintain their corporate identity as Coca-Cola, even to the extent of legal battles with rival firms, who misuse the Coca-Cola brand name. The well-known script logo has scarcely changed since 1886, when Frank M. Robinson, bookkeeper to the creator of Coca-Cola, Dr John T. Pemberton, penned it. The freehand copies of the script have been tidied up and the logo containing the trade mark script has changed shape from time to time. The company has issued a style guide worldwide and ruled that only faithful reproductions may be used. Corporate identity has also been associated with the pack (the bottle with the badge).

The logotype

The *logotype*, usually shortened to logo, is a special way of presenting the name of the company. Strictly speaking, symbols are special, distinctive designs or shapes like the torch of British Telecom, the red rose of the New Labour Party, or the Nike Swoosh. Name displays and symbols are often loosely called logos. Many logotypes are based on a signature or handwriting, such as Boots, Cadbury's, Canon, Ford, Coca-Cola and Kellogg's. Others use a distinctive typography, like

Guinness and Kodak. The logotype may be accompanied by a symbol or, like a number of motor car badges, name and symbol may be combined (e.g. BMW and VW), whereas the Mercedes-Benz symbol appears alone on the bonnet, as does the symbol for the Jaguar. These designs are also usually registered trade marks. Some symbols last for years, then disappear only to return when an advertising agency decides on a revival. Obscure symbols should be avoided since, although they may be distinctive, they are not meaningful. Figure 28.4 provides examples of the world's top five brands, identified in a survey undertaken by MORI, amongst UK Captains of Industry, commissioned by Wolff Olins (2002).

GlaxoSmithKline required a new logo and corporate identity after the merger between its constituent companies, SmithKline Beecham and

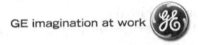

Mercedes-Benz

Figure 28.4 The world's top five brands (2002). Logos reproduced with kind permission. 'Coca-Cola' and 'Coke' are registered trademarks of The Coca-Cola Company and are reproduced with kind permission from The Coca-Cola Company. Microsoft is a registered trademark of Microsoft Corporation.

GlaxoWellcome. This task was undertaken by top agency, Futurebrand. They came up with a logo designed to resemble a heart rather than a pill, as some have said. The intention was to connote a more caring company amongst its publics.

Futurebrand also worked on the logo of Microsoft's online operation, MSN.com, providing it with a separate identity from its parent by virtue of its association with a multicoloured butterfly, presumably to connote an image of innovation, dynamism and multifacetedness.

A client of Interbrand, Barclays, had had PR problems in Spring 2000, when the closure of several hundred branches was announced, including many in rural areas at a time when an ad campaign emphasized its 'bigness', starring Anthony Hopkins and other 'big' stars. It was perceived by many consumers as promoting its arrogance more than its pedigree, worldliness and expertise. Interbrand was commissioned to 'bring a breath of fresh air' to high street banking, by opening up the branches with large glass frontages. The specially commissioned Big Life photography, in use throughout the identity programme from ATM machines to print and literature, gave the brand even more energy (Interbrand, 2000). More recently, Barclays advertising agency Bartle Bogle Hegarty have introduced a new slogan; 'fluent in finance' is a strap line used to embody Barclays as the money experts (Figure 28.5). This strategy, according to the company, is intended to shift Barclays' positioning from one of brawn power (the 'Big' ads of old) to brain power, as recently expressed in the Samuel L. Jackson TV commercials.

Corporate identity may be associated with a trade character, some of which seem to live on forever, like Johnnie Walker, the Michelin rubber man and the black horse of Lloyds TSB.

Egg, the Internet bank set up by Prudential Insurance and since floated on the London Stock Exchange, commissioned Wolff Olins to develop its brand image. Whilst its previous advertising was best characterized as a bit madcap (it portrayed customers falling in love with Egg and vice versa), the new image is more irreverent but still highly consumer oriented after it ditched its advertising agency HHCL in favour of Mother to attract a broader audience

Figure 28.5 The Barclays Logo and Slogan. Reproduced with kind permission of Barclays Bank PLC.

13 August 2001

Egg appoints Wolff Olins

Egg has appointed brand consultancy Wolff Olins to further develop its brand. The consultancy was appointed after a three-way pitch.

Egg's chief marketing officer, Nick Cross said, 'We've built a very strong business. The next phase will be to develop internationally and leverage the brand further. Wolff Olins will work with us to position Egg for the future.'

Wolff Olins will work towards strengthening Egg's position and developing a powerful visual expression. The work will start immediately and will influence the brand gradually over the coming months.

Since entering the market as the UK's first Internet-only bank, Egg has constantly innovated and taken the position as consumer champion. Since it began trading in 1998, Egg's offer has expanded, becoming broader and more sophisticated. The Egg brand will increasingly be associated with innovative new services inside and outside the UK. Egg has already gained over 1.7 million customers, and is listed on the London Stock Exchange.

'We are delighted with this opportunity to work with the team at Egg. We will start by clarifying the brand idea in preparation for their growth. It's a very exciting time,' says Nikki Jones, Wolff Olins consultant on the project.

Wolff Olins' clients include Heathrow Express, Credit Suisse, Tate, Goldfish, Orange, Britannic Group, Sky, Powwow and World Gold Council.

For more information, please contact:

Alice Huang, Wolff Olins (t)+44 (0) 20 7551 4621

or e-mail: publicrelations@wolff-olins.com

Figure 28.6 Press release announcing Egg/Wolff Olins branding campaign. Reproduced with the kind permission of Wolff Olins.

Source: http://www.wolff-olins.com/Press2001egg.htm, accessed 24 July 2002.

(Bashford, 2001). Figure 28.6 outlines a press release announcing the tie-up.

Figure 28.7 outlines the new logo and the Egg message 'what's in it for me?', showing its irreverent consumer focus.

egg™

Figure 28.7 The Egg logo and slogan. Reproduction of this Egg logo and trade mark is only with permission of Egg plc.

Corporate advertising

We sought to distinguish public relations from advertising in Chapter 1. Why then does public relations sometimes resort to corporate advertising? In planning public relations campaigns, it is necessary to choose the best media for transmitting the message most effectively. When it is necessary to control the content of the message, and when, where and how it is to appear, the answer is corporate advertising. Corporate advertising is used to:

1. Establish a corporate image.
2. Announce financial results.
3. Contest political policies, e.g. nationalization (as used to happen under Labour governments).
4. Contest or support a takeover bid.
5. Position a company regarding issues of the day.

Points 2 and 4 really belong to financial PR, and point 3 verges on propaganda. This chapter considers the importance of corporate advertising in developing the corporate image. Following the aggressive and knocking advertising used in takeover battles, the Takeover Panel of the London Stock Exchange issued restrictions, which took effect on 7 April 1986. These restrictions apply to advertisements about takeover offers and defences, but exclude product or corporate image advertisements not bearing on an offer or potential offer. A number of companies have become the prey of predators simply because shareholders and financial institutions did not know how good they were, and because their share prices had fallen due to lack of confidence in the money market. Their financial public relations had been neglected, and probably they had done no corporate advertising until it was too late. Then, in desperation, they indulged in expensive and often useless last-ditch defensive advertising.

Corporate advertising is sometimes used as a way of augmenting financial PR. It has the advantage of making a company very visible and better understood, but it is also used to influence a number of its publics simultaneously. It may be very necessary when the full extent of a company's activities are not fully or widely known, amongst a number of its publics, or when an organization's general image amongst various publics is poor.

For example, Aeroflot has hired Identica Partnership to revamp its image after decades of being saddled with a poor reputation for safety. Its first supersonic plane, the Tupolev TU-144, crashed at the Paris Air Show. 'In 1994, the International Passengers Association said Aeroflot was the world's worst airline, adding that only a fool with no personal regard for safety would fly it' (Arnold, 2001b). It tried to change its image through a corporate identity scheme in 1997, incorporating dressing flight crew in traditional Russian dress and serving Russian food. It also spent £2.6 million on a disastrous ad campaign, created by Russian agency Premier SV, featuring flying pink elephants, as research had demonstrated that Russians like them! Most people associated the flying elephant with the hapless Dumbo, whose flying was less than perfect (Arnold, 2001c). Aeroflot needs to work on ensuring its safety record, and removing this prejudice amongst its publics, before it can seriously increase its market share of international Russian flights.

Slogans

Certain evocative advertising slogans, because they have been retained for so long, also become part of a company's corporate identity. Although Guinness has not used the slogan *'Guinness Is Good For You'*,

Table 28.2 Famous taglines by company/agency and date

Company	Tagline example	Date – Agency
British Airways	'The world's favourite airline'	1983 – Saatchi & Saatchi
BMW	'The ultimate driving machine'	1975 – Ammirati & Puris
Federal Express	'When it absolutely, positively has to be there overnight'	1982 – Ally & Gargano
L'Oreal	'Because I'm worth it'	1967 – McCann Erickson
KFC	'Finger lickin' good'	1952 – Ogilvy & Mather
Heinz	'Beanz Meanz Heinz'	1967 – Young & Rubicam
Nike	'Just do it'	1988 – Wieden & Kennedy
Avis	'We try harder'	1962 – Doyle Dane Bernbach

Source: Examples from http://www.adslogans.co.uk/hof/2trplo.html

first developed in 1929 by S. H. Benson, in British advertising for many years, many people still remember it. Another type of slogan, the strapline or signature slogan, has become internationally adopted. The same strapline may be used, or a new one may be created for each advertising campaign. These usually appear at the end of an advertisement, and may also be used as a jingle in TV commercials. They go beyond corporate identity to try to sum up the corporate image in a few words. Table 28.2 highlights some of the more memorable slogans used by various companies, the date and by whom they were first developed.

Many were still in use at the start of the millennium. L'Oreal, Avis and Heinz have all recently advertised using these slogans. More recently, British Airways took low-cost carrier easyJet to court for adapting its slogan to 'The Web's Favourite Airline' (easyJet). BA lost the court action. This was all the more notable because easyJet had adopted the tactic of using knocking copy advertising against BA to differentiate its service.

Constant repetition of the slogan in corporate advertising does make the strapline more memorable and ensures its importance as part of a corporate identity scheme, thereby contributing to the corporate image. Primarily, they are the creations of imaginative copywriters. Nevertheless, if such a slogan is intended to be permanent, the public relations manager or public relations consultant should be consulted at the visual and draft copy stage because of the obvious public relations implications. It is important to ensure that the slogan is in tune ('on message') with the public relations message, especially in a corporate image campaign. A slogan must be credible to be effective, and not just a gimmick.

Chapter 29

Public relations in political context

LEARNING OBJECTIVES

At the end of this chapter you will be able to:

■ define public affairs and lobbying, and the differences between them;
■ explain the lobbying process and how it works;
■ understand how public relations is used by governments and political parties.

Defining public affairs and lobbying

In the political context, various terms are used to denote the public relations function. Public affairs, regulatory affairs, government relations or, when work is outsourced to an agency, lobbying, all come under the rubric of political PR. Each of these functions actually has slightly different roles. For instance, public affairs departments might generally subsume government relations, or they might formulate policy in public relations programmes. White (1991, p. 55) defines public affairs as: 'A specialist area of practice within public relations concerned with those relationships involved in public policy-making, legislation and regulation that may affect the interests of organizations and their operations.' Conversely, lobbying, according to Cutlip et al. (1994, p. 17), is defined similarly as: 'The specialized part of public relations that builds and maintains relations with government primarily for the purpose of influencing legislation and regulation.'

What then is the difference between lobbying and regulatory affairs? Or lobbying and government relations? Generally, whilst government relations departments might monitor government legislation to see how it impacts upon their sponsors (their firm or their client), regulatory affairs usually deals with specific government regulatory bodies such as the ITC (for the independent television industry), or OFTEL (the telecommunication regulator), or OFWAT (the water industry regulator). Lobbying efforts, by contrast, deal with these and other areas.

Because legislation is such a technical area, and because few firms have the capability to understand and influence leglislation, lobbyists are often hired. Moloney and Jordan (1996) outline the main reasons why:

- For representation (advocacy) for clients to government decision makers.
- For strategic advice to clients on how a campaign should proceed.
- For political administrative support for their clients.

The public relations manager who requires discourse with government has to decide whether he or she has the expertise, money and manpower to handle it alone. Of course, if the company is constantly involved in political matters, a full-time in-house service will be justified. But many companies engage in political public relations only occasionally, or only when a special issue arises. It may then pay to use either the regular advisory or the ad hoc services of a political public relations consultancy. For example, if a company is being investigated by the Competition Commission, a consultancy might be called in.

Yet another way of lobbying is through a trade association or professional body, of which the company or individual may be a member. A member may approach such a society, or the society may itself initiate matters as a pressure group on behalf of its members. For instance, the Advertising Association has negotiated with the European Commission over attempts to lay down rules about advertising that were contrary to British custom, and out of line with the British Code of Advertising Practice. Some of the EC proposals were seen to be unworkable, including interpretations of what may be considered misleading in an advertisement. Another example is the Direct Marketing Association's lobby campaign on EU distance selling directives. The British Medical Association has lobbied on a number of medical subjects, and not just on behalf of doctors. In such cases, it is far better for the spokesperson of the industry to do the lobbying.

It is often said that only those with enough money can indulge in political lobbying. On the other hand, democracy works best when the government can discuss its proposals with appropriate interest groups.

When the National Health Service scheme was first introduced, in the post-War Attlee government, it was possible for the government to negotiate with the medical profession, but not with the patients; they had no representative body. Nowadays, agriculture and education policy initiatives, for instance, are seldom developed without the input of the National Farmer's Union (NFU), or protracted negotiations with dissatisfied teachers' trade unions. There have been many successful examples of lobbying – for instance, that of the Shopping Hours Reform Council (SHRC), consisting mainly of large supermarket chains, who managed to lobby the then Conservative government to make Sunday trading legal in July 1994 (see Harris et al., 1999). PriceWaterhouse and Coopers & Lybrand managed to persuade the European Union competition authorities that it was better able to serve the EU's enlargement agenda as the merged entity, PriceWaterhouseCoopers, than as separate companies in auditing Eastern European member state firms (Hatcher, 1998) when they accede to the EU in 2004.

In the USA, the capital, Washington, DC, is a hotbed of lobbying activity as Political Action Committees (PACs), which channel corporate and individual donations, representing numerous interests, pounce on Capitol Hill in legislative session. Brussels, however, is fast expanding as a lobbying centre in its own right and is now reputed to be the largest lobbying centre in the world (Harris et al., 1999). In the British context, the Meat and Livestock Commission have been lobbying hard to overturn an illegal French ban on British beef, maintained long after the EU's own ban was removed. This campaign was eventually successful only because the British government pushed the EU to take the French government to court to sue for damages. The French government rescinded their ban before they had to pay any damages.

An organization may conduct public relations in the political context in the following ways:

1. A specialist lobbyist can be engaged, either permanently or as the need arises.
2. Some of the larger public relations consultancies offer political services, often having MPs or others with a high degree of political influence as director and/or advisers.
3. A Member of Parliament may be paid a fee to give political advice on matters of importance to an organization.
4. The in-house public relations manager may handle political lobbying directly.
5. An association may lobby on behalf of members, e.g. the NFU, Universities UK (the body representing vice-chancellors and principals of universities) or the Countryside Commission, for instance.

6. A Member of Parliament may be invited to join the board of directors of the company to help the company lobby the government directly.

It should be remembered that political and parliamentary public relations is a very broad term, and it could embrace local government, quasi-autonomous non-governmental organizations (quangos), civil service chiefs, members of the Westminster parliament, Scottish parliament, Welsh Assembly and the North Ireland Legislative Assembly, government, members of parliaments and assemblies from all parties, members of the House of Lords, MEPs of all EU countries at the European Parliament in Strasbourg, Ministers at Luxembourg, Commissioners and others at Brussels, and even MPs and Ministers in other countries. However, in spite of this array of political figures, it is often more effective to work with a small number of sympathetic politicians who are prepared to take up one's cause.

The side of public affairs that monitors the working of government in parliament is termed 'parliamentary liaison'. This is sometimes confused with attempts by the government to present its case to the public, but the term has the opposite meaning. The expression 'parliament' is itself a broad one. It can mean the business of the house such as at Question Time when the Prime Minister is asked questions (for which there are prepared answers), and supplementary questions, debates and the reading of bills. Much occurs outside the chambers of the Commons and the Lords. In the legislative process in the UK, interest groups are usually informally, and formally, consulted by government departments, particularly in the process of drawing up White/Green Papers, which are effectively government proposals at differing stages of advancement for new laws and political administrative procedures. They also have extra-parliamentary influence, through dealings with MPs, at the committee stage (clause-by-clause scrutiny in standing committee), report stage (at which amendments are considered) and the third reading stage (when the final version is debated) in the House of Commons. The process in the Lords is similar.

Generally, when working with civil servants at Whitehall or with ministers or parliament, it is important to:

- identify and prioritize the issues;
- get to know the appropriate officials;
- put together a planning and contacts grid;
- identify key ministers, Opposition frontbenchers and other interested MPs;
- read the press (Morris, 2001).

Morris argues, however, that successive governments never work in the same way, so there is a learning curve at the start of each electoral cycle.

A political public relations consultancy can provide clients with services such as advice on when various issues have been awarded parliamentary time for discussion or debate, and they can also supply clients with copies of Hansard, White Papers, Green Papers, Bills and other publications, with interpretations and advice as necessary. Consultancies sometimes employ experienced politicians (e.g. Hill & Knowlton) to help in understanding, and working with, this complex process.

Many interests, such as farming, medicine and motoring, have groups of MPs who are particularly qualified or interested in them, and some MPs represent constituencies in which businesses have their premises or plants. Trade unions also frequently sponsor particular MPs. When Devonport Management Ltd., through its consultant, The Rowland Company, lobbied government to award it the Trident submarine refiting contract, it focused on 'a wide range of stakeholders in the decision ... the MoD and the Navy, Treasury, Number 10, and other ministers who could influence the decision – DTI, Environment, Employment, Chairman of the Conservative Central Office, and parliament, especially MPs in the South West and those with defence and public spending interests' (Andrews, 1996). Partly because The Rowland Company managed to link constituency issues in the Portsmouth area, such as unemployment, and the future election of local constituency MPs with Devonport's winning of the contract, it won against the favoured competition from the Rosyth dockyard in Scotland.

Political public relations does not involve bribing MPs to speak on behalf of an issue, although this did happen when Conservative MP, Neil Hamilton, allegedly accepted brown envelopes stuffed with cash from Mohammed Al Fayed, the Chairman of Harrods. This issue dogged the Conservative Party throughout the 1997 British General Election, and despite a spirited media campaign from Hamilton himself, in and out of court, the 'cash for questions' scandal probably acted as the straw that broke the camel's (government's) back in their subsequent electoral demise. Despite the Labour government's denouncements of the Tories' activities in this regard, they courted their own bad publicity when it was subsequently determined that the Labour Party had accepted a £1 million donation from the Formula One supremo, Bernie Ecclestone. This at a time when motorsport's governing body, the Federation de l'Automobile (FIA), was lobbying ministers to contest a proposed EU ban on tobacco sponsorship, arguing that it would simply drive the sport, its £900 million export value, its 50 000 highly skilled and 150 000 part-time workers to the Far East (Abrams and Butler, 1997). The EU subsequently delayed the tobacco sponsorship ban, whilst the

Labour Party eventually returned the £1 million donation, when news of it was leaked to the press.

Fortunately, cases of bribery and corruption are rare in British politics. If MPs do speak on a subject with which they are financially connected, they are expected to declare their interest, and there is a register of MP's private interests. Members of Parliament often do have other sources of income, such as journalism, broadcasting, directorships and legal practices. Some are directors of public relations consultancies, or receive retainers from public relations consultancies and companies for advisory services only. Both the Institute of Public Relations and the Public Relations Consultants Association maintain a register, publicly available, of member MPs so engaged. When MPs were asked in November 1996 if they thought political consultancies helped or hindered organizations in obtaining contact with MPs, 64 per cent thought that they helped and only 9 per cent believed they hindered (McLeod, 1997).

Criticism is sometimes made of MPs who receive substantial fees for consultancy services, on the grounds that they are paid salaries to serve as MPs and should not receive other payments. This line of argument is false criticism, since any MP may well have other income as a farmer, lawyer, journalist, public speaker or company director, provided he or she is not a member of the government, when any conflicting interests would have to be renounced. However, the line of argument that suggests that MPs shouldn't accept fees to influence a system that they themselves are part of is more convincing.

Brief cases in lobbying: PriceWaterhouseCoopers and Camelot

The PriceWaterhouse/Coopers & Lybrand merger

PriceWaterhouse and Coopers & Lybrand announced their merger plans on 17 September 1997. It wasn't until almost a year later, on 1 July 1998, that they formally merged to form PriceWaterhouseCoopers, the world's largest professional services firm, after nearly a year of assuaging regulators' fears. They had decided to merge to:

- provide their clients with significantly enhanced geographic coverage;
- strengthen their ability to invest in emerging markets by spreading the enormous costs involved across a significantly larger base, eliminating duplicate investments;

- raise the level of their investment in the latest and best technology, and thereby position themselves to better offer innovatory solutions and invest in an intellectual capital base capable of offering world-class expertise (Hatcher, 1998).

However, because the market for professional accountancy services (e.g. tax compliance, management consulting, and corporate finance advisory and insolvency services) was intensely competitive and dominated by a relatively small number of companies, the case was referred to the Merger Task Force of DG IV (the Competition Commission, effectively) of the EU Commission. Public affairs activity was used in the process to:

1. Organize and manage task forces.
2. Gather data and intelligence about external perceptions.
3. Communicate benefits of the merger to stakeholders.
4. Support national administrations at member state level.
5. Counter actual or possible misconceptions (White, 2001).

The public affairs activity was fundamental in providing PriceWaterhouse and Coopers & Lybrand with the information necessary to make a rational, expert, persuasive case to the EU competition authorities that it was in their (the EU's) best interests to accept the merged institution, because it would then be better able to audit and provide professional services for East European nations intent on joining the EU.

The renewal of Camelot's National Lottery licence

The deadline for submissions for the licence to operate the United Kingdom's National Lottery was the 29 February 2000. Two companies were bidding: Camelot, the incumbent operator, and The People's Lottery (TPL), a consortium led by Sir Richard Branson. Problems started to occur for Camelot when its electronics partner, GTECH, discovered a glitch in its software. This badly affected their bid and the National Lottery Commission (NLC – the licensor) sought clarification of various undertakings advanced by Camelot, which were designed to sort out the software problem. The NLC then wrote separate letters: one to TPL explaining how it needed to improve its bid and one to Camelot stating they felt GTECH's software was fit for the purpose. Then, the NLC decided to announce that it was scrapping the original bidding process (perhaps because the decision deadline had lapsed two months previously). It then subsequently announced that it was to work only with TPL as its preferred bidder. It was at this point that public affairs activity within Camelot became frenetic. Camelot applied for a judicial review, and won it. The judge later ruled that the NLC action was an abuse of power. It eventually issued an apology to Camelot and two months later it was declared the preferred bidder over TPL.

Camelot had won, but it had not been easy. They had had to manage a situation in which the shareholders wanted more profit and enhanced reputation, the players wanted more, 'smaller' prizes, retailers wanted more terminals installed, government wanted greater revenue for good causes, and the public wanted a not-for-profit operation. These last two items probably indicate why the NLC originally ruled Camelot out of the bidding: because TPL declared its aim to run the lottery as a not-for-profit operation with more prizes for the consumer. Camelot had managed this turnaround through regional roadshows, by writing articles, through briefings and dialogue with government and special interest groups, by attending party conferences, through conducting opinion polls and disseminating research papers, correspondence with MPs, by throwing charity events and their 24/7 newsroom.

Several lessons emerge from these campaigns which apply to lobbying more generally. The first is never to be daunted by initial pessimism and statements made by governments or officials. It is always better to work with politicians rather than against them. Nevertheless, politicians are elected and thus they can be swung by grassroots arguments (petitions and constituent letter writing campaigns), especially if an election is pending. The second lesson is to make full use of the media to buttress the lobbying case. This provides the campaign with the ability to resonate their message and build public awareness of the issue. The third lesson is that it is important to determine what the overlap of understanding is between the body being lobbied and the lobbyist. This overlap of understanding is better known as 'the identification of rhetoric' in literary academic circles. In the PriceWaterhouseCoopers case, the company had cleverly linked its merger objective with the EU's desire to enlarge itself by taking in Eastern Europe. They argued that only a merged professional services company would be able to properly audit the influx of East European companies that would occur as a result of the EU enlargement initiative. In the second case, Camelot, after initially being ruled out of the bidding, took legal action to ensure that it was placed back in the running for the National Lottery licence. Once it was back in the bidding, it was able to capitalize on the poor behaviour of the NLC, and it was able to reassure the NLC that ultimately it could offer more money for good causes using a profit-oriented model than TPL could with a not-for-profit model.

Party political and government public relations

One author has suggested that the public relations activity indulged in by modern Western political parties and governments is a political marketing–propaganda hybrid (O'Shaughnessy, 1999). By that, he means that parties often seek to persuade people to believe in their issues using a unidirectional, manipulative communication process. But public relations is also a legitimate activity used to explain policy to citizens and other stakeholder groups, and to make a party understood for what it does or does not stand for.

A government may indulge in propaganda on behalf of its country, and this is especially true in wartime, when propaganda is issued to boost the morale of the civilian population, or to undermine the morale of the enemy. The US, after Islamic fundamentalist terrorists attacked major targets in New York, Pennsylvania and Washington, DC on 11 September 2001, has been engaged in a campaign to win the hearts and minds of European and Middle Eastern allies in its Afghan bombing campaign. The US president was said to be stunned at the extent of anti-American sentiment in Arab nations, although his government did eventually make statements to Arab nations using Al-Jazeera television, the very medium used by Osama bin Laden himself, the Al Qaeda chief and financier, to announce jihad against the West. In Germany, although public support did not exist to support the US effort in Afghanistan, Chancellor Gerhard Schroeder nevertheless agreed to contribute 4000 troops, showing that public opinion is not always slavishly followed by governments (*The Economist*, 2001a). Bush's propaganda effort has, as its core, the desire to maintain the unity of the world anti-terrorist alliance. It is for this reason that he has mentioned that he could support an eventual Palestinian state (*The Economist*, 2001b), though not under the leadership of Yasser Arafat.

After the bombing of the World Trade Center in September 2001, the US began 'fighting' a diplomatic and media campaign to attack Iraq, perhaps because President Saddam Hussein was managing to convince his own citizens that US-led food sanctions were directly to blame for hundreds of thousands of deaths of Iraqi children (*The Economist*, 2001b), rather than his own failure to make his military establishments available to UN inspectors (the reason for the sanctions). Perhaps it was also because of his support for Al Qaeda terrorists, whom he was allegedly bankrolling, but this could well be American propaganda.

Propaganda was used to devastating effect to convince the German population of the need to eradicate the Jews, through the use of cinema by propaganda minister, Goebbels (e.g. *Der Juder* – 'The Jew') to portray the Jewish people in a contemptuous manner. Hitler (1925, p. 166), showing his sickening understanding of persuasion early on, argued that the first axiom of all propagandist activity is that it should be one-sided and subjective. Propaganda, however, was used by the British military in India during the Second World War to maintain the morale of their South Asian troops fighting against the Japanese. Special information lectures and pamphlets were organized that outlined the vicious and inhumane methods used by the Japanese to torture prisoners. But pamphlets were also distributed showing the meagre rations of the Japanese soldiers, with testimonials by the Japanese soldiers themselves on how badly they were treated by their superiors. This was an attempt to float the idea that South Asian soldiers working for the British Army had a good lot, generally. British Military Intelligence monitored post-cards and letters sent to relatives and friends to determine the morale of their South Asian troops. Bhattacharya (2000) argues that it was partly because of the information this monitoring provided that the British military decided to pull out of India, rather than send in British troops to support the Raj, and keep India within the British Empire. The information gleaned from the troops' correspondence outlined the lack of loyalty they felt towards the British crown.

We often have the party of the government in power using propaganda to boost its fortunes, but government also use public relations to help the electorate to understand its policies, legislation and public services. The Central Office of Information (COI) provides creative services for ministries, departments and government agencies, and arranges for the appointment of advertising agencies. This is carefully costed so that the COI pays its way. At one time, the COI provided exporters with many free services through the overseas distribution (via High Commissions abroad) of news stories, photographs and films. Today, the COI has to operate more cost-effectively, and most overseas information work is conducted by the COI as commissioned by the Department of Trade and Industry, which now has its own export publicity unit.

Examples of campaigns conducted by the COI include: public service advertising for military recruitment; new employment initiatives; health campaigns (such as the AIDS awareness campaign of the 1980s); and more controversially, privatization in the late 1980s and early 1990s (initiated by the Conservative Party) and issues close to Labour's 2001 election campaign (recruitment of nurses and police). These latter campaigns incurred unprecedented government spending for the months of March and April, when the election was only a couple of months away. This period of the year has always previously been a relatively quieter period in the government communications calendar. Government communications advisers can play significant roles in the development of a nation's political agenda. Witness the role played by Dick Morris, largely regarded as having rescued Bill Clinton after the 1994 mid-term elections in which his party suffered significantly, as did Clinton's image itself, in developing Clinton's agenda for the 1996 Presidential Election. Adrianne Foglia, foreign press aide to former Colombian President Andres Pastrana, turned US perceptions of the Andean country's drug enforcement operations around by making the defence minister available for the US press, and several of his department's studies highlighting the fight against paramilitaries and its human rights concerns (Dudley, 2001). This was important because the US subsequently advanced a $1.3 billion aid package in June 2000.

For the latter purpose, government departments make use of chief information officers and their public relations staff. Over the last century, these positions have been staffed by civil servants, so as not to mix party and government publicity generation. In the last two decades, however, Number 10 has gained increasing control over the public relations officers of various government departments. The Central Office of Information was brought under the control of Margaret Thatcher's formidable press secretary (now Sir) Bernard Ingham. Shortly after the British General Election, Alastair Campbell (Blair's Labour Party communications supremo turned government communications strategist) presided over the replacement of 18 out of 20 heads of information in the various government departments in the first two years of government (*The Economist*, 2002a). In March 2002, perhaps the worst example of a government department's press relations was when Jo Moore, Stephen Byers' spin doctor, suggested in an e-mail that the week after 11 September 2001 would be a good time to 'bury' bad news because the media would be dominated by reportage of the terrorist events in the US. This e-mail was subsequently leaked to the press. The UK Transport Secretary engineered the resignation of his press secretary Martin Sixsmith and Ms Moore shortly after, but not before damaging his own image substantially. He had announced the resignation of Martin Sixsmith even though Sixsmith had not resigned! He also lied on television about his role in blocking Mr Sixsmith's search for an alternative job (*The Economist*, 2002b). His tattered reputation did not withstand a subsequent train disaster at Potter's Bar and he duly resigned.

Local government public relations officers are engaged in information services about the proposals and decisions of the individual council, and about the services and amenities provided to local residents. Various authorities have priorities for information providers that can include public transport, car parking, entertainment, markets, libraries, art galleries and museums, parks and recreation grounds, street and shopping centre planning, industrial estates, and in some cases special subjects such as exhibition centres, holiday attractions, airports and seaports. Local authorities are often trading enterprises that require constant public relations support.

The lobbying/political fund-raising link

The British political parties' annual conferences, particularly prior to a general election, provide companies with opportunities to raise awareness of their concerns and interests. In 1996, the year before the election campaign in Britain, there were around 100 commercial exhibitors at the Conservative, Labour and Liberal Democrat conferences. These exhibitors made a net contribution to party funds of approximately half a million pounds. In subsequent years, these conferences have grown, raising increasing funds for the Labour Party, in particular. Because of the Liberal Democrats' important role in local government, they frequently had multiple retail grocers exhibiting at their conference. This business–political influence is often more pervasive in newly developing democracies. In an interview in January 1998 between one of the authors and a US Democratic political consultant, the consultant explained that she:

> ... had worked in elections where people are trying to buy the country because they have a corporate goal that they're trying to achieve. [Sometimes] they want access to oil reserves for their company, which is very common. I mean you'd be amazed at what people will get for oil rights.

On the other hand, it could be argued that companies do have a legitimate right to represent themselves. Another US Democratic political consultant, interviewed in January 1998, outlined this very point:

> You can't write a law in such a way that the National Rifle Association and the AFL-CIO (America's Labour Union) or Philip Morris or General Motors are going to [say], 'You got me! I'm going to stop trying to influence policy.' You can't. It's too important, they are going to find a way. Maybe they should.

The role of lobbying, with Dianne Thompson, Chief Executive, Camelot Group plc

Dianne Thompson is Chief Executive, Camelot Group plc, the operator of the National Lottery in the United Kingdom. After working in a variety of marketing positions at The Co-operative Wholesale Society, ICI Paints and Sterling Roncraft, she became a lecturer at Manchester Polytechnic for seven years, during which time she founded and ran her own advertising agency. Later she became Managing Director of Sandvik Saws and Tools, before moving to London to take up the post of Director of Marketing at Woolworths and later Marketing Director for the Signet Group. Dianne took over as Chief Executive of Camelot after the company was finally awarded the second licence in December 2000. Prior to the licence award, she had led the business through a successful judicial review, after the company was excluded from the bidding process to run the National Lottery. She was named Veuve Clicquot Businesswoman of the Year for 2000 and was voted 2001 Marketer of the Year by the Marketing Society.

Interviewer: What would you say your prime role is now as head of Camelot? What are the key roles you have played?

Dianne: My key functions are as lobbyist, motivator and strategist, because I am responsible for the strategic development of the business. I find that, because of the type of organization we are, we are a private company operating in a very public space, there are very many stakeholders in the National Lottery. So our role is to raise money but then obviously we hand it over to a variety of government quangos [quasi-autonomous non-governmental organizations], who then distribute the money. We have a regulator in the National Lottery Commission and we have a sponsoring department in the Department of Culture, Media and Sport. So, we have a lot of interaction with government officials, with our regulator and with the distributing bodies as well.

Interviewer: You obviously have a strong relationship with the government. Can you tell me what that involves?

Dianne: It changes over time. There are two things that make us a very unique company. Firstly, we are the only organization that has a regulator that is there to look after one organization only. Most other regulators, be it Ofgas – or the new Ofcom [the regulators for the Gas and Telecommunications industries respectively] when it gets created through the Communications Bill – will have a whole variety of companies and operators that they have to look after. One of the main things that a regulator is actually regulating in those other markets is price. Our regulator regulates the operation of the National Lottery only and there is only one National Lottery operator. We have a dedicated regulator and price is not one of the things they are regulating, so that makes us quite unique.

The second thing that makes us unique is that we operate on a seven-year licence and our relationship with our stakeholders changes at different stages during that seven-year process. When we went into the bidding process for the second licence, which was in February 2000, we went into bid mode in 1998. The distributing bodies then had an edict from government saying they could not talk to us because that would potentially be seen as an unfair advantage for the incumbent and our relationship with the department itself changed in those last years because they had to be seen to be absolutely fair and to be keeping us at arm's length. That was a real disadvantage to the National Lottery because it means that we had to put the development of the National Lottery on hold because we didn't have access to the people we needed to be talking to. So, it was a flawed process and that is something the government are looking [to review] for the third licence period. Our relationship with the Department of Media, Culture and Sport is probably stronger now than it has ever been, because everybody seems to realize that it is in everybody's interest for Camelot to be successful. The more successful we are, the more money we raise for good causes and the more the nation benefits. At the end of the day, whether you are a regulator or an operator the point is to get as much money as possible in a socially responsible way without causing problems for our players to the benefit of the nation.

Interviewer: Let's look at the second licence bidding process. This was certainly played out in the media as farcical and a little bit unfair [to Camelot], and I think this is largely due to the efforts by your group to portray it as unfair. Can you give me some idea how you managed this?

Dianne: When we actually submitted our bid in February 2000, we were quietly confident that we would win. Not because we were arrogant and certainly not because we were complacent. We had worked for over two years on the bid, it was 15 000 pages long, it weighed a quarter of a ton, and 150 people had worked on it virtually non-stop. So, it had been a huge undertaking for this organization, but it was a bid we were proud of. We had a good track record. We were the youngest company ever to get Investors in People [human resource development accreditation], the youngest to have got ISO 9001 [a quality management kitemark], we were only the sixth company to get the British Securities Standard BS7799 [a financial standard], so we had lots of ticks in lots of boxes where external organizations had looked at us as a business and said we were doing well. We had also been ranked the most efficient lottery in the world for four out of the last five years by an external company in the States, where efficiency means returning the most money to the government and good causes. We had had no major problems in terms of IT.

We had raised more than we said we would. We said we would raise £9 billion in the first licence and in fact we raised £10.5 billion. We had written a good bid, so we were quietly confident. We had a press launch on 28 February 2000, to talk about some of the highlights of our bid and the bid was submitted on the 29th. I met Sir Richard Branson [chairman of the Virgin Group and The People's Lottery, the rival bidder for the National Lottery franchise] for the first time on the 29th, when we actually met on the sofa of *GMTV* [a morning ITV programme]. It's worth mentioning that, because our then Chairman, Sir George Russell, had always said we should never ever do an interview with Sir Richard as he is obviously a past master at public relations. Because we had had such a good day on the Monday, the 28th, my head of external affairs, when we got the call from *GMTV* asking if we would go on, said we should really do it. We went on and it went well. We didn't tell my Chairman until it was over; that could have been very career limiting. The bid went in, it was fairly quiet and we were expecting to get to hear [the decision] in July and then it was deferred. It was eventually the

23rd of August when we got the news. The news was that the Commission felt that neither bid was good enough and they decided to stop the process between the two bidders and create a new process where they negotiated with one bidder only, which was Sir Richard [Branson]. It came as a real shock to us and having to go back to head office with my then boss, and tell our staff around the country that not only had we not won but we had lost our jobs as well, that was awful. I think it will turn out to be the worse day of my career.

We had prepared our PR strategy and we had decided that if we won we would put out a short statement and if we lost we wouldn't say anything. Because it was such a bizarre decision, it was felt we had to say something. So, I got whisked back into London feeling very wobbly to read this statement saying we couldn't really understand it, it was a big shock, and we were going to take stock and decide what to do. On the Thursday, we met with our lawyers. They said we hadn't much chance of winning a judicial review, at most a 20 per cent chance, and the Board said it was our call. I do believe passionately in fair play. If we had lost in a fair fight, of course, I would have been disappointed, but that's life. This [decision] was so unfair. If neither bid was good enough why not give both of us a month to try to come up with a better one and that is what I couldn't accept. They should have said, 'The People's Lottery bid is better than Camelot's and we believe they will do a better job.' Then I would have been astonished and distraught but I could have lived with that.

We decided to fight [their decision] and then the most unbelievable thing in our history happened. We changed from being 'fat cats' to the underdog. Our PR strategy was very simple. I met my Director of External Affairs each day and we reviewed what had been in the press that morning, whether there was anything we had to rebut, and we put a very efficient rebuttal system in. Anything that was inaccurate we challenged, absolutely anything. In the past, we had been a bit *laissez-faire* about it. Things that had been inaccurate or not very nice, we often had let go, but we didn't this time; we challenged everything. Sometimes, it would just be a letter to an editor saying 'not for publication'. We did find, over time, that the media stopped being quite so aggressive. The big turning point was when we got permission to have a judicial review.

From the media's perspective, I know the media didn't particularly want Camelot to win, but the big story for them was Sir Richard Branson losing. Sir Richard, the billionaire tycoon, very successful, very charismatic, and then this little northern working-class woman, the imagery was just brilliant from a media point of view. In fact, Sir Richard had undergone an interesting transition from being the underdog, the people's champion, the person who always took on the big institutions, to almost becoming the villain of the piece. So, a fascinating shift occurred in the media.

It would have been easy to fall into the trap of thinking that the media wanted us to win because they liked Camelot. But it was just a great story for them. Our strategy was good. We met every morning, we reviewed all the papers, decided what messages would go out, at what time, and in which media we would release them. [We mainly targeted] the newspapers in the fight back, but we did some TV stuff. We did things I thought I would never do. I did *Newsnight* a couple of times. It was quite a daunting experience.

Interviewer: Tell me about that. You had obviously made a decision to target those particular shows. Why?

Dianne: In our fightback there were several things we had to achieve. We had to win the judicial review, which against the odds we did. But we also then had to get a ground swell of opinion amongst opinion formers about the fact that Camelot was much maligned and was in fact a much better organization than people ever gave us credit for. If we had been much more popular with the general public we might not have found ourselves in the situation that we did. It was not the general public who would have been able to change the decision though, so it had to be people in government. So, obviously something like *Newsnight* has a fantastic reach to that target audience. It was very daunting. Usually, what the interviewers on these programmes are doing is showing their own intellectual prowess and how good they are at giving interviewees a tough time. I have a lot of respect for David Frost because he is equally effective in getting a lot of interesting things out of his interviewees, but he does it in a far more gentle style. I think that is why most of the senior politicians are happy to go on the *Breakfast with Frost* programme. They know they will be asked tough questions but not in an aggressive way.

We decided to go on *Newsnight* because we thought it was the right target market, it had the right interviewers and we had some significant landmarks to talk about. The first interview we did was about the judicial review but what I did learn as a result of this was preparation, preparation, preparation. We had all our key statements, what our line was on every issue, and I had some very aggressive media training. Sometimes the media training is harder than the actual interview! It is incredibly valuable and we were prepared. This was the day we had got the judicial review, so I was on a high and it went very well. Once you have done an interview and it goes well, it gives you the confidence to do it again.

Interviewer: There must have been a number of times when you thought there was no hope at all?

Dianne: Absolutely, because as I said earlier we were quietly confident we would win and we had done everything we could within our power to make sure we were in a position to win. And we didn't win! So, we could not help but think, 'is there a different agenda here?' It was a matter of principle for me. We have raised to date over £12.6 billion for good causes: money that was not here a few years ago. Eight hundred people here have worked their socks off to deliver this for Britain and they had been treated badly. If we didn't win, we were still going to go out with our heads held high and it really helped the morale of the staff here to know we were not just going out with a whimper.

Interviewer: It seems to me that ultimately you were not awarded the contract because you had a poor image amongst the public.

Dianne: That was never given as a public reason. You can imagine if the lottery had gone to The People's Lottery rather than Camelot that there would have been a huge popular roar from the general public because Sir Richard [Branson] is a well-respected businessman. He is still the people's champion, the people's hero, so I think it would have been a very popular decision for the National Lottery Commission to have taken. If we had been in as popular a position as he was, it might have ended differently the first time around.

Interviewer: Do you deal with the public relations and the various regulatory agencies in-house or with external consultants?

Dianne: We do most of it in-house, although from time to time we use external consultants. We have a Head of Government Relations who is Sarah Kennedy, the wife of Charles Kennedy [Leader of the Liberal Democrats], and I have just appointed a new Director of Corporate Communications, who is joining us from ITN, so we do most of it ourselves.

Interviewer: When would you consider using an external consultancy?

Dianne: The advantage of having internal consultants is that it is my people who are building relationships directly with members of parliament, government officials or civil servants. That is very valuable to us as it means we have direct access rather than going through a third party and we are meeting them on a regular basis. If you are meeting government or civil servants only a couple of times a year, you don't build that level of expertise in-house. That would be when to use external consultants. For example, there has been a review on gaming regulation so we used external help there.

I have press cuttings delivered at home every morning because, on two or three occasions, I have been doorstepped [caught by journalists at home] as I have been leaving the house. Now, I read what's in the press before I go out. In the three and a half years I have been having the cuttings delivered at home, there has only been two days when there hasn't been something [about us in the press]. It's not always negative but when you have that sort of level of media frenzy around you then you need your own in-house team.

Interviewer: Can you give me an insight into how public relations is changing?

Dianne: The Camelot approach to public relations is that, in everything we do, we are absolutely open and transparent. That sometimes gets us into trouble. The whole 'fat cat' row was about directors' bonuses which were paid in 1996 and then were in our accounts in 1997. Because we are not a listed company, we do not need to list direct emoluments to directors. But, because of the nature of the business that we run, the view has always been – from the day Camelot was founded – that we should be open and honest about everything. We have never had a policy of 'no comment' even when we know the answer will probably get us some bad publicity. We are always open and honest. We operate a 24-hour newsroom day and night, so journalists know they can get hold of somebody. That is the way we believe in doing business.

I think what is happening, looking at it from a broader perspective, is that there has been a tendency for PR to be seen as the work of spin doctors, particularly in 1997 when New Labour first came into power. I think it all started about that time. The general public is more aware that PR is there in the background trying to change opinion or mitigate situations. I think the whole industry is becoming more open and transparent.

Interviewer: OK, we'll end there. Thanks.

Chapter links

Appendix 1

IPR Code of Conduct

Section A

IPR Principles

1. Members of the Institute of Public Relations agree to:
    (i) Maintain the highest standards of professional endeavour, integrity, confidentiality, financial propriety and personal conduct.
    (ii) Deal honestly and fairly in business with employers, employees, clients, fellow professionals, other professions and the public.
    (iii) Respect the customs, practices and codes of clients, employers, colleagues, fellow professionals and other professions in all countries where they practise.
    (iv) Take all reasonable care to ensure employment best practice including giving no cause for complaint of unfair discrimination on any grounds.
    (v) Work within the legal and regulatory frameworks affecting the practice of public relations in all countries where they practise.
    (vi) Encourage professional training and development among members of the profession.
    (vii) Respect and abide by this Code and related Notes of Guidance issued by the Institute of Public Relations and encourage others to do the same.

Principles of Good Practice

2. Fundamental to good public relations practice are:

Integrity
- Honest and responsible regard for the public interest.
- Checking the reliability and accuracy of information before dissemination.
- Never knowingly misleading clients, employers, employees, colleagues and fellow professionals about the nature of representation or what can be competently delivered and achieved.
- Supporting the IPR Principles by bringing to the attention of the IPR examples of malpractice and unprofessional conduct.

Competence
- Being aware of the limitations of professional competence: without limiting realistic scope for development, being willing to accept or delegate only that work for which practitioners are suitably skilled and experienced.
- Where appropriate, collaborating on projects to ensure the necessary skill base.

Transparency and conflicts of interest
- Disclosing to employers, clients or potential clients any financial interest in a supplier being recommended or engaged.
- Declaring conflicts of interest (or circumstances which may give rise to them) in writing to clients, potential clients and employers as soon as they arise.
- Ensuring that services provided are costed and accounted for in a manner that conforms to accepted business practice and ethics.

Confidentiality
- Safeguarding the confidences of present and former clients and employers.
- Being careful to avoid using confidential and 'insider' information to the disadvantage or prejudice of clients and employers, or to self-advantage of any kind.
- Not disclosing confidential information unless specific permission has been granted or the public interest is at stake or if required by law.

Maintaining Professional Standards

3. IPR members are encouraged to spread awareness and pride in the public relations profession where practicable by, for example:

- Identifying and closing professional skills gaps through the Institute's Continuous Professional Development programme.
- Offering work experience to students interested in pursuing a career in public relations.
- Participating in the work of the Institute through the committee structure, special interest and vocational groups, training and networking events.
- Encouraging employees and colleagues to join and support the IPR.
- Displaying the IPR designatory letters on business stationery.
- Specifying a preference for IPR applicants for staff positions advertised.
- Evaluating the practice of public relations through use of the IPR Research & Evaluation Toolkit and other quality management and quality assurance systems (e.g. ISO standards); and constantly striving to improve the quality of business performance.
- Sharing information on good practice with members and, equally, referring perceived examples of poor practice to the Institute.

Interpreting the Code

4. In the interpretation of this code, the Laws of the Land shall apply.

Section B

Regulations governing complaints relating to Professional Conduct

1. Definitions

For the purpose of these Regulations the following words and expressions shall have the meanings set against them, unless the context otherwise requires:

committees the Professional Practices Committee and the Disciplinary Committee;

complaint facts or matters, other than those which are sub judice, coming to the attention of the Secretary indicating that a member of the Institute may have become liable to disciplinary action in accordance with Articles 12–18 (Disciplinary Powers) of the Articles of Association of the Institute, whether the member works with a consultancy, a commercial organization or otherwise;

complainant a person who brings a complaint;

defendant a member against whom a complaint has been lodged;

member a member of the Institute at the time the matter complained about occurred.

Note: It is a condition of membership that members remain subject to disciplinary proceedings in relation to their professional activities during such time as they are members, even though they may subsequently have ceased to be members;

parties (in relation to hearings of the Disciplinary Committee) the Professional Practices Committee and the defendant;

professional practices committee representative (in relation to hearings of the Disciplinary Committee) the person appointed to represent the Professional Practices Committee and to support the complaint.

Other words and expressions defined in the Memorandum and Articles of Association of the Institute shall have the meanings there assigned to them. The singular includes the plural and vice versa.

2. Professional Practices Committee and Disciplinary Committee

(a) The Professional Practices Committee and the Disciplinary Committee constituted in accordance with the Articles of Association of the Institute shall meet as required to investigate and hear complaints against members.

(b) The quorum of the Professional Practices Committee shall be not less than four and of the Disciplinary Committee shall be not less than three.

(c) A member of either of the Committees retiring from that Committee shall, unless the Council otherwise resolves, continue to be a member of the Committee for the purposes of any proceedings before the Committee not completed at the date of his or her retirement.

(d) A member of either of the Committees shall abstain from taking part in the consideration of a complaint if he or she has had previous dealings with the defendant personally or professionally or has taken part in the previous consideration of the complaint or any aspect of the complaint.

(e) Before the date of any hearing before either of the Committees the defendant shall be informed of the identity of the members of the Committee and shall have the right to give notice to the Chairman objecting to any of the members, stating his or her objections.

(f) Upon receipt of the notice mentioned in paragraph (e) of this Regulation, the Chairman, if satisfied that the objection is properly made, shall require the member in question to abstain from taking part in the proceedings. The defendant shall be informed of the identity of any alternate appointed in the place of that member and shall have the like right to give notice of objection.

(g) The Chairman of each Committee shall be present throughout the hearing of a complaint before that Committee. If any other member of the Committee for any reason is absent from any part of the hearing of a complaint, he or she shall take no further part in the hearing.

(h) The proceedings of either of the Committees shall be valid notwithstanding that one or more of the members other than the Chairman becomes unable to continue to act, so long as the number of members present throughout the substantive hearing of the complaint is not reduced below the quorum and continues to include the Chairman.

(i) Any duty or function or step which, pursuant to the provisions of these Regulations, is to be discharged or carried out by the Chairman of either of the Committees may, if he or she is unable to act for any reason, be discharged or carried out by any other member nominated in writing by the President for any specific purpose.

3. Assessors

(a) The Chairman of either of the Committees may direct that in considering a complaint the Committee shall sit with a legally qualified assessor.

(b) Likewise, the Chairman of either of the Committees may direct that in considering a complaint, the Committee shall have the assistance of one or more technical assessors, who appear to the Chairman to have knowledge or experience which would be relevant to assisting the Committee in considering any particular complaint.

(c) No assessor shall be appointed who has taken part in any process of resolution under Regulation 6 (duty to conciliate).

(d) No assessor shall form part of either of the Committees. It shall be for each Committee alone to determine the issues before it.

4. Complaints

(a) Any person (whether a member of the Institute or not) or any committee of the Council, or the Council itself, may bring a complaint against a member.

(b) It shall be the duty of every member of the Institute, where it is in the public interest to do so, to bring a complaint against a member. In deciding whether it is in the public interest to bring a complaint, regard should be paid to such guidance as the Council may give from time to time.

(c) The Secretary shall maintain a register of all complaints received and the decision of the Professional Practices Committee and, if relevant, the Disciplinary Committee thereon.

(d) On receipt of a complaint the Secretary shall make such enquiries of the complainant as may be necessary in order to clarify any matters of uncertainty and to identify the specific clause or clauses in the Code of Professional Conduct to which the complaint has reference.

(e) The Secretary shall also ensure that the complainant is aware of these Regulations and the Institute's disciplinary powers and in particular the Secretary shall explain that the defendant will be notified of the complaint in order that he or she may exercise the right of reply. The Secretary shall also draw attention to the provisions of Regulation 5 (confidentiality).

(f) If the complainant wishes to proceed with the complaint, the Secretary shall send details of the complaint to the defendant and invite him or her to submit written observations. The Secretary shall draw to the defendant's attention the provisions of Regulation 5 (confidentiality).

(g) The defendant's written observations shall be forwarded to the complainant, and, unless the complainant with the consent of the defendant withdraws the complaint, to the Professional Practices Committee.

(h) Any complaint shall be placed by the Secretary before the Professional Practices Committee as soon as reasonably practicable but no later than eight weeks after the complaint was received, except with the consent of both the complainant and the defendant.

5. Confidentiality

(a) Once a complaint has been made and communicated by the Secretary to the defendant, the substance of the complaint and all related correspondence, statements and submissions of the complainant and the defendant and all proceedings before and findings of the Professional Practices Committee shall be treated with complete confidentiality by both the complainant and the defendant, and all public discussion and disclosure avoided.

(b) Any breach, or alleged breach, of paragraph (a) of this Regulation which comes to the notice of the Professional Practices Committee shall be considered by the Committee, which may cause further investigation to be made. Any breach, or alleged breach, may itself give rise to a further complaint being laid before the Committee.

(c) In any case where there has been public discussion or disclosure of the substance of a complaint before receipt of the complaint by the Professional Practices Committee, the Committee shall, in considering the complaint, take into account the nature of and justification for such public discussion or disclosure, which may itself give rise to a further complaint being laid before the Professional Practices Committee.

(d) The requirement of confidentiality extends to all members of the Professional Practices Committee without limit of time.

6. Duty to conciliate

The Professional Practices Committee shall, in all proper cases, explore the possibility of resolving any grievance which has given rise to a complaint by conciliation, mediation, arbitration or otherwise, subject to the consent of the complainant and the defendant, and shall, whenever possible, make arrangements to provide the machinery for such resolution.

7. Power to demand information

(a) Each of the Committees shall have power to call for, and it shall be the duty of every defendant to provide, such information, including papers and records, as the Committee considers necessary to enable it to discharge its functions.

(b) The power in paragraph (a) of this Regulation shall not extend to information relating to any process of resolution under Regulation 6 (duty to conciliate).

8. Professional Practices Committee and Disciplinary Committee

(a) If a complaint is not resolved by the Professional Practices Committee under Regulation 6 (duty to conciliate), the Committee shall consider whether a complaint discloses a prima facie case for disciplinary action. If it considers that it does, it shall:
   (i)   refer the complaint to the Disciplinary Committee; or
   (ii) proceed as in Regulation 9 (consent orders); or
   (iii) proceed as in Regulation 10 (letters of advice); or
   (iv) order that no further action be taken on the complaint.

If it considers that the complaint does not disclose a prima facie case for disciplinary action, it shall order that the complaint be dismissed.

(b) Before taking any decision under clause (a) of this Regulation the Professional Practices Committee shall be satisfied that the defendant has been given an opportunity either of submitting written representations to it or, if the defendant desires to do so, of appearing before the Committee in person. The Committee shall have the power to require the defendant to attend before it and to request the attendance of witnesses. If the defendant fails to attend or otherwise avail him or herself of the rights of the defendant under these Regulations, the Committee may proceed in the absence of the defendant.

(c) If a complaint has not been resolved under Regulation 6 (duty to conciliate), a defendant appearing before the Professional Practices Committee may at the discretion of the Chairman be represented by a solicitor, counsel or friend and may at the discretion of the Chairman call witnesses on his or her behalf and examine and cross-examine any witnesses called to give oral evidence.

(d) The Professional Practices Committee may, at the discretion of the Chairman, adjourn its considerations from time to time to seek further information, or to give the defendant sufficient opportunity to consider and answer further information or to satisfy itself that all aggravating or mitigating circumstances have been taken into account, or otherwise.

(e) In deciding whether a complaint ought to be referred to the Disciplinary Committee the Professional Practices Committee shall be entitled to take into account any facts or matters which may have been considered by the Professional Practices Committee on previous occasions in relation to the defendant in respect of which no complaint was referred to the Disciplinary Committee.

(f) If the Professional Practices Committee refers a complaint to the Disciplinary Committee it shall do so by sending to the Disciplinary Committee a full statement of the offence or offences alleged, specifying the sub-section or sub-sections of Section A of the Code of Professional Conduct alleged to have been infringed, together with a summary of the facts and matters which were before the Committee and a summary or copy of any representation made by the defendant to the Committee. A copy of the complaint referred to the Disciplinary Committee shall be given to the defendant.

9. Consent orders

(a) If the Professional Practices Committee decides that a prima facie case has been made out against a defendant in accordance with

Regulation 8 and if, after considering all the circumstances including the past record of the defendant, the Professional Practices Committee further decides that the case is one which is appropriate to be dealt with under this Regulation, the Professional Practices Committee may, with the agreement of the defendant

  (i) make one or more of the following orders:

    (A) that the defendant be reprimanded;

    (B) that the defendant be severely reprimanded;

    (C) if the complaint relates to work within a consultancy, that within such time as the Professional Practices Committee thinks fit, the defendant return to a client all or part of the fee which the client has paid or pay over to a client funds which have been retained by the defendant in or towards payment of a fee; and

  (ii) include in any such order a direction that the defendant pay to the Institute a sum by way of costs arising subsequent to any attempt to resolve the complaint under Regulation 6 (duty to conciliate), such payment to be made within 28 days of the date the Professional Practices Committee so directs, unless some other date is determined by the Committee.

(b) Before making any order under paragraph (a) of this Regulation the Professional Practices Committee shall first give written notice to the defendant:

  (i) specifying the order or orders which it is considering making and the direction it is considering giving with the defendant's agreement; and

  (ii) stating that, if the defendant does not give his or her agreement to the proposed course within 21 days, the case shall be referred to the Disciplinary Committee, which, if it finds against the defendant, will have a wider range of orders available to it.

(c) If within the period stated the defendant gives his or her written agreement to the Professional Practices Committee proceeding as proposed in the notice given under paragraph (b) of this Regulation, the Committee shall make the order or orders and give the direction specified in the notice. The Committee shall also report the decision to the Council, which shall cause it to be published in the same manner as a decision of the Disciplinary Committee.

(d) If the defendant fails within the time stated to give written agreement to the Professional Practices Committee proceeding as proposed in the notice given under paragraph (b) of this Regulation, the Professional Practices Committee shall proceed to refer the complaint, formulated in accordance with paragraph (f) of Regulation 8, to the Disciplinary Committee, and report to the Council that it has done so.

(e) The breach of any order under paragraph (a)(i)(C) or a direction under paragraph (a)(ii) of this Regulation may itself give rise to a further complaint being laid before the Professional Practices Committee.

10. Letters of advice

(a) The Professional Practices Committee may decide to issue a letter of advice to a defendant if it considers that a complaint laid before it has arisen because of the inefficient management of the defendant's business or the business in which the defendant is employed. By this letter the Professional Practices Committee may require the defendant to obtain advice from such source or sources as the Professional Practices Committee may prescribe and (in the absence of good reason to the contrary) duly to implement the advice so obtained. Where relevant, the Committee may draw the attention of the defendant's employer to the contents of the letter of advice and seek the employer's assistance in the implementation of advice received by the defendant.

(b) Any breach of a requirement under paragraph (a) of this Regulation may itself give rise to a further complaint being laid before the Professional Practices Committee.

11. Joint consideration of complaints

Either of the Committees may, at the discretion of the Chairman, consider together more than one complaint against the same member, and consider together complaints against more than one member.

12. Cases of urgency

In cases where the Chairman of the Professional Practices Committee considers that the public interest demands a more urgent resolution of a complaint, he or she shall be entitled to exercise the powers of the Committee in demanding information and taking forward consideration and resolution of the complaint, in consultation with one or more members of the Committee, and shall report his or her actions to the Committee as soon as reasonably practicable.

13. Publicity in relation to the Professional Practices Committee

(a) The Chairman of the Professional Practices Committee may at any time make such public announcement as he or she sees fit in relation to the consideration by the Committee of any complaint which in his or her opinion is a matter of public concern. Except as mentioned in paragraph (c) of Regulation 9 (consent orders), no other public announcement shall be made in relation to any matter before the Professional Practices Committee.

(b) No public announcement under paragraph (a) of this Regulation shall refer to anything disclosed in any process of resolution under Regulation 6 (duty to conciliate).

14. The Disciplinary Committee

(a) The Disciplinary Committee shall meet as necessary to hear and determine complaints, formulated in accordance with paragraphs (f) of Regulation 8, referred to it by the Professional Practices Committee.
(b) Regulation 5 (confidentiality), adapted as necessary, shall apply equally to the Disciplinary Committee.
(c) In any case where the Disciplinary Committee considers it reasonable to do so, it may:
  (i) amend a complaint formulated by the Professional Practices Committee;
  (ii) formulate a new complaint relating to any information which comes to the notice of the Disciplinary Committee in the course of proceedings on any complaint referred to it;
  (iii) remit any complaint to the Professional Practices Committee for amendment or for the addition or substitution of any other complaint or complaints, provided that:
    (A) the Committee is satisfied that the defendant will not by reason of such an amendment suffer any substantial prejudice in the conduct of his or her defence; and
    (B) the Committee shall, if so requested by the defendant, adjourn for such time as is reasonably necessary to enable him or her to meet the complaint as so amended.

15. Further evidence and representation

The Professional Practices Committee may after referring a complaint to the Disciplinary Committee instruct the Secretary to make such enquiries, assemble such evidence and request the complainant to supply such further information and documents relating to the complaint as it thinks fit and may instruct a solicitor and/or counsel to act as Professional Practices Committee Representative if it thinks fit.

16. Convening of the Disciplinary Committee

(a) As soon as practicable after a complaint is referred to the Disciplinary Committee, the Committee shall issue a convening notice giving not less than eight weeks' notice to the parties of the date, time and place appointed for hearing the complaint.
(b) The convening notice shall also set out details of the procedure to be followed at any hearing and contain notice of the rights of the defendant to appear before the Disciplinary Committee in person

and/or by a solicitor, counsel or friend, to submit evidence and to make other written submissions, to call witnesses on his or her behalf at the discretion of the Chairman and to examine and cross-examine any witnesses called to give evidence.

(c) The convening notice given to the defendant shall be accompanied by copies of any documents which the Professional Practices Committee intends to adduce in evidence.

(d) An application for postponement of a hearing which has not commenced shall be determined by the Chairman of the Disciplinary Committee in his discretion.

17. Pre-hearing procedures

(a) Not less than 28 days before the date fixed for the hearing the Chairman of the Disciplinary Committee may direct the defendant to state in writing within such time as may be specified:

  (i) whether the defendant accepts all or part of the allegations in the complaint and, if the defendant does not accept all of them, on what grounds he or she denies all or part of them;

  (ii) whether the defendant accepts the facts as stated in the summaries referred to the Disciplinary Committee under paragraph (f) of Regulation 8 and, if not, the grounds on which such facts are disputed;

  (iii) if the defendant accepts all or part of the allegations in the complaint, the grounds on which any plea for mitigation will be made; and

  (iv) whether or not the defendant intends to attend and/or be represented at the hearing and the identity of any representative.

(b) The defendant's response to the direction referred to in paragraph (a) of this Regulation shall be drawn to the attention of the Disciplinary Committee at the conclusion of the hearing, if relevant, on the question of costs.

(c) At least 21 days before the date fixed for the hearing, the defendant shall serve on the Disciplinary Committee two copies of a paginated and indexed bundle of all documents on which he or she intends to rely unless the documents have already been included among the documents served under paragraph (c) of this Regulation. The Disciplinary Committee shall forthwith send one copy of the bundle to the Professional Practices Committee Representative.

(d) Either party may inspect the documents served by the other party within 14 days of the service.

(e) Unless the Chairman of the Disciplinary Committee otherwise directs, no witness may be called nor document produced by either party without at least 21 days written notice being given to the Disciplinary Committee. In the case of witnesses, such notice shall include the name and address of the witness and a copy of the statement of his or her evidence, in order that the Chairman of the Disciplinary Committee may decide whether such evidence is material to the proceedings. The Chairman of the Disciplinary Committee shall as soon as practicable give a direction accordingly.

(f) Nothing in this Regulation shall preclude the reception by the Disciplinary Committee of the evidence of a witness a copy of whose statement has not been duly served, or of a document not duly served, provided the Disciplinary Committee is of the opinion that the defendant is not materially prejudiced thereby, or on such terms as are necessary to ensure that no such prejudice arises.

(g) At any time before the hearing the Chairman of the Disciplinary Committee may direct the defendant to:

(i) send an answer to the complaint in writing to the Disciplinary Committee within 14 days, subject to any extension of time if in the opinion of the Chairman of the Disciplinary Committee there is good and sufficient reason for an extension;

(ii) provide such further information and documents relating to the complaint as the Chairman considers necessary for the just and expeditious handling of the case;

(iii) appear in person at a pre-trial review in accordance with Regulation 18 or at the hearing before the Disciplinary Committee at the time appointed for the review or hearing.

(h) At any time before the hearing the Chairman of the Disciplinary Committee may direct that either of the parties indicate which of any information supplied by the other party is not accepted or whether either party wishes to challenge the authenticity of any document supplied by the other party.

18. Pre-hearing review

(a) The Chairman of the Disciplinary Committee either of his or her own motion or on the application of either party may direct that there be a pre-hearing review conducted by him or herself for the purpose of giving directions and of taking such other steps as he or she considers suitable for the clarification of the issues before the Disciplinary Committee and generally for the just and expeditious handling of the case.

(b) The directions to be given and steps taken by the Chairman of the Disciplinary Committee may concern, but not be limited to, the following matters:

(i) whether the hearing should be held in private or in public;

(ii) whether more than one complaint should be considered together by the Disciplinary Committee;

(iii) application to strike out allegations;
(iv) attendance of witnesses;
(v) admission of documents;
(vi) admission of facts;
(vii) the estimated duration of the hearing;
(viii) such other matters as he or she deems expedient for the just and expeditious conduct of the hearing.

(c) The Chairman of the Disciplinary Committee shall cause a record to be served on the parties setting out the directions given, admissions made and steps taken at the pre-hearing review.

(d) The parties may, in advance of the date fixed for any pre-hearing review, agree upon the directions to be made and/or steps to be taken at the pre-hearing review and shall notify the Chairman of the Disciplinary Committee of such agreement. Following such notification the Chairman of the Disciplinary Committee may, if he or she thinks fit, make directions in the terms agreed and/or direct that no pre-hearing review is required.

(e) For the avoidance of doubt, the Chairman of the Disciplinary Committee may:
  (i) adjourn the pre-hearing review from time to time as he or she considers appropriate;
  (ii) upon the application of either party or of his or her own motion, and either with or without further preliminary hearings, give such further directions or take such further steps as he or she considers necessary for the just and expeditious conduct of the proceedings, including extending or abridging any time limit governing the procedures of the Disciplinary Committee on such terms as he or she thinks just.

19. Procedures at hearings of the Disciplinary Committee

The order in which a hearing before the Disciplinary Committee will normally proceed, subject to the discretion of the Chairman of the Committee, shall be as follows:

(i) The defendant will be called before the Committee.
(ii) The Chairman of the Committee will make the members of the Committee known to the defendant. If the defendant is accompanied by others he or she will make them known to the Committee, or the representative of the defendant will make him or herself and those with him or her known to the Committee.
(iii) The procedure to be followed will be explained by the Chairman of the Committee.
(iv) The complaint will be read and the defendant's written answer taken into consideration.

(v) The Committee will put to the defendant any questions arising out of the complaint and the evidence in support of the defendant's written answer which the Committee considers pertinent.

(vi) The defendant (or his or her representative) will be given the opportunity to address the Committee.

(vii) After the Committee has heard the defendant (or his or her representative) and any witnesses, the defendant and any persons with him or her will be asked to withdraw while the Committee makes its findings on the complaint.

(viii) The defendant (and those with him or her) will be recalled and the Chairman of the Committee will pronounce its findings on the complaint. If the finding is against the defendant, he or she (or his or her representative) will be invited to address the Committee in mitigation.

(ix) The defendant (and those with him or her) will again be asked to withdraw while the Committee decides on the nature of the report to be made to the Council.

(x) The defendant (and those with him or her) will be recalled and the decision of the Committee, to be embodied in a report to the Council, will be pronounced.

20. Adjournment

(a) Subject to the provisions of the following paragraph, the Disciplinary Committee shall sit from day to day until it has arrived at a finding and, if any allegation has been found proved, until the decision of the Committee is pronounced.

(b) Notwithstanding the provisions of paragraph (a) of this Regulation, the Disciplinary Committee may, if the Chairman decides that an adjournment is necessary for any reason, adjourn the hearing for such period as he may decide.

21. Evidence and standard of proof

(a) The proceedings of the hearing before the Disciplinary Committee shall be governed by the rules of natural justice, subject to which the Committee may:

(i) admit any evidence, whether oral or written, whether direct or hearsay, and without being bound by any enactment or rule of law relating to the admissibility of evidence in proceedings before any court of law;

(ii) give such directions with regard to the conduct of and procedure at the hearing, and with regard to the admission of evidence thereat, as it considers appropriate for securing that the defendant has a proper opportunity of answering the charge or otherwise as shall be just;

(iii) exclude any hearsay evidence if it is not satisfied that reasonable steps have been taken to obtain direct evidence of the facts sought to be proved by the hearsay evidence.

(b) The standard of proof is satisfied on a balance of probabilities.

22. Hearing in private or in public

The hearing before the Disciplinary Committee shall be in private unless either:

(i) at a pre-hearing review or otherwise it has been directed that the hearing shall be held in public; or

(ii) the defendant has made an application that the hearing shall be held in public, and the Chairman in his discretion does not consider that for any reason the circumstances and nature of the hearing make a public hearing undesirable.

23. Absence of defendant

If the defendant does not attend at the time and place appointed for the hearing, the Disciplinary Committee may nevertheless proceed to hear and determine the complaint, provided that the Committee is satisfied that the relevant procedure has been complied with and the defendant has been duly served, in accordance with Regulation 29 (service of documents), with the documents required under paragraph (f) of Regulation 8 and Regulations 16 (convening of the Disciplinary Committee) and 17 (pre-hearing proceedings).

24. Non-compliance of defendant

(a) If, having been required under these Regulations to answer a complaint in writing, to provide further information or to appear in person before the Disciplinary Committee, the defendant fails for whatever reason so to do, the Disciplinary Committee shall be empowered at its discretion to postpone its findings on the complaint and to report to the Council that it has decided that the defendant should be suspended for such period as the Disciplinary Committee thinks fit for conduct inconsistent with his or her status as a member.

(b) The power of the Disciplinary Committee to decide that a defendant should be suspended under paragraph (a) of this Regulation notwithstanding, a defendant who fails to comply with these Regulations or any direction under these Regulations may be deemed by the Disciplinary Committee to be conducting him or herself in a manner inconsistent with his or her status as a member and the proceedings may be determined by a report by the Disciplinary Committee to the Council that it has decided that one of the range of measures open to the Council under Article 12 should be exercised against the defendant without the formulation of any further complaint for that purpose.

25. The finding of the Disciplinary Committee

(a) At the conclusion of the hearing, the finding of the Disciplinary Committee on each allegation included in the complaint shall be set down in writing and signed by the Chairman and all members of the Committee present.

(b) If the members of the Committee are not unanimous as to the finding on any allegation, the finding to be recorded on that allegation shall be that of the majority.

(c) If the members of the Committee are equally divided as to the finding on any allegation, the finding to be recorded on that allegation shall be that which is the most favourable to the defendant.

(d) The Chairman of the Committee shall then pronounce the Committee's finding on the allegation or allegations as stated in Regulation 19 (procedure at hearings of the Disciplinary Committee).

26. The decision of the Disciplinary Committee

(a) If the Disciplinary Committee shall have found the allegation or any of the allegations included in the complaint proved, after hearing any representations by or on behalf of the defendant, the Committee shall set down in writing its decision as to how the Council should exercise its powers under Article 12.

(b) If the members of the Committee are not unanimous as to the decision, the decision to be recorded shall be that decided by the majority.

(c) If the members of the Committee are equally divided as to the decision, the decision to be recorded shall be that which is the most favourable to the defendant.

(d) The Chairman of the Committee shall then announce the Committee's decision in the form of a report to the Council, indicating how the Council should exercise its powers under Article 12 or that no action should be taken against the defendant.

(e) If the defendant has not been present throughout the proceedings, the report to the Council shall include a statement that the provisions of Regulation 23 (absence of defendant) have been complied with.

27. Costs

(a) The Disciplinary Committee shall have power to make and report to the Council such decision as to direction for costs against a defendant as it shall think fit.

(b) Upon deciding on such direction, the Disciplinary Committee shall either itself determine the amount of such costs or appoint a suitably qualified person to do so on its behalf.

(c) Any costs directed to be paid by a defendant shall, unless some other date is determined by the Disciplinary Committee, be paid to the Institute within 28 days of the date the Council so directs.

(d) Subject as aforesaid, all costs and expenses incurred by the Committees in connection with these Regulations shall be borne by the Institute.

28. Record of proceedings

Unless the Chairman of the Disciplinary Committee in his discretion decides in any particular case to make a record of the proceedings at a hearing in any other manner, he or she shall take a handwritten note of the proceedings. A copy of the Chairman's note of the proceedings (or of any other record of the proceedings made in the discretion of the Chairman) shall be made available to the defendant if he requests one within three months of the date of the hearing and reimburses the cost of supplying the same.

29. Service of documents

(a) Any documents required to be served on a defendant arising out of or in connection with investigations or proceedings under these Regulations shall be deemed to have been validly served:

   (i) if sent by registered post, or recorded delivery post, or receipted hand delivery to:

      (A) the address registered by the defendant with the Institute; or

      (B) an address to which the defendant may have requested in writing that such documents be sent (including the address of his or her legal adviser); or

      (C) in the absence of any such request, his or her last known address;

   (ii) if actually served on the defendant;

   (iii) if served in any way which may be directed by the Chairman of either of the Committees.

(b) For the purpose of this Regulation 'receipted hand delivery' means a delivery by hand which is acknowledged by a receipt signed by the defendant.

(c) A copy of all notices and directions served and given by the Disciplinary Committee on and to either party shall be sent to the other party.

(d) The accidental omission to send or deliver a notice or other communication to, or the non-receipt of a notice or other communication by, either party shall not invalidate any investigation or proceedings to which such notice or communication relates.

30. Disposal of papers

The record of each set of proceedings before each of the Committees, including a copy of all written representations made by the defendant, shall at the conclusion of the proceedings (whether the complaint is upheld or dismissed) be delivered to the Secretary's custody for disposal as and when the Council determines.

31. Curing of irregularities

Any irregularity resulting from failure to comply with these Regulations during the course of any proceedings hereunder shall not of itself render the proceedings void, but the Chairman of either Committee may, and shall if he or she considers that either party to the proceedings may have been prejudiced, take such steps as he or she thinks fit before the conclusion of the proceedings to cure the irregularity, whether by the amendment of any document, the giving of any notice, the taking of any step or otherwise.

32. Disputes

If any question or difference shall arise with regard to the interpretation or application of these Regulations or on any matter whatsoever concerning the conduct of the hearing of a complaint, it shall be referred to and settled conclusively by the President, who shall take whatever advice thereon considered necessary.

Source: reproduced by kind permission of the Institute of Public Relations, http://www.ipr.org.uk

Global Protocol on Public Relations Protocol – Summer 2002

Declaration of principles

A profession is distinguished by certain characteristics or attributes, including:

- mastery of a particular intellectual skill through education and training
- acceptance of duties to a broader society than merely one's clients/employers
- objectivity
- high standards of conduct and performance.

We base our professional principles therefore on the fundamental value and dignity of the individual. We believe in and support the free exercise of human rights, especially freedom of speech, freedom of assembly, and freedom of the media, which are essential to the practice of good public relations.

In serving the interest of clients and employers, we dedicate ourselves to the goals of better communication, understanding, and cooperation among diverse individuals, groups, and institutions of society. We also subscribe to and support equal opportunity of employment in the public relations profession and lifelong professional development.

We pledge:

- To conduct ourselves professionally, with integrity, truth, accuracy, fairness, and responsibility to our clients, our client publics, and to an informed society;
- To improve our individual competence and advance the knowledge and proficiency of the profession through continuing education and research and where available, through the pursuit of professional accreditation;
- To adhere to the principles of the Global Protocol on Ethics in Public Relations.

Protocol standards

We believe it is the duty of every association and every member within that association that is party to the Global Protocol on Ethics in Public Relations to:

- Acknowledge that there is an obligation to protect and enhance the profession.
- Keep informed and educated about practices in the profession that ensure ethical conduct.
- Actively pursue personal professional development.
- Accurately define what public relations activities can and cannot accomplish.
- Counsel its individual members in proper ethical decision-making generally and on a case specific basis.
- Require that individual members observe the ethical recommendations and behavioral requirements of the Protocol.

We are committed to ethical practices, preservation of public trust, and the pursuit of communication excellence with powerful standards of performance, professionalism, and ethical conduct.

Advocacy

We will serve our client and employer interests by acting as responsible advocates and by providing a voice in the market place of ideas, facts, and viewpoints to aid informed public debate.

Honesty

We will adhere to the highest standards of accuracy and truth in advancing the interests of clients and employers.

Integrity

We will conduct our business with integrity and observe the principles and spirit of the Code in such a way that our own personal reputation and that of our employer and the public relations profession in general is protected.

Expertise

We will encourage members to acquire and responsibly use specialized knowledge and experience to build understanding and client/employer credibility. Furthermore we will actively promote and advance the profession through continued professional development, research, and education.

Loyalty

We will insist that members are faithful to those they represent, while honoring their obligations to serve the interests of society and support the right of free expression.

Advancing the Protocol

We believe it is the responsibility of each member association to draw upon its own member's experiences to expand the number of examples of good and bad practice so as to better inform members' ethical practices. Experiences should be broadly shared with other members within the association and with the Global Alliance so as to build up case histories that may assist in individual cases throughout the world.

Prepared by the Global Alliance Code of ethics project team:

Jean Valin APR, Fellow CPRS, Canada
Don LaBelle, APR, Fellow CPRS, Canada
Chris Skinner, APR, South Africa
Jim Lukaszewski, ABC, APR, Fellow PRSA, United States
Nigel O'Connor, IPR, United Kingdom
Toni Muzi Falconi, Italy
Ulli Sats, Estonia

Source: reproduced with kind permission from the Global Alliance for Public Relations and Communication Management 2003 (www.globalpr.org).

References

Abrams, F. and Butler, K. (1997). How Blair's ear was bent by the king of Formula One. *The Independent*, 6 November, Section 7.

Ace, C. (2001). *Successful Marketing Communications*. Oxford: Butterworth-Heinemann.

Adkins, S. (2000). Why cause-related marketing is a winning business formula. *Marketing*, 20 July, p. 18.

Andrews, L. (1996). The relationship of political marketing to political lobbying: an examination of the Devonport campaign for the Trident refitting contract. *European Journal of Marketing*, 30 (10), 68–91.

Anon. (1991). *Hutchinson Concise Encyclopedia*, 2nd edn. London: Random Century.

Anon. (1999a). Enjoying benefits of healthy returns. *Marketing*, 27 May, p. 55.

Anon. (1999b). Case study: Lloyds/TSB merger. *Marketing*, 4 November, p. 36.

Anon. (2000a). Boom time in city fuels financial PR. *Marketing*, 25 May, p. 65.

Anon. (2000b). Internal communications. *Marketing*, 6 June, p. 19.

Anon. (2001a). Best integrated campaign. *Marketing*, PRCA Frontline Awards Supplement, September, p. 9.

Anon. (2002a). Tough times alert PR to weak spots. *Marketing*, 16 May, pp. 27–30.

Anon. (2002b). Event awards 2002: best use of exhibitions. *Marketing*, 22 October, accessed via www.brandrepublic.com, 16 January 2003.

Anon. (2002c). Event awards 2002: best product launch. *Marketing*, 22 October, accessed via www.brandrepublic.com, 16 January 2003.

Anon. (2002d). City PR fights tough climate. *Marketing*, 16 May, p. 37.

Anon. (2002e). Crisis management for directors: preparing for the unexpected. *CA Magazine*, **135** (4), 56.

Anon. (2002f). General Motors recalls 1.9 million vehicles. *Quality*, **41** (5), 12–14.

Anon. (2002g). Sky TV signs up Sony as sponsor of movie service. *Marketing*, 6 June, p. 3.

Anon. (2002h). Briefs. *Marketing*, 19 December, p. 5.

Anon. (2002i). Identity slow ends fee bonanza. *Marketing*, 13 June, p. 13.

Anon. (2002j). Mattel loses suit over song about 'blonde bimbo' Barbie. *Ottawa Citizen*, 25 July, p. E8.

Arnold, M. (2001a). Is Ben and Jerry's losing its Bohemian appeal? *Marketing*, 3 May, p. 17.

Arnold, M. (2001b). Can Aeroflot become a credible airline brand? *Marketing*, 26 July, p. 17.

Arnold, M. (2001c). Aeroflot looks to shed worst airline image in revamp. *Marketing*, 19 July, p. 17.

August, M., Bower, A., Butler, R. and Fonda, D. (2001). Unhappy meals. *Time*, **158** (8), 17.

Baines, P. (1998). Unpublished Consultancy Report. FLS Aerospace Advertising Effectiveness Study, Middlesex University, London.

Baines, P. R. and Harris, P. (2000). Kite-flying: the role of marketing in the post-BSE British beef export industry. *British Food Journal*, **102** (5/6), 454–64.

Ballantyne, D. (2000). Internal relationship marketing: a strategy for knowledge renewal. *The International Journal of Bank Marketing*, **18** (6), 274–86.

Bashford, S. (2001). Is Egg right to aim for a mainstream image? *Marketing*, 8 November, p. 13.

Bashford, S. (2002). Castrol raises staff awareness with game. *Marketing*, 4 July, p. 10.

BBC (2002). Jobs section, http://www.bbc.co.uk/jobs/, accessed 10 February.

Bejou, D. and Palmer, A. (1998). Service failure and loyalty: an exploratory empirical study of airline customers. *Journal of Services Marketing*, **12** (1), 7–22.

Belch, G. E. and Belch, M. A. (2001). *Advertising and Promotion: An Integrated Marketing Communications Perspectives*, 5th edn. London: McGraw-Hill Irwin.

Bell, S. (1999). Coke pays the price for a mishandled crisis. *Marketing*, 24 June, p. 15.

Bennett, R. (1999). Headteacher characteristics, management style and attitudes towards the acceptance of commercial sponsorship by state-funded schools. *Marketing Intelligence and Planning*, **17** (1), 41–52.

Bernays, E. L. (1952). *Public Relations*. Oklahoma: University of Oklahoma Press.

Bettinghaus, E. P. and Cody, M. J. (1994). *Persuasive Communication*, 5th edn. London: Harcourt Brace.

Bhattacharya, S. (2000). British military information management techniques and the South Asian soldier: Eastern India during the Second World War. *Modern Asian Studies*, **34** (2), 483–510.

Bird, J. (2000). The benefits of cybermeetings. *Marketing*, 1 July, accessed via www.brandrepublic.com, 16 January 2003.

Black, S. (ed.) (1995). *The Practice of Public Relations*. Oxford: Butterworth-Heinemann.

Blackhurst, C. (2000). How the city was spun. *Management Today*, February, pp. 58–65.

Blythe, J. (1999). Visitor and exhibitor expectations and outcomes at trade exhibitions. *Marketing Intelligence and Planning*, **17** (2), 100–108.

Boulton, A. (1999). Private interview with Adam Boulton from Sky News, April.

Brennan, R. and Baines, P. R. (2002). Ethical aspects of drug pricing: GlaxoSmithKline and anti-retroviral drugs in South Africa. *Proceedings of the Academy of Marketing Conference*, July, Nottingham University, Nottingham.

Brierley, S. (2002). *The Advertising Handbook*, 2nd edn. London: Routledge.

Briggs, W. and Tucson, M. (1993). PR versus marketing. *Communication World*, March. San Francisco: IABC.

Britton, J. (2002). Two children's books recalled. *Publishers Weekly*, **249** (8), 18.

Campbell, T. (1999). Crisis management at Coke. *Sales and Marketing Management*, **151** (9), 14.

Cantwell, J. E. (2000). Rating agency evaluations: what really matters. *AFP Exchange*, **20** (2), 6–10.

Center, A. H. and Jackson, P. (2003). *Public Relations Practices*, 6th edn. Englewood Cliffs, NJ: Prentice-Hall.

Chambers, L. (1999). Seminars through prospects' eyes. *On Wall Street*, **9** (5), 66.

CIA (2003). *World Factbook*, http://www.cia.gov/cia/publications/factbook/, accessed 8 January 2003. Washington, DC: Central Intelligence Agency.

Coombs, W. T. (1998). An analytic framework for crisis situations: better responses from a better understanding of the situation. *Journal of Public Relations Research*, No. 10, pp. 177–92.

Cowlett, M. (2001a). Financial PR deals with time of crisis. *Marketing*, 13 December, p. 25.

Cowlett, M. (2001b). PRs benefit from forward planning. *Marketing*, 28 June, p. 37.

Cowlett, M. (2002). How innovative PR benefits marques. *Marketing*, 17 January, p. 25.

Cox, V. and Spickett-Jones, G. (1999). Adoption and diffusion processes. In *Marketing Communications* (Kitchen, P., ed.), pp. 189–210. London: Thomson Business Press.

Cutlip, S. M., Center, A. H. and Broom, G. M. (1994). *Effective Public Relations*, 7th edn. Englewood Cliffs, NJ: Prentice-Hall.

Dann, S. and Dann, S. (2001). *Strategic Internet Marketing*. Milton, Queensland: John Wiley & Sons Australia.

Davies, S. (2002). The precautionary principle and food policy. *Consumer Policy Review*, **12** (2), 65–72.

Dignam, C. and Murphy, C. (2002). How to steal the World Cup. *Marketing*, 9 May, pp. S12–S13.

Dittrick, P. (2002). US oil, gas companies reassessing post-Sept. 11 security risks. *Oil and Gas Journal*, **100** (16), 24–30.

Dolbow, S. (2002a). Sunglass Hut eyes sunny weather. *Brandweek*, **43** (23), 6.

Dolbow, S. (2002b). Men in Black 2 alien-chasers wear Rockport shoes to step ahead. *Brandweek*, **43** (23), 6.

Dowling, G. (2001). *Creating Corporate Reputations*. Oxford: Oxford University Press.

Doyle, P. (1995). Marketing in the New Millennium. *European Journal of Marketing*, **29** (12), 23–41.

Dudley, S. (2001). Colombia's secret weapon. *Colombia Journalism Review*, **40** (3), 58–60.

Duncan, T. (2002). *Integrated Marketing Communications: Using Advertising and Promotion to Build Brands*, international edn. London: McGraw-Hill.

Egan, J. (2001). Political marketing: lessons from the mainstream. *Journal of Marketing Management*, **15** (6), July, 495–504.

Eisenberg, D. and Zagorin, A. (2000). Anatomy of a recall. *Time*, **156** (11), 28–32.

Elkin, T. (2002). Video games try product placement. *Advertising Age*, **73** (20), 157.

Erickson, B., Lind, E. A., Johnson, B. C. and O'Barr, W. M. (1978). Speech style and impression formation in a court setting: the effects of powerful and powerless speech. *Journal of Experimental Psychology*, **14**, 264–79.

Ewing, J. and Capell, K. (2002). World Cup: sponsors need to get in the game. *Business Week*, 17 June, p. 52.

Fan, Y. and Pfitzenmaier, N. (2002). Event sponsorship in China. *Corporate Communications: An International Journal*, **7** (2), 110–16.

Fishman, C. (2001). Business fights back: crisis and confidence at Ground Zero. *Fast Company*, No. 53, pp. 108–13.

Ford Motor Company (2000). Questions and answers from the Ford Call Centre for Firestone Inquiries, www.ford.com, 12 August. In O'Rourke, J. (2001). Bridgestone/Firestone, Inc. and Ford Motor Company: how a product safety crisis ended a hundred-year relationship. *Corporate Reputation Review*, **4** (3), 255–64.

Fraza, V. (2001). A joint approach. *Industrial Distribution*, **90** (10), 57–9.

Freitag, A. (2002). International coverage of the Firestone tyre recall. *Journal of Communication Management*, **6** (3), 239–56.

Friedman, W., Chura, H., Elkin, T. and Halliday, J. (2002). 'Minority Report' stars Lexus, Nokia. *Advertising Age*, **73** (24), 41.

Fry, A. (2000). Why sponsors are great fans of sport. *Marketing*, 30 March, pp. 41–2.

Fry, A. (2001). How to profit from sponsoring sport. *Marketing*, 16 August, pp. 25–6.

Gander, P. (2002). Seen and heard? *Marketing Week*, **25** (14), 35.

Gifford, G. (1999). Cause-related marketing: ten rules to protect your non-profit assets. *Nonprofit World*, **17** (6), 11–13.

Goddard, C. (1999). Creating a format for living brands. *Marketing*, 8 April, accessed via www.brandrepublic.com, 16 January 2003.

Gofton, K. (2001). City PRs maintain positive approach. *Marketing*, 17 May, p. 59.

Goldman, D. (2001). Is Fay Weldon's *The Bulgari Connection* good advertising? *Adweek*, **42** (46), 16.

Gould, P. (1998). *The Unfinished Revolution: How the Modernisers Saved the Labour Party*. London: Little and Brown.

Gray, R. (2001). How to build a caring image. *Marketing*, 3 May, pp. 35–6.

Grönroos, C. (1994). From marketing mix to relationship marketing: towards a paradigm shift in marketing. *Management Decision*, **32** (2), 4–20.

Gummesson, E. (1987). The new marketing: developing long term interactive relationships. *Long Range Planning*, **20** (4), 10–20.

Guth, D. W. (1998). Public relations in the new Russia. *PR Strategist*, **4** (3), 51–4.

Hackley, C. A. and Dong, Q. (2001). American public relations networking encounters China's Guanxi. *Public Relations Quarterly*, **46** (2), 16–19.

Hallahan, K. (2000). Inactive publics: the forgotten publics in public relations. *Public Relations Review*, **26** (4), 499–515.

Harris, P., Gardner, H. and Vetter, N. (1999). 'Goods over God' lobbying and political marketing: a case study of the campaign by the Shopping Hours Reform Council to change Sunday trading laws in Britain. In *Handbook of Political Marketing* (Newman, B. I., ed.). London: Sage Publications.

Harrison, S. (2000). *Public Relations*, 2nd edn. London: Thompson Learning.

Hatcher, M. (1998). The presentation of a complex case to the European Commission (Aspects of EU Merger Control with Reference to the Case of Price Waterhouse/Coopers and Lybrand). In *The Proceedings of the 5th International Public Relations Symposium*, Lake Bled. Slovenia: Pristop Communications.

Hayes, R. (2001). The importance of crisis management. *Intermedia*, **29** (4), 36.

Haywood, R. (2002). PRs should have good ideas but integrity is vital. *Marketing*, 7 March, p. 22.

Herbig, P., O'Hara, B. and Palumbo, F. A. (1998). Trade show: who, what, why. *Marketing Intelligence and Planning*, **16** (7), 425–35.

Hiscock, J. (2002). The brand insiders. *Marketing*, 23 May, p. 24.

Hitler, A. (1925). *Mein Kampf*. London: Pimlico Press (originally published in 1925, translated by Ralph Mannheim).

Hollis Press and Public Relations Annual. Sunbury-on-Thames: Hollis Directories.

Holtzhausen, D. R. (2000). Postmodern values in public relations. *Journal of Public Relations Research*, **12** (1), 93–114.

Hunt, T. and Grunig, J. (1994). *Public Relations Techniques*. New York: Holt, Rineholt & Winston.

Interbrand (2002). http://www.brandchannel.com/start.asp, accessed 23 July.

IPR (2002). Excellence Awards Winners: Glas Cymru – selling 'not-for-profit' to the City, www.ipr.org.uk./excellence/winners.htm, accessed 30 July.

Jefkins, F. (1990). *Public Relations for Your Business*. London: Mercury Books.

Jefkins, F. (1994). *Public Relations Techniques*, 2nd edn. Oxford: Butterworth-Heinemann.

Jefkins, F. and Yadin, D. (1998). *Public Relations*, 5th edn. London: Pitman.

Kamalipour, Y. R. and Rad, M. M. (1997). Public relations in Iran: from Persian Empire to Islamic Republic. *International Public Relations Review*, June, pp. 27–31.

Kitchen, P. J. and Daly, F. (2002). Internal communication during change management. *Corporate Communications: An International Journal*, **7** (1), 46–53.

Kleinman, M. (2000). Tobacco ads saved – but not for long. *Marketing*, 12 October, p. 9.

Kleinman, M. (2002a). Imperial Tobacco in colour rebrand ahead of ad ban. *Marketing*, 12 December, p. 1.

Kleinman, M. (2002b). Philips is to launch 007 shaving range. *Marketing*, 4 April, p. 3.

Kotler, P. (2000). Future markets. *Executive Excellence*, **17** (2), 6.

Kotler, P. and Mindak, W. (1978). Marketing and public relations: should they be partners or rivals? *Journal of Marketing*, October.

Lazersfeld, P., Berelson, L. and Gaudet, H. (1948). *Propaganda and Communication in World History*, Vol. 2. Honolulu: University of Hawaii Press.

LSE (2002a). http://www.londonstockexchange.com/distributors/regulatory_news.asp, accessed 29 July.

LSE (2002b). *RNS: User Guide*. London: London Stock Exchange.

LSE (2002c). RNS welcomes FSA announcement setting date for commercialisation of its news distribution. Press Release, 25 January. London: London Stock Exchange.

LSE (2002d). *A Practical Guide to Investor Relations*. London: London Stock Exchange.

LSE (2002e). *Investor Relations*. London: London Stock Exchange.

MacMillan, K., Money, K. and Downing, S. (2002). Best and worst corporate reputations – nominations by the general public. *Corporate Reputation Review*, **4** (4), 374–84.

MacNamara, J. R. (1992). Evaluation of public relations: the Achilles heel of public relations. *International Public Relations*, IPRA, **15** (4).

Mandelson, P. (1988). Marketing Labour: personal reflections and experience. *Contemporary Record*, **1** (4), 11–13.

Mazur, L. (1999). Unleashing employees' true value. *Marketing*, 29 April, pp. 22–3.

McLeod, J. (1997). The changing role of parliamentary lobbyists. *Journal of Communication Management*, **1** (4), 374–8.

McMains, A. and Mack, A. M. (2001). Johnnie Walker NBC plug: content or commercial. *Adweek*, **42** (51), 2.

Metcalfe, K. and Rose, H. (2001). Maximize the launch with public relations. *Pharmaceutical Executive*, Successful Product Management II supplement, October, pp. 16–18.

Miller, H. (2001). Name and shame. *Director*, **55** (1), 55.

Mitroff, I. I. (2001). Crisis leadership. *Executive Excellence*, **18** (8), 19.

Moloney, K. and Jordan, G. (1996). Why companies hire lobbyists. *The Service Industries Journal*, **16** (2), 242–58.

Morris, P. (2001). Dealing with Whitehall and Westminster. *Hawkesmere Seminar on Lobbying*, Berners Hotel, London, 4 April.

Murphy, C. (2000). Instilling workers with brand values. *Marketing*, 27 January, pp. 31–2.

O'Malley, L. and Patterson, M. (1998). Vanishing point: the mix management paradigm reviewed. *Journal of Marketing Management*, **14** (8), 829–51.

O'Rourke, J. (2001). Bridgestone/Firestone, Inc. and Ford Motor Company: how a product safety crisis ended a hundred-year relationship. *Corporate Reputation Review*, **4** (3), 255–64.

O'Shaughnessy, N. (1999). Political marketing and political propaganda. In *Handbook of Political Marketing* (Newman, B. I., ed.), pp. 725–40. London: Sage Publications.

O'Sullivan, T. (2002). Do the ads add up for the sponsors? *Financial Times*, Business of Sport Survey, 28 May, p. VI.

Palmer, A. (2000). Co-operation and competition; a Darwinian synthesis of relationship marketing. *European Journal of Marketing*, **34** (5/6), 687–704.

Pearson, C. (2002). A blueprint for crisis management. *Ivey Business Journal*, **66** (3), 63–9.

Pierach, J. (2002). PR must evolve to gain a seat at the table. *Brandweek*, **43** (19), 41–2.

Prabhaker, P. R. (2000). Who owns the on-line consumer? *Journal of Consumer Marketing*, **17** (2), 158–71.

PRSA (2002). Code of Conduct, http://www.prsawest.org/code.html, accessed 29 July. In *Public Relations Journal*, June 1995, pp. 22–5.

Public Relations Yearbook. London: FT Business Information/Public Relations Consultants Association.

Raeburn, P. (2002). The credibility gap in drug research. *Business Week*, 24 June, p. 78.

Reiss, A. H. (2000). Corporate sponsorship: a growing area of arts concern. *Fund Raising Management*, **31** (8), 46–7.

Resnicks, J. T. (2002). A matter of reputation. *Pharmaceutical Executive*, **22** (6), 74–84.

Rogers, D. (2002a). Npower to unveil cash for schools internet initiative. *Marketing*, 25 April, p. 3.

Rogers, D. (2002b). Nescafé targets teens with £9.5m Hollyoaks tie-up. *Marketing*, 25 April, p. 1.

Rogers, M. R. (1995). *Diffusion of Innovations*, 4th edn. London: Macmillan.

Schramm, W. (1955). *The Process and Effects of Mass Communications*. Urbana, IL: University of Illinois Press.

Sen, F. and Egelhoff, W. G. (1991). Six years and counting: learning from crisis management at Bhopal. *Public Relations Review*, **17** (1), 68–93.

Seringhaus, F. H. R. and Rosson, P. J. (1998). Management and performance of international trade fair exhibitors: government stands versus independent stands. *International Marketing Review*, **15** (5), 398–412.

Shimp, T. A. (2000). *Advertising, Promotion: Supplemental Aspects of Integrated Marketing Communications*, 5th edn. Orlando, FL: Dryden Press.

Sky News (2002a). AOL shares dive after probe revealed, http://www.sky.com/skynews/article/0,,30400-12054959,00.html, accessed 29 July.

Sky News (2002b). WorldCom files for bankruptcy, http://www.sky.com/skynews/article/0,,15410-12047168,00.html, accessed 29 July.

Smith, P. R. (2002). *Marketing Communications: An Integrated Approach*, 3rd edn. London: Kogan-Page.

Spaeth, T. (2002). The name game. *Across the Board*, **39** (2), 27–31.

Sriramesh, K. and Vercic, D. (2001). International public relations: a framework for future research. *Journal of Communication Management*, **6** (2), 103–16.

Stewart, K. (1998). An exploration of customer exit in retail banking. *International Journal of Bank Marketing*, **16** (1), 6–14.

Theaker, A. (2001). *The Public Relations Handbook*. London: Routledge.

The Economist (2001a). Special Report: Relaunching the propaganda war – Fighting terrorism; the battle for hearts and minds. *The Economist*, **361** (8247), 19.

The Economist (2001b). Leaders: The propaganda war – The propaganda war; fighting terrorism. *The Economist*, **361** (8242), 11–2.

The Economist (2002a). Britain: Byers beware; Government. *The Economist*, **362** (8262), 54–5.

The Economist (2002b). Leaders: The disgraceful Stephen Byers; Britain's Government. *The Economist*, **362** (8262), 15.

Till, B. D. and Nowak, L. I. (2000). Toward effective use of cause-related marketing alliances. *Journal of Product and Brand Management*, **9** (7), 472–84.

Ugboajah, F. (1985). *Mass Communication Culture and Society in West Africa*. Munich: Hanz Zell Publishers (imprint of K. G. Saur).

UKCS (2003). UK Copyright Act 1988, UK Copyright Service, http://www.copyrightservice.co.uk/copyright/intellectual_property.htm, accessed 15 February.

Ulmer, R. R. (2001). Effective crisis management through established stakeholder relationships. *Management Communication Quarterly*, **14** (4), 590–615.

Vence, D. L. (2002). Event marketing. *Marketing News*, **37** (1), 13.

Walker, D. (2000). Product recalls. *Target Marketing*, **23** (6), 34.

Wally, S. and Hurley, A. E. (1998). The torch stops here: Olympic sponsorship and corporate reputation. *Corporate Reputation Review*, **1** (4), 334–5.

Webb, J. R. (2000). *Understanding and Designing Marketing Research*, 2nd edn. London: Thompson Learning.

Webster, K. K. (2002). Branding your employees, brand papers, www. brandchannel.com, accessed 3 August 2002.

Welch, D. (2001). Firestone: is this brand beyond repair? *Business Week*, **3736** (48), 48.

Western Union (1985). When every second counts – crisis communications planning. *Company Document*, Upper Saddle River, New Jersey.

White, J. (1991). *How to Understand and Manage Public Relations*. London: Business Books.

White, J. and Mazur, L. (1995). *Strategic Communication Management: Making Public Relations Work*. London: Addison-Wesley/Economist Intelligence Unit.

White, R. (2001). Case Study: PriceWaterhouseCoopers. *Hawkesmere Seminar on Lobbying*, Berners Hotel, London, 4 April.

Williams, D. (2002). Weaving ethics into corporate culture. *Communication World*, **19** (4), June/July, 38, 48.

Wilson, J. (2001). Building an effective in-house operation. *Hawkesmere Seminar on Lobbying*, Berners Hotel, London, 4 April.

Wolff Olins (2002). What value can a strong brand add in difficult economic times. MORI Captains of Industry Survey, www.wolff-olins.com, accessed 23 July.

Worcester, R. and Mortimore, R. (1999). *Explaining Labour's Landslide*. London: Politico's.

Worcester, R. M. and Mortimore, R. (2001). *Explaining Labour's Second Landslide*, p. 221. London: Politico's Publishers.

Workinpr.com (2002). *Hiring a Public Relations Firm: A Guide for Clients*, http://www.workinpr.com/industry/agency/pr_hire.asp, accessed 1 August.

Wright, H. and Fill, C. (2001). Corporate image, attributes and the UK pharmaceutical industry. *Corporate Reputation Review*, **4** (2), 99–110.

Index

Lightning Source UK Ltd.
Milton Keynes UK
UKOW02f1122040414

229415UK00003B/54/P